Savage Frontier

Volume III
1840–1841

Other Books by Stephen L. Moore

Savage Frontier: Rangers, Riflemen, and Indian Wars in Texas. Volume II: 1838–1839. Denton, TX: University of North Texas Press, 2006.

Spadefish: On Patrol With a Top-Scoring World War II Submarine. Dallas, TX: Atriad Press, 2006.

Eighteen Minutes: The Battle of San Jacinto and the Texas Independence Campaign. Plano, TX: Republic of Texas Press, 2004.

Savage Frontier: Rangers, Riflemen, and Indian Wars in Texas. Volume 1: 1835–1837. Plano, TX: Republic of Texas Press, 2002.

Taming Texas. Captain William T. Sadler's Lone Star Service. Austin, TX: State House Press, 2000.

With William J. Shinneman and Robert W. Gruebel. *The Buzzard Brigade: Torpedo Squadron Ten at War.* Missoula, MT: Pictorial Histories Publishing, 1996.

For more information, visit www.stephenlmoore.com

Savage Frontier

Volume III
1840–1841

Rangers, Riflemen, and Indian Wars in Texas

Stephen L. Moore

UNIVERSITY OF NORTH TEXAS PRESS

DENTON, TEXAS

Manufactured in the United States of America

10 9 8 7 6 5 4 3 2 1

Requests for permission to reproduce material from this work
should be sent to:

Permissions
University of North Texas Press
PO Box 311336
Denton, TX 76203

The paper used in this book meets the minimum requirements
of the American National Standard for Permanence of Paper for
Printed Library Materials, Z39.48.1984.

Library of Congress Cataloging-in-Publication Data

Moore, Stephen L.
Savage frontier III: rangers, riflemen, and Indian wars in Texas/
Stephen L. Moore.
p. cm.
Includes bibliographical references and index.
ISBN-10: 1-57441-228-0 (cloth:alk. paper)
ISBN-13: 978-1-57441-228-4 (cloth: alk. paper)
ISBN-10: 1-57441-229-9 (pbk: alk. paper)
ISBN-13: 978-1-57441-229-1 (pbk. alk. paper)
1. Indians of North America—Wars—Texas. 2. Indians of North
America—Texas—Government relations. 3. Texas Rangers—
History. 4. Frontier and pioneer life—Texas—History. 5. Texas—
Politics and government—1836–1846. I. Title
E78.T4 M675 2006
 976.4—dc21
2002000480

*Cover design by Lindsay B. Behrens, based on Alan McCuller's Vol. I
creation. Layout and typesetting by Stephen L. Moore.*

Contents

Volume 3

Prologue

The first two volumes of *Savage Frontier* traced the evolution of the Texas Rangers during the revolution and in the post-revolutionary period, during which ranging companies began to operate within formal militia brigades. Other military forces on the Texas frontiers during the period of 1835–1839 included army, militiamen, mounted volunteers, and even allied Indian scouts and rangers.

Spurred by President Mirabeau Lamar's ethnic cleansing policy, the year 1839 was a record year for Texas Indian battles and for casualties. Thirty-three Texans had been killed and another fifty were wounded in conflicts with the Indians. In return, they claimed to have killed several times as many Native Americans. Texas military forces managed to drive most Shawnees and Cherokees across the Red River borders out of Texas—in line with Lamar's objective of ridding the country of Indians.

Kelsey Douglass, Edward Burleson, and Thomas Rusk were key leaders during 1838 and 1839. In 1840, command of the Texas Militia passed from Rusk—a veteran frontiersman—to Felix Huston, who had never been in an Indian fight.

By the end of 1839, only three companies of Texas Rangers remained in service. The Texas Militia would continue to be called up as needed, but the largest force in operation was the army's Frontier Regiment, or First Regiment of Infantry. Headed by Colonel Edward Burleson—and later Colonel William Cooke—the Frontier Regiment would be involved in much of the frontier action in 1841. The army also worked to negotiate the release of civilian hostages held by the Comanches and other Indian tribes.

One such attempt to release prisoners turned violent in San Antonio on March 19, 1840. Twelve Comanche chiefs and eighteen other Indians were killed at an old courthouse that became known as the Council House.

Later that summer—after acquiring more weapons—the Comanches made a retaliatory raid to the coast of Texas, killing, stealing cattle, and burning buildings in their path. Neophyte militia general Huston had his first big battle when these Comanches were engaged at Plum Creek in August 1840 during their retreat northward. Some of the more seasoned frontiersmen believed that Huston's inexperience prevented a crushing defeat of the Comanches.

John Henry Moore, who had led ranger expeditions in 1835 and 1839, led another ad hoc ranger expedition in the fall of 1840. This time, he surprised a large Comanche village on the Colorado River and killed most of its inhabitants. These deadly clashes in 1840 insured that the Comanches would remain stirred up against Texas settlers for many years.

The Texas Militia had little serious effect on the state of the Texas frontiers throughout the rest of the year. The army's Frontier Regiment's largest contribution was the building of a military road from the Austin area up to the Red River border—a road which roughly parallels the modern Interstate 35. This advancement helped to further open up settlements, but also further stirred relations with the Indians of northern Texas.

Militia leaders James Smith and Edward Tarrant—the namesakes of Texas counties—made new expeditions in 1841 into the areas of the Cross Timbers and the modern Dallas-Fort Worth areas to attack the Indians who had settled there. Another county namesake—Captain John Denton—was killed on one of these offensives in the area of the present Dallas—Fort Worth metroplex.

Ranging companies under John T. Price, Antonio Perez, and Jack Hays operated during the early months of 1841, but these units soon gave way to a new frontier force. Twenty special county "minuteman" companies were authorized for 1841. Traditional Texas Ranger companies during the previous six years had been commissioned to serve from three to twelve months in the field. In contrast, the newly authorized county minuteman companies could not stay in the field longer than fifteen consecutive days and their men could not serve more than four months

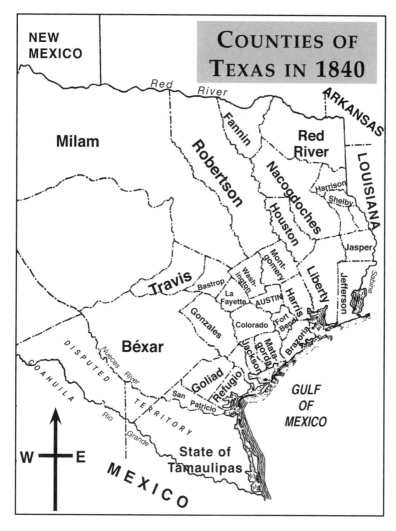

COUNTIES OF TEXAS IN 1840

total. Fifteen of the twenty county companies are known to have formed, while three companies were never formed. If the other two counties did organize minuteman companies, the records of their existence have not been found.

Some of these units found conflict with frontier Indian tribes from the Red River area down to the southern coastal areas of Texas. Other units served less reputably, preying on traders and rustling cattle in the southwest. Famed Texas Ranger leader Jack Hays led the Béxar County Minutemen after his ranging unit was disbanded. Early rangers historian Walter Prescott Webb wrote in 1935 of Hays that "under his leadership the best tradition of the Texas Rangers was established." More recently, Robert Utley wrote in his ranger history, "John Coffee Hays resonated through history as the ideal Texas Ranger, the one above all others every Ranger strove to emulate."[1]

Volume III of *Savage Frontier* seeks to straighten out the record on the early service of legendary Texas Ranger Jack Hays. His own 1840s written testimony later helped create much confusion for historians. He did not hold a formal ranger command in 1840, as one of his biographers has written. Use of his muster rolls, ranger pay rolls, and official reports helped to straighten out the true dates of his frontier battles. The much-debated battle at Enchanted Rock is also explored.

The introduction of the Colt repeating pistol in several engagments during these two years marked a major change in frontier warfare. The war of extermination of the Texas Indians did not end with President Lamar's administration. The so-called "savages" of the Texas frontier had become the hunted in many cases, and deadly raids on their villages became more frequent. As with the previous volumes of *Savage Frontier*, Volume III does not seek to justify the persecutions or prejudices that prevailed in this time. My own ancestry includes militiamen, Texas Rangers, and also a Cherokee great-great-great grandmother.

For the continuation of the *Savage Frontier* series, I thank Ron Chrisman and his staff at the University of North Texas Press for their confidence. For his unwavering support, research assistance, and advice, Donaly Brice of the Texas State Archives deserves many kudos. Donaly was also kind enough to share some of his illustrations and research from his excellent book, *The Great Comanche Raid*. Special thanks are due to James Haley for his critical review of an early draft of the manuscript. Byron Johnson, Director of the Texas Ranger Hall of Fame and Museum in Waco, granted permission for inclusion of several key images for this volume. Finally, thank you to Patrick Lemelle of the University of Texas Institute of Texan Cultures at San Antonio and Jane Boyd of the University of Texas at Austin's Center for American History for their work in providing several key illustrations.

CHAPTER 1

The Comanches

Four unknown riders made their approach to the outskirts of San Antonio as the sun set low into the afternoon sky. Three wore the accoutrements of Comanche Indians—breechclout, leggings, moccasins, and buffalo skin robes to ward off the cool winter air. The fourth horse bore a small young captive, secured to his horse to prevent his escape.

The four riders were hailed by San Antonio citizens as they neared the edge of town. The Comanches cried out loudly for "Colonel Karnes," demanding to speak with him.

The Indians were told to wait with their prisoner while someone was sent to fetch Karnes. The three Comanches who had thus entered San Antonio on January 9, 1840, sought to speak to a man familiar to their people from previous peace negotiations.

Although known to the Indians to seek peace, Colonel Henry Wax Karnes had also led several campaigns against the Comanches and other warlike Texas Indian tribes. A hero of the Texas Revolution, twenty-eight-year-old Karnes had consistently served as a leader of cavalry forces in and around the San Antonio area in the years following the battle of San Jacinto.

These Comanches were part of the Penateka ("Honey Eaters") tribe, one of twelve regional bands of Comanche. Also known as the Wasps, the Penatekas survived largely on bison meat, and had migrated to the North Texas plains around 1700. As many as 40,000 Comanches had inhabited Texas soil in the peace of the

1780s, but epidemics that included cholera reduced their number to around 12,000 by the late 1830s.[1]

San Antonio was heavily populated with Tejanos, Texas natives of Mexican ancestry. The old Alamo mission still stood—the compound whose fall had inspired the "remember the Alamo" rallying cry of the Texas Revolution. At times during the years following, various army troops had used the grounds for a fortress. The city itself was now an epicenter of activity in the growing Republic of Texas. To the west, traders moved toward the Rio Grande to ferry goods to and from Mexico. In the Hill Country north of San Antonio, the Comanches ranged over miles of unsettled land. They were accused, sometimes unjustly, of preying upon helpless travelers or plundering the traders who became more numerous each year. San Antonio was the largest community in close proximity to villages of the Penateka Comanches, who desired many of the items traded in that town.

The three Comanche riders were brought into town before Colonel Karnes on January 9 with their prisoner. In a letter written the next day, Karnes related the demands of the Indians.

> On being introduced into my presence, the most distinguished amongst them—who appeared to be a priest—stated that he was deputed by his nation to solicit a peace. He further states, that eighteen days since, his tribe, in a general council, elected a distinguished Chief to treat with the Texians, who will visit the settlements on his return, should his report be favorable to him. He says that the nation will accept of peace on any terms, being sensible of their inability to contend with the Texian forces.[2]

Although encouraged by the desires of the Comanche nation to request a peace agreement, Henry Karnes was certainly at least a little wary. The Comanches were not afraid of Texas forces, as they had yet to incur any serious losses from fights with Texas frontiersmen or rangers.

The Comanches also stated to Karnes that they had rejected presents from the Cherokees, and also from the Centralist Mexican military command, who had sent emissaries among their people. Both parties sought to use the Comanches to stir up a general war against Texas settlers. Again, the word that the

Comanches had rebuffed the two opportunities to rise up against the Texans was taken with a grain of salt by Karnes.

"These statements may be true, but their known treachery and duplicity induces me to put but little faith in them," wrote Karnes. The Indians left their captive behind, a young boy later identified as John Horn. His family had been attacked in April 1836, in the Nueces River valley. Thirteen men were killed, leaving two women and their young children to be taken prisoners by the Comanches. Mrs. Horn was ransomed in 1839 by traders, but her young son had been a prisoner so long that he had lost most of his ability to use the English language. He was at first believed to be a young Mexican man because of his appearance.[3]

Karnes decided not to hold the three Comanches as hostages. In good faith, he would send them back to their nation with the word that he was willing to treat with them. As was the usual custom, he presented the Indians with gifts of peace offerings to show his good intention. Henry Karnes had proved to be a man of his word in previous negotiations.

This time, he made his demands clear to the Comanches. "I told them that the Government would not enter into any treaty without the release of the American captives, and the restoration of all stolen property."[4]

The Comanche priest took the message that Colonel Karnes desired to treat with the "principal chiefs" of their nation. The Indians promised Karnes that they would indeed gather their leaders and would return to San Antonio "in twenty or thirty days." The following day, January 10, Colonel Karnes wrote to Texas Secretary of War Albert Sidney Johnston of his meeting with the Comanches. He was, at the very least, skeptical of their true desire for peace and the promise that they would bring in all of their white prisoners.

Karnes suggested that Johnston should immediately select "one or two commissioners to meet them here." His own "indispensable business" required Karnes to make an immediate trip to New Orleans. In his absence, he requested that the commissioners treat with the Comanches in San Antonio.

Karnes further felt that the commissioners should be "accompanied by a force sufficient to justify our seizing and retaining those who may come in as hostages, for the delivery of such American captives as may at this time be among them."

This statement showed the determination of Karnes to bring about an end to the depredations and kidnappings. If the Comanches failed to bring in the promised American prisoners, he advocated that all of their chiefs be held as hostages. It was a plan that set a new precedent in Indian negotiations, and one that led to great bloodshed.

Although it would be days before Karnes' letter made it into the hands of Secretary Johnston in Austin, its message would be taken to heart. In Karnes' defense, he was hoping to use the Republic's Frontier Regiment to recover Anglo captives without a fight. The Penateka Comanches, however, would rather die than surrender and be held publicly as prisoners.

State of the Texas Frontier System: January 1840

On the day that the Comanches rode into San Antonio, Colonel Edward Burleson was leading the Texas Army back toward Austin. At age forty-two, Colonel Burleson was already something of a legend in Texas. He had led militia forces in Missouri and Tennessee years before coming to Texas in 1830, where he had soon become lieutenant colonel of the militia in Stephen F. Austin's municipality. A hero of the Texas Revolution and the battle of San Jacinto, Burleson was also respected as a fearless Indian fighter.

His Frontier Regiment of Texas had been created in early 1839 to build frontier outposts and to protect the outlying settlements of Texas from Indian depredations. Consisting of a First Regiment of Infantry, a First Regiment of Cavalry, and an artillery division, Burleson's Frontier Regiment had been successful thus far in carrying out President Lamar's objective of driving out Indian tribes deemed to be hostile to Anglo Texian settlers. Burleson's men had fought with the Texas Militia and Texas Rangers during the Cherokee War of 1839, driving most of the Cherokees and Shawnees across the Texas borders. His army companies had also constructed and manned several frontier outposts during 1839.

Recruiting had continued during late 1839, until the Frontier Regiment numbered a little under 450 men by the start of 1840, which was about half of its designated strength. Colonel Burleson

Capt. Roberts' Rangers: September 16, 1839–March 16, 1840

Captain:
Mark R. Roberts
First Lieutenant:
Daniel R. Jackson
Second Lieutenant:
William E. Wiley
First Sergeant:
James Martin
Second Sergeant:
Gibson May
Third Sergeant:
Alexander McKinney
Fourth Sergeant:
Charles Quillen [1]
First Corporal:
Santiago Eusses

Privates:
John Anderson
Reed Anderson
Jonathan Anthony
Spencer Asberry
Carter Bean
Carter Bourland
Nicholas Cantu
William R. Caruthers
Jesse Case
Thomas Cousins
Jesse Cox
John Davis
William Dillingham
Jesse Francis
Thomas F. Gilbert
Isaac Houston
Samuel Johnson

Jesse Kuykendall [2]
Peter Maroney
Jackson McFarland
Charles McManus
Jackson Morrison
H. Morse
Samuel Moss
David Mouser
Henry Mouser
David Pettit
William C. Rice
E. C. Rogers
James Rutland
John L. Scantling
James Seymore
John Seymore
William H. Stark
John Stephen Sr.
John Stephens Jr. [3]
Joseph Strickland
J. P. Thruston
William C. Twitty
William Tyler
John Van Dine
Whitfield Viles
William Winlock

[1] Substitute for company's original second sergeant, William Bailey.
[2] Substitute for William W. Boone.
[3] Substitute for R. Beck.

Source: Texas State Archives.

had led a little more than 200 of his troops out from Austin in December 1839 in company with Lipan scouts, under Chief Castro, and Tonkawa scouts under Chief Plácido. They fought a band of Comanches on Christmas Day and made their way back to Camp Caldwell near Austin by January 12, 1840.

Aside from this regular army, Texas was patrolled at the beginning of 1840 by only three companies of true Texas Rangers.

Capt. Black's Mounted Rangers: October 22, 1839–Jan. 29, 1840

Captain:
George K. Black
First Lieutenant:
Henry Rodgers
Quartermaster:
James S. Gillett
First Sergeant:
John S. Thompson
Second Lieutenant:
William James
Surgeon:
John L. Douglass

Privates:
John Arnold
Leonard A. Ashmore
Thomas Avon [1]
Edward Burns [1]
A. G. Conner
Uriah Conner
David Cook [1]
Elihu D. Cook [1]
Joseph Thomas Cook Sr. [1]
Joseph Thomas Cook Jr. [1]
Joseph Dickerson [2]
George S. Downs
William L. Dupree [1]
Solomon K. Flynn
George N. Gibson [1]

Benjamin P. C. Harrill
Peter W. Holmes [2]
Willis D. Howell [1]
Benjamin A. James
Joshua Leach
Samuel A. McNutt [1]
Marcus P. Mead [1]
J. H. Moore [1]
Abraham Myers [2]
Nathaniel Newman [2]
David O'Kelly
N. S. Outlaw
F. D. Pickens [2]
Richard Pollard
Stephenson Ramsey
John Henninger Reagan [2]
John Rowan
Milton Rowan
Jose Silvia
French Smith
Conrad Snider
Miles Stacey
Benjamin F. Ward
George Washington Welsh [2]
Samuel W. Wilds

[1] Enlisted into company on Dec. 1, 1839.
[2] Enlisted January 10, 1840.
Source: Texas State Archives.

They were commanded by captains Mark R. Roberts, George K. Black, and John William Lane. Roberts, who had settled along the Red River shortly after his arrival in Texas in March 1836, had taken command in September 1839. His fifty-two-man company operated out of Camp Warren in Fannin County.

Captain Black's Nacogdoches County Mounted Rangers of the Third Militia Brigade were mustered into service on October 22, 1839. Black had served on General Thomas Rusk's 1838 expedition into the Cherokee Nation and had been first lieutenant of Captain Peter Tipps' company during the 1839 Cherokee War. His ranger company had twenty-six rangers at its formation, with another dozen joining on December 1.

Capt. Lane's Mounted Rangers: August 15, 1839–Feb. 16, 1840

Captain:
John William Lane

Privates:
T. H. Anthony
Francis C. Baker
William H. Bobo
Henry Bull
Hulett H. Farmer
John Ferguson [1]
E. Frazier [1]
Gabriel Frazier
Hezekiah George
L. M. Grace [1]
J. G. Hayes
Henry B. Kelsey [1]
Daniel Minor [1]

Joseph Moore
Josephus Moore
A. Joseph L. Page
Elias Page [1]
Albert E. Ray [1]
Henry Reel
Jacob Taylor [2]
M. H. Ussery
Isaac Walters [1]

[1] Served from Sept. 23–Dec. 24, 1839.
[2] Served from Aug. 15, 1839–February 16, 1840.

Source: F. C. Baker PD, R 135, F 36–71; William Lane PD, R 167, F 250–73. Partial roster created via search of Republic era records.

While in service, Captain Black's rangers constructed Cook's Fort in the former Cherokee territory where Chief Bowles' tribe had recently been ejected. The company ranged the areas of present Houston and Nacogdoches counties while they built Cook's Fort during the winter of 1839–1840. The site was about three miles northwest of the present town of Rusk, located in Cherokee County. It was named for Joseph Thomas Cook Sr., a member of Captain Black's company. Cook, who lived in the community of Douglass outside of Nacogdoches, had also served in Captain Michael Costley's 1836 ranger company which had worked on Fort Houston.[5]

An additional seven men enlisted under Captain Black on January 10, 1840, likely to participate in a scout or expedition that moved out. Black's rangers were back in Nacogdoches on January 29 and—having completed their three-month enlistment with a week to spare—his unit was disbanded.

The third Texas Ranger unit still in existence at the turn of the year served in the Fourth Militia Brigade under Captain John William Lane. His men had been organized on August 15, 1839, in the wake of the Cherokee War. Some of his unit completed three months of service on Christmas Eve 1839 and were discharged. At least seven of his company continued to serve into

February of 1840, however, and were the only rangers in service in North Texas at the time.

The life of a ranger in 1840 was not for everyone. Former New Yorker Nelson Lee spent his early years at sea before coming to Texas in 1840. He became involved with various ranger companies and scouting expeditions shortly after his arrival. In his 1859 memoirs, he describes the characteristics of the early Texas Rangers.

> The condition of affairs necessarily resulted in bringing into existence the Texas Rangers, a military order as peculiar as it has become famous. The extensive frontier exposed to hostile inroads, together with the extremely sparse population of the country, rendered any other force of comparatively small avail. The qualifications necessary in a genuine Ranger were not, in many respects, such as are required in the ordinary soldier. Discipline, in the common acceptance of the term, was not regarded as absolutely essential. A fleet horse, an eye that could detect the trail, a power of endurance that defied fatigue, and the faculty of "looking through the double sights of his rifle with a steady arm,"—these distinguished the Ranger, rather than any special knowledge of tactics.[6]

With these three ranger companies, Colonel Burleson's Frontier Regiment was left to defend all of the frontier of Texas in early 1840. Two days after his regiment had reached Camp Caldwell, Burleson went on into Austin on January 14. Since becoming the Republic's capital, Austin boasted a population in January 1840 of 711 men, women, and children, plus another 145 slaves.[7]

Upon his arrival, Burleson learned of an uproar within Congress concerning his most recent Northwestern Campaign. From John Bowles' camp, he had retrieved the military hat of the late Chief Bowles, who had been killed in the 1839 Cherokee War campaign in present Van Zandt County. With some of the plunder, Burleson sent along the "cocked hat of the distinguished friend of General Sam Houston, Colonel Bowles."

Colonel Burleson sent Bowles' hat to Colonel Hugh McLeod, the adjutant general, with a special note. Since the hat had originated from Houston, "I especially request you to present it to him from me as a compliment."

Sam Houston was insulted and called for the dismissal of Hugh McLeod from office. The debate raged for some time, but Houston eventually withdrew his resolution when no member of the House would agree to vote for it. In the protest, it was revealed that Chief Bowles had been given a vest and sword by Sam Houston, but that the hat was a gift from an agent of the Mexican government.[8]

Burleson's Northwestern Campaign and the recent ventures out against the Comanches by Henry Karnes and John Neill's forces had somewhat calmed the central Texas frontier. Such strong showings of force had convinced frontier hostiles that raids on the inadequately defended Mexican settlements further south were more desirous.

Upon his return to Austin, Colonel Burleson decided that the frontier was in "a prosperous condition" and that his services were no longer necessary as supreme commander of the Frontier Regiment. Writing to President Mirabeau Lamar on January 29, Burleson tendered his resignation to spend time with his wife and children. He remained in Austin several more days to assist in the transfer of command to his number two man, Lieutenant Colonel William Fisher.[9]

As events unfolded, Burleson's resignment would be short-lived. Increased depredations by the Comanches and several major happenings with the Indians during the upcoming weeks would cause him to reconsider his resignation.

President Lamar's administration continued to support the frontier Indian wars into 1840. Although the value of the Republic's currency was rapidly declining, the Fourth Congress held the hope that they might be able to secure a foreign loan. To support Texas military forces in 1840, the Congress appropriated $1,620,169 on February 3, 1840. Fisher's army was allowed $1,056,369, only slightly less than the 1839 appropriation —which had not been fully spent.[10]

The appropriations were clearly broken down by infantry, cavalry, and for all army expenses that could be incurred. The funding provided for twelve infantry companies of up to 494 private soldiers and seven cavalry companies of up to 392 mounted cavalrymen each.

These military appropriations were given in spite of the fact that the Republic of Texas' currency value was on a steady decline. The recently elected Fourth Congress had seen progress with the new army's organization and with the Indian offensives that Lamar's forces had carried out on the frontier in late 1839. There was a rising tide of voters, however, who were not happy with other aspects of President Lamar's administration.

Mexico had never fully recognized Texas' independence and the Mexicans had hinted that they would again try to establish sovereignty over Texas. Lamar had tried in vain to obtain a five-million-dollar loan to control the rising inflation and financial insecurity in Texas, but had come up empty handed.[11]

In spite of these political failures, President Lamar's military policies remained largely supported going into 1840, allowing his army and ranger forces to continue their frontier war.

Johnston orders Fisher to San Antonio

From Austin, Secretary of War Albert Sidney Johnston issued orders on January 30 to Lieutenant Colonel William Fisher, the First Regiment's new commander. A native of Virginia, Fisher had fought with the Texas Army during the Texas Revolution. He then served a year as secretary of war before receiving his latest commission in January 1839, to serve as the number two man in charge of the Texas Army. With Colonel Burleson's temporary resignation in place, Fisher was responsible for carrying out Secretary Johnston's orders.

Johnston gave details of the Comanches' visit with Henry Karnes in San Antonio earlier that month. He instructed Fisher to take command of the pending peace negotiations with the Comanches, who had promised to return to San Antonio within thirty days with their principal chiefs. "You will designate, and take command of three companies of the 1st Regiment, who will be immediately marched to San Antonio."[12]

If the Comanches came in with the requested prisoners and delivered them, this act was to be "regarded as an evidence of their sincere desire for peace." The Comanches were to then be treated "with kindness and be permitted to depart without molestation." Before allowing them to leave, Fisher was to warn them about molesting the settlements any further and against attacking surveyors. "Their own happiness depends on their good or bad conduct toward our citizens," wrote Johnston.

Should the Comanches *not* bring in prisoners with them, Fisher was ordered to arrest the Indians and hold them hostage. In this case, "some of their number will be dispatched as messengers to the tribe to inform them that those retained will be held as hostages until the prisoners are delivered up, when the hostages will be released." A further instruction was: "It has been usual, heretofore, to give presents. For the future such custom will be dispensed with."

Following this military order—according to Colonel Karnes' suggestion—President Lamar sent Colonel McLeod, the adjutant general, and Colonel William G. Cooke, the First Regiment's quartermaster general, to act as commissioners to treat with the Comanches when they appeared. These men moved to San Antonio to await events.

During February, Lieutenant Colonel Fisher communicated with the Comanches. He told them not to come in to San Antonio without bringing all of their prisoners. The Comanches promised to arrive at the appointed time.[13]

On February 18, 1840, President Lamar ordered the Frontier Regiment to move its artillery, small arms, ammunition, and other military stores from Houston to Austin, the new capital. Everything was shipped from Galveston to Linn's Landing on Lavaca Bay, where it would be transported north to Austin over land. This ordnance did not reach Austin until May, and it would be more months before proper new workshops were built out.[14]

William Fisher had about 450 able men between his nine infantry companies as of February 1840. He opted to send more than 175 soldiers into San Antonio for the Comanche meeting: Captain William Davis Redd's Company A, Captain Mark Lewis' Company E, and Captain George Thomas Howard's Company I.

Company I was commanded by Captain Benjamin Y. Gillen through the end of February, before Captain Howard received transfer orders to take over. Gillen's men had departed Camp McLeod near Austin on February 3 and arrived at the Mission San José on February 12. By month's end, his company was down to fifty-three men, having lost four to desertion during February.

Redd's forty-eight-man company had reached Mission San José by February 29 and taken up station. They joined Captain John Kennymore's fifty-man Company C at the Mission San José near San Antonio. Captain Lewis' seventy-man Company E would not reach San Antonio until the second week of March.

Redd's company had seen its share of difficulties during the month. After arriving at Mission San José on February 10, privates William Andrew and Calvin Post had deserted on the night of February 20. On February 14, he had sent a small group of soldiers from the three companies at the post to Gonzales to fetch supplies for the post. On their return from Gonzales on February 28, the small party was attacked by Indians at a point only two and a half miles from San Antonio. Two privates—Henry Douglass of Company A and Richard L'Estrange of Company I—were killed. Private C. A. Root of Company A was wounded by a shot in the small of the back. Root's fellow soldier William Kelly also survived, as did Private Augustus Kemper of Company C. This trio returned to Mission San José the following day.[15]

Lieutenant Colonel Fisher's other five companies remained stationed on the frontier. Captain Mark Blake Skerrett's Company H—recruited in late 1839 in Galveston—was sent from Camp Lamar near Austin in early 1840 to the Cherokee Nation in East Texas. Skerrett's number two man was First Lieutenant John S. Sutton, a Delaware native who had recently left the United States Military Academy. Their unit was smaller, numbering fewer than thirty men.[16]

Skerrett took over Fort Scott from Second Lieutenant Abram H. Scott, who was commanding the post with a small detachment of Company E upon Skerrett's arrival in February 1840. Fort Scott was the old Fort Lamar in Smith County, which had been built during the 1839 Cherokee War by Captain Clendenin's First Infantry company. The original post was hastily assembled in July 1839 around the homestead of Elisha DeBard. Lieutenant Scott had been stationed at the Neches Saline with a detachment of troops in early 1840 in present Smith County.

Lieutenant Scott purchased pork for his troops and corn and forage for their horses from Benjamin Vansickle on February 25, while encamped on the Neches. He bought additional food and supplies for improving the old Fort Lamar from John Durst's company, including axes, and a cross cut saw. By March 25, Fort

Lamar had been renamed Fort Scott, as evidenced by a claim for tobacco, clothing, and food furnished by Durst to Company H's troops. This claim was signed by both Scott and Captain Skerrett.[17]

Sometime after April 30, 1840, Fort Scott was renamed Fort Skerrett in honor of its new commander. It was located in southwestern Smith County, about five miles southwest of the present town of Flint. Skerrett's company would remain on operation in East Texas until July 1840.

By the end of February, Company B's thirty-seven men were under acting command of Second Lieutenant Collier Hornsby on the San Gabriel River. Captain Adam Clendenin had been given a temporary furlough on February 7. Captain John Holliday, commanding the fifty-two-man Company D, remained stationed at Fort Burleson as of the end of February. Holliday had endured five soldiers—Corporal Hugh Vance and Privates James Hall, John Herron, William Sweener, and John W. Scott—deserting his post on February 4. A sixth man, Private M. R. Alderman, skipped out on February 18.

The winter of 1840 was tough on the men of the First Regiment of Infantry. On the night of February 21, a number of men of Company G deserted their post at the old Little River Fort, a camp north of the city of Austin. Some of these men were captured within days near the town of Nashville on the Brazos River by three citizens. Those captured were Corporal Jacob McMindus, Sergeant Oliver P. Gale, Private Charles Ladoucer, Private Josiah R. Edgar, and Private James W. Brown, the acting corporal of the guard that night.[18]

Also at the post with Company G was Captain James January's sixty-three-man Company F, recently returned from the turn-of-the-year Northwestern Campaign under Colonel Burleson. They reached the Little River Fort on January 13, but deserted the post on February 10 "on account of the failure of subsistence stores." Of all the First Regiment companies, January's unit suffered the most from lack of provisions and had the highest desertion rate. Between January 20 and February 17, forty-two enlisted men—two-thirds of his unit—had deserted. With a splintering command, January marched back to the Little River Fort on February 20 to organize the remnants of the two companies. By the following day, only fifteen had been apprehended and returned to their companies.[19]

Company E—a forty-three-man unit under the charge of Lieutenant William Dunnington—was called up from Camp Caldwell on February 22 to help deal with the situation. Dunnington's own company had lost two of its number on February 12, when Privates John Connolly and Amos Donaldson deserted from Camp Caldwell. Company E moved first to Nashville and then on to Camp Cazneau on Onion Creek near Austin, arriving on March 5.

Captain Mark Lewis was named acting commander of Company E on February 26. Twenty-one former members of Company G were moved into Captain Lewis' command. At least two others—Privates John Stein and Jacob Mushback—deserted from Camp Cazneau on February 27 before a court martial board could be convened.[20]

By order of Adjutant General Hugh McLeod, a court martial board was held on February 29 at Camp Cazneau, near the city of Austin. The board was assembled at the camp of Company E at 11:00 a.m. President of the board was commissary general of subsistence Colonel William Cazneau. The other board members were Colonel Jacob Snively, Captain George Howard, Captain Lewis, and Lieutenant A. C. Holmes of Company E. Lieutenant Dunnington of Company E was appointed to act as special judge advocate.[21]

The court martial board found the men guilty of desertion and the five were sentenced to be shot to death. President Cazneau, in reading the defenses of the prisoners, felt himself

> compelled to admit, that the temporary want of supplies, and the extreme difficulties attending the transportation when procured, added to the inclemency of the winter, at times when the troops were suffering; though offering no justification of the crime, affords some apology for the exercise of the prerogative of mercy. The prisoners urge as their only hope, and the President admits it, contrary to the stern, but just arbitration of the law; because he believes that as the alleged cause of their desertion are now removed, they will fulfill their pledge to the court, and by their future fidelity redeem themselves from the odium of their past conduct.[22]

Cazneau later addressed the army troops and gave them an admonition about such desertion. Sergeant Gale was demoted to private and was transferred with Private Brown into Company B. The other prisoners from the former Company G were pardoned, released from their arrest, and were returned to duty in Company E of the First Regiment. It would be several months before a new Company G could be organized from new recruits at Galveston.

Greer's Rangers and the Travis Guards

The three remaining Texas Ranger companies from 1839 were discharged during early 1840 and new companies were formed as needed. The first new ranging company to be formed under the authority of the War Department was that of Captain Thomas N. B. Greer. A Tennessee native and a veteran of San Jacinto, Greer had emigrated to Texas in 1835 with his brother, Andrew Greer. By request of President Lamar, he organized his "Boggy and Trinity Rangers" on February 22, 1840.[23]

Captain Greer mustered his company into service under the Third Militia Brigade of General James Smith the following day. His Boggy and Trinity Rangers engaged themselves in the building of a new frontier outpost. The two-story blockhouse was similar to Fort Houston, with the upper floor extending over and beyond the lower floor's walls. This enabled sharpshooters on the second floor to shoot anyone approaching the first floor walls. Captain Greer's rangers built "Fort Boggy" on the north bank of Boggy Creek, about two and one-half miles north of present Leona, and five miles south of Centerville, in present Leon County. A state historical marker now locates the spot.[24]

Captain Greer's rangers served three months, being discharged on May 23 by General Smith, but were not paid. In 1842, Captain Greer was still trying to collect on a compensation claim from the Texas government. President Houston, however, chose to return the bill to the House of Representatives without his signature. Thomas Greer never collected his money. He was killed by Indians in June 1842 on the Trinity River, near the settlement of Alabama in Houston County.[25]

While Greer's men found no Indians to contest, attacks on settlers were more prevalent farther west in the Hill Country

---

Capt. Greer's Boggy & Trinity Rangers: Feb. 23–May 23, 1840

Captain:	James Erwin
Thomas N. B. Greer	James L. Erwin
First Lieutenant:	John Erwin
Thomas Robbins	William H. Howell
Second Lieutenant:	Jefferson Y. Jones
Elisha H. Whitton	John Karner
Orderly Sergeant:	R. B. King
John Byrnes	James Marshall
Second Sergeant:	Benoni Middleton
A. G. Rogers	Thomas J. Middleton
	William B. Middleton
Privates:	James P. Philpot
James C. Bloodworth	William Robbins
James Bozeman	Robert Rogers Sr.
Thomas B. Bozeman	Robert Rogers Jr.
James Byrnes	Stephen N. Rogers
Harvey Capps	William Surles
William B. Capps	
John R. Chatham	Partial muster roll constructed by author's
James W. Easton	research of Republic of Texas audited
Alexander R. Erwin	military claims and pension papers.
George M. C. Erwin	

---

area. Most depredations during the early month of 1840 involved the stealing of horses or settlers' property. The *Brazos Courier* reported in its March 3, 1840, issue that the friendly Tonkawas were believed to have killed a man named Kaughman, who was hunting on Williamson Creek near Austin.[26]

Wayne Barton and a friend discovered Kaughman's body and reported plenty of Indian signs, the trails leading eastward toward Webber's Prairie. On the same night that Kaughman was killed, four horses were stolen from William Barton at Barton Springs.

Colonel McLeod wrote to Edward Burleson—recently retired from leading the Frontier Regiment—on March 7. McLeod knew of the special relationship Burleson had with Chief Plácido of the Tonkawas. He asked Burleson to immediately meet with this tribe and bring them in to Austin to answer charges that the Tonkawas had been conducting raids and murders. According to McLeod, Burleson's presence was "required by the President" for this meeting.[27]

Plácido—whose name meant "Can't Kill Him"—was the son of a Tonkawa warrior and a Comanche woman whom his father had taken captive. He and his Tonkawas had been loyal to Texas settlers since first participating in James Long's 1819 expedition to help fight the Spanish Army. Plácido became chief of the Tonkawas in 1823 and had since scouted for the Texas Rangers and militiamen when requested. Tonkawas were enemies with the Comanches and their associated bands, and were known to remove scalps from their enemies after a battle.[28]

Edward Burleson considered Plácido and his Tonkawas his friends and chose not to believe the charges against them. Gathering Chief Plácido and his Indians, Burleson was bound with them for Austin when word arrived of another depredation. On the night of Friday, March 13, a butcher named Ward and an English yardman named Headley were murdered within the city limits of Austin, this time by the Comanches without any doubt. The Tonkawas were thus cleared of the guilt and remained on friendly terms with the Texans.

As a result of this depredation, a stockade was built around the capitol building in Austin to protect the government officials. Burleson then gathered a small party of volunteers and rode out from Austin to search for the Comanche attackers. He followed their trail toward Brushy Creek and the San Gabriel River, where he picked up another very fresh trail.

This trail led him to the Colorado River and back to within about eight miles of Austin. The *Austin City Gazette* of March 18 included a report from Burleson in which he stated that the Comanches at this point "appeared to have scattered." Burleson's volunteers soon returned to Austin without any encounters. During his time out, however, the Comanches had moved up to San Antonio for their peace talks with the Texas commissioners.

Perhaps in response to these fresh depredations, a new company was formed in Austin on March 1, 1840, called the Travis Guards in honor of the Alamo's fallen hero William B. Travis. Like the former Milam Guards of Houston, the Travis Guards helped protect local citizens, the capital city's government, and the president from attack. The company was uniformed, issued rifles and swords by the government, and operated in the same fashion as volunteer militia.

Capt. Woodhouse's Travis Guards: March 1, 1840 Original Roll

Captain:
M. H. Nicholson [1]
First Lieutenant:
Matthew P. Woodhouse [2]
Second Lieutenant:
Alfred W. Luckett
First Sergeant:
Alexander S. Patterson
Second Sergeant:
A. G. Johnson
Third Sergeant:
John W. Hann
Fourth Sergeant:
C. R. Sossaman
First Corporal:
Thomas Bryson
Second Corporal:
Allen E. Brown
Third Corporal:
M. H. Beaty
Secretary:
J. Y. Burney
Treasurer:
John H. Yerby
Surgeon:
Richard F. Brenham

Privates:
Charles J. Babcock
William B. Billingsley
George W. Bonnell
John Henry Brown
Samuel Browning
William Clark
D. S. Dickinson
George J. Durham
Jacob Eberly
James F. Edrington

George W. Evans
Thomas Gales Forster
Alexander T. Gayle
Joseph Harrell
James C. Harrellson
Bird Holland
Thomas H. Hord
William S. Hotchkiss
William H. Hunt
P. J. Hunter
Archibald C. Hyde
Henry J. Jewett
James F. Johnson
William Henry H. Johnston
Albert G. Kimbell
Alexander C. MacFarlane
Louis F. Marguerat
James D. Martin
William H. Murrah
Shadrach W. Pipkin
William Renney
William H. Sandusky
H. P. Savery
John M. Shreve
John F. Smith
William K. Smith
John Milton Swisher
James Underwood
Lorenzo Walker
Charles J. Webb

[1] Resigned.
[2] Elected captain. Served until later replaced by Captain Joseph Daniels.

Source:*Constitution and By-Laws of the Travis Guards: Adopted March First, 1840*. Austin: Cruger and Bonnell's Print, 1840, 15–6. From the collections in the Center for American History, The University of Texas at Austin.

In its bylaws, the Travis Guards professed themselves to be in service for "establishing protection, insuring domestic tranquility, and providing for the common defense and general prosperity of our city." Unlike Texas Rangers, this company would not stay in the field continually, but would operate more as militiamen, being called out as needed.[29]

The Travis Guards were unique in that they held regular meetings and drills. The company had its own secretary and a treasurer. Members paid a hefty five-dollar initiation fee to join and a three-dollar tax at the expiration of every quarter. When not in the field, the company met on the last Monday of each month and held parade on the first Saturday of every month. Members of the Travis Guards who were called to duty with the Texas Navy or Army would still be considered honorary members.

When the company passed its original constitution and bylaws on March 1, 1840, Captain M. H. Nicholson was voted into command by his companions. The men then proceeded to elect their other officers by ballot. Among the company was George Washington Bonnell, who had been major of the volunteer battalion in which the Milam Guards had once served. Another Travis Guard, Jacob Eberly, had commanded a company during the Texas Revolution. Private Alexander C. MacFarlane would be elected Travis County's sheriff during 1840.

The *Austin City Gazette*'s Wednesday, March 4, issue announced that "a number of the young men of this city have enrolled themselves as a volunteer military company." They had already framed their constitution and planned to meet that Friday evening to complete their officer organization. Captain Nicholson soon resigned his command of the Austin company, and Captain Matthew Woodhouse was elected to succeed him. Woodhouse had served as a first lieutenant in the First Regiment of Infantry of the Texas Army in 1837 and as first lieutenant of Captain James Ownby's rangers during the 1839 Cherokee War.

The *Gazette* also gave a pretty fair summary of what Captain Woodhouse's Travis Guards would mean as full-time security for Austin's residents.

A company of this kind has long been wanted at this place, and, under the direction of efficient officers, cannot fail of rendering essential service to this section of the country. It cannot otherwise than prove the means of inspiring confidence among our citizens as guaranteeing that, in case the hour of danger should again arrive, there will always be a well-organized and disciplined body, on the spot, as a nucleus round which all may rally for mutual protection and defense.

CHAPTER 2

The Council
House Fight

March 19, 1840

On the morning of March 19, two Comanche runners entered San Antonio and announced the arrival of a party of sixty-five men, women, and children. This peace party included many chiefs and warriors, plus one old man and about thirty-two women and children. The only prisoner they brought along, however, was one fifteen-year-old girl—Matilda Lockhart—whose appearance was shocking.

Matilda—the niece of early Texas Ranger Captain Byrd Lockhart—had been captured by Comanches near the Guadalupe River on December 9, 1838, with four other children. After fifteen months of captivity and abuse, the teenage girl was not a pretty sight. Local San Antonio resident Mary Ann Maverick saw Matilda that day and recorded her condition in her memoirs.

> She was in a frightful condition, poor girl, when at last she returned to civilization. Her head, arms and face were full of bruises, and sores, and her nose actually burnt off to the bone—all the fleshy end gone, and a great scab formed on the end of the bone. Both nostrils were wide open and denuded of flesh. She told a piteous tale of how dreadfully the Indians had beaten her, and how they would wake her from sleep by sticking a chunk of fire to her flesh, especially to her nose, and how they would shout and laugh like fiends when she cried. Her body had many scars from fire, many of which she showed us.[1]

21

Colonel Henry Karnes was out of Texas on business when the Comanches appeared as promised in San Antonio with Matilda Lockhart. Lieutenant Colonel Fisher was present with three companies of the First Regiment of Infantry: Captain William Redd's Company A, Captain Mark Lewis' Company E, and Captain George Howard's Company I. Howard had turned command of his Company D over to Captain John Holliday.

Also present in San Antonio this day was Colonel Lysander Wells, head of the army's cavalry, with several of his men. Wells had joined the cavalry during the Texas Revolution, fought at San Jacinto, and had held cavalry commands since 1837. Of key note is the fact that some of Wells' men had recently received the new Colt "Patent Arms" repeating revolvers that were only just beginning to enter Texas by 1840.

Samuel Colt's revolving firearm was patented on February 25, 1836, and was produced in his Patent Arms Manufacturing Company in Paterson, New Jersey. His fourth production model

Colt Paterson repeating firearms began making their presence known on the Texas frontiers by 1840. Some of the Texas Army's cavalrymen, including Major Lysander Wells, had Colt No. 5 repeating pistols at the Council House Fight. Shown left to right are: an 1838 model .52-caliber revolving carbine; a .36-caliber Patent No. 5 "Texas" model Colt revolving pistol; and an 1837 model ring-lever action .52-caliber revolving rifle. *Photo by Tom Knowles, courtesy of the Texas Ranger Hall of Fame and Museum.*

was actually his fifth patent, and was thus known as Colt's Patent No. 5. Of its one-thousand production run, many of these Colts were shipped to Texas. It therefore became known as the Texas Paterson. In early Texas documents, this five-shooter was more commonly referred to as the "Colt Patent Revolver," as his weapons were then known as Patent Arms.[2]

The Texas Paterson was a light caliber (from .28 to .36), five-shooter, cap-and-ball firearm with a four-and-one-half-inch octagonal barrel. In addition, the concealed trigger only dropped into view when the gun was cocked. Five chambers in the cylinder each contained a separately-loaded powder and ball. With all five chambers loaded with powder and balls, only a layer of protective grease prevented the powder blast of one shot from igniting the others and causing the entire cylinder to explode. The hammer was pulled back manually to turn the cylinder and cock the gun.[3]

As fast as the shooter could work the hammer and trigger, he could discharge five rounds at his opponents. When all five shots were spent, the barrel was removed. The chambers were charged by pouring powder into the cylinder, followed by the insertion of the bullets, sealing the chambers, capping the percussion cap nipples, and replacing the barrel.

The original purchase of the Colt Patent Arms had been made in 1839 for the use of the Texas Navy. Some of the navy's pistols would eventually find their way into the hands of Texas Rangers. Another order of these five-shooters was placed for the First Regiment's cavalrymen. Among the ordnance documents of the Texas Army, there are surviving papers which show that several orders were placed for Colt carbines with bullet molds and other accessories. Fifty were ordered by the army on August 3, 1839, at a unit cost of fifty-five dollars. This order also called for fifty belt pistols, with loading levers, bullet molds, and equipment, at a cost of thirty-five dollars each. A second order on October 5, 1839, called for forty more belt pistols, thirty carbines, and fifty rifles, with their respective accessories. For each order, an insurance premium was paid to insure that the orders made their way safely across the frontier to the Texas Army.[4]

An Ordnance Department memo from March 20, 1840, lists five cases of these Patent Arms in Galveston awaiting shipment to Austin for the army's use. Sixteen Patent Arms were being

The Council House in San Antonio, as sketched by artist Raymond Vásquez. It was in this old courthouse building on March 19, 1840, that Texas leaders attempted to negotiate with Comanche leaders for the release of captives taken during depredations. Courtesy of Richard G. Santos, San Antonio, Texas.

shipped to one of the First Regiment companies that was raised by the War Department in February 1840. Army ordnance returns for the First Infantry companies May–June 1840 show that they had thirty Patent Arms. The Paterson carbines and rifles could fire from five to eight shots of larger caliber (.36 to .58), depending on the model.[5]

Wells' cavalrymen were in town but were not immediately part of the proceedings with the Comanches who appeared for their promised negotiations. The twelve senior leaders of the Indians were led into the San Antonio Courthouse, which became known as the "Council House." The courthouse was a one-story stone building which adjoined the stone jail house on the corner of Main Plaza and Calabosa (Market) Street. Both were stone buildings, one story, with flat roofs and dirt floors. The yard in the rear of the courthouse later became the city market on Market Street in San Antonio. This courthouse was erected in the 1740s as part of a building known as the Casas Reales. The building was rich in history. It had once served as the headquarters of the first Spanish governor of Texas. By 1840, the ancient buildings had undergone much reconstruction before becoming San Antonio's jailhouse and courthouse. A new page in the courthouse's history was to be written on March 19, 1840, as it served as the "Council House" for the Comanche negotiations.[6]

In the courthouse yard, the young Indians and the women remained while their leaders met with the Texan commissioners. "The young Indians amused themselves shooting arrows at pieces of money put up by some of the Americans," wrote Mary Maverick. In the meantime, the twelve principal chiefs of the Comanches were asked to take seats on a platform at one end of the room in the courthouse. Present to conduct the questioning at this hearing were Colonel Fisher, Colonel Hugh McLeod, the adjutant general, and Colonel William Cooke, who was quartermaster general and acting secretary of war at the time.[7]

Like William Fisher, Hugh McLeod and William Cooke were both staunch supporters of President Lamar's Indian policies. McLeod had campaigned with Thomas Rusk in 1838 and had fought in both the Kickapoo and Cherokee wars in East Texas in 1839, taking an arrow in the thigh during the latter.

The first order of business on March 19 for these Texas commissioners was to determine where the other prisoners were. The Texans firmly believed that the Comanches were holding no fewer than thirteen white captives. They had brought in only Matilda Lockhart. The abused teenager was brought before the commissioners for questioning on this point, as McLeod related to President Lamar in a letter the next day.

> The little girl was very intelligent and told us that she had seen several of the other prisoners at the principal camp a few days before she left, and that they brought her in to see if they could get a high price for her, and, if so, they intended to bring in the rest, one at a time.[8]

Turning from poor young Lockhart to the Comanche leaders, Colonel Fisher opened his questioning by trying to determine what had become of the other twelve captives: "Where are the prisoners you promised to bring in to the talk?"

Chief Muguara, who had held the last talk with Colonel Karnes, replied, "We have brought in the only one we had. The others are with the other tribes."

"A pause ensued," wrote McLeod, "as this was a palpable lie, and a direct violation of their pledge, solemnly given scarcely a month since." Observing the silence which fell over the Council House negotiators, Chief Muguara spoke up again.

"How do you like the answer?" he demanded.

The commissioners were already angered by the visual signs of abuse on Matilda Lockhart's face and body. The arrogance of the Comanche leaders at this point in refusing to discuss their other captives ended the chance for a peaceful resolution.

Colonel Fisher then decided to exercise his orders to hold the Indian leaders hostage until terms could be negotiated for the others' release. He ordered Captain George Howard's Company I into the room to prevent the Comanches from leaving. Captain William Redd's Company A was ordered to the rear of the building, where the younger Comanches were assembled. As the guards took their posts, the talks continued for a few moments, according to McLeod.

> During the execution of this order, the talk was re-opened and the terms of a treaty, directed by your excellency to be made with them in case the prisoners were restored, were discussed, and they were told the treaty would be made when they brought in the prisoners. They acknowledged that they had violated all their previous treaties, and yet tauntingly demanded that new confidence should be reposed in another promise to bring in the prisoners.

Fisher then told the twelve Comanche chiefs that they were now prisoners of Texas for coming to San Antonio without their prisoners. "Your women and children may depart in peace, and your braves may go and tell your people to send in the prisoners," Fisher explained.[9]

The interpreter, a Tejano familiar with the Comanche language, was reluctant to translate Fisher's statement as to their prisoner status. Only upon Colonel Fisher's demand did the interpreter utter the Penateka translation of the sentence. "We told the chiefs that the soldiers they saw were their guards, and descended from the platform," wrote Hugh McLeod. "The chiefs immediately followed." Before the Texans could depart the courthouse, the Indian leaders bolted from their seats.

One Comanche chief sprang for the Council House's back door and attempted to pass by the sentinel, Private Martin Kelly. The soldier presented his musket, but the Comanche drew his knife and stabbed Kelly, wounding him severely. A mad rush was then made for the door.

Captain Howard seized one of the Indians and received a severe stab wound in the side during the process. Howard ordered his sentinel to fire upon them, which he immediately did. The Comanche who had stabbed Howard fell dead to the floor. "They then all drew their knives and bows, and evidently resolved to fight to the last," related Colonel McLeod.

"Fire if they do not desist!" shouted Lieutenant Colonel Fisher.

The Indians rushed the Texan guards and a general fight immediately broke out. Musket smoke and shouts filled the room as a hand-to-hand melee ensued. John Hemphill—a lawyer from South Carolina who had just been confirmed in January as judge of the Fourth Judicial District of the Republic of Texas—was present in the Council House and was attacked by one of the chiefs. Judge Hemphill was forced to defend himself and he disemboweled his opponent with his bowie knife. Lieutenant William Dunnington was shot through with an arrow, but managed to fire his pistol into the face of one of the chiefs before he collapsed, mortally wounded. Within moments, all of the twelve Penateka Comanches' chiefs were killed, stabbed, or shot down at close range.

Captain Howard, seriously wounded during his stabbing, was unable to lead his men. He passed acting command of his soldiers to Lieutenant Benjamin Gillen, who had been the original commander of Company I.

The war whoops that rang out from the Council House were instantly understood by the other Indians in the San Antonio courthouse yard. Captain Redd—whose Company A was posted in the rear of the Council House—was attacked by the twenty younger Comanches in the yard. Some of the Indians raced to take cover in the stone houses surrounding the Council House. They began firing upon the Texan soldiers with bows, arrows, and a few rifles.

Company A's First Lieutenant Edward Adams Thompson, who had served under Captain Clendenin during the 1839 Cherokee War, was wounded. At least two civilians, Judge Hugh Thompson and young George W. Cayce, were immediately shot by arrows from the younger Comanches. Cayce, standing near

---

The "Council House Fight": March 19, 1840

Killed in Action:	Wounded:
Company A:	*Company A:*
Frederick Kaminsky, Pvt.	Edward Adams Thompson, Lt.
Company E:	*Company I:*
William M. Dunnington, First Lt.	George Thomas Howard, Capt.
Robert G. Whitney, Pvt.	Martin Kelly, Pvt.
Non-Military:	Mathew Caldwell, Capt.
George W. Cayce	
Joseph L. Hood, judge	*Non-Military:*
Hugh Miller Thompson, judge	Judge James W. Robinson
Unnamed Hispanic man	Thomas Higginbotham
	John C. Morgan, deputy sheriff
	_____ Carson

---

the door of the courthouse, "was shot and instantly killed at the beginning of the fight, and fell by the side of Captain Caldwell," wrote Mary Maverick.[10]

The younger Comanches raced around the back of the courthouse and were confronted by Captain Redd's infantrymen. Private Frederick Kaminsky of Company A and four Comanches were killed in this sharp exchange. Judge Joseph Hood was shot full of arrows as he started down from the jailhouse porch. Others were killed or wounded as the excited Comanches fought for their lives. Near the entryway to the Council House, Robert J. Whitney—who had joined Company E on October 3, 1839, in Galveston—was also killed. Thomas Higginbotham, a neighbor of the Mavericks, ran from his house and was severely wounded before he could reach the street.[11]

Colonel Lysander Wells, head of the army cavalry, carried one of the new Colt repeating pistols. Ill-trained on how to shoot this new pistol, the startled Texan had his wedge improperly placed and his gun would not fire. An Indian grabbed the barrel, jerked it loose, and left Wells cursing his luck and the new gun. In the continuing fight, Wells fought hand to hand with his Comanche foe. He finally pulled one of his lap pistols and "fired into the Indian's body," killing him. Another of Wells' cavalrymen, young Henry Clay Davis, used his new Colt pistol to kill another Comanche who was wielding an arrow as a dagger.[12]

Captain Mathew "Paint" Caldwell was present in San Antonio, visiting the Samuel Maverick family at this time. A forty-two-year-old Gonzales resident and signer of the Texas Declaration of Independence, Caldwell had fought Indians on the Rio Blanco in April 1835, and had been wounded during the Béxar siege later that year. He had been nicknamed both "Old Paint," because of his spotted whiskers, and "the Paul Revere of the Texas Revolution," for riding from Gonzales to Bastrop to call men to arms. He served as a recruiter of rangers during the revolution and commanded the Gonzales County Rangers during 1839. Caldwell later joined the First Regiment of Infantry as a commander of scouts, serving on Edward Burleson's Northwestern Campaign during December 1839–January 1840.

Paint Caldwell had wandered unarmed down toward the San Antonio courthouse at the time the action ensued with the Comanches. According to an account published in the *Telegraph and Texas Register*, Caldwell ducked into a nearby house to look for a weapon.

No one was at home, and he passed into the back yard. There he was confronted by an Indian warrior, who made ready to shoot him. Caldwell stooped down and picked up a rock, which he threw, hitting the warrior on the forehead, slightly stunning him. Caldwell continued to throw stones, hurling them so fast, that for dodging, the Indian did not get a chance to take aim and let fly an arrow.

As Caldwell continued to hold the Comanche at bay with rocks, John Dabney Morris—the twenty-four-year-old district attorney for Béxar's Fourth Judicial District—came into the enclosure. A former lawyer from Virginia, Judge Morris fortunately was armed this day with a single-shot, three-inch barrel pistol. Caldwell, nearing exhaustion, called, "Shoot him, John."

Morris did as requested, moving to within point-blank range for the ineffective belt pistol before putting a shot through the Comanche's heart. Paint Caldwell was wounded early in the fighting by a gunshot through the right leg. He later believed that he may have been struck by the shot from a Texas soldier. In the initial panic of fleeing Indians, some of the First Regiment soldiers were firing wildly.[13]

An early artist's rendering of the deadly fight with Comanche chiefs inside San Antonio's Council House on March 19, 1840. Originally published in 1912 in DeShield's *Border Wars of Texas*.

Those Indians who were not killed in the fighting directly surrounding the Council House climbed walls and fled through the streets of San Antonio. Deputy Sheriff John C. Morgan was standing in the back yard of a residence when three Comanches scaled the wall and attacked him. Morgan would prove to be more of a fighter than his aggressors might have imagined. A former Texas Ranger who had served both in Captain Sterling Robertson's 1836 company and later in Colonel Coleman's ranger battalion, Morgan had also served in Captain Deaf Smith's 1837 cavalry company which had fought Mexican soldiers near Laredo.

The three Comanches surprised Morgan and wounded him. During the struggle, he managed to grab a rock and fracture the skull of one of his assailants, killing him. Morgan then grabbed an axe and retreated into the house, taking cover behind an open door. According to the *Telegraph*'s account, "The two remaining Indians attempted to follow him, and he killed them with terrific blows, dealt with the axe."

Some of the Indians ran up Soledad Street toward the San Antonio River. Several passed across the yard of the Samuel Maverick homestead. Mary Maverick shouted for her husband and her brother, Andrew Adams, who quickly retrieved their firearms. Caught up in the action, Mary had gone out into the street, without thinking of her own safety.

Mike Chevallie, a second lieutenant of the First Regiment, shouted to her, "Are you crazy? Go in or you will be killed."

In her memoirs, Mary Maverick related the bravery of one of her family's servants in the face of the fleeing Comanches.

One had paused near Jinny Anderson, our cook, who stood bravely in front of the children, mine and hers, with a great rock lifted in both hands above her head, and I heard her cry out to the Indians, "If you don't go 'way from here I'll mash your head with this rock!"[14]

The Comanche paused to consider the woman only for a moment before dashing down the bank into the river. He swam for the opposite shore, but he was shot and killed by Andrew Adams before he cleared the other bank.

A small party of the younger Comanches escaped across the river, but were pursued by Colonel Wells and his mounted men. All of the Indians were killed. Only one of their party—a renegade Mexican traveling with the Indians—managed to escape. A single Comanche took refuge in a stone house, refusing every opportunity offered him to surrender. He killed or wounded several during the day. The Texian soldiers even sent in an Indian woman to tell him to surrender and spare himself. The Comanche refused and continued to shoot throughout the late afternoon.

After night fell, Anton Lockmar and another young Béxar man climbed up on the roof with a ball of rags soaked in turpentine. He lit the rag ball on fire and dropped it through the chimney in the stone house's roof. The burning rag ball landed squarely on the Comanche's head and stuck there. "Thus, in a blaze of fire, he sprang through the door and was riddled with bullets," wrote Colonel McLeod.[15]

McLeod's report says thirty chiefs and warriors were killed, plus three women and two children, for a total of thirty-five casualties. Two old men and twenty-seven women and children were taken prisoner, for a total of twenty-nine prisoners. They were locked in the city jail for safekeeping. Only the one Mexican man who had been traveling with the Comanches managed to slip away during the fighting and make his escape. More than one hundred horses and a large quantity of buffalo robes and peltries were taken by the Texans.

The Texans had suffered fifteen casualties. Those dead included Lieutenant Dunnington, two judges, two First Regiment soldiers, and two civilians. Wounded were captains George Howard and Paint Caldwell, plus two soldiers, two civilians, another judge, and Béxar's deputy sheriff. Captain Caldwell was assisted back to the Samuel Maverick homestead, where he was attended to by the town's Russian physician, Dr. Edmund Weideman.

> Dr. Weideman came and cut off his boot and found the bullet had gone entirely through the leg, and lodged in the boot, where it was discovered. The wound, though not dangerous, was very painful, but the doughty captain recovered rapidly and in a few days walked about with the aid of a stick.[16]

Lieutenant Thompson was in much worse shape. He had been shot through the lungs and was taken into Madam Santita's house on Soledad Street. "That night he vomited blood and cried and groaned all night," wrote Mary Maverick. "I shall never forget his gasping for breath and his agonizing cries."

Dr. Weideman stayed with the army lieutenant during the night, leaving only on occasion to tend to some of the other wounded men. Thompson was not expected to live until daybreak, but he did. His strength returned, and within weeks he walked out of San Antonio on his own power.

Perhaps because of his dedicated work in saving Lieutenant Thompson, Dr. Weideman was later hired as a surgeon for the First Regiment of Infantry. Still, the townspeople found him to be very strange. A man of about thirty-five years of age, he spoke fluent English, Russian, and other languages. "The Emperor of Russia had sent him to Texas to find and report anything and everything, vegetable and animal grown in Texas," recalled one San Antonio citizen.[17]

Considered morbid by some, Dr. Weideman collected the bodies of some of the Comanche victims in his cart. He selected the heads of one Comanche woman and man as specimens. He also selected two bodies to boil and preserve as skeletons for scientific study. When he dumped the boiled water into a ditch on the night of March 20, townspeople began calling him "diabolo," "demonio," and other names.

The captured Comanches were put into the jail—on the corner of Market Street adjoining the courthouse—for several days. The army leaders continued to treat with their captives to work on further peace solutions. Colonel Fisher made an agreement with the captives—who were acting for their Nation—that a twelve-day truce would be maintained with the Comanches.[18]

In accordance with the stipulations of this treaty, one Indian woman, the widow of a chief, was released on March 20, the day following the Council House battle. She was mounted on a horse, given provisions, and allowed to return to her people. The Texans had good reason to believe that the Comanches still held at least fifteen Americans and several Mexican prisoners. The Indian woman was ordered to tell her tribe to return these captives and that the Texans would return the twenty-seven other Comanche captives they now held.

The Indian woman rode off quickly to carry out her mission, but would not be seen again. The Comanches had sent in this delegation to conduct peaceful negotiations, and all of their men had been killed. The mood of the negotiations had collapsed due to the Indians' arrogance and lies concerning their captives. The testimony and visual evidence of torture displayed by young captive Matilda Lockhart certainly had incensed the Texas negotiators. She also told of other hostages being held in camp, a clear violation of promises made by the Comanches. Henry Karnes had originally suggested to Secretary of War Johnston that the Comanches should be seized and held hostage if they did not fully cooperate. Johnston, of course, had ordered William Fisher to do just that.[19]

The Comanches were known to avoid capture, so Karnes, Johnston, and Fisher certainly were aware of the terrible fight they might have faced if they tried to arrest these Indian leaders. The Council House Fight did not kill all of the leading chiefs of the Comanches. Muguara was the most influential leader present, yet he was not even head of his band, the Penateka. Thus the killing of these minor chiefs simply gave the senior Comanche leaders no reason to trust any future peace talks with the white men.

For the Texians and the local newspaper editors, the Council House Fight was a justified battle due to the poor condition of the young captive the Comanches had brought in. The Indians had been given notice to bring in other captives and could have simply surrendered. When word of the event made it back to the Comanches and their affiliated bands, the deaths in San Antonio would be considered nothing but a massacre. Forgiveness was not an option.

The Penateka Comanches now had a score to settle.

CHAPTER 3

Spring Expeditions

April–July 1840

Nine days after their Council House losses, a war party of at least two hundred Comanches rode down to San Antonio on March 28 looking for a fight.

Chief Isomania, veteran of an earlier fight with frontiersman Jack Hays, boldly came into town with another Comanche. They rode into the San Antonio public square, tauntingly circling around the plaza on their horses. The two paraded some distance down Commerce Street and back again, shouting all the while for the Americans to come out and fight them.[1]

Chief Isomania was nearly naked, his body streaked black with war paint. In front of the local saloon on the northeast corner of the public square, he halted his horse. Rising in his stirrups, he angrily shook his clenched fist and shouted defiantly. Mary Maverick wrote in her memoirs, "The citizens, through an interpreter, told him the soldiers were all down the river at Mission San José and if he went there Colonel Fisher would give him fight enough."[2]

Chief Isomania did just that. He and his war party rode up to the mission, located four miles below town, and dared the soldiers to come out and fight. Colonel William Fisher was confined to his bed due to a fall from his horse and Captain William Redd was in acting command of the post.

Captain Redd stated that he must hold true to the twelve-day truce promised at the Council House. Redd hoped to work out the release of other American captives. He would be happy to fight after the twelve days. The disgusted Indians denounced Redd's men as "liars" and "cowards" and rode away, Isomania being the last to leave town.

Lieutenant Colonel Fisher wrote:

> I saw one of the principal war chiefs, Isamini, who is well known here and sustains a great reputation for bravery. He appears to be evidently anxious to become reconciled to the whites; and it appears that in a council held by them the evening before they came in town, he killed a Comanche Indian for endeavoring to excite the Comanches to offensive measures. They have gone on the Pinto trail toward the head of the Pedernales.[3]

Captain Howard Negotiates Prisoner Release

The Comanches remained in the San Antonio area throughout the truce period. On April 3, Chief Piava—an unusually heavy-set chief—rode into San Antonio with an Indian woman. They announced that the Comanches had brought in white captives for exchange. According to Captain George Howard, Chief Piava was offered "bread, brown sugar candy cones (peloncillo), and a beef" for his information.[4]

The following day, April 4, talks were opened between Howard's First Regiment soldiers and the party of Comanches. In a letter written on April 8, Colonel Fisher described how a

> party of Comanche Indians, about thirty in number, made their appearance in the neighborhood of San Antonio and expressed through their messengers a desire to effect an exchange of prisoners. Being at the time confined to bed, unable to move, in consequence to a severe fall which I had received, I dispatched Captain Howard, in command of "C" and "F" companies, First Infantry, to San Antonio with instructions to effect an exchange.[5]

The captains of the First Regiment moved frequently between commands during 1840. George Howard, now in temporary command of Captain James January's Company F, took his men and Captain John Kennymore's Company C into town to negotiate the prisoner release.

> I marched to the town with the company of Captain Kennymore and my own, early on the morning of yesterday, the fifth instant.
> The Indian called Piava, well known as a crafty and treacherous Comanche, of some influence, came in and proposed an exchange of prisoners. I assented and requested him to bring in such Texian prisoners as they had, and we would exchange one for one.[6]

Captain Howard and Chief Piava carried on their negotation talks for some length, during which "Piava displayed nothing but suspicion and a design to obtain some advantage in the exchange."

Finally, the two leaders agreed that two San Antonio citizens would return with Piava to the Comanche party with an Indian woman and a child of about nine years age, both of whom had been captured at the Council House Fight. Damasio and Antonio Pérez were sent with Chief Piava and the two former Comanche captives. They returned a half hour later from the Indian camp with two captives.

One was a Mexican child "about twelve years old, and unknown to any person here." The other captive was well known––six-year-old Elizabeth Putman—who had been kidnapped from the Guadalupe River in December 1838. The soldiers found that Elizabeth did not speak English, was covered in bruises, and her nose was partially burned off from cruelty.

About fifteen minutes later, Chief Piava returned with two other captives, a boy kidnapped from San Antonio in 1836, and a little girl who had been taken from the Carlos ranch near Goliad in 1838 or 1839.

Captain Howard was anxious to retrieve all of the American captives from these Comanches.

> By this time, I had discovered from the captives in our hands that several American and a number of Mexican captives had been left in their camps, and that they had

here (after having effected the exchange of the above named four), but five more prisoners, vis: an American boy, a Mexican girl, taken from this place, and three boys from the other side of the Rio Grande.

Piava was extremely anxious to purchase a certain squaw we had; but having discovered her value, and that they had prisoners of ours which they had failed to bring in, I refused to deliver her, trusting that with her we should yet be able to effect the release of the other prisoners in their hands.[7]

The Indian woman desired by Chief Piava was "a squaw whose arm had been broken in the fight on the 19th." When Howard asked Piava why he selected her, he found that the woman had been wife of a great chief killed in the fight and that she had "muchas mules, muchas mules."

Howard made a proposition to free more Americans. Piava was to allow two Texans to enter their camp to select any two captives they desired. In return, Piava's Comanches would be allowed to select any two Comanche prisoners he wished to be released from the First Regiment's hold. The only exception made to him was the Indian woman he desired.

It was a high stakes game being played by the Texas soldiers and the frontier Indians. Human lives were exchanged like cards. Any aggressive moves by one party might have caused the other player to fold his hand and take his chips home with him.

Howard selected Dr. Shields Booker and San Antonio citizen Cornelius Van Ness to make the prisoner selections for the Texans. Booker had served in the Texas Army during the San Jacinto campaign and had treated the wounded during the 1839 Cherokee War. Van Ness, a thirty-seven-year old formerly from Vermont, had once served as a secretary of legislation to his father, the U.S. minister to Spain from 1829 to 1837. With his brother George Van Ness, he had moved to San Antonio in 1837, where he had been appointed district attorney of the Fourth Judicial District. Shortly after Chief Piava had departed, Dr. Booker and Van Ness set out with Captain Howard and several mounted and armed citizens.[8]

They approached to within about three hundred yards of the Comanche camp. There, Howard's men were met by Piava and principal Chief Isomania, who had been one of the chiefs who had negotiated with Albert Sidney Johnston in 1838. The Comanche leaders were accompanied by a half dozen of their younger men, who stood with their bows strung and firearms ready.

The five prisoners were brought out and shown to the Texan party. According to Howard, the resulting negotiations "exhausted nearly an hour, during which we were at one moment almost at blows." Calm was finally restored enough to agree with Chief Isomania for the purchase of Booker L. Webster (who had been a captive of the Comanches since 1839), the Mexican girl, and one of the other Rio Grande captives.

Booker Webster was known to still be among the Comanches, because his thirty-two-year-old mother had just escaped from their camp about the time of the Council House Fight. She fled with her three-year-old daughter and spent days going through the wilderness, before reaching San Antonio on March 26, 1840. There, the local women cleaned her and began nursing her back to health.[9]

The party returned to San Antonio, where they made the exchange for three of their Comanche prisoners. Captain Howard's report continues.

> In the course of a talk which I had with Piava, I told him that if he would bring in the other Texian prisoners in their camps, we would give them the remaining captives we had. He said *he* was a friend of the Americans; but a portion of the Comanches wanted to fight.
>
> I told him that we were willing to make *peace* or *war*, and if they wished war, we were ready, and upon the first manifestation of hostilities on their part, we should save them the trouble of coming so far to attack us, but would march our men up to their houses and fight them there.[10]

Chief Piava remained fixated on freeing one specific Comanche woman being held by the First Regiment. He promised to go buy other Texian prisoners and bring them in to effect her release. George Howard's soldiers had successfully managed to secure the peaceful release of seven young Comanche prisoners, in return for releasing an equal number of the Indians they had taken at the Council House Fight.

The two parties separated on April 5, 1840, with the understanding that the Comanches were to return once they had rounded up more American prisoners from other camps. Piava appeared worried that he would not find enough Americans to exchange one-for-one, but Howard offered to accept "runaway negroes" that were being held among the Comanches "if after his return I was satisfied he had no more prisoners."

Whether Chief Piava's men would honestly return with more captives was doubtful. "I do not think any reliance is to be placed in their word," Captain Howard wrote to Lieutenant Colonel Fisher on April 6.

Former captive Booker Webster—returned with a shaved head and painted in Indian colors—offered intelligence on Comanche activities. Once they had received news of the bloody Council House fight, Webster said the Comanches "howled and cut themselves with knives, and killed horses, for several days." They then took thirteen of their American captives and "roasted and butchered them to death with horrible cruelties." They spared Booker Webster and six-year-old Elizabeth Putman, only because they had been previously adopted into the tribe. The three other Putman children were apparently with other bands of Comanches and were spared from this killing.[11]

After this little event, the Comanches remained quiet around San Antonio for several months. They regrouped and other men stepped up to fill the positions vacated by their slain chiefs. In due time, they would strike back against the Texans.

The prisoners taken at the Council House Fight eventually managed to escape. From the city jailhouse, the captives were later moved to the Mission San José, to be guarded by the First Regiment. They were then later moved to Camp Cooke at the head of the San Antonio River. The prisoners never trusted the kindness that they were offered, and they gradually escaped as the lax security permitted. Several of the Indian women and children were taken into San Antonio homes to work and live, but they ran away as soon as they were able.[12]

Most of the settlements of Texas were quiet from Indian depredations during early 1840. Former ranger commander George

Bernhard Erath found so little Indian activity in Milam County that he worked earnestly at his surveying business during the first five months of the year. Some of Erath's surveying expeditions carried him far into northern Texas, although without injury, as he later wrote.

> The two expeditions I made up to the first of May were more profitable than any before, notwithstanding I had employed for extra guard about double the hands needed. The contracts I had made were with New Orleans landowners, who were willing to pay good money for surveying. Texas money was taken at its value in New Orleans, where all goods imported to Texas were bought. I saw nothing of Indians during these two expeditions, although a hundred miles out from the settlements. But in June, with only ten men, I found myself forced to return on account of Indians.[13]

The most serious threat to the settlers came in the form of a new rumored invasion of Texas by neighboring Mexico. The Texas diplomatic agent sent to Mexico to settle defense and boundary issues reported in mid-February that the Mexican government was delaying. Soon thereafter came the rumors that Mexico intended another invasion.[14]

Such news prompted President Lamar to order the first and second militia brigades to be kept ready at a day's notice. He had not called out any expeditions since Burleson's Northwestern Campaign that had ended during the first days of January.

On April 3, Lieutenant Colonel Fisher—commanding the detachment at Mission San José near San Antonio—sent a messenger to the secretary of war in Austin. Fisher reported that the Federalist Army had fought and lost a bloody fight against the Centralist Army at Santa Rita de Morelos on March 24–25. The Federalist movement was strongest in the northern states of Mexico, where the leaders had broken away from Mexico's Centralist government in an effort to reinstate the Constitution of 1824. Jesús Cárdenas was chosen president and General Antonio Canales was commander-in-chief of the Federalist Army.[15]

Following the defeat at Morelos, General Canales' remaining forces had retreated into Texas, arriving on the Medina River by

April. William Fisher was informed that if General Canales or any other Federal armed force commander should show himself in San Antonio, he was to be warned that he was not permitted to organize or recruit forces within Texas for the purpose of prosecuting war against the Mexican government.[16]

Adjutant General McLeod sent clarifying orders to Fisher on April 4. The Federalist troops were to be allowed to avail themselves of Texas for safety and protection, and could purchase supplies and food from within Texas. They could do no more, unless Texas was directly invaded by the opposing Centralist army. Under such an attack, Fisher was to use his Frontier Regiment to help expel the raiders. General Canales and his Federalist troops would fight alongside Fisher under the Texas flag. In order to prepare for such a possible defensive action, Lieutenant Colonel Fisher was ordered to reinforce his garrison at San Antonio. By early April, Fisher had about 160 men at the old Mission San José, organized into three companies.[17]

During May, General Canales made a trip from Austin to Houston and Galveston to secure clothing, provisions, and supplies for his Federalist troops to use in another expedition. Canales' senior military commanders included Colonel José María Jesus Carbajal, Major Luis López, Colonel José María Gonzáles, and Juan Nepomuceno Molano. The Federalist agents secured their goods at Galveston and used the steamboat *Constitution* to haul them to San Patricio on the Nueces River.[18]

Colonel George Hockley of the Ordnance Department entered into an arms contract with Tryon Son & Company of Philadelphia on April 3, 1840, for the Texas government. He ordered the manufacturing and furnishing of 1,500 muskets and their accoutrements to be delivered in parcels of one hundred. They were to be paid for upon each delivery. Hockley was able to renegotiate with the company to furnish these arms at a discounted rate equivalent to what the U.S. military paid for arms when purchased in contracts of thousands of muskets per year. Tryon Son & Company's records would later reflect that ordnance deliveries of muskets had been made to Texas on at least the following dates: October 13, November 14, and December 11, 1840, and January 23, February 27, and March 26, 1841.[19]

★ ★ ★ ★ ★

Captain Jackson's Fannin County Rangers

The political unrest caused by the Federalist and Centralist armies had less effect upon the citizens of Texas' more northern frontier. There, the settlers still feared raids from bands of Indians along the Red River.

In North Texas, another new ranger company was formed in Fannin County to help keep the peace. Captain Daniel R. Jackson mustered in a twenty-nine-man unit on March 28, 1840, by the order of Major William M. "Buckskin" Williams, the former first lieutenant of Captain John Emberson's 1839 ranger company. Daniel Jackson was an eligible bachelor and a diehard ranger. He was a private in Captain Nathaniel Journey's 1839 rangers and served as first lieutenant of Captain Mark Roberts' Fannin County rangers from September 16, 1839, to March 16, 1840.

Shortly after the disbanding of Captain Roberts' company, Jackson was called upon to raise his own ranger unit for service

---

Capt. Jackson's Fannin County Rangers: March 28–Sept. 28, 1840

Captain:
Daniel R. Jackson
First Lieutenant:
John M. Gann
Second Lieutenant:
Joshua B. Sharpless

Privates:
Spencer Asberry
John Barker
Carter Bourland [1]
Archibald Carter
John H. Davis
Mitchell George
James J. Holcomb
A. P. Houston
Isaac Houston
Joseph Hunter
William Hunter
Charles Jackson
James Jeffries
Jesse Kuykendall
T. L. Larrimore
Luther Luster [1]

William Lyles
Peter Maroney
James Martin
R. R. McIntire
Alexander McKinney [2]
David Pettit
Isaac Reed
William M. Rice [3]
John L. Scantling
James Seymour
John Seymour
Joseph Sowell
Joseph Strickland [4]
John Van Dine
Samuel Wychard [5]

[1] Enlisted June 15, 1840.
[2] Enlisted June 28, 1840.
[3] Enlisted May 28, 1840.
[4] Enlisted May 22, 1840.
[5] Served as replacement for Carter Bourland from April 28.

Key source: Joseph Hunter PD, R 163, F 624.

in Fannin County. Among the provisioning vouchers for his company is one dated April 2, 1840, at Fort Coffee on the Red River, which shows delivery of coffee, corn, and provisions. It also shows that his rangers received three dozen gun flints for their muskets and three boxes of percussion caps. This has led to some speculation that the Colt Paterson five-shooters were working their way into the hands of Texas Rangers by early spring 1840. This receipt, however, only offers that as a possibility.[20]

Percussion caps were not uncommon in Texas by 1840, as many older muskets had been converted to cap-and-ball rifles. The 1835 ranging company of Captain Daniel Friar had also purchased both gun flints and boxes of percussion caps for its mixed assortment of rifles.

Jackson's rangers were paid $25 per month, or $150 for the full six months of their service period. Jackson signed discharges as "Capt. Rangers" on September 28, 1840, in Fannin County. While serving as captain of his ranger company, Captain Jackson was married to Susannah Lee on July 27, 1840. Only a little less than a year after his marriage, this early northern Texas ranger leader would pass away on June 11, 1841.[21]

Burleson Readies an Expedition

In the weeks following the Council House fight, Edward Burleson was called upon to lead another Indian expedition into the Comanche country to keep the peace. He had his share of difficulties, and on April 2, announced that "it is impossible to get the necessary supplies all in readiness for the intended expedition against the Indians before Tuesday the 7th." Burleson planned to leave on that date for a tour of "six weeks or two months."[22]

Changes in the military leadership appear to have stalled out this Burleson campaign. Neither of his military superiors—new Secretary of War Branch Archer nor new Major General Felix Huston of the militia—had any Indian-fighting experience whatsoever. Huston had been elected into the Texas Militia's senior position in late 1839 and had succeeded Thomas Rusk in 1840. Fifty-year-old Archer, a physician who had come to Texas in 1831 from Virginia, had vast legislative experience, but even less military background than Huston.

Burleson was troubled with conflicting assignments from neophyte frontier commanders Archer and Huston. On April 10, he was ordered to go after a band of Comanches in the Walnut Creek area near Austin. Chief Plácido and his Tonkawas had spotted the Comanches near Walnut Creek. Hugh McLeod ordered Burleson to "select from Captain Pierce's company a detachment of the best mounted" men and to proceed with them, and some of Plácido's Tonkawas, to scour this area. Burleson received simultaneous orders on April 10, the second dispatch calling for him to take the Pitkin Guards to San Antonio. There, he was to call up the militia of Béxar County and work on the exchange of prisoners with the Comanches. [23]

Twenty-four-year-old Captain John Constantinus Pierce was in command of a mounted volunteer company from Harris County known as the "Pitkin Guards." Pierce's company was named after John W. Pitkin of Houston, who had organized the unit for Texan frontier defense. The Pitkin Guards had been enrolled in Houston for three months' service on March 7, 1840, under orders of Brigadier General Edwin Morehouse, commander of the Second Brigade of the Texas Militia.[24]

While the company was organizing and gearing up to move out, it remained at "Camp Pitkin" just outside Houston through at least March 18. The company's first lieutenant, Ebenezer B. Nichols, was also the company's acting quartermaster. He managed to procure from Buckman Canfield 525 pounds of beef "for the use of the mounted company of infantry raised by order of the War Department of the 18th February 1840."[25]

Captain Pierce's company moved out from Camp Pitkin for deployment under orders to supplement the regular garrison at San Antonio. They were camped at Camp Nichols on March 25, 1840, where William P. Bird furnished beef to the company. This camp was located near San Felipe in Austin County and was probably named for First Lieutenant Nichols.[26]

Just as quickly as he had given Burleson two conflicting sets of orders, Colonel McLeod countermanded both directions the following day, April 11. Burleson and Captain Pierce were ordered to remain in Austin for further orders. These did come on April 23 from Secretary Archer. He ordered the company "of Capt. C. Pierce to accompany the surveyors appointed to run the line between Travis and Béxar Counties."[27]

Capt. Pierce's Pitkin Guards: March 7–June 6, 1840

Captain:
Constantius Pierce
First Lieutenant:
Ebenezer B. Nichols
Second Lieutenant:
Harvey R. Marks
Orderly Sergeant:
Robert Leslie Heckle
Second Sergeant:
Francis S. Wilson
Third Sergeant:
John Lemon
Fourth Sergeant:
Timothy F. Hart
First Corporal:
Thomas V. Mortimer
Second Corporal:
S. T. Smith
Third Corporal:
A. B. Sutherland
Fourth Corporal:
G. W. Chambers

Privates:
E. C. Alexander
E. E. Backus
Lemicks E. Banks
Henry Barcheskey
Henry Barker
P. V. Bickford
William Bishoff
Marquis Booth
Marcus Boyce
John C. Champion
John B. Couteau
Edmund P. Crosby
Adrian Deckler
Joseph Dewey
Alfred S. Donovan
Addison Drinkwater [1]
James Duncan
Herman Ehrenberg
Joseph Emerson
William H. Emory [2]
Dell M. Eustace

D. Fallon [3]
O. Fallon
Robert R. Fleming
Simon Frazier [1]
John G. Hadnot
Lawrence Hefferman
Joseph Hobson
E. W. Jackson
Fred R. Johnson
L. D. Justice
William H. Kennedy
Robert Kilgore
John G. Knapp
Nicholas Lardner
George Leila
Samuel Mason
Robery May
_____ Mentig [4]
Jacob Miller
Alexander H. Moore
H. V. Morell
Peter Moss
William Nagle
Joseph Nelson [5]
Alfred Nightingale
William Oltman
John O'Meara
Edward Padloup
Milton Perry
William F. Powell
James A. Prestwood
John Rahm
Fidel Secholzea
John Siberia
John T. Vance
William Winkler
George Young

[1] Joined April 13 at Austin.
[2] Deserted April 15.
[3] Dishonorably discharged April 24.
[4] Deserted March 19.
[5] Dishonorably discharged April 22.
Source: Texas State Archives.

When this mission was complete, Pierce was to march his men to San Antonio and report to the commander of the post Mission San José for further orders.

Pierce's Pitkin Guards were stationed at Mission San José during late April and early May. During May, most of the Frontier Regiment troops stationed at Mission San José were ordered to move out to Mission Concepción and to Camp Cooke. The Pitkin Guards were then ordered back to Mission Concepción. A provisions document signed by Lieutenant Nichols for blankets, rifles, cups, and canteens places the company at this post on June 19.[28]

In early June, thirteen companies were ordered into service to protect Austin from an expected Mexican attack. These rumors eventually proved to be unfounded, but Major General Felix Huston found it a good opportunity to raise men.

These rumors kept the Pitkin Guards in service beyond their original three-month enlistment which ended on June 6. Nichols' June 19 provisions receipt also mentions "the late Capt. Pierce," whose departure left the company in the hands of Nichols as of mid-June. Captain Nichols' new senior officers were First Lieutenant S. T. Smith, Second Lieutenant Francis Wilson, and First Sergeant P. V. Bickford. The revamped Pitkin Guards would serve through August 27, 1840.

Nichols' men remained in service based on word the Texas government received in late May 1840 that General Valentin Canalizo, the Mexican military commander in Matamoros, was again attempting to incite the Indians to wage war on the whites. Canalizo sent emissaries into Texas, primarily to visit the Comanches. He hoped to take advantage of the recent Council House Fight and to remind other Indians of the Cherokee expulsion and the killing of Chief Bowles.[29]

Branch Archer called for the militia to form up to repel the Indians. Although they saw no action, their rise to force during early June almost certainly was noted by the Mexican spies, who may have cautioned the Comanches to hold off on their attack. The great raid of August was thus likely put off from happening in early June due to the militia's show of force.

General Huston tried to promote an expedition up the Brazos River against the Indians during June. President Lamar was no friend of Huston, as Huston—who just missed the battle of San Jacinto in 1836—had challenged war hero Lamar's command of the army following the Texas Revolution. Lamar ordered the militia to disband, thus greatly disappointing Huston.[30]

Colonel Wheeler's Campaign

In May 1840, Secretary of War Branch Archer issued a proclamation ordering the Texas Militia to enter into service to exterminate all Indians from Texas. The proclamation was soon deemed to be illegal and impractical since it called all able-bodied men into service and prevented them from raising corn for their families.[31]

Archer divided the Republic into five militia districts. The first covered all of the territory west of the Colorado River. The second was between the Colorado and Brazos rivers. The third was between the Brazos and Trinity. The fourth was between the Trinity and Sabine rivers. The fifth militia district was for the counties bordering the Red River. Secretary Archer designated a rendezvous site for each district and ordered the militia of each district to meet at the appointed place on June 1, 1841. They were to encamp there until receiving further orders. Two of the key areas of rendezvous were Nashville-on-the-Brazos and the Colorado River town of La Grange.[32]

Most of the districts decided that Archer's proclamation was illegal and chose to ignore it. From the Second District, a few men of Washington County met on the east bank of the Colorado River between La Grange and Bastrop. After discussing their options for a day or two, these men unanimously voted to return home. Some of those participating in this campaign would call it the "Archer Campaign."[33]

The Third Militia District rendezvoused on June 1. A few of the militiamen were from Navasota County, but the vast majority were from Montgomery County, which in 1840 comprised the areas of present Grimes, Walker, Montgomery, and Madison counties. These men elected Colonel Francis A. B. Wheeler—the first settler in 1825 of Montgomery County—to lead their regiment. Wheeler selected Uriah Case to serve as his command clerk, officially appointing him on June 27, 1840, as clerk of the Third Regiment, Second Brigade, Texas Militia.[34]

According to volunteer William Physick Zuber, a San Jacinto veteran, the rendezvous site was on the west bank of the Brazos River near Nashville in present Milam County.

I was one of those men, and we were about 300 in number. A few men from Navasota County rendezvoused with us, but they soon returned home. The rest of us waited for further orders. Some of our men returned home nearly every day, so that by the first of July, we were reduced to about 150 men.

At that time, Senator Beden Stroud, a wealthy bachelor who represented the counties of Robertson and Milam, owned and resided on a plantation covering the site of the present city of Calvert, eighteen miles northeast of our encampment. Stroud had two neighbors in limited circumstances, Mr. [Joseph M.] Tidwell and David Hollis, who lived on farms adjacent to each other and northwest of Stroud's plantation. Settlements extended farther up the Brazos and Trinity rivers, in and near their respective bottoms, but on the dividing ridge between those rivers there was not a habitation between Stroud's plantation and the settlements on the Red River.[35]

While the Third Militia District troops were gathering near Nashville, Indian depredations around the south-central Texas area greatly excited the settlers. On June 2, an Irishman employed by Mr. Sherrod of Robertson's Colony was shot. Another attack occurred near Austin on June 10. The *Austin Gazette* of June 15 reported: "A party of about forty Indians, supposed to be of the Cherokees, and their associate bands, came down on Brushy Creek, about twelve miles north of this city, last week." The Indians killed a man and stole a number of horses.[36]

The Travis Guards departed Austin on Monday, June 10, to pursue the raiders. General Burleson was also ordered to raise a volunteer company and cooperate with the Travis Guards in scouring the country for Indians. Captain Nicholson's company was in the field for a six-day scout for these Indians. They found the mutilated corpse of a man named Rogers, but the Indians had scattered and were not found. The Travis Guards reached Austin again on June 15.

The company stayed on the ready and held its regular meetings. On Independence Day, July 4, 1840, the Travis Guards were paraded in town, followed by an oration by Private Thomas Gales Forster. Also, at this time in Austin there was an artillery company under a Captain Mulhausen, which had been formed in June to help support the capitol. Neither unit appears to have had direct encounters with Indians during the summer of 1840.

The Third Militia Brigade remained idle in camp near Nashville during the first two weeks of June 1840. Colonel Wheeler held command over the various companies, but he found his job a difficult one. As the days passed without action, his 300-odd men quickly began to dwindle. Men returned home daily and the entire Navasota County company departed. The majority of the men from Militia Beats 3, 4, and 5 departed for home. Men found needs at home to be more pressing than to remain in volunteer service without action.[37]

During this idle time, another Indian depredation occurred very close to their area around June 24, 1840. A band of forty Indians came down from the Indian territory in northern Texas toward the residence of the Joseph Tidwell family. This party was later believed to be Cherokee and Kickapoos, but may have included some Kichais and Wacos as well. At his nearby residence, Senator Stroud heard the Indians yelling and believed that they must have killed the Tidwell family. After arming his servants and instructing them how to defend themselves in case of attack, Stroud rode to Colonel Wheeler's camp of the Third Militia District near present Calvert.[38]

Stroud reached camp and reported on the raiding Indians during the night. "As soon as it was light enough to find our horses, we saddled up and marched for the scene of the tragedy," wrote William Zuber.[39]

Colonel Wheeler's force numbered roughly 150 men in a very ragged collection of units. As of June 18, none of Montgomery County's Beat No. 4 company's officers remained. Wheeler had thus merged the remaining men, including the No. 5 company, into the remnants of Beat No. 2 company under Captain William R. Sanders. At the time Wheeler's camp began to mobilize for action, only two other companies remained. They were Montgomery County's Beat No. 1 company under Captain Thomas Pliney Plaster and Captain Bensen Risenhoover's Beat

No. 6 company. Plaster, a lieutenant of rangers during the Texas Revolution, had fought with the Texian artillery at San Jacinto.[40]

The companies at Nashville were supplied 472 pounds of beef by local resident John C. Pool on June 25, 1840, which was likely the date that they marched out to track the raiding Indians. This beef was provided to the mixed company of Captain Sanders.[41]

Wheeler's three companies reached Stroud's neighbor's home on Tidwell Creek, located at the site of present Calvert, about noon. They found that the Indians had killed Joseph Tidwell and captured his wife and three children. Tidwell had been plowing his field when the attack occurred. The militiamen soon found the Indians' trail and followed it back toward Indian territory.[42]

Colonel Wheeler's Montgomery County militiamen were joined by a nine-man volunteer unit from Robertson County under Captain Eli Chandler. This group included Beden Stroud, his nephew Logan A. Stroud, and former cavalry company commander John Goodloe Warren Pierson. The Robertson and Montgomery county militiamen tracked the Indians into the higher country, as Private Zuber later recorded.

> We followed the trail for eight or ten days, subsisting on the flesh of buffaloes that our best hunters killed.
> At the head of the Navasota River, our commanding officer, Colonel Wheeler, and about half our regiment turned back. The remainder of us chose to proceed, and we elected J. G. W. Pierson our captain.[43]

Private John Park of Captain Sanders' company lost a horse during the expedition. His horse was "under guard in the Indian country" at the time. During the night, a panic was sounded and one of the sentinels fired a shot that struck and killed Park's horse, valued at $75.[44]

Several days after Wheeler's half of the regiment had turned back for home, Pierson's party encountered Indians. Overnight intelligence from scouts gave Eli Chandler the confidence that his men could overtake the Indians if they moved forward. Chandler and Captain Sanders moved through the camp, awakening those men with the most reliable horses. They planned to move out swiftly in the night to attempt to recover the Tidwell family captives from the Indians.

The Archer Campaign
June 18–July 12, 1840

Colonel Commanding:
Francis A. B. Wheeler
Quartermaster:
William N. Mock

Clerk:
Uriah Case

Capt. Plaster's Company, Beat No. 1

Captain:
Thomas Pliney Plaster
First Lieutenant:
Charles Teas

Privates:
Thomas B. Bozeman
William W. Byers
Jesse Clary
Washington Clary
John Copeland
Martin Copeland
John T. Eubanks
Craner Foard

John Gibony
James R. Jones
M. Gordon McGuffin
James Phifer
Robert S. Raburn
Charles B. Ridgell
Henry Smock
Clement Waters
John J. Whitesides
L. Wilson

Source: author's research of Republic of Texas audited claims and public debt papers.

Capt. Risenhoover's Company, Beat No. 6

Captain:
Benson Risenhoover
First Lieutenant:
Christopher C. Edinburgh

Privates:
William Barker
Alfred Cato Jr.
James Clark
Hillary M. Crabb

Craner Foard
William H. Fowler
Daniel Fuller
John McAdams
John D. Murphy
Samuel R. Smith

Source: author's research of Republic of Texas audited claims and public debt papers.

Capt. Chandler's Robertson County Company

Captain:
Eli Chandler

Privates:
John Goodloe Warren Pierson
Logan A. Stroud
Beden Stroud

Source: The memoirs of William P. Zuber say that this small Robertson County company consisted of nine men in total. See Zuber, *My Eighty Years in Texas*, 107–9.

Capt. Sanders' Company, Beat No. 2

Captain:
William R. Sanders
First Lieutenant:
William E. Kennard
Second Lieutenant:
William McCoy
Orderly Sergeant:
Dickerson Garrett
Third Sergeant:
Elisha Anglin
Fourth Sergeant:
Jesse Smith
Third Corporal:
Wesley Fisher

Privates:
Henry Alston
Samuel Andrews
Yarborough Baker
Silas H. Bates
Alpheus A. Bogart
Adam R. Bowen
William Bowen
Josiah J. Brantly
Foster Brigance
Harvey Brigance
Jackson Crouch
Bailey Daniels
Edward B. Davis
Thomas Dunham
Davis S. Files
Rufus Grimes
Abram Helm
Absolom Henson
Joseph Henson

Jesse Johnson
Benjamin Jones
James Jones
Lewis Jones
Thomas B. Kelofer
Marcus L. Kennard
Thomas J. McCullum
William Miller
Azariah G. Moore
Ross Morris
John C. Palmer
John Park
John C. Pool
Elijah P. Robinson
Leonidas Sanders
William Stewart
John D. Taylor
Miles N. Taylor
Hugh Vandevender
Henry Walker
Martin West
Richard Williams
Richard S. Willis
John Winters
William Physick Zuber

Source: author's research of Republic of Texas audited claims and public debt papers. Many of Sanders' men were added to his company on June 18 from other militia beats by orders of Colonel Wheeler. John Winters, for example, was former second lieutenant of Beat No. 5's company.

Chandler and Sanders told the volunteers "that we should ride fast and try to overtake the enemy in one day," recalled William Zuber. "We left the rest of our squad asleep."[45]

The small pursuit party had only gone about two miles before the others in camp awoke and saw their companions departing. Five or six others rode and caught up with the group, but the rest had to follow slowly. With about thirty advance mounted men in

Captain   Thomas
Phiney Plaster (1814-
1862) was a veteran of
both San Jacinto and
Captain Louis Franks'
1836 ranger company.
He commanded one of
the militia companies
on Colonel Wheeler's
1840 expedition.
*Courtesy of the San
Jacinto Museum of
History,   Houston,
Texas.*

the lead—including Captain Chandler's nine Robertson County
men—the party rode fast through the Cross Timbers approaching
the present Dallas–Fort Worth area.

The Indians discovered the militiamen and eluded them by
riding up the bed of a running creek where the water spoiled their
tracks. "We continued on the trail they had made when coming
down," wrote Zuber. "And so we unconsciously got ahead of the
enemy."

That evening, the party arrived at a point where three streams
came together to form Nolan's Fork, a branch of the Brazos.
They made camp there without food or fire. "Here we found that
all of our horses, including mine, were so broken down that we
could go no farther in pursuit," wrote Zuber. Reluctantly, the men
decided to return home. They commenced the retreat ride slowly
the next morning, resting their worn horses.[46]

About noon, they rejoined the balance of their party under
Captain Pierson and proceeded toward home. Along the return
route, they met General Felix Huston, "with his colored servant

and four or five citizens of Robertson County, the latter bringing biscuit and flour for our relief and hunger," wrote Zuber.

They returned to Beden Stroud's Robertson County plantation, where they found Colonel Wheeler and the others who had previously turned back. The men camped at Stroud's that night, with General Huston in command. Camp guards were stationed about the camp. The following morning, Huston issued an honorable discharge to each man for eighteen days' service, from June 25 to July 12.

The volunteers were discharged at "Camp Near Stroud's" on July 12. It is evident from these discharges how fragmented the companies had become during the Wheeler expedition. First Lieutenant Charles Teas was acting commander of Captain Plaster's Montgomery County company and he signed most of the discharges for his men. First Lieutenant Christopher Edinburgh was acting commander of Captain Risenhoover's unit at the time discharges were signed on July 12.[47]

Later in 1840, a Choctaw Indian named Jim White helped to orchestrate the release of the Tidwell captives from the Choctaw Nation on Red River. The Indians took Mrs. Tidwell and the children to Holland Coffee's trading post, where their release was successfully negotiated. The *Texas Sentinel* in Austin reported in its October 24, 1840, edition that Mrs. Tidwell and two surviving children had finally received their freedom.[48]

Although the Wheeler Expedition failed to bring the Indians to combat, the Tidwell family captives were later ransomed. Mrs. Joseph Tidwell later wrote to Senator Stroud, telling of her capture, her ransom, and her situation at her brother's home in Arkansas. She said that the Indians had killed her six-week-old baby on the first day of their return. She also wrote of the fatiguing rides, during which the Indians had treated her kindly. She was warned that they would kill her rather than let her be rescued.

Lieutenant Wells' Rangers

Lieutenant Moses Wells commanded a detachment of volunteer rangers at Fort Wells from April into July, 1840. His fortified home had been built during the early 1830s on the Colorado River in Austin's Little Colony. The simple fort had no block-

Lieutenant Wells' Rangers: April 9–July 9, 1840	
Second Lieutenant:	S. Benjamin Gray
Moses Wells	Joshua Moody
Privates:	Source: author's research of Republic
Christopher Brimer	of Texas audited claims and public debt
John Daniels	papers.

house and only three cabins built close together for protection. It was located in the western part of Bastrop County, almost at the Travis County line. It was on the north side of the Colorado River, located approximately three miles southeast of Webberville.[49]

Adjutant General Hugh McLeod certified on May 9, 1840, that "Moses Wells is a second lieutenant of Rangers, in command of a detachment posted twelve miles above the city of Austin." One of Wells' men, Benjamin Gray, had previously served as a ranger in the Austin area in 1839 under Captain John Garrett.[50]

Paid military claims for Privates Joshua Moody and John Daniels show that they served three months under Lieutenant Wells and were paid twenty-five dollars per month. Wells wrote that both men were privates "of my company of rangers who w[ere] enrolled on the 9th day of April 1840 to serve for the period of three months." Wells discharged his company from service at Austin on July 9, 1840, signing as "2nd Lt. Commanding."[51]

After disbanding his unit, Lieutenant Wells brought two of the unit's public horses back into Austin to return to the war department and was paid twenty dollars on July 19. Wells' rangers apparently served without any noteworthy conflict while protecting the Colorado River settlements near Austin.[52]

Stout and Stout's Red River Ranger Companies

In the Red River area, Captain William B. Stout again commanded rangers during 1840. His unit operated as rangers in the First Regiment, Fourth Brigade, Texas Militia. His men were enrolled for service on April 22, and commenced their service on May 2, 1840, for a three-month duration.

Capt. Stout's Red River Rangers: May 2–August 2, 1840

Captain:
William B. Stout
First Lieutenant:
David L. Ross [1]
Second Lieutenant:
Joseph D. Lilly
First Sergeant:
Mansell Walter Matthews
McQuery H. Wright [2]
Second Sergeant:
William C. Twitty [2]
Third Sergeant:
James Morrison [2]
Quartermaster Sergeant:
William H. Hinton

Privates:
Daniel Adams
Hodge Adams
Peter Adams [3]
William Adams
James Bailey [4]
John Baldin
George Birdwell [3]
Ezereh Brackeen
William Brackeen [5]
Basdale Caison
John E. Chisum

John C. Gahagen
William G. Grinder
Martin D. Hart [6]
William T. Henderson [6]
Jacob Hushaw
Thomas Jouett [6]
William A. Matthews
Jackson Mays [3]
Wily B. Merrill [7]
Daniel Montague [6]
_____ Moody
Garret F. Pangburn [6]
A. C. Pick
Daniel Rattan
Littleton Rattan
Eli J. Shelton
Charles M. Straly
S. W. Westbrook

[1] Elected on May 18, 1840.
[2] Promoted on May 13.
[3] Enrolled May 23.
[4] Enrolled May 22. Did not serve.
[5] Enrolled May 15.
[6] Enrolled April 28 for 18 days.
[7] Enrolled May 3 for 10 days.

Source: Texas State Archives.

Coincidentally, his brother Henry also took command of a Red River area ranger company several weeks later. Together, the brothers Stout patrolled with their ranger units in northern Texas' Fourth Militia Brigade. Major Buckskin Williams was in charge of all ranging units operating in this militia brigade, which also included Captain Daniel Jackson's Fannin County Rangers.

Captain Henry Stout's rangers were enrolled for a three-month duration on June 11, 1840. His men ranged in the southern areas of Red River and Lamar counties. At the time his company was discharged on September 10, 1840, it was camped at "Camp Sherman" on Cypress Creek. This camp is believed to have been

Capt. Henry Stout's Red River Rangers: June 10–Sept. 10, 1840	
Captain:	Anderson Coots
Henry Stout	David Coots
Second Lieutenant:	Hugh H. Hill
Joseph D. Lilly	Levi Jordan
Orderly Sergeant:	Martin G. Miller
James M. Patton	John H. Milligan
	Thomas J. Ripley
Privates:	Tilman Smith
R. S. Anderson	Thomas R. Starnes
Amos C. C. Bailey	John Wadkins
Francis Blundell	
J. H. Blundell	Source: Partial roster based on author's search of audited claims and public debt papers.
Solomon Blundell	

near Fort Sherman in the extreme southwestern area of present Titus County.[53]

Fort Sherman had been built by Captain William Stout's 1838 rangers and was located near present Farm Road 21's bridge over Cypress Creek. The fort stood about one mile north of the bridge and thirteen miles southwest of present Mount Pleasant.

Assistant quartermaster Levi Jordan provided for Henry Stout's company. He wrote to Major Williams on July 2, informing him of his company's first month activities and requesting how to handle furnishing such extras as coffee and sugar.

> The Capt.'s men is making a desperate fuss about my not furnishing them coffee and sugar. I went to the lake with the view of buying some of both until I could get an answer from you, though found none nearer than Shreveport, and there Texas funds is only worth $14 per hundred.[54]

Jordan brought his supplies to Fort Sherman, the operating base for Captain Stout's rangers. He sent his note to Major Williams with courier R. S. Anderson, who was under orders to collect funds to help the company operate. Jordan stated that he would come up at the first of August to make his next report to Williams in person. "The number of the company is 32," he said of Henry Stout's rangers, signing his location as "near Fort Sherman."

Captain William Stout affirmed that his men furnished their own horses and equipment on his muster roll of May 2, 1840. This was signed at Camp DeKalb (formerly known as Fort Lyday) near the North Sulphur River in Red River County.

Among the men he had managed to sign up were some veterans of the Red River service. Among those initially agreeing to serve for a limited eighteen-day expedition were William T. Henderson, Martin D. Hart (a former 1838 mounted gunman corporal), Thomas Jouett (an 1838 Montague campaign veteran), Garret Pangburn (from the 1838 Dallas-area attack), and former militia lieutenant colonel Daniel Montague.

Captain Stout's company was disbanded on August 2, 1840, at "Camp Davis." His rangers had been at Camp Davis as early as June 22. He signed the discharges of his men as the "Red River Rangers." Camp Davis was likely near Camp Sherman, in an area of Red River County close to Sulphur River or Cypress Creek.[55]

Frontier Regiment: May–June 1840

During the early part of May, Colonel Edward Burleson made a tour of the detachments of the First Regiment of Infantry which were stationed at Mission San José in San Antonio.

During his visit, two of his leading officers had a quarrel about the Council House Fight. Major Lysander Wells of the cavalry was bitter toward Captain William Redd for not fighting Chief Isomania's Comanches on March 28. Isomani had brought a large group of Indians into town to fight, but Redd had orders at that time to maintain a twelve-day truce.

In an insulting letter, Major Wells apparently called Captain Redd a "dastardly coward," among other things. Wells also complained that Redd was under the influence of a "petticoat government," making insinuations about a certain woman from Georgia who was living with him out of wedlock. Lysander Wells had his letter signed by others from San Antonio before presenting it to Redd.

Captain Redd was furious, and challenged Wells to a duel the following morning. At 6:00 a.m. on May 10, 1840, two of the Texas Army leaders met where the Ursuline Convent now stands near the Alamo.[56]

Major Lysander Wells (1812–1840) and a fellow First Regiment officer, both San Jacinto veterans, participated in a pistol duel at their San Antonio army base on May 10, 1840. Both Wells and Captain William Davis Redd fatally wounded each other. (Previously published in Wharton's *San Jacinto: The Sixteenth Decisive Battle.*)

Two other Texas Army leaders, Albert Sidney Johnston and Felix Huston, had duelled in 1837. They both had old horse pistols. Three years later, the weapons were much better. In fact, Major Wells' cavalry is known to have been armed with the new Colt Patent Arms repeating pistol as of 1840.

"I aim for your heart," announced Redd.

"And I for your brains," countered Wells.

Béxar citizen Mary Maverick later recorded the deadly results of the army leaders' duel.

> They fired. Redd sprang high into the air and fell dead with a bullet in his brain. Wells was shot near the heart, but lived two weeks, in great torture, begging every one near him to dispatch him, or furnish him a pistol that he might kill himself and end his agony.
>
> Dr. Weideman nursed him tenderly. In Captain Redd's pocket was found a marriage license and certificate showing that he was wedded to the girl—also letters to members of his own and her families, speaking of her in the tenderest manner, and asking them to protect and provide for her.[57]

Thus ended the lives and careers of two valiant Texan fighters. Both had fought on the battlegrounds at San Jacinto, Wells leading the cavalry into battle and Redd as an infantryman. Both were buried just outside the Catholic cemetery in San Antonio, in what is now known as Milam Square.

Later in May, while Burleson was still in Béxar, Private John Robinson of Captain Howard's Company C committed "an indignity" to one of the female Comanche prisoners, the wife of one of the slain Comanche chiefs. Colonel Burleson ordered a court martial. The Frontier Regiment soldier was "whipped, had his head shaven, and with an ample coat of tar and feathers, was drummed out of camp" on May 20.[58]

The regulars at San Antonio were an unruly bunch during May 1840. The previously good record of the Frontier Regiment was blackened by this soldier's actions, the duel of the officers previously mentioned, and a mutiny that occurred in that month. They were angry that they had not been paid, and that many of them had not been stationed, as promised, at points on the frontier where the men could cultivate land, which they would be given at the close of their enlistments.[59]

The mutiny was serious enough that Captain Woodhouse's Travis Guards from Austin were sent rushing to San Antonio to help. The local First Regiment command, however, was still strong enough that most of the troops rallied behind their leaders. Five of the leading mutineers were jailed and two deserters were shot before the uprising was ended.

Following his inspection tour, Colonel Burleson rode back to Austin, arriving there on June 3. Two days later, yet another embarrassing episode occurred between First Regiment officers. John W. Smith wrote to Colonel Cooke from San Antonio on June 5, "I have just learned of a meeting this afternoon between Lieutenant [Robert R.] Scott and [Edward S.] Ratcliffe in which the latter was wounded (shot through the calves of the legs)." Ratcliffe—a native of Mobile, Alabama, who had served under Captain Mark Lewis in the 1839 Cherokee War—survived the wounds from his duel and served well into 1841 with the Frontier Regiment.[60]

President Lamar continued to use Henry Wax Karnes as a frontier leader in the San Antonio area. In June 1840, Lamar authorized Karnes to raise a volunteer force "under certain conditions not calculated to embarrass the Government." Karnes' volunteers were hoped to be used to avoid "any further military operation in the West" concerning the Federalist wars. Lamar hoped to extend Texas jurisdiction "to the Rio Grande, chastizing the Indians in that section—repelling such marauding parties as may be committing these depredations, this side of the River."[61]

Colonel Karnes arrived in Austin on June 13 in company with Captain George Howard and Lieutenant William Houghton of the First Regiment. There, the trio conferred with Secretary of War Archer. Karnes then moved on to Houston to meet with President Lamar concerning the increased Indian depredations in the vicinity of San Antonio, partly brought on by Centralist agents who were operating among the Comanches.[62]

Captain Howard, commanding Company C of the First Regiment, was stationed at Mission Concepción during June 1840. When he went into town, he left ten of his company under the acting command of his brother, Second Lieutenant John C. Howard, and First Lieutenant Mike Chevallie at Hondo Creek Station. Company muster rolls show that these ten were "on detached service to Rio Jonde." The station held by Chevallie and Howard was likely at or near the crossing of the road to Presidio del Río Grande, in the southern part of present Medina County. The remote site west of San Antonio certainly would have given them time to report any incoming hostile Indian bands.[63]

In Houston, Karnes and Lamar met and Karnes was ordered to raise a regiment of volunteers "to operate immediately upon the extreme western frontier." His troops were to establish "national jurisdiction to the Rio Bravo," and to ward off any intrusions by the Centralist forces gathered at Laredo. In the event he should end up operating in conjunction with regular military forces, Colonel Karnes was to devolve upon the colonel of the regular army until a brigadier general was appointed to take joint command. Lamar noted to Karnes on June 23, that he hoped that adequate volunteers could be found to avoid drafting any more regulars to deal with the Texas border wars issues.[64]

Karnes put out a call for volunteers from Houston on June 24, which was published in the *Telegraph and Texas Register* on July 1, 1840. He called for volunteers "well armed and mounted" and for four to six companies of infantry. The volunteers would rendezvous within thirty days at San Antonio, where they would be enrolled for six months' service. Field officers would be appointed by President Lamar, but Karnes promised the volunteers that they could elect their own company officers. Karnes advertised that he was "looking for troops to protect Laredo and that vicinity to develop a military force closer to the Rio Grande."[65]

Karnes targeted "Indians, Mexicans, and other lawless ban- ditti" who had broken up trade between Texas and friendly settlements beyond the Rio Grande. By mid-July, five hundred men from Washington County were reported to be ready to join him. Another one to two hundred men from Fayette and adjoining counties were also preparing to turn out for Karnes' call.[66]

★ ★ ★ ★

Summer Depredations and the "Border Guards"
Following the return of the Wheeler Expedition, General Felix Huston was ordered to Nashville at the end of June 1840 to take command of the troops stationed there. According to Captain George Erath, Colonel Wheeler's Montgomery County regiment rendezvoused at Nashville on the Brazos about July 1 by orders of the secretary of war.

Erath wrote that he

> was employed to carry or rather guide a bearer of dis-
> patches to the war department at Austin by order of the
> Secretary of War. I remained two or three days at Austin
> for the purpose of guiding Major Gnl. Felix Huston to the
> ground of rendezvous, who was momentarily expected
> and when he arrived, proceed to Nashville, took command
> of said regiment.[67]

By the time Huston reached Colonel Wheeler, the latter had already concluded his ineffective militia expedition into the areas north of Robertson County. Prior to joining these troops, inexperienced Indian fighter Felix Huston had boldly pledged on June 22 that he would "end the Indian war by the 1st of January." After reaching the camp of Wheeler, however, he found that what few men remained did not care to make another long summer expedition without sufficient food and supplies.[68]

Secretary Archer soon changed his mind about calling up the militia any further. He apparently felt that Wheeler's brief expedition and the advertised campaign had done the job in spreading fear among the Comanches, causing them to cast aside ideas of retaliating for the Council House Fight. The few remaining companies of the Texas Militia were thus ordered to disband. This whole affair was dubbed the "Archer War" by bitter critics of the Lamar administration.

With or without the Texas Militia in operation, the Indian depredations did not cease during the summer of 1840. In fact, they became more random and more frequent. Secretary of State James Mayfield was wounded by an Indian in early June in the middle of Austin while escorting a lady home from a party. Secretary of War Archer ordered the creation of a supplemental company to assist the Travis Guards, who had returned from their posting in San Antonio in early June.[69]

In response to this order for a new mounted company to help defend Austin, the "Border Guards" were organized in Houston on June 18, 1840, for six months' service. The company's commander was Captain James Decatur Cocke. Born about 1815 in Richmond, Virginia, he was a printer with the *Mobile Chronicle* before moving to Texas in 1837 to attempt to publish a newspaper. During 1838, he served as Quartermaster of Major George Bonnell's First Regiment, Second Brigade of the Texas Militia. In the fall of 1839, he had run unsuccesfully against Dudley W. Babcock for the post of Colonel, First Regiment, 2nd Brigade, Texas Militia.[70]

Captain Cocke's company was furnished by the government. The men without weapons were issued older muskets from the government arsenals in Houston. Local citizens in Galveston and Houston provided horses for his soldiers. Captain Cocke was in Galveston on June 17, where John A. Settle furnished two horses for the company. Private John Moore also acquired his horse in Galveston on June 17 from Charles B. Hammond.[71]

Other men, such as privates James P. Sherwood and William H. Henderson, supplied their own horses and equipment without government pay. Larkin B. Smith was later paid $175 for the purchase of two horses and mountings which he supplied to privates Harlan L. Leaf and John M. Coughlin on June 20, at Houston.[72]

Captain Cocke's Border Guards completed their organization and then proceeded in early July toward Austin to report for service in protecting the frontier. The Indian depredations against Texas settlers were plentiful during the summer months, particularly around the Austin and San Antonio areas.

On June 21, Indians killed several young men who were between the Guadalupe River and San Antonio in the lower country. Among those killed was a young man of the Lockhart family. Another young man, Josiah Powers, was captured but managed to escape.[73]

Claiborne Osborn was buffalo hunting in Williamson County with his brother Lee Osborn, James Hamilton, and several other men when they were attacked. Claiborne Osborn and Hamilton were riding apart from the others when they were chased by Indians. Osborn's horse was wounded and it fell, throwing him to the ground. Hamilton raced to round up the other men to help as the Indians descended upon Osborn. By the time the hunters returned en masse to chase away the Indians with their firepower, Osborn was seriously wounded. Indians were beating and stabbing him and had partially removed his scalp. Osborn later settled near Webberville in Travis County and his scalp was carefully replaced and healed.[74]

In present Grayson County, Dr. Edward Hunter's family was attacked at their home during the summer of 1840. Hunter's place was located in the Red River valley about eight miles below Old Warren and a few miles west of Choctaw. While Dr. Hunter and his son were away from home on business, Indians raided their homestead. They attacked two of his daughters who had gone to the creek to fetch water. One girl was killed and the other was taken prisoner.[75]

They carried her back to her own house, where they scalped and killed Mrs. Hunter. They allowed the family's servant woman to live, but ransacked the Hunter home, ripping open feather beds and looting the valuables. They tore open the doctor's medical bags and scattered his pills and medicines all over the house. Just before dark, the Indians gathered their spoils and their female prisoner and departed.

Dr. Hunter's son rode up as they were departing. One of the Indians put the Hunter daughter on his horse and rode rapidly away. They rode all night with her, scattering into smaller groups to confuse any followers, until they reached their village.

Hunter went into the dark house, made a light, and looked at the disheveled mess. To his horror, he soon found the scalped corpse of his mother in the ruins. Alone, he staggered to his horse and rode through the night to the nearest neighbors, who were several miles away. The details of the Hunter family depredation were later written down in 1885 and 1886 by Mary A. E. Shearer, the granddaughter of early Grayson County pioneer Daniel V. Dugan. By her grandfather's account, Shearer related that young Hunter "roused the neighbors and started rangers in pursuit of the Indians."[76]

The closest ranger company operating in Grayson County at this time in 1840 was that of Captain Daniel Jackson. The Indians had many hours' head start and Jackson's rangers were unable to catch up with them. They searched the house and did not find either girl and at first assumed that both had been carried away. By chance, someone discovered the body of the girl by the creek the next day.

The poor daughter was made a slave to the Indian women of the tribe. Among other hardships, she had to scrape and clean the scalp of her own mother for her captors. Her kidnappers moved her from one band of Indians to another during the next six months. They finally made a good trade to the Choctaws. Word eventually reached brother Hunter that a white girl of about her age had been sold to the Choctaws. He went to the Nation and managed to secure her ransom.

Despite the presences of Captain Jackson's rangers, the present Grayson County area near Old Warren suffered other Indian attacks in 1840. William McIntyre lived near the Red River on 3,000 acres near Shawneetown, several miles above Choctaw. Near his home, Indians killed neighbor William C. Moody and mutilated his body. Soon thereafter, two of William McIntyre's boys were killed and scalped while out hunting near Choctaw. In a separate attack, two brothers named Sewell who lived in Warren were attacked by Indians while checking their horses. One was fatally shot and the other brother managed to kill an Indian before escaping.[77]

William Clopton's place near Austin suffered a depredation on July 4. He had sent one of his black servant girls out to call in the cows from pasture along Gilleland Creek. Her calls attracted the attention of Indians, who slipped up toward her in the tall grass and shot her through with arrows. Perhaps she was shot from a distance where the Indians could not see her face, for they seldom ever killed a black person. In any event, they scalped her.[78]

In the summer weeks of 1840, Comanches attacked many other Texas settlers. Among other vicious assaults were those on: Michael Nash near Bastrop, former ranger Joseph Weeks at Kenney's Fort, Gilbert H. Love in Robertson County, a man named Ladd on the San Gabriel River, James Campbell on the Guadalupe, Bat Manlove in Travis County, San Jacinto veteran Leander Calvin Cunningham on the San Marcos River, Henry Earthman in Fayette County, and many others.[79]

In late June, "a considerable number of horses" were stolen by Indians in the vicinity of Bastrop. Several head of cattle were also killed by the marauders. The crime was immediately charged against the Indians, although a traveler in the area reported seeing two white cowboys in company with a small party of Indians. The man reported the whites and Indians with "a large number of horses in a hurry along the Gotcher Trace."[80]

It is indeed possible that white men were assisting the Indians in robbing some of the settlements. During the early 1840s, horse and cattle robbing were equally conducted by Mexican, white, and Indian marauders.

About the same time, around July 1, Captain Mark Lewis had a number of his company's horses stolen from camp on Walnut Creek near Austin. Lewis' Company E of the First Regiment of Infantry had departed Camp Cooke on June 6 and had taken up station at Austin as of June 24. The *Texas Sentinel* in Austin reported on July 4, 1840, that Captain Lewis' company had been robbed by Indians "a few nights ago."[81]

Lewis' company set out in immediate pursuit. He trailed the Indians closely and soon recovered all of his horses, together with several belonging to the enemy. They also captured all the Indians' supplies and camp equipage. The Indians hurriedly fled their campground and escaped without any apparent casualties.

Citizen James Lester wrote to President Lamar on July 16, 1840, from La Grange. He had been in Austin, where he found the people anxious for frontier protection. Lester suggested that Lamar order the raising of a frontier force of "three hundred mounted men for the purpose of making an expedition against the Indian villages up the Colorado & Brazos rivers." Lester volunteered that John Henry Moore "would be the most suitable person to command it."[82]

★ ★ ★ ★ ★

Cunningham's Clash: July 4, 1840

Although placed out on the frontier to deal with Indian hostilities, the Frontier Regiment of Texas had seen no action since the Council House Fight.

Captain Clendenin had gone on furlough February 7, 1840, from his Company B of the First Regiment, turning over acting command to Second Lieutenant Collier C. Hornsby. Clendenin next took command of the new Company A, which had lost its commanding officer, Captain Redd, on May 10 during the duel with Major Wells at Mission San José. Company A, as related, had been involved in the Council House Fight in March.

Clendenin left the bulk of his company at Mission Concepción on June 25 under First Lieutenant Daniel Lewis. Captain Clendenin was accompanied by Corporal James Chaplin and a dozen of his private soldiers: Barney Cannon, Aaron Crawford, George Chyler, Robert Foster, Thomas Kane, George H. Kidd, James B. Lee, Michael Smith, Patrick Smith, Frederick Showman, James Sloan, and Edward Stroll.[83]

Captain Clendenin's Company A detachment was accompanied by Captain John R. Cunningham, an adventurous San Antonio lawyer who had raised nineteen volunteer men. This mini expedition penetrated deep into Comanche country on the upper Frio River. Among those who served under Cunningham were: James H. Brown, José Maria Espinosa, James M. Jett, John James, James W. Gray, Antonio Lockmar, William H. Daingerfield, Wilson J. Riddle, Béxar County Judge John Hemphill, and Martin Delgado. James listed these men as serving under Captain Cunningham and Major George Thomas Howard.

John James, twenty-one, had sailed to Texas from England to join the revolution. Arriving too late for the war, James had settled near San Antonio and taken up surveying. He later wrote:

> The time occupied in making the campaign was six or seven weeks. I recollect James H. Brown, James M. Jett (whose horse was killed by a shot from an Indian in the head) and James W. Gray, John Hemphill (our Judge), José Maria Espinosa and myself messed together during the trip.[84]

On the morning of July 4, Adam Clendenin and John Cunningham divided their forces and set out in different directions. Captain Clendenin would return to San Antonio without encountering any Indians, but Cunningham's Tonkawa guide, Antonio, spotted an Indian trail within an hour after the companies had separated.

In his report, written five days later, Captain Cunningham described his advance on the Comanches:

> We followed it for about six miles, when we came to the Indian camp. The sign was still hot, and showed that they had an acquisition of six to their numbers. I dispatched Antonio, the Tonkawa, ahead. We followed at a brisk pace.
>
> The trail crossed the Frio to the west bank, in about five miles, and struck the river, rather bearing towards the Leona, into the prairie. Supposing the trail to continue down, upon the bank of the river, and expecting every moment to come down upon the Indians, we neglected to supply ourselves with water. The trail gradually led us from the water, until it was too far to return.
>
> The suffering of the men and the horses was immense for nine hours in the heat of the day; and what made it worse for us, we knew we had to fight before we could get water, as the Indians, in all probability, would encamp upon the first they came to.[85]

Between 5:00 and 6:00 p.m., Antonio returned with news that he had located the Indians' camp ahead, near water. He gave their number as twenty, which made the odds fair for Cunningham's nineteen men. He quickly made plans to attack. Four men would go with Antonio to stampede the Comanches' *caballado*. Captain Cunningham, with the other fourteen men, dismounted and prepared to advance on foot.

"They were instructed strictly, in both languages [English and Spanish], not to fire without the signal for a charge," wrote Cunningham. All went as planned, with the front five men advancing beyond the center of camp. They came within twenty paces of the Comanches, where the captain halted them, waiting for the rear file men to close up before signaling to attack.

"We were still undiscovered, as the Indians were busily engaged in saddling up their horses for the evening's march," wrote Cunningham. Just as the captain was beginning to rejoice on his good fortunes, one of the rear files of his main party fired his gun—either by accident or in alarm at their close proximity to the Indians.

Captain Cunningham watched in horror as the Indians immediately broke for cover. "Charge!" he cried. "Fire!"

The company immediately rushed in, discharging their weapons on the fleeing Comanches. The Indians returned fire with guns and arrows, but did no injury. Cunningham kept his men on the charge for six hundred yards, following the Comanches into a thicket.

> The Indians rallied several times, and bravely and nobly covered the retreat of the wounded. I saw several severely wounded myself, and some of my company, in whose word I have the utmost confidence, saw many more.
>
> Towards the close of the action, but three Indians were left to cover the retreat. This they did nobly, under the fire of ten or twelve as good shots as ever cocked a rifle. One of the three had his left leg and thigh broken by some one of fifty shots, which must have been leveled at him. He fell upon his horse's neck, and all put out for a more agreeable place.

In the initial charge, volunteer James Jett was thrown from his horse. A skilled shot from one of the Comanches struck his horse "in the head," killing him, but leaving Jett unhurt.[86]

The other Texans pursued on foot as far as their fatigue and thirst would allow. The remaining Indians escaped on horseback and Captain Cunningham called a halt. He ordered his men to return to the Indian camp and to take on water.

In the Comanche camp, they found an "abundance of meat —buffalo, horse, cow, and venison." Many guns, saddles, and baggage were also taken. "We ate, drank, and rested for a moment," wrote Cunningham.

He then ordered a bonfire made of the Indians' goods. The Texans also captured sixteen horses and mules from the camp.

With darkness setting in, Captain Cunningham's men continued their march to the Rio Frio, where the water tasted much less muddy than that from the stream near the Indian camp. The site of their battle had been about eight miles west of the Frio River, and about the same distance above the Presidio Rio Grande Road.

Among the horses and mules taken was a mule that had once belonged to Vincente de la Garza, which had been stolen some time before when de la Garza was on his way from the Presidio toward San Antonio. When stolen from him, de la Garza's mule had been laden with silver eagle money dated 1840.

When Cunningham had ordered the charge, some of his men had stayed to pillage the Indian camp. Among them was "a Welchman by the name of Davis." On Davis, Captain Cunningham found "a quantity of new eagle money, which he acknowledged he stole from the Indian camp."

The captain was quick to make an example of Davis.

> I had him properly punished. He was stripped of his shirt, his back and arms painted, his head covered with a red-flannel cap, with flowers, and rode, with his face to the rear of a no-tailed mule through the public squares of [the] principal streets of town, the company marching, in silent procession, behind. The guilty scamp was then turned loose in the center of the square. He was left by the light of the moon.[87]

Cunningham's nineteeen-man volunteer company reached San Antonio on July 7. In his July 9 report to Captain Clendenin, Cunningham felt that his men narrowly missed killing all of the Comanches. He felt confident "that if we had one man less, or if all had obeyed the commands, not one Indian would have escaped." He was unable to say for certain how many Comanches had been killed, but only that many of their number had at least been severely wounded.

He felt that among those present when the Texans attacked were "the celebrated [chiefs] Is[o]mani and Piava (the fat fellow)." It was the first Indian skirmish of any kind since March's Council House Fight in San Antonio.

Capt. Barkley's Mounted Rangers: July 4–October 4, 1840

Captain:
Robert Barkley
First Lieutenant:
Daniel Woodlan
Second Lieutenant:
Henry Mullens
Second Sergeant:
John N. Sullivan
Fourth Sergeant:
J. J. Munchew
Battalion Quartermaster:
John F. Graham

Privates:
Edward Abshire
Spencer Adams [1]
Jeremiah Bailey
R. W. Battiouex
Matthew R. Birdwell
Alexander Bowin
James W. Brown
Robert P. Brown
Samuel Burris
Holmes Byfield
John Cochran
Latchlin Dew
Wiliford Dew
Francis Dietrich
George S. Downs
John Ford

Henry Garner
James M. Gillitt
William Griffin
Benjamin P. C. Harrill
T. H. Hill
William Perry Matteson
Daniel C. McFarland
J. A. N. Murray
E. K. Oliver
John Pate
J. L. Shields
J. M. Shields
Samuel R. Stephenson
Berry A. Stone
Thomas Strahan
John Tomlinson
Joel Walker
Jesse Wilson
Richard Wist
Joseph Wood
Joseph P. Wood
Christopher G. Woods

[1] Originally under Capt. Sterne. Discharged by Lt. Woodlan on October 4.

Source: Texas State Archives.

Major Durst's Nacogdoches Battalion

In the Texas Militia's Third District, there were much fewer Indian depredations and killings during the summer of 1840 than what was experienced in other districts. The fact that two large companies of Texas Rangers patrolled the vast areas of Nacogdoches County certainly helped to quell such uprisings.

General James Smith of the Third Brigade, long associated with ranging units in his area, commissioned Major James H. Durst to oversee a two-company battalion. In a draft held in Nacogdoches on July 4, the companies elected Captain Adolphus Sterne and Captain Robert Barkley, a recent immigrant, to

Capt. Sterne's Mounted Rangers: July 8–October 16, 1840

Captain:
Adolphus Sterne
First Lieutenant:
Sidney P. Brown
Second Lieutenant:
William Graham
First Sergeant:
William B. Williams
Second Sergeant:
John S. Thompson
Third Sergeant:
Samuel W. Wilds
First Corporal:
William L. Dupree
Second Corporal:
Eli Casey

Privates:
Ezekiel Ables
Spencer Adams
John M. Bates
Thomas P. Brockman
Archer Browning
Lemuel Caldwell
William R. Carnes
Sam Chatham
Henry Conner
Jenkins Cox
Reuben C. Crawford
Moses Durst
Lopez Faliciano
William Francisco
Absolom W. Gibson

Samuel G. Hanks
John Hunter
Henry Jeffrey
William Jones
Thomas M. Lindsey
William Perry Matteson
H. B. McBroom
Joseph Meredith
John C. Morrison
N. S. Outlaw
John M. Page
Richard Pollard
Peter C. Price
James B. Read
Milton Rowan
John T. Russell
Alexander Sandling
David B. Sikes
Jose Silvia
Joseph Smith
William Smith
William Squires
Isaac Stokely
Peter G. Townsend
William Henry Vardeman
Reuben Webb
J. G. Wells
Benjamin M. White
James Williams
John A. Williams
Baalam Yeargin

Source: Texas State Archives.

take command. Sterne had first opened a mercantile house in Nacogdoches in 1826 and was arrested during the Fredonian Rebellion for resisting the Mexican government. During the Texas Revolution, he traveled to New Orleans to help recruit for the war. Captain Sterne had fought during the 1839 Cherokee War and became postmaster of Nacogdoches in 1840. As ranger captains, Sterne and Barkley were paid seventy-five dollars per month and were to patrol the county for three months' time.[88]

Major Durst appointed former Tennessean John F. Graham of Barkley's unit to serve as his battlion quartermaster to supply goods for both Barkley and Sterne's companies. During the course of their service, some of Captain Sterne's rangers elected to draw provisions against their future pay. Shoes were issued at $1.50 value and tobacco was distributed at $1 per plug.[89]

Reuben Webb, a private of Captain Sterne's company, served as a guide for Captain Barkley's company while they were out in the field. Neither of Major Durst's ranging units engaged in any sustained conflict with Indians that can be found in extant records. When Barkley's company was discharged in October, Webb and a few other members of Sterne's company, such as Spencer Adams and William Matteson, actually received their discharges by Lieutenant Daniel Woodlan of Captain Barkley's company. A twenty-six-year-old saddler from Missouri who had recently arrived in Nacogdoches, Woodlan had become acting commander of the company during the fall.

The unpaid militiary claims of such rangers as Privates Benjamin C. P. Harrell and J. L. Shields show that these Nacogdoches rangers were discharged on October 4, in "Nacogdoches County" by General James Smith, Third Brigade, and Lieutenant Woodlan.[90]

Death of Henry Karnes

Colonel Henry Karnes remained committed to recruiting hundreds of volunteers for his new western frontier regiment. He was intent on fighting Indians and trade bandits who were harassing settlers and traders between San Antonio and the Rio Grande. He had started calling for volunteers on June 24 and was in San Antonio by late July, preparing for the rendezvous of troops.

Karnes wrote a letter to General Antonio Canales of the Federalist Army on July 26 from Béxar.

> The volunteers under my command will be here in a few days from this date, and at their arrival I shall make all the necessary preparations for a rapid march to Laredo. I shall wait here only [for] the general orders of the Government. Meantime the pretentions of the Federalists

to the territory between the Nueces and the Rio Grande have wounded the feelings of the President and have also excited the indignation of the people.[91]

Karnes warned Canales and his Federalists that he planned to march to Laredo with his forces. He promised to then follow the Rio Grande to its mouth and "plant the standard of Texas on its eastern bank" in Mexican soil. General Canales penned a stinging reply from Lipantitlán on August 4 in which he vowed that "I shall never suffer that the flag of Texas" be planted in Mexican soil. "To effect it, it will be necessary to pass over our corpses and those of all other Mexicans," he wrote.[92]

It is unknown whether Colonel Karnes ever received Canales' letter. Karnes was stricken with typhoid or yellow fever during the early days of August. While he lay sick in San Antonio, he allowed Quartermaster Robert Neighbors of the Frontier Regiment to provision the army troops from his own crops. Soldiers under Captain Adam Clendenin, commanding nearby Camp Cooke, cut corn from Karnes' labor of land near Béxar.

Feeling well enough to travel, Colonel Karnes decided it was important to make one last trip to Houston. He planned to visit with President Lamar on his upcoming military expedition to Laredo. Against Dr. Edmund Weideman's advise, Karnes set out for Houston in a light wagon. He suffered a relapse on the first day out, however, and was taken back to San Antonio.[93]

Henry Wax Karnes never recovered. He died on August 16, 1840. Mary Ann Maverick, present during Karnes' last days, wrote admiringly of the frontier leader in her memoirs.

> Colonel Karnes was a short, thick-set man with bright red hair. While he was uneducated, he was modest, generous, and devoted to his friends. He was brave and untiring and a terror to the Indians. They called him "Capitan Colorado" (Red Captain) and spoke of him as "Muy Wapo" (very brave). Four or five years before he died, he was taken prisoner by the Comanches, and the squaws so greatly admired his hair of "fire" that they felt it and washed it to see if it would fade; and, when they found the color held fast, they would not be satisfied until each had a lock.

A veteran of the 1835 battle for San Antonio, a hero of the battle of San Jacinto, and a constant cavalry and ranger commander in the years following Texas' independence, Henry Karnes' fighting spirit was an inspiration to future leaders on the Texas frontier.

CHAPTER 4

The Great
Comanche Raid

August 1840

The Comanches of central Texas were stirred up to a fever pitch. They had not forgotten how their chiefs had been killed in San Antonio in March. They had tried to provoke a fight in the week after the Council House affair, but the Texas soldiers had refused to fight them on account of the temporary truce. Captain Cunningham's little party had fired into another Comanche camp in early July. By late July, the Comanche leaders were planning a bold offensive against their white aggressors.

The Indian offensive was reportedly encouraged by General Valentin Canalizo, the military commander of northern Mexico, who was headquartered in Matamoros. Dr. Branch Archer, the Texas secretary of war, had given a warning to the country in June of the dangers of attack. Since no attack had come, one early settler recalled, "the occasion became derisively known as the 'Archer war.'"[1]

Canalizo's spies had likely cautioned the Indians to delay their attack until Colonel Wheeler's militia regiment broke up in mid-July. The Penateka Comanches mourned their thirty dead during the spring months of 1840, and then moved north by May 1840 in search of allies. The Anglo-Texans erroneously perceived that the Comanche threat had subsided during the early summer months, when in fact they were busily acquiring firearms for battle. The Comanches even held a peace council with their old enemies, the Cheyennes and Arapahos, during the summer near

77

Bent's Fort on the upper Arkansas River outside Texas territory. The Comanches and their allied Kiowas smoked peace pipes for two solid days to judge each other's sincerity.[2]

Soon thereafter, the Comanches and Kiowas offered their new friends large numbers of horses. In exchange, they asked for guns, blankets, and kettles. The Cheyennes then introduced the Comanches and Kiowas to William and Charles Bent, the brothers who ran the trading post at Bent's Fort. With a new trading partner shaping up, the Comanches then broke camp and headed south back into Texas, taking along some of the extra guns and munitions they had been able to acquire.[3]

The party of Comanches and Kiowa numbered more than six hundred as they descended into Texas again. They also moved in company with a small number of Mexican citizens who were loyal to their cause. The senior surviving leader of the Penateka Comanches was Chief Buffalo Hump, who now led what would be the largest of all southern Comanche offensives. During the night of August 4, they descended from the Hill Country above San Antonio, San Marcos, and Austin and began their march to the coast to avenge their fallen chiefs.[4]

As the Comanches moved down south from their territory, they made a glancing blow against the fortified structure known as Kenney's Fort. This was located in the southern part of present Williamson County, on the south bank of Brushy Creek. The site was located about two and one-half miles east of present Round Rock, north of Austin.[5]

Kenney's Fort had been built in 1839 by Dr. Thomas Kenney and Joseph Barnhart. Some twenty-five miles north of the new capital of Austin, Kenney's was a single blockhouse containing several small cabins. Its eight-foot stockade helped protect the local settlers from Indians.

Although the exact date is unrecorded, Kenney's Fort was attacked by a passing band of Indians in August 1840. One of those stationed at the fort was Joseph Weeks, who had served in the 1836 ranger company of Captain John Tumlinson and under Captain Micah Andrews in 1837. Weeks noted what he at first perceived to be an owl hooting in the night.

Dr. Joel Ponton was seriously wounded on August 5, 1840, by the Comanches who were making their way into lower Texas coastal settlements. *Courtesy of Mrs. Fannie Ponton, Corpus Christi, Texas.*

When the owl was answered by other hoots from various directions, Weeks quickly deduced that the calls were being made by human voices. A messenger was sent racing to the nearest settlements for help.[6]

Shortly thereafter, the Indians made an attack on Kenney's Fort, where they were met by intense rifle fire. The settlers suffered one man killed and another wounded in the action, but they managed to prevent the Indians from overrunning their blockhouse. A number of Indians were believed to have been killed and wounded before the attackers gave up the fight.

The messenger arrived with a party of about fifty volunteers the next morning, but the pursuit party found that they were too late to catch the Indian body.

Ponton and Foley Attacked: August 5

The first notice that the Comanches were on the move came on August 5, 1840. Dr. Joel Ponton and Tucker Foley were citizens of the Lavaca neighborhood (now Halletsville). They were en route to Gonzales, on the road from Columbus. Just west of Ponton Creek—west of present Halletsville in Lavaca County—and east of Gonzales, the two were attacked by a band of twenty-seven mounted Comanches.[7]

Both Ponton and Foley suffered from poor family luck in Texas. Foley had previously lost two brothers, one with James

Fannin in the 1836 Goliad Massacre and another to Mexican marauders in 1839. Dr. Ponton's father, William Ponton, had been massacred by Indians near his own home on Ponton Creek in 1834.[8]

As the Comanches rushed toward Ponton and Foley on August 5, the two men wheeled their horses and raced for their lives. The Indians chased them for about three miles back toward Ponton Creek. The Comanches raced after Dr. Ponton, discharging arrows along the way. One passed through his hat and two lodged in his back. Once his horse became too badly wounded to run, Ponton abandoned the dying creature and hid in a dense thicket.

The Indians momentarily left Ponton and continued their pursuit of Foley. He tried to hide in Ponton Creek, but was discovered and captured by the Indians. They immediately cut off the soles of his feet and made him walk barefooted on the rough ground back to the spot where they knew Ponton was hiding. They forced him to call to Ponton to emerge from his hiding spot, but Ponton refused. The Comanches tortured and slowly mutilated poor Foley, as Ponton silently listened to his friend's agonized screams. Finally, the Indians speared and scalped Foley and left his mutilated body.[9]

Ponton waited until the Indians were long gone before emerging from his hiding spot. Although painfully wounded, he managed to crawl through the bottomland thickets and made his way back home to the Lavaca settlements during that night, August 5.

The sight of Dr. Ponton and the tale he told of the murder of Tucker Foley was enough to energize the community. Captain Adam Zumwalt was elected to take command of the Lavaca River settlers' volunteer pursuit party. Zumwalt was among a number of settlers from Missouri who had located to the Lavaca River between 1829 and 1837.[10]

Among those who joined Zumwalt's party were his son, Thomas K. Zumwalt, and veteran ranger Cicero Rufus Perry, who was in town visiting the Sherrill family. Other known members of Captain Zumwalt's company were W. H. Baldridge, Henry Bridger, Anthony Brown, Wilson Clark, Patrick Dougherty, Mason B. Foley (brother of the murdered Foley), Stewart Foley, Richard Heath, John W. Hinch, David Ives, David Kent, Mark H. Moore, Jesse Robinson, John McKinney, Montreville Rountree,

Arthur Sherrill, John Smothers, William Smothers, Richard Veal, and Isaac K. Zumwalt.[11]

Zumwalt organized thirty-six men and they set out west toward Gonzales for the scene of the attack on the morning of August 6. Tucker Foley's naked, mutilated body was found about two miles from the present town of Moulton in Lavaca County. John McKinney dug a grave with his butcher knife, wrapped Foley in a cotton saddle blanket, and buried him under a large live oak tree. Zumwalt's company then took up the trail of the Comanches and began tracking their movements.[12]

Another man who noticed the increased Indian activity was thirty-seven-year-old Baptist preacher Zachariah N. Morrell. He had been in Texas since the Texas Revolution and had traveled about during his preaching. Most recently, Reverend Morrell had traded for land on the Guadalupe River, thirty miles above Victoria. He took his wagons to Bastrop, loaded them with lumber, and deposited this on his new land on the Guadalupe to build a home with.

> On my return, between the Guadalupe and Lavaca rivers, I saw clouds of smoke rise up and suddenly pass away, answered by corresponding signs in other directions. We passed with the wagons just in the rear and across the track of the Indians as they went down. From their trail I thought, and afterwards found I was correct, that there were four or five hundred.
>
> The trail was on the dividing ridge between Lavaca and Guadalupe rivers. I trembled for the settlements below; for I knew this meant war on a larger scale than usual.[13]

Reverend Morrell soon found out about the Ponton/Foley depredation from the Lavaca area settlements on August 7. He was immediately anxious to spread the word to Colonel Edward Burleson and the citizens living along the Colorado River valley near his home of LaGrange. "My oxen were in fine condition," wrote Morrell. "I drove thirty miles in twelve hours."[14]

His oxen wagon crossed the Indian trail at noon and he reached home at La Grange at midnight.

In view of the long race before me, I tried to sleep
some, while a horse was being secured. At four o'clock
in the morning I was in my saddle, intending to reach
Colonel Ed. Burleson's at daylight, twelve miles off, on
a borrowed horse, as I had no horse in condition for the
trip.

Borrowing a fine sorrel from Dick Chisholm, Reverend
Morrell set out from La Grange during the early morning hours of
August 8. He reached Burleson's house near Bastrop around sun-
rise. Word of the new killing and the large body of Comanches
moving toward the settlements was enough to move the old
Indian fighter to action.

Saddling up, he joined Morrell for the ride back into Bastrop.
The First Regiment's leader quickly began organizing forces to
make a stand against the Indians. Sending Morrell as a rider on
to Austin to spread the word and to raise more forces, Burleson
worked on recruiting along the Colorado. He had none of his
army troops anywhere in the area, so would have to make the
most of the available citizens and the militia.

Volunteer Forces Unite: August 6–7

In early 1840, the area moving northwesterly between
Gonzales and the new capital of Austin was almost completely
uninhabited. Two recent settlers, Isham J. Good and John A.
Neill, did live on Plum Creek between the two towns.[15]

The mail carrier from Austin to Gonzales happened upon a
large, fresh Indian trail crossing the road in the vicinity of Plum
Creek. The Indians appeared to be bearing down toward the coast
of Texas. The mail carrier arrived in Gonzales and reported this
startling find.

The local militia was under the command of Captain Mathew
"Paint" Caldwell, who had been wounded in March in the Council
House Fight. On August 5, Caldwell happened to be away with
some of his men tracking other Indians who had been reported
west of the Guadalupe River. This courier brought the word
into Gonzales on Thursday, August 6. Ben McCulloch therefore
organized a twenty-four-man volunteer party to investigate the

Captain Benjamin McCulloch (1811–1862) organized one of the first volunteer companies to go in pursuit of the Comanches who raided Victoria and Linnville. He had manned one of the cannon at San Jacinto and would later serve as a Texas Ranger captain. Ben McCulloch was a brigadier general for the Confederacy when he was killed in action during the Civil War.
Texas State Library & Archives Commission, 1983/112-R-485-1.

tracks. McCulloch sent word at once to the settlements along the Guadalupe and Lavaca rivers. He asked for those citizens to come to the assistance of those from Gonzales in cutting off the body of Indians.[16]

One of Captain McCulloch's volunteers was twenty-eight-year-old Washington D. Miller, who had graduated from the University of Alabama in January 1836, with an engineering degree. Miller originally practiced law after moving to Gonzales in 1837, but his career in Texas would eventually include stints as legislator, postmaster general, newspaper editor, and private secretary for Sam Houston. In a letter to the *Telegraph and Texas Register*, Miller related why McCulloch could only raise two dozen men.

> A larger number would have moved out, but for the very short notice of the intended expedition and the great difficulty of procuring horses the Indians having about a week [before] stolen a majority of the best in the neighborhood.

Ben McCulloch was an experienced leader who had directed several Indian expeditions in his time already. Ironically, he was suffering in August from a wound by a fellow Texan. He had been challenged to a duel by Colonel Reuben Ross on October 6, 1839. The two met about two miles north of Gonzales, with rifles, at forty paces. Ross, an experienced duelist, fired at the word and struck McCulloch in the underside of his right arm. The wound was painful, but not deadly. Ross, being a surgeon, felt that the duel had been settled and then assisted McCulloch with his paralyzed right arm. The two became friends, but Ben McCulloch would be forced to keep his right arm in a sling for many months. Although Ross and McCulloch promised that their differences had been settled, Ben's brother Henry McCulloch had a further dispute with Ross later that year, in which Henry McCulloch fatally shot Ross at Gonzales on Christmas Eve 1839.[17]

Captain McCulloch's volunteers rode out from Gonzales at 4:00 p.m. on August 6 for the Big Hill settlement, about sixteen miles east of town toward the Lavaca River. This extended ridge, rising to almost 600 feet, separated the waters of the Peach creeks of the Guadalupe from the heads of Rocky, Ponton's, and other Lavaca River tributaries. It was also known as McClure's Hill. McCulloch's men reached this point and made camp for the night.[18]

McCulloch's Gonzales men located the great Indian trail early on the following morning, August 7. Private Washington Miller wrote on August 17 of their movements.

> Early this morning we came upon the trail which appears large and well trodden from which it is estimated there must be several hundred Indians. At this juncture a party of thirty six men from the upper La Vaca, and in the lead of Capt. A. Zumwalt, joined us.[19]

Collectively, the McCulloch and Zumwalt companies numbered sixty men. The Gonzales and Lavaca men continued south toward Victoria in pursuit along the Indian trail, spreading out their scouts ahead, left and right, "in constant expectation of soon meeting our savage foe."

About noon on August 7, the scouts made out a company of horsemen advancing toward the trail. A mutual reconnaissance took place and the new horsemen were found to be a company from other settlements. Word of the Indians had also made it down to the Cuero settlements on the Guadalupe River in present DeWitt County. Captain John Jackson Tumlinson Jr., the thirty-six-year-old veteran ranger commander whose father had helped inspire the Texas Rangers, took command of sixty-five men who volunteered from the Cuero and Victoria settlements.[20]

Captain Tumlinson's men joined those of captains Zumwalt and McCulloch shortly after noon on August 7, bringing their numbers up. "With our force now augmented to one hundred and twenty-five men, we push ahead in a brisk trot," wrote Miller.

Tumlinson's Cuero and Victoria men brought news that the Comanches had attacked the town of Victoria the previous day. Only after the Indians had moved out of town that night were the men able to go for help. Tumlinson, who had commanded rangers since the Texas Revolution, took charge of all that he could muster and had set out down their trail, expecting to encounter the main body at any moment.

By mutual agreement, the three company leaders agreed to give acting command to Captain Tumlinson, likely due to his vast experience in the ranging service. By late day, camp was made for the night, as Washington Miller recorded.

> Having reached a creek called Bushy (or Brushy), it is deemed advisable to diverge a few miles to the right, in the direction of the Guadalupe, for the purpose of intercepting them if they have taken that passage. We encamp about four miles from the trail, and send out scouts to the river at Tuscaloosa and back to the trail, with orders to ascertain whether they have yet passed up.

Captain Tumlinson's 125 men made a force sizable enough to engage the Comanches. The trouble was that they were too far behind to stop the raids that were already occurring.

The Victoria and Linnville Raids: August 6–8

At about 4:00 p.m. on August 6, the 500-plus Comanche party under Chief Buffalo Hump appeared on the outskirts of Victoria. They first killed four black servants of Thomas H. Poage at Spring Creek, above Victoria. The townspeople were completely oblivious to the danger as the Indians approached. Some even thought that a friendly group of Lipans were riding into town at first. Not until the Indians began yelling and riding toward the citizens did the realization of the true danger sink in.[21]

As the panic set in, the Victorians fled for their lives. A small party of the men, numbering thirteen, hurried to the suburbs to confront the attacking Indians. This group included Dr. Arthur Gray, William McMin Nuner, and Mr. Daniels. Although too small in number to stop such a massive Comanche force, the men hoped to at least buy time for their wives and children to flee to safety. The citizen party had no chance against the number. Gray, McNuner, and Daniels were killed.

Victoria resident John Joseph Linn, who had established a wharf and warehouse at Linnville in 1831, later wrote,

> Some Mexican traders were in Victoria at the time, and had about five hundred head of horses on the prairie in the immediate vicinity of town. All these the Comanches captured, besides a great many belonging to citizens of the place.[22]

The victorious Indians retired from town and camped that night on Spring Creek. There, they killed a settler named Varlan Richeson and two black men, and they captured a black girl. They had secured about fifteen hundred horses and mules on the prairie in front of Victoria, a large portion of which belonged to "Scotch" Sutherland, who had just arrived en route east.[23]

Unlike most Comanche raids, this time they did not ride away for their homes with their plunder. During the night, a group of men from Victoria who still had horses left town in search of reinforcements. They passed close by the Indian camp en route to the Cuero settlement in De Witt County, where Captain Tumlinson's volunteer company was raised.[24]

On Friday, August 7, the Comanches moved from Spring Creek, moving the three miles back into Victoria. A party of men returning from Jackson County happened across their force about a mile from town along the Texana road. Pinckney Coatsworth Caldwell—a longtime quartermaster for the Texas Army—and a Mexican man were killed. The other two men of the party, Joseph Rodgers and Jesse O. Wheeler, raced into Victoria with the Indians closely pursuing.

This was the site of the early port town of Linnville (now Placedo), which was burned by the Comanches on August 8, 1840. *Photo courtesy of Donaly Brice.*

The Comanches proceeded to burn one house and rob several others, but they were quickly discouraged from doing any more execution. The local men were now well armed and they put up enough heavy gunfire to convince the Comanches to move on. They opted to move down toward the lower coastal settlements, rounding up more cattle as they went.

From Victoria, the party rode south to Nine Mile Point. Near this little settlement, settler Cyrus Crosby had gone into Victoria early on August 7, leaving his family behind. During his absence, the Comanches captured his twenty-five-year-old wife, Nancy Darst Crosby, and her child. Nancy Crosby was the daughter of Jacob C. Darst, a Gonzales Mounted Ranger who had died in the Alamo in 1836. Nancy Crosby's mother, Elizabeth Bryan, was a relative of Daniel Boone's wife, Rebecca Bryan Boone. That evening or during the early morning hours of the following day, Nancy Crosby's child became hungry and began crying. When the mother was unable to quiet the child, one of the Indians grabbed the baby, threw it down on the ground, and speared it before the horrified mother.[25]

The Comanches then deflected to the east, across the prairie in the direction of Linnville. They camped for a portion of the night on Plácido Creek, on the Benavides ranch about twelve miles from Linnville. There, they killed a teamster named Stephens.

They failed to discover a fortunate Frenchman who hid above them in a giant live oak tree, covered in the moss and foliage. The death toll now stood at sixteen, including Tucker Foley from two days previous.[26]

Merchant William G. Ewing was traveling from Linnville to Victoria that night. He noticed a great number of campfires along Plácido Creek and spotted Stephen's empty wagon. Ewing moved on to Victoria, guessing that the camp was that of Mexican traders bound for Linnville. Only after arriving in Victoria did he learn that the Indians had already attacked that town. Ewing was upset to find how closely he had passed such a large Comanche camp in the night.[27]

Before dawn on August 8, the Comanches approached the town of Linnville. This coastal town was the key shipping point for much of the goods between southwest Texas and Mexico. Somehow the inhabitants of the town had received absolutely no warning yet of what had happened in Victoria. The Indians made their appearance on the Victoria road "about 8 o'clock" on the morning of Saturday, August 8, according to one eyewitness.[28]

Seeing the large herd of horses approaching, they had at first believed this to be a large band of friendly Mexicans arriving with horses to sell. The Indian riders approached in the shape of a half moon and began riding at full speed. Only as the killings began did the townspeople realize the horrible truth.

Moving into the edge of town, the Indians killed a citizen named Joseph O'Neill and two black servants of Major Hugh Oran Watts. Caught without guns or any form of defense, the people of Linnville frantically took to the water to save themselves. Many swam out to their sailboats, which were anchored in shoal water about one hundred yards from shore. Also in the bay was Captain William G. Marshall's steamer *Mustang*, aboard which many found refuge.[29]

In attempting to reach the sailboats, Major Watts, the customs collector for the port of Linnville, was killed in the water. His young bride, the family black servant woman, and the woman's little son were all captured. Watts had been married but twenty-one days to Juliet Constance Ewing Watts, a recent emigrant to Texas from Ireland.[30]

William H. Watts, brother of Major Watts, wrote of the killings at Linnville.

The citizens had no other alternative but to flee to the bay, where the rest of them were saved by getting into a lighter. Mr. and Mrs. Watts, being in the lowest house, and not hearing other Indians so soon as the rest, could not make their escape.[31]

The Indians found an immense amount of goods in the warehouses of Linnville. This merchandise was destined for San Antonio and the Mexican trade. The Comanches rapidly packed these goods onto their horses and mules, a task which consumed the better part of the day.

John Linn, who had escaped the Comanches in their raid on Victoria the previous day, owned a warehouse near the water in Linnville. He suffered the loss of all of his merchandise.

In my warehouse were several cases of hats and umbrellas belonging to Mr. James Robinson, a merchant of San Antonio. These the Indians made free with, and went dashing about the blazing village, amid their screeching squaws and little Injuns, like demons in a drunken saturnali, with Robinson's hats and Robinson's umbrellas bobbing about on every side like tipsy young balloons.[32]

At least one citizen could not stand seeing the destruction and looting. Judge John Hays became so angered that he grabbed a gun and leaped into the bay, vowing to kill an Indian. Wading toward shore, the judge shouted at the Indians and threatened them to come within range of his gun. The Indians apparently respected the gun, and did not come within range. Judge Hays was eventually convinced by friends to return to the safety of the boat. Upon examination, his gun was found to be unloaded.[33]

Late in the day, every building of Linnville except one warehouse was set afire and burned down. The horrified citizens could only watch in anger from their sailboats offshore as their happy little settlement was looted and literally burned to ashes.

William Watts, whose brother had been killed, wrote:

The Indians appeared to be perfectly contented, and remained in town till after dark, burning one house at a time. They destroyed nearly all the goods and all the houses; also, a large number of cattle and calves, which they drove into pens and burned, or cut to pieces with their knives and lances.

The citizens remained in sight of town all day witnessing the shocking scene of the destruction of their property without being able to make any resistance, having no guns or any means of defense. Some of the citizens returned next morning and buried the dead. The remainder continued on to the pass, where they were kindly treated by Mr. [Elijah] Deckrow, boarding officer of that place.[34]

During the late afternoon of August 8, the Comanche band began their jubilant departure from the Texas coast. They withdrew from Linnville across a nearby bayou and made their camp for the night. In their wake, they left twenty dead and two towns ransacked. They had taken five prisoners, all women and children. Although a long delay in coming, the Comanches certainly now felt some revenge for their previous losses at San Antonio's Council House.

Their route of retirement toward the Texas Hill Country was a path that would pass up the west side of Garcitas Creek, about fifteen miles east of Victoria. The return to their more northern hunting grounds would not, however, go uninterrupted.

Captain John Tumlinson's 125-man pursuit party returned to the trail on August 8. His scouts had returned at daybreak with no news of the Indians. Tumlinson's volunteers rode the trail throughout the day, without stopping, until they arrived at Victoria about sunset. As they were approaching Victoria on August 8, the Comanches were in the act of terrorizing Linnville.

By nightfall, news that Linnville was under attack had made it to Victoria. Washington Miller, his Gonzales company commander Ben McCulloch, and Victoria volunteer David Murphree compiled their thoughts upon entering town.

We find the inhabitants in much agitation, and under apprehension of further molestation from Indians. Many families are assembled in houses centrally situated, and eligible for defence; the nine-pounder is mounted at an angle of the square, and every preparation made for the worst. It is well ascertained that some five or six individuals of the town and neighborhood have been killed, and that some fifteen hundred head of horses have been driven off. We hear, also, that Linnville is destroyed and many of its inhabitants massacred.

Our men are cordially received and handsomely treated by the citizens of Victoria, which inspires us with increased good feeling towards them as a community, and with a lively regard for their protection and safety.[35]

The men under captains Tumlinson, McCulloch, and Zumwalt rested for a short time and took on supplies as they listened to the tales of horror from the Victoria citizens. They found the local citizens barricaded against a new attack. Approximately twenty-five of Tumlinson's overall party were left at Victoria, some with worn horses. In return, he received an equal number of new recruits, keeping his strength at 125 men.[36]

The Tumlinson battalion moved east of Victoria on the Texana road, making camp about midnight. The location was on Casa Blanca Creek, a small tributary of the Garcitas from the west. George Kerr was dispatched as a courier for more recruits from Texana. Kerr rode to Kitchen's ranch, on the east side of the Arenosa, near the tidewater junction with the Garcitas. There, he found Captain Clark L. Owen of Texana with a forty-man volunteer company. Owen, thirty-two, had previously commanded a Texas Army company during 1836.

The following day, August 9, Kerr wrote a letter from Lavaca to Colonel John Moore in La Grange. He relayed the news of the Indian attacks and informed Moore that "about 45 men left Victoria on the evening the Indians attacked Victoria." Kerr asked for assistance from La Grange. "Let Burleson be informed of this and move on to intercept the Indians between the Guadalupe and La Baca, passing by [Williamson] Daniels."[37]

During the early morning hours of August 9, Captain Owen's company was approached by the retreating Comanche war party. The hundreds of campaigning Indians passed between the camps of Owen and Tumlinson, making it impossible for the two to

unite. Captain Owen sent out three of his men as scouts—John
Sutherland Menefee, a Dr. Bell, and a man named Nail.

These three were attacked and chased by the Comanches on
Arenosa Creek in Jackson County. Dr. Bell was killed and Nail
escaped only by the sheer speed of his horse. He fled towards the
Lavaca settlements and escaped. John Menefee, a San Jacinto veteran and Texas congressman, was struck in the body with seven
arrows piercing him. He somehow managed to escape and hide
in some drift brush along the creek bank until the Comanches
passed on. Menefee walked and crawled to a nearby ranch the
following day. He had managed to pull the seven arrows from
his own body. Although suffering from serious blood loss, he
survived, and would keep the seven arrows in his Jackson County
home for years.[38]

During the morning on August 9, Captain Tumlinson's
scouts reported the massive body of Comanches returning from
Linnville. His men diverged from the Texana road and crossed
a large prairie, with Casa Blanca Creek on their left. They rode
roughly seven miles further until they finally came in sight of
their adversary after 10:00 a.m. They were located about five
miles south of DeLeon's ranch and were issuing from the woods
onto the verge of the prairie.

The Indian pack animals were heavily laden with booty.
Tumlinson's companies rode out to intercept the Comanches on a
level, treeless prairie. Tumlinson's right flankers were more than
a mile away from his main body at the time of the Indian sight-
ing. The Indians passed between his forces and thus cut off this
detachment of his men temporarily.[39]

He advanced his Texan volunteers upon the Indians in parallel divisions. Captain McCulloch's Gonzales company and
Captain Zumwalt's Lavaca companies held the right closest to
the Comanches. Captain Tumlinson's own Cuero and Victoria
men were about twenty paces to the left. The Comanches, armed
with shields, guns, lances, bows, and quivers, were mounted and
prepared for the Texan charge.[40]

Gonzales volunteer Washington Miller found the Comanches
to be "hideously bedaubed after their own savage taste." Some
wore feathers. Others were "sporting huge helmets of buffalo or
elk horns —armed with glistening shields, with bows and quivers with guns and lances, and mounted on their chargers, dash-

ing about with streamers" flying behind them. He estimated the Indian party to number "from 400 to 500."

Tumlinson preferred to dismount his men for an attack as he approached. As the Indians moved forward, a large number of their warriors encircled the Texans. This move was to keep the Texans at bay while other Indians herded their large droves of horses forward. While the Comanches continually circled his men, some of Captain Tumlinson's party grew impatient.

Alfred Kelso, sheriff of Gonzales, drew first blood this day. His target was a daring turkey-plumed Comanche chief with a lance and shield. As the Comanche moved tauntingly close, Kelso dropped him from his horse with a well-directed shot.[41]

William Riley Wood later wrote that he was among those who fought the battle "at Garcitas Creek with the Indians in 1840 under J. J. Tumlinson at the time the Comanche Indians burned Linnville." The firing continued between the Texans and the Indian party for about twenty minutes. The battle never became general, due to the lack of a charge by the volunteers. During the skirmishing, Benjamin H. Mordica of Victoria—one of the twenty-five new men who had joined Tumlinson the previous day—was killed. In addition, three Texan horses were wounded.[42]

Washington Miller continues:

> They whirl about us and around us, exhibiting the most admirable feats of horsemanship and, being continually in motion, they were the less liable to be struck by our balls. But it was seldom they withdrew from their daring sallies without leaving upon the ground some indubitable evidence of the skilled use of our arms. Discovering the fate of several of their number, they became more wary, and kept at a more respectful distance. Those among them using rifles and escopetas dismount and play upon us from the grass, at about one hundred and fifty paces.[43]

Captain Ben McCulloch insisted that a charge should be ordered to scatter the Indians. He felt such action was the only chance of victory against such superior numbers. Sensing hesitancy in his ranks, leader John Tumlinson would not commit to the full charge. He knew full well that many of his less courageous men might not follow, thus badly stretching out the Texans.

After skirmishing for about twenty minutes, the Texans failed to bring on the real battle. They had only wasted enough time for the Comanches to successfully slip their pack animals past them. One of Tumlinson's Victoria men claimed that the Comanches lost "four of their most conspicuous warriors." He claimed that others were wounded and that "the enemy left three of their dead" on the field before retreating.[44]

Captain Tumlinson allowed his men to move to a nearby stream to take on much-needed water. While the Texans quenched their thirsts, the Comanches who had kept them at bay joined the main body of retreating Indians. The Indian force was now literally moving right back up the path they had come down on—the same path that Tumlinson's men had followed down.

The volunteers found the weather to be excessively hot and their horses were pretty much worn down. Tumlinson decided it would be foolish to charge after the Indians this day without fresh horses. Charging the Indians would also send them fleeing. He therefore decided that the best course of action was to maintain a slow pursuit in their wake. If possible, a more aggressive action might be taken against them once they reached some timber, where the Texans could use the cover to their advantage.

With one man killed and three horses wounded, the 124 remaining men under Tumlinson, Zumwalt, and McCulloch began a slow pursuit of the Comanches. A courier was sent back toward Texana to urge more volunteers to join up. Proceeding northwesterly, the main Texan body reached Chicolete Creek late on August 9, some twenty miles above the Casa Blanca. Scouts showed that the Comanches had made camp just ahead, so Tumlinson ordered his men to camp for the night also.

At Chicolete Creek, a command division occurred. Captain McCulloch, seething with anger that he had been unable to bring Tumlinson to force a charge all day, decided that the Texans had missed their golden opportunity.

Ben McCulloch turned his Gonzales company over to his lieutenant and departed with three of his trusted men—Archibald Gipson, Barney Randall, and Alsey S. Miller. McCulloch rode hard for Gonzales throughout the night. He was determined to find more men who would aid him in fighting the Indians. He dispatched Gipson with a note to the Colorado River to raise up Edward Burleson to join with recruits. McCulloch asked Burleson to designate the crossing at Plum Creek as the rendezvous site for the volunteers that could be raised.[45]

The parties under Zumwalt, Tumlinson, and the remaining Gonzales volunteers made camp on August 9. The following day, they continued to follow the retiring Comanches. Just after daybreak on August 10, courier George Kerr and Captain Clark Owen's remaining thirty-seven men from Texana joined up. The gallantry of John Tumlinson was never questioned. His pursuit party stayed after the Comanche for days, hoping to effect a rendezvous with a large Texian force which could effectively challenge such a large number of Indians.

Alsey Silvanus Miller was one of only four men who fought in both the August 9 Comanche skirmish and in the ensuing Battle of Plum Creek. *Courtesy of Mrs. Lucy Ainsworth, Luling, Texas.*

During the day on August 10, his 160-plus men found the Indians "drawn up in a very imposing line, upon the crest of a ridge, to our left." Wash Miller wrote, "We make for them—they fly in disorder, man and beast, bag and baggage—their object is what we apprehended, to elude us by flight."[46]

Some of the fleeing Comanches dropped their plunder along the trail. Tumlinson ordered the Texans with the freshest horses to ride hard through the night to get ahead of the advancing Indians. The best option now seemed to move the men ahead who had the best horses and set up an ambush at Plum Creek.

Despite this hope, Tumlinson's party would not be able to make the rendezvous. Of his original command, none would make the Plum Creek rendezvous to stage an organized fight. Only the four who split from him on August 9 would be successful in making this fight.

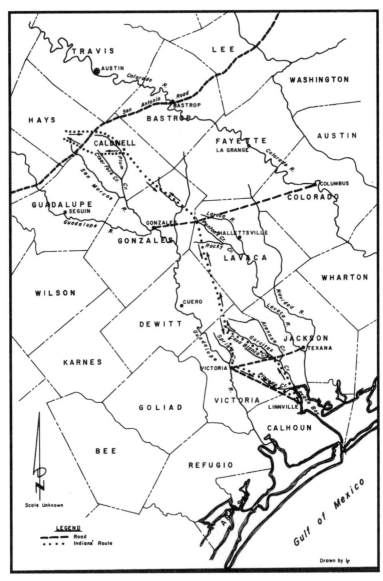

This map, drawn by Linda Fields, shows the route of the Comanches to the Texas Gulf Coast and the paths of Texan forces which pursued them. Courtesy of Donaly Brice, from his book *The Great Comanche Raid*.

CHAPTER 5

"If We Can't Whip 'em, We Can Try!"

August 1840

Ben McCulloch was determined to organize a group of men who would aggressively seek out a fight. As he neared Gonzales, he dispatched Alsey Miller to find Captain Mathew Caldwell, who was returning with a group of men from chasing other Indians.[1]

Arch Gibson, also dispatched as a courier by McCulloch, rode hard to the Bastrop area, where he reached Colonel Edward Burleson at noon on August 10. Burleson had orders from Secretary of War Branch Archer, but immediately decided that this crisis overrode any standing military orders.

Burleson wrote Archer on August 10: "I am now raising all the volunteers in [my] power to go to their assistance." He planned to ride out the following morning, in company with some of his trusted Tonkawa scouts.[2]

Burleson called a meeting and the men agreed to try to intercept the Indians at Isham Good's cabin on Plum Creek, about twenty-seven miles below Austin. Burleson dispatched riders to round up volunteers.

Across the river from Burleson's Mount Pleasant plantation, Thomas Monroe Hardeman and Susan Burleson, cousin of Edward Burleson, were enjoying their wedding ceremony. Guests from many miles away had assembled to watch the wedding. One of Burleson's riders appeared just as the happy party was enjoying a toast to the bride. Just as quickly as the horseman dashed into the yard with the warning from Colonel Burleson, "the table was deserted" as the able men raced to help.[3]

Monroe Hardeman, now distantly related to Colonel Burleson by marriage, was elected Major of the volunteer troops now assembled from the Bastrop area. Branch Archer received Burleson's letter on August 11 and he quickly authored a reply. Due to the severity of the crisis, Burleson received orders from the government which "placed this expedition under your command. The responsibility rests upon you."

It is doubtful that he received these orders until after his men had returned to town, for his party moved out on the morning of August 11 to meet other volunteers at Plum Creek.

Jonathan Burleson had rounded up Chief Plácido and twelve of his Tonkawa scouts. They set out at 10:00 p.m. on August 11 to join up with Colonel Burleson's main forces. Plácido and his men ran on foot throughout the night, Plácido keeping one hand on Jonathan Burleson's knee as he trotted with his Tonkawas alongside.[4]

While he awaited the return of Captain Caldwell, Ben McCulloch assisted the Gonzales citizens in raising another volunteer company. Captain James Bird, a veteran of Captain Stephen Townsend's 1836 rangers, was elected to command the thirty additional Gonzales volunteers. Among those now in his number were Ben McCulloch, his brother Henry McCulloch, and Barney Randall.

Some of the pursuit party formerly under Captains Tumlinson, Zumwalt, and McCulloch made it into Gonzales on August 11. These men had ridden hard during the night to try and get ahead of the Comanches. Wash Miller wrote that they had reached McClure's Hill at sunrise on August 11

> with most of our horses worn down with the extraordinary fatigue of yesterday and last night, having travelled some sixty or seventy miles. Here we quit the trail, and make for Gonzales for the purpose of feeding our horses, and as many of us can, joining the force supposed to be on Plum Creek. It is plain that our sole reliance is to take

advantage of them in Plum Creek bottom, where they will little expect to see us, and which is looked to as the ground where, of all others, they may effectually be chastised.[5]

As Captain Bird was gathering his volunteers, Henry McCulloch was sent out ahead to scout for the Comanche. He rode out to Big Hill, fourteen miles east of Gonzales, to view the passing cavalcade. He saw them pass and noted Captain Tumlinson's pursuit party still in tow. McCulloch then rode hard to alert his brother and Captain Bird. Bird's men departed Gonzales at once toward Plum Creek, with about thirty men and Ben McCulloch's three men. "There we resolved to attack them," wrote Nelson Lee, who departed Gonzales with McCulloch and Bird's company.[6]

Even as Bird's force departed Gonzales, two other companies were converging on that town and narrowly missed joining him. One, of course, was the returning scout party under Captain Paint Caldwell. The second was another volunteer party from the Lavaca settlements under Captain Lafayette Ward.

The men of Lavaca had been awakened on the night of August 7 by a courier who raced into the settlements with the news that Victoria had been attacked by Indians and that many citizens had been killed. Twenty-two volunteers gathered on the Lavaca River at the home of James Kerr, one of Texas' earliest militia leaders. They elected Captain Ward into command and departed on August 8.

The youngest volunteer of Captain Ward's Lavaca company was nineteen-year-old John Henry Brown, a nephew of James Kerr who worked in the newspaper business. During his life, Brown would collect and write extensively on the Texas-Indian wars, much from his personal experience.

Brown related his company's move to catch the Indians and Texian volunteers.

Reaching the Big Hill, and finding the Indians had not passed up, the opinion prevailed that they had crossed over and were returning on the west side of the Guadalupe. [Captain Ward's company] hastened on to Gonzales where the old hero, Capt. Mathew Caldwell, had just arrived.

Early historian John Henry Brown (1820–1895) worked at a small newspaper as a teen before coming to Texas. Brown fought at Plum Creek in 1840 and served as a county minuteman in 1841. From Brown's *Indian Wars and Pioneers of Texas.*

He adopted the same view, and announced that the Indians would recross the Guadalupe where New Braunfels now stands. In an hour, he was at the head of thirty-seven men, making our united number fifty-nine. We followed his lead, traveled all night, and at sunrise on the 10th, reached Seguín.[7]

As Caldwell and Ward's companies reached the Seguín area on the morning of August 10, they encountered courier Robert Hall, another Gonzales man. Hall, who had served under Paint Caldwell in the past, had departed from Gonzales with Captain Bird's recruits. He was sent back to find Caldwell's men to relay the word of the attacks on Victoria and Linnville. John Henry Brown noted Hall arrive "on foaming steed" to announce that the Indians were retreating directly up the trail they had made on their way down.[8]

Captain Caldwell announced that his forces must move at once to meet the Indians at Plum Creek. "After rest and breakfast, and strengthened by a few recruits," wrote Brown, "we moved on and camped that night at the old San Antonio crossing of the San Marcos."

The eager Ben McCulloch and the other Gonzales volunteers under Captain James Bird were first to reach Plum Creek with their approximately thirty-three men.

Captains Ward and Caldwell moved out from the San Marcos River on the morning of August 11 to effect a rendezvous. John Henry Brown of Ward's company recalled:

The 11th was intensely hot, and our ride was chiefly over a burnt prairie, the flying ashes being blinding to the eyes. Waiting some hours at noon, watching for the approach of the enemy after night, we arrived at Good's cabin, on the Gonzales and Austin road, a little east of Plum Creek.[9]

Arriving at Isham Good's cabin from Austin about the same time was Major General Felix Huston, leader of the Texas Militia, with his aide, Major John Izod, and Captain George Howard of the First Regiment. Huston arrived on the evening of August 11 "and found Capt. Caldwell encamped on Plum Creek with about one hundred men." The three companies moved two or three miles and made camp for the night on Plum Creek, above the return trail of the Indians. The men slept at midnight, sending out pickets to watch the Indian trail for signs.[10]

Robert Hall, twenty-six, recalled, "Capt. Caldwell asked me to take a good man and scout to the front and see if I could see anything of the Indians." He selected John Baker, and the pair rode through the night toward the advancing Indian force.[11]

"Men and horses were greatly jaded," wrote Brown, "but the horses had to eat while the men slept."[12]

The Battle of Plum Creek: August 12, 1840

Henry McCulloch and two or three other scouts remained out during the overnight hours, watching for the approaching Comanches. They did not have long to wait. At daylight on August 12, one of McCulloch's scouts rushed back to report that the Comanches were approaching from about three miles below. The spies reached Felix Huston's camp about 6:00 a.m.[13]

Paint Caldwell, being respected as a brave Indian fighter, made a brief speech to the volunteers. Despite only being about one hundred in number, he felt that they must challenge the Comanches before they passed. "They must be attacked and whipped before they reach the mountains," he said. Once the Indians could reach the safety of the mountainous thickets above Plum Creek, Caldwell saw no use in following them any further. "If we can't whip 'em, we can try."[14]

Within twenty minutes, every man was mounted and in battle line. Captain Caldwell, "in the bigness of his heart," rode out in front of the men and suggested that General Huston take command.[15]

Although most of the men silently wanted the veteran Caldwell to lead the fight, some gave their "aye" to the offer. Those opposed did not speak out. Huston was respected as a military man, although most knew that he had no direct experience with fighting Indians. "I was requested to take the command, which I did," wrote Huston, "with the consent of the men."[16]

Huston's hundred-man command moved forward about three miles from Good's cabin, across one or two ravines and glades, organized under command of captains Caldwell, Bird, and Ward. They entered a small, open space well concealed from the larger prairie by a thicket of trees and bushes along a creek branch.

Another stroke of luck arrived in the form of two advance riders from another Texan volunteer party. Owen Hardeman and Hutchinson Reed of Bastrop rode up to General Huston with the news that Colonel Edward Burleson was right behind them. He had gathered eighty-seven volunteers and thirteen Tonkawa Indians. The settlers were all mounted, while Chief Plácido's Tonkawas were on foot. Hardeman and Reed announced that Burleson's men were within three or four miles, advancing at a gallop.

From available records, it does not appear that Colonel Burleson brought his First Regiment troops with him in his haste to gather volunteers. The lone exception was Major George Howard, who had arrived with General Huston and now served as one of his aides. Howard had passed the word to the mounted "Border Guards" company of Captain James Cocke, whose unit operated from San Antonio under Howard's direction. According to General Huston, Burleson had organized his forces under Colonel Henry Jones, Lieutenant Colonel Joseph Wallace, and Major Thomas Monroe Hardeman.[17]

Burleson's men had paused only for a few short hours during the night. One of his Bastrop volunteers was seventeen-year-old John Holland Jenkins, who had served in the Texas Revolution.

> Every now and then we met runners, who were sent
> to bid Burleson to come on. We rode until midnight, then

Major General Felix Huston (1800–1857), commander of the Texas Militia. Although he had never been involved in an Indian fight, the more veteran Texans agreed to let Huston, a former Mississippi lawyer, have command at Plum Creek. *Texas State Library & Archives Commission, 2000/1-29-1.*

Major Thomas Monroe Hardeman (1814–1862), a division commander under Colonel Edward Burleson at Plum Creek. Hardeman's horse was shot by an arrow during the battle. *Center for American History, UT-Austin. CN Number 02711 a, b. Prints & Photographs Collection, circa 1850s.*

halted to rest our horses. Very early the next morning we were again on the warpath, still meeting runners at regular intervals beseeching us to hurry.[18]

With the ability to double his fighting forces, Huston ordered his men to halt until Burleson could catch up. During this delay, Huston drew up a battle plan. He would spread his forces to form a "hollow square," the front side of which would be open. Burleson's hundred troops would form the right side of the square, while Captain Caldwell would take the left side. Forming the rear line would be Major Thomas Hardeman, commanding the companies of captains Bird and Ward.

As with most early Texas battles, the accounts of this campaign have to be weighed carefully. Zachariah Morrell wrote that the companies gathered included ones under the command of William B. DeWees, Ad Gillespie, and Christopher "Kit" Acklin, among others. DeWees himself also later wrote of being in command of a company that fought at Plum Creek, a fact that battle veterans John Henry Brown and Jim Nichols called false. Reports of the Plum Creek battle, in fact, make no mention at all of companies formally commanded by DeWees, Gillaspie, or Acklin.[19]

From the rear of the square, Private Brown soon caught sight of Chief Buffalo Hump's approaching Comanche party.

> During this delay we had a full view of the Indians passing diagonally across our front, about a mile distant. They were singing and gyrating in diverse grotesque ways, evidencing their great triumph, and utterly oblivious of danger. Up to this time they had lost but one warrior, at the Casa Blanca.[20]

The Comanches had killed twenty people in their offensive to the Texas coast. They had three women and two young children as hostages, an immense booty of stolen goods, and an estimated *caballado* [Spanish for herd of horses] of 2,000 captured horses and mules.

The Texans were impressed with the number of Comanches approaching them and were amused at their attire. Jim Nichols of Seguín found them in "gaudy array." He noted one Indian "with a two-story bee gum silk hat on his head with at least ten yards of each color—red, green and blue ribbon—one end of each tied around his hat, [and] the other end loose streaming in the air behind."[21]

Robert Hall of Gonzales felt that the Comanches had been long preparing for this raid. "They all had new white shields, and many of the warriors had long tails to their headgear." With their stolen shoes and clothes, including shirts worn backwards, the column of Indians "presented a ludicrous sight."[22]

John Jenkins, riding with Burleson's Bastrop volunteers, also noted the Indian with the "stovepipe hat" and the cloth coat buttoned on backwards. "They seemed to have a talent for finding and blending the strangest, most unheard-of ornaments," Jenkins wrote. Among the buffalo and buck horns which the Comanches wore on their heads, he noted that "one headdress struck me particularly. It consisted of a large white crane with red eyes."[23]

Before Colonel Burleson's volunteers arrived, the advance force of the Comanches had passed the front of General Huston's concealed men. Behind the main crowd came other Indian stragglers who were herding bunches of stolen animals from the heavy timber in the rear. From the Big Hill near Gonzales on to Plum Creek, this area of Texas was heavily wooded. Beyond Plum Creek, there was an open prairie which led toward the hill country area of Austin. The trail of the Indians paralleled the Clear Fork of Plum Creek.[24]

John Henry Brown estimated the total number of Indians to be "about 1,000" against the two hundred Texians and Tonkawas preparing to attack them. General Huston found the parade of Indians was "extending nearly a quarter of a mile into the prairie."[25]

As soon as Colonel Burleson's men reached Huston, his men were quickly informed of the open square battle formation and were ordered to deploy. Without a moment to lose debating who should be in command, Burleson—although certainly the most experienced Indian fighter on the scene—graciously accepted militia leader Felix Huston as the Texan commander who would lead this fight.

The Texan troops now advanced at a trot. This pace was steadily increased to a gallop. The main body of retreating Comanches had advanced about a mile and a half ahead during the time that Burleson was allowed to arrive.

"As soon as we ascended from the valley on to the level plain, they had a full view of us, and at once prepared for action," recalled Private Brown.[26]

Small groups of the Comanche broke away to gallantly clash with the approaching Texans. Brown recalled "heroic acts" performed by Andrew Neill, Ben and Henry McCulloch, Alonzo Sweitzer, Hutch Reed, Arch Gibson, and Columbus DeWitt during the early fighting.

The large open prairie that was the site of the initial skirmishing with the Comanche war party later became known as Comanche Flats. This area is in present Caldwell County, about five miles southeast of Lockhart.[27]

During the approach of the main Indian body, four Texans were sent to spy on their movements. As they approached Buffalo Hump's Comanches, the Indian rear guard turned to meet the spies. As the Comanches approached, Dr. Alonzo Sweitzer fired on them, killing one of their number. The other Indians of the rear guard turned and fled into the main body of the war party.[28]

Battle of Plum Creek: August 12, 1840
Texan Forces

Major General Commanding
Felix Huston
General's Staff:
Maj. James Izod
Capt. George Thomas Howard
Capt. Andrew Neill

Regimental / Unit Commanders:
Col. Edward Burleson
Col. Henry Jones
Lt. Col. Joseph Washington Elliott Wallace
Maj. Thomas Monroe Hardeman
Capt. James Bird
Capt. Matthew Caldwell
Capt. Lafayette Ward

Volunteer Participants:
Christopher B. Acklin
Col. _____ Anderson
John Baker
Robert Emmett Bledsoe Baylor
Edward Beatty
Joseph Beitel
James T. Belknap
Col. Peter Hansbrough Bell
Judge Edmund Bellinger
Miles Squire Bennett
Andrew Jackson Berry
James Berry
John Bates Berry
Joseph Berry
Jesse Billingsley
Jonathan Bird
William Birdwell
Sion Record Bostick
Charles Braches
Dr. Caleb S. Brown
Dr. David F. Brown
John Hawkins Brown
John Henry Brown
Jonathan Burleson
Joseph Burleson Jr.
Jesse Burnam

William Owen Burnam
William J. S. Carter
Whitfield Chalk
William A. Clopton
Owen N. Cordell
Rev. Thomas Washington Cox
William H. Cushney
John Washington Darlington
David S. H. Darst
James Milford Day
Gordon Dees
William Bluford DeWees
Christopher Columbus DeWitt [1]
William Duty
Felix B. Earnest
Dr. James Fentress
Daniel Boone Friar
Thomas Galbreath
Archibald Gibson [1]
James Gibson
Isham Jones Good
James P. Gorman
George W. Grover
Robert Hall [1]
Eli Skaggs Hankins
Owen Bailey Hardeman
William P. Hardeman

John B. Harvey
Charles Haynes
John Coffee Hays
John Harvey Herron
Benjamin Franklin Highsmith
Abraham Webb Hill
Joseph Hornsby
Jacob Jackson Humphreys
John Husbands
John Holland Jenkins
Joseph Lawrence
Nelson Lee [1]
Addison Litton
Frank M. Litton
John Litton [2]
John McCoy
Benjamin McCulloch
Henry Eustace McCulloch [1]
Samuel McCulloch
James P. Magill
William Harrison Magill
James F. Martin
Alsey Silvanus Miller
James L. Mills
William Washington Moon
Rev. Zachariah N. Morrell
James Moss
Matthew Mark Moss [2]
David Murphree
George Neill
James Wilson Nichols [1]
John W. Nichols
Thomas R. Nichols
Charles A. Ogsbury
William Sanders Oury
James Patton
Thomas J. Pilgrim
Chief Plácido
Elijah R. Porter
Barney Randall
Wilson Randle
Henry Prentice Redfield
Samuel Hutchinson Reed [1]
James Ogden Rice
Alexander Roberts
Lemuel M. Rodarmel

Henry Rogers
John A. Rogers Jr.
John A. Rogers Sr.
Samuel C. A. Rogers
William L. Scarborough
Josiah Shaw
Thomas W. Short
Ezekiel Smith
French Smith
James N. Smith
John L. Smith
John Smothers
Andrew Jackson Sowell
John N. Sowell
Darwin M. Stapp
Oliver H. Stapp
Isaac Phillip Stem
Dr. Alonzo B. Sweitzer [1]
James A. Sylvester
Creed Taylor
Barry Thompson
Alfred S. Thurmond
Charles Wagoner
William Alexander A. Wallace
Judge Edwin Waller
Jesse O. Wheeler
David N. White
John C. White
John M. White
Newton White
Peter White
Sam Addison White
Simon C. White
Caleb Wilburn
Henry C. Winchel
Charles John Wright

[1] Wounded during battle.
[2] Per subsequent veterans paper research by Donaly Brice supplied to author.

Primary source: Donaly Brice, *The Great Comanche Raid*, 69–70. Cicero Rufus Perry removed from original list per subsequent research by Brice.

Capt. Cocke's "Border Guards": June 18–August 28, 1840	
Captain:	Francis Lambert
James Decatur Cocke	Harlan L. Leaf
Orderly Sergeant:	_____ Lloyd
Alfred A. Smith	John Moore
First Corporal:	_____ Morris
Samuel Purcell	William C. Oglevie
	James P. Sherwood
Privates:	John R. Slocumb
Lewis Beardsley	Gotlip Wolf [DeWolf] *
John F. Coughlin	
John Daly	* Killed in action August 12.
Quintan M. Douglass	
_____ Harrold	Source: Partial roster compiled by author's research of Republic of Texas audited claims and public debt papers.
William H. Henderson	
C. F. Houston	

At about the same time, some of General Huston's men noticed another group of Anglo riders being chased by a portion of the Comanche war party. This was later discovered to be Captain James Cocke's mounted volunteer Border Guards. Dispatched from San Antonio by Major Howard, Cocke's company had accidentally come upon the Indians' advanced guard without realizing the full strength of the Comanche party.

Cocke's company took up position in a small grove of live oaks. They dismounted and prepared to attack the approaching small group of Comanches. When Cocke's men spotted the main body of Indians appear behind the advanced guard, they swiftly mounted their horses and retreated. In the rush, Gotlip Wolf [called DeWolfe in a contemporary newspaper account] was left behind by both his horse and his company mates. The Comanches quickly overtook DeWolf and killed him.[29]

The Border Guards, small in number, fell back away from the advancing Comanche forces. They did not engage the Indians any further until they encountered another force which was moving toward the area to intercept the Indians: Colonel Juan Seguín's party of Federalist volunteers. According to the *Austin Sentinel*, "they joined their force and immediately pursued after the Indians. The Border Guards deserve much credit for the promptitude with which they acted on this occasion."[30]

Comanche Flats in present Caldwell County. This was the site of the initial contact between Comanche and Texan forces at Plum Creek. Photo courtesy of John Anderson, originally published in Donaly Brice's *The Great Comanche Raid.*

One of Cocke's men was sent to Austin the following day with a Caddo Indian prisoner and news of the previous day's action. "Capt. Cocke of the Border Guards and six others were missing at the time the express left," reported the *Sentinel*, "but it is to be hoped that they have not been killed."

The Indians soon became aware of the other, larger force of Texans under General Huston. They began to have minor skirmishes with various members of Huston's collective forces, while the main body of the Indians continued to drive their livestock and plunder northwesterly toward their home camps.

The distance between the opposing forces closed until the Comanches halted their northwestward retreat at a place later known as Kelley Springs. The Texan forces continued to edge closer to them as the Indians took up a position in a point of oak trees on their left. Behind them was the Clear Fork of Plum Creek. To their left, and impeding their line of retreat, was a small boggy branch. This branch was only boggy for a short distance, which the advancing right body of the Texans easily avoided.[31]

When within about two hundred yards of the Indians, Huston ordered his men to halt and dismount from their horses on the open plain of present Kelley Springs. The various units began to form the "hollow square" that General Huston had planned.

Kelley Springs in Caldwell County. The Comanches halted their retreat at this location and the heaviest fighting of the Battle of Plum Creek ensued. Photo courtesy of John Anderson, originally published in Donaly Brice's *The Great Comanche Raid.*

Some of Huston's veteran rangers and Indian fighters were not happy that they were asked to dismount rather than charge into the Indians' midst. As the Texans tied off their horses, a small band of Comanches then began circling around them. Using their shields for cover, they dashed in on horseback and fired. "A handsome fire was opened," wrote Huston, as the Comanches were observed "cavorting around in splendid style, on front and flank, finely mounted, and dressed in all the splendor of Comanche warfare."[32]

In the early skirmishing, the taunting Comanches wheeled their horses away when the distance narrowed to eighty yards or less. They discharged their guns and arrows at the Texans, circled and moved in again and again. There was no destruction on either side, due to the lengthy distances. Henry McCulloch, from Captain Caldwell's company, took this opportunity to dash across the battlefield on foot and take position behind a ten-inch-diameter mesquite tree.[33]

McCulloch managed several effective shots on the Indians before he was discovered and taken under fire. Bullets struck the tree around him until his brother Ben McCulloch rode forward and advised him to fall back for safety.

Jim Nichols of Seguín saw one of the chiefs riding toward McCulloch during this action. As he raised his rifle to shoot, Nichols was struck in the hand by an Indian's rifle ball. He later wrote that the "ball struck me in the hand between my fore and middle finger, ranging towards and lodging in or near the wrist joint, where it remains to this day."[34]

Nichols fired at the same instant he was struck, and he claimed to have killed the horse of the Comanche chief wearing the buffalo helmet. He claimed that his shot ripped through the chief's thigh, crippling him. The chief could only manage to hop after climbing off his downed mount. "While thus exposed, old John McCoy shot and kilt him," Nichols wrote in his journal.[35]

Among the Texans gathered on the battlefield on August 14 were three Baptist preachers, Robert E. B. Baylor, Thomas W. Cox, and Zachariah Morrell. The latter, having returned to Burleson's command from his courier services, marveled at the opening acts of the battle. Like all other witnesses, he noted the Comanche with the top hat, umbrella, and the elegant coat, "hind part before, with brass buttons shining brightly right up and down his back."[36]

Morrell also noted that "The Indian and others would charge towards us and shoot their arrows, then wheel and run away, doing no damage." This was done several times within range of some of the Texans' guns.

During the early skirmishing, Henry McCulloch was also credited with saving the life of Colonel Sweitzer, a man previously among his enemies. Sweitzer, having advanced to fire on an Indian, was rushed by eight to ten Comanches and was severely wounded. An arrow passed through his arm and pinned it against his body. McCulloch, with Arch Gibson and Alsey Miller at his side, spurred their horses forward to slow the advancing Comanches.[37]

In return, Sweitzer was credited with shooting an Indian who had advanced on McCulloch as he reloaded his gun. Both Sweitzer and McCulloch had helped save each other that day, although neither had a word of thanks for the other.[38]

According to John Henry Brown:

> From the timber a steady fire was kept up, by muskets and some long range rifles, while about thirty of our men, still mounted, were dashing to and fro among the mounted Indians, illustrating a series of personal heroisms worthy of all praise. In one of these Reed of Bastrop had an arrow

driven through his body, piercing his lungs, though he lived long afterwards.[39]

Among the dismounted Texans, several were wounded and a number of their horses were killed. Nichols says that Samuel Hutchinson Reed was "hit with six arrows in the body and legs and finally his horse fell, pierced through with a ball." He claims that Reed had run his horse into the thickest portion of the Indians and became a standout target.[40]

Jim Nichols was impressed with the riding and fighting ability of the Comanches.

> Lying flat on the side of their horse with nothing to be seen but a foot and a hand, they would shoot their arrows under the horse's neck, run to one end of the space, straighten up, wheel their horses, and reverse themselves, always keeping on the opposite side from us. The line of warriors just behind these chiefs kept up a continuous firing with their escopetos, doing no damage. But they had some fine rifles taken at Linnville, and those done all the damage.[41]

During the skirmishing, the Comanches continued to herd their captured horses and mules onwards. The more experienced Indian fighters—namely Burleson, Caldwell, and McCulloch—were eager to charge into their midst and prevent their escape.

About half an hour after dismounting, the Texans scored a climactic kill which greatly inspired the men. Reverend Morrell claims that the shot was made by "an old Texan, living on Lavaca," who asked him to hold his horse. Moving as close as he safely could to the spot where the Comanches consistently wheeled their horses back around, the man waited patiently for one particular chief. As the chief turned his horse and briefly raised his shield, the Texan shot him.[42]

(Facing page) "Battle of Plum Creek." Sporting war paint and stolen clothing, more than five hundred Comanches are met in battle by Texan forces at Plum Creek on August 12, 1840. *USTA's Institute of Texan Cultures, No. 088-0055. Artist: Lee Herring. Courtesy of Mr. William Adams.*

Some of Captain Zumwalt's company may have been involved at Plum Creek. Mason Foley, brother of the slain Tucker Foley, claimed to have brought back his brother's horse and rifle, retrieved from an Indian he killed in battle. John Smothers of Zumwalt's company may have killed the Indian chief Morrell mentions above. Judge Paul Boethel, in *A History of Lavaca County,* relates from Lucy Turk that her grandfather Smothers was in the battle. She says her grandfather shot

> an old chief [who] kept daring all of them. He kept circling all around. He was decorated all over in ribbons made of calico, feathers in his hair. He was riding a big paint horse, and he kept daring them all, and Grandpa Smothers shot him off of his horse.[43]

This particular Indian chief, wearing a tremendous head dress, was "exceedingly daring" according to John Henry Brown. As he was struck by the Texan's bullet, the chief fell forward on the pommel of his saddle, but his slumping body was caught by a comrade on either side. Holding their chief on his horse, the Comanches rushed him away toward the oak trees.[44]

Brown felt that the chief was either dead or dying, for the Indians "set up a peculiar howl," a loud, mournful wail. At this instant, "Old Paint" Caldwell shouted out to Felix Huston, "Now, General, is your time to charge them! They are whipped!"[45]

Ben McCulloch's biographer wrote that he and his brother Henry advised the general to make the charge. It is likely that the neophyte general heard the plea to call for a charge from several of the battle-wise Texans present.[46]

Huston ordered the charge and the Texans rushed forward. Jim Nichols, having just fired his rifle, did not have time to reload it before charging. He returned his rifle to its holder at the horn of his saddle. From his brace of pistols, "I drew one of them with my left hand and was amongst the foremost in the charge."[47]

During the fighting, Robert Hall of Gonzales had been impressed with the courage of rookie Indian fighter General Huston. "He rode right with the line, and never flinched under the most galling fire." As the Texans charged, Hall was hit in the thigh by a bullet.

It made a terrible wound, and the blood ran until it sloshed out of my boots. I was compelled to dismount, or rather I fell off of my horse. After a moment I felt better and made an effort to rejoin the line of battle. I met an Indian, and was just in the act of shooting him when he threw up his hands and shouted, "Tonkaway!"[48]

One of the Gonzales volunteers, Nelson Lee, later claimed he had also been wounded by a gunshot early during the Plum Creek battle.

As I approached with another detachment of my comrades from a different direction, a buckshot struck me near the elbow, passing up the arm to the shoulder blade, where it yet remains. It was my bridle arm, causing me to drop the rein, and in consequence, my horse unexpectedly bore me directly into their midst.[49]

At the time that General Huston finally ordered the charge, the Comanches quickly broke into smaller parties and ran, but they continued fighting and firing all the way. A good many of the Comanches were killed who were slowed by the boggy branch of the creek. Brown reported that the Indians "were killed in clusters for ten or twelve miles, our men scattering as did the Indians, every man acting as he pleased. There was no pretense of command after the boggy branch was passed."[50]

General Huston agreed on the lengthy pursuit in his report.

The Indians did not stand the charge, and fled at all points; from that time there was a warm and spirited pursuit for fifteen miles; the Indians scattered, mostly abandoning their horses and taking to the thickets. Nothing could exceed the animation of the men, and the cool and steady manner in which they would dismount and deliver their fire.[51]

As he rode across the battlefield in pursuit, Jim Nichols noted one particular Indian's body. The Comanche had on red top boots, blue cloth pants, and a coat that he was wearing backwards with "the hind part before and buttoned up behind."[52]

Early ranger and scout Robert Hall (1814–1899), who had helped to lay out the town of Seguín in 1838, was wounded at the Battle of Plum Creek. *Lawrence T. Jones Collection, courtesy of Lawrence T. Jones III, Austin, Texas.*

At the boggy creek, Nichols found the bank "literally bridged with packs, dead and bogged down horses and mules." John Jenkins found the pack mules "bogged down so close together that a man could have walked along on their bodies dry."[53]

Nichols saw two Indians climbing the bank on the other side. Pulling his large Derringer belt pistol, he and a number of other Texans opened fire on the fleeing Comanches. Both fell.[54]

Some Texan parties pursued fleeing Comanches as far as twelve miles from the Plum Creek battlefield. In one of these running isolated fights, John Henry Brown killed a Comanche wearing a buffalo skin cap surmounted with the horns. "He was dead when I dismounted to secure the prize, which was soon afterwards sent by Judge John Hays to the Cincinnati museum, and was there in 1870."[55]

During the running fight, the Indians resolved to kill their hostages. Jim Nichols, racing forward during the charge, witnessed "an old Indian squaw" shoot Juliet Watts through the breast with an arrow. The Indian woman "then ran for her horse, but received the contents of my holster before she could mount."[56]

The black servant woman who had worked for the Watts family was also shot through with an arrow and dumped, along with her little boy. Another captive, Nancy Darst Crosby, worked herself free during the retreat and tried to take cover in a small thicket. Before she could reach this cover, a Comanche delivered a fatal lance thrust through her chest. Robert Hall, who rode upon this scene, found the Watts' servant woman and her child hiding in the grass near Mrs. Crosby. "Bless God, here is a white man once more," the Watts' servant exclaimed when Hall found her.[57]

Chief Plácido and his twelve horseless Tonkawas were especially brave during the battle. They could only mount themselves by vaulting into the saddle of slain Comanches. According to one eyewitness, Plácido and his Tonkawas "were all mounted in a marvelously short time after the action commenced."[58]

Ben McCulloch rode his strong horse "Pike," and led a pursuit of some of the fleeing Comanches. Leading about thirty of the best mounted men, he raced ahead to a miry branch to ambush some of the Indians as they tried to ride through the mud. Henry McCulloch shot one Indian from his horse.[59]

A number of the Comanches crossed the muddy creek and continued their flight. The McCulloch brothers, Alsey Miller, and Columbus DeWitt were the first Texans across the mire to race after their foe. Henry McCulloch fired at a fleeing chief and wounded his horse. The chief turned to fire his bow, but McCulloch was quicker, dropping the chief with his lap pistol.

The running fight continued. Alsey Miller had a hand-to-hand engagement with one Comanche and managed to come out the victor. Miller was racing upon a Comanche chief, preparing to fire, when his gun misfired. Nichols claims that this was "a repeating rifle" and that Miller had failed to revolve the large brass cylinder far enough after his first shot. Miller and the chief rode directly into each other, the chief attempting to launch an arrow into the Texan. Miller swung his rifle and hit the Indian in the head. Passing each other, the Comanche went for another arrow from his quiver as Miller frantically adjusted the cylinder on his Patterson rifle to catch. Miller quickly made the repeating rifle's cylinder catch and delivered a death shot to the chief.[60]

DeWitt, with one shot remaining in his pistol, charged to point-blank range before delivering his final deadly blast. In other close encounters, both Ben and Henry McCulloch reportedly killed another Comanche each. The pursuit continued until they had chased the Indians to the timber on Morrison's Creek, a tributary of the San Marcos River.[61]

The Indians fled toward the hill country above San Marcos, pursued by volunteers for twelve to fifteen miles in some cases.

The pursuit ceased between the present towns of San Marcos and Kyle.[62]

Colonel Burleson's brother, John Burleson, was among the approximately twenty-five pursuers of the fleeing Indians. He shot and killed one Comanche who was riding a horse noted by several from Bastrop to be the fine race horse of the late Matthew Duty. Known as the "Duty roan," this horse had been taken when Duty was killed by Indians near Bastrop in 1836.[63]

In the aftermath of the battle, Jenkins says that "a Mr. [William] Carter found a fine Indian baby, which had been left in the retreat" in a thicket.[64]

Joe Hornsby and John Jenkins from Bastrop, riding ahead of Colonel Burleson's troops during the mopping up action, spotted some thirty Indians ahead. Hornsby at first thought they might be friendly Tonkawas, but seeing their shields realized what they had encountered were Comanches. Jenkins doubled back to alert Colonel Burleson, who was about two hundred yards behind.

Burleson's men approached to within thirty steps of the Comanches before he ordered his men to fire. For a moment, John Jenkins felt that his "time had 'come,' sure enough." While reloading on the ground after his first shot, a Comanche moved on him with his gun presented. Joe Burleson Jr., nephew of the colonel, shot the Indian down. Only afterwards did they find that he was bravely bluffing the Texans with an unloaded gun.[65]

During the chase of these Comanches, Jenkins saw Colonel Burleson and Major Monroe Hardeman in action against a Comanche who shot arrows at his pursuers as he ran.

> General Burleson rushed at him with pistol presented, when an arrow from the Indian would have killed him if he had not stepped back. Then the warrior made another shot at Monroe Hardeman, which missed him, but was driven eight inches into his horse. The hardy warrior made a brave and persistent fight, and even after he was knocked down, drew his last arrow at me, the man nearest to him. I killed him just in time to save myself.[66]

There, the exhausted Texans dropped the pursuit. The McCullochs, DeWitt, and Miller continued scouting on ahead up the San Marcos and across to the Clear Fork of Plum Creek.

They found an abandoned child of two to three years of age and an Indian woman who had been left behind.

The foursome took these two and returned back to camp about sundown, where they met General Huston, Colonel Burleson, and Captain Caldwell.[67]

The Texans killed Indian men and women alike during the frantic chase. Nichols admitted to shooting two Indian women, one of which was fleeing on a horse, carrying a bow and arrow, and looked like a man. After he had discharged his rifle and all three belt pistols, Nichols sat down near the boggy creek to reload his arms. As he was doing so, he witnessed an Indian woman fall wounded from her dying horse. "I discovered she had been shot through both thighs," and was unable to walk. Nichols finished loading his guns and was preparing to ride off, when two other Texans from Seguín raced across the field on their horses.

Ezekiel Smith and his son, French Smith, discovered the wounded Indian woman and stopped. Nichols watched in disgust at the cruelty of one of his fellow volunteers.

> The old man got down, handed French his panting horse to hold, saying at the same time, "Look thare, French," pointing to the old wounded squaw with her long flabby breasts hanging down as she had recovered a sitting posture.
>
> He drew his long hack knife as he strode towards her, taken her by the long hair, pulled her head back and she gave him one imploring look and jabbered something in her own language and raised both hands as though she would consign her soul to the great spirit. [She] received the knife to her throat, which cut from ear to ear, and she fell back and expired. He then plunged the knife to the hilt in her breast and twisted it round and round like he was grinding coffee, then drew it from the reathing body and returned the dripping instrument to its scabbard without saying a word.[68]

French Smith was shocked at his father's act, but both men mounted their horses and continued the pursuit. Nichols was equally shocked with Ezekiel Smith, a member of the Methodist church for twenty-seven years and a noted Sunday school teacher. "I still sat there on my horse a few seconds longer, wondering if there was another man in America that claimed to be civilized that would act so cruel." Another fighter on the battlefield, John Jenkins, felt that Smith had treated the Indian woman "with almost inhuman and unmanly cruelty" in her death. "I do not think there was a single man from Bastrop who would have stooped to so brutal a deed."[69]

The Texans began returning to the main battlefield after the pursuit was dropped. Large numbers of horses and mules were herded in during this return. By mid-afternoon, the men herded the animals back to about where the action had first commenced. Here, camp was made for the night. "A welcome shower proved refreshing about this time," wrote John Henry Brown.[70]

General Huston's report simply states Texan losses as being "one killed and seven wounded—one mortally." The Texans took care of their wounded. Jim Nichols wrapped his bleeding hand with a bolt of yellow silk he found discarded on the battlefield. He joined up with his brother Thomas Nichols and they rode over to see Dr. Brown of Gonzales. Hutch Reed was suffering from the arrows shot into his body. Nichols watched as Brown extracted the arrows from Reed and dressed his wounds. Then several of Reed's friends put him on a blanket and moved him "to the point of timber to find a shade, for it was an awful hot day."[71]

Nichols listed the other wounded as: Robert Hall in the thigh; Henry C. Winchel in the arm; James Gibson (brother of Arch Gibson) in the shoulder; Mrs. Juliet Watts; Hutch Reed in six places in "body and legs and a rifle ball went through his body"; Nichols in the hand; and two more men slightly wounded with flesh wounds. Hall named some of the other wounded as Columbus DeWitt, Dr. Alonzo Sweitzer, and Henry McCulloch. Following the battle, Hall had a friend pull the arrow from his own thigh.[72]

Aside from the volunteer militiamen who had been wounded, two women had been shot by the Comanches and dropped for dead. Daniel Darst was grief-stricken, as his sister Nancy Darst Crosby was fatally speared through the chest. Another of the Texan volunteers who came upon the woman in her dying moments was her own husband, Cyrus Crosby. According to one account, Crosby reached his dying wife Nancy "just in time to soothe with endearing offices her last moments."[73]

The other white female discarded by the Comanches was Juliet Constance Ewing Watts. She had emigrated to Texas with her brother William G. Ewing in September 1839, and had married Hugh Watts on July 18, 1840, only three weeks before Major Watts was killed.[74]

Reverend Morrell found the badly wounded Mrs. Watts and helped retrieve her from the woods where she lay. The poor woman was struggling in vain to remove the arrow shaft from her breast. Dr. David F. Brown of Bastrop was summoned to her side, where Reverend Morrell held Mrs. Watts' hands as Dr. Brown tried to extract the arrow. Among others who gathered at the scene of this operation were Tom and Jim Nichols, who followed along with Dr. Brown. Jim Nichols recalled that the pain of trying to extract the arrow was more than Watts could bear.[75]

Robert Hall, wounded during the Texan charge, was also near as the arrow was extracted from Mrs. Watts.

> She possessed great fortitude, for she never flinched, though we could hear the breastbone crack when the arrow came out. She turned over on her side and bled a great deal, but she soon recovered. She was the wife of a custom house officer, and I think her maiden name was Ewing.
>
> She asked for Mrs. Crosby and told us that the Indians whipped the poor woman frequently and called her a "peon," because she could not read. They had stolen several books, and when in camp at night they would gather around Mrs. Watts and ask her to explain the pictures and read to them.[76]

Among those who helped console poor Juliet Watts on the Plum Creek battlefield was her brother, William G. Ewing, a merchant of Linnville who had joined the pursuit parties and arrived late in the day with Colonel John Henry Moore.

After the twelve- to fifteen-mile pursuit of the fleeing Comanches had ended, the Texans made their way back to the original battleground. They found Mrs. Crosby's body and buried her under a large oak tree, about one and a half miles west of present Lockhart. The Lockhart Masonic Lodge in 1850 later provided funding to have the remains of Mrs. Crosby reburied.[77]

Texan Casualties of August 12, 1840
Battle of Plum Creek

Capt. James D. Cocke's Border Guards

Name		Remarks:
Pvt.	Gotlip [de]Wolf	Killed in action.

Major General Huston's Command

Name	Remarks:
Columbus DeWitt	Unspecified wound.
James Gibson	Shot in the shoulder.
Robert Hall	Shot in the leg with arrow.
Nelson Lee	Shot in the elbow.
Henry Eustace McCulloch	Unspecified wound.
James Nichols	Shot in the hand.
Samuel Hutchinson Reed	Severely wounded by several shots.
Dr. Alonzo B. Sweitzer	Shot in the arm with an arrow.
Henry C. Winchel	Shot in the arm.

The Texan camp was made on the battlegrounds on the south side of Clear Fork Creek close to the water. It was surrounded on all sides except one with stands of timber and dogwood brush, opposite or slightly below the main battleground. All of the captured Indian booty was deposited here and the horses and mules were corralled nearby.[78]

Among the stolen goods now found included tobacco, black silk, calico sheeting, clothing, eating utensils, and books. Perhaps the most unusual item found among their haul were baby alligators packed in the Indians' bundles. Some men thought the Comanches were carrying them back as either curiosities or proof that they had actually gone as far as the coast.[79]

There was at least some indication that the Comanche offensive raid may have been encouraged by Mexican leaders. When the booty was divided, James N. Smith received a beaded shot bag with Roman cross designs on it. Inside the bag, Smith found a letter written by a Mexican to one of the Indian chiefs. The Mexican stated that he would meet the chief "at Corpus Christi or Lynvill [sic]."[80]

Perhaps due to the failure of Mexican officials to contribute support to the Comanches during their August offensive, the Comanches would carry out a major depredation into Mexico in

Dr. David F. Brown of Bastrop tended to the wounded after the Plum Creek battle and helped extract the arrow from Juliet Ewing Watts. *Courtesy of Mrs. Helen Rugeley, Austin, Texas.*

Alexander "Buck" Roberts fought at Plum Creek and was father of future Texas Ranger Captain Dan W. Roberts. *Courtesy of Kenneth J. Hyman, Leander, Texas.*

October 1840. More than four hundred Comanches penetrated deep into the Mexican states of Coahuila and Nuevo Leon, burning ranches and villages along their path. Many women were captured, along with thousands of head of livestock. In the state of Nuevo Leon, roughly seven hundred civilians were killed. Coahuila suffered equally.[81]

General Huston's report shows that the Texans had conservatively killed at least forty Indians and taken "a squaw and a child" as prisoners. He also noted that his men had taken "upwards of two hundred horses and mules, many of them heavily packed with the plunder of Linnville and the lower country."[82]

In the final post-battle tally, the Texans triumphantly raised the casualty rate to more than eighty Comanche chiefs and warriors on August 14. Eight or ten Comanche bodies were found in the San Marcos River. Several other Indian bodies were located as far away as the San Antonio Road. Others likely died later from their wounds after being carried away.[83]

Huston credited Major Izod, Colonel Bell, Captain Howard, and Captain Neill for acting as his volunteer aids and in rendering "essential service." He further credited Colonel Burleson, Captain Caldwell, Colonel Jones, Lieutenant Colonel Wallace, and Major Hardeman and "each of the captains commanding

companies" for acting "with the utmost courage and firmness."
He felt that his men had engaged at least 400 Comanches.[84]

Squads of new men continued to arrive all afternoon and into
the night. Colonel John Henry Moore arrived in company with
Captain Clark Owen and about 150 other men. General Huston
noted that "Colonel Moore joined us this evening with about 170
men, horses very hard ridden." Owen's men had been following
the Indian trail for days. This group included the companies of
captains John Tumlinson, Adam Zumwalt, and Clarke Owen.
General Huston planned to send men in pursuit of the Indians
the next day, but the horses were too exhausted to resume the
pursuit.

Among those arriving with Colonel Moore was Hamilton P.
Bee. He was mortified to find that his company had arrived "at
the battle ground a few hours after the fight." Bee found the militia general to be very satisfied with his first battle.

> Gen. Felix Huston of course makes it out a second
> Waterloo. I am glad he was in it, being the first fight he
> has been in, although it was the general opinion that if
> Burleson had been in command much more execution
> would have been made.[85]

One of the volunteers from Bastrop, thirty-year-old San
Jacinto veteran John Harvey, fought at Plum Creek. In his later
years, he shared Bee's opinion of the fight this day.

> We had two old Indian fighters along, viz, Ed Burleson
> and Paint Caldwell, and think that if either had command-
> ed, we would have done more execution. But Huston was
> commander of the Texas forces in that battle, and hearing
> of their vast numbers supposed that the Indians would halt
> and give us battle in a regular way and made his arrange-
> ments accordingly.
> But the Indians were too smart for us, and made their
> own arrangements as to fight. They outgeneraled us, but
> we whipped the red man.[86]

With Plum Creek, John Harvey had been in three Indian
fights in his six years in Texas. "I care not to be in another."

Around the campfires on the night of August 12, the Texans talked for hours about the great Comanche battle and the victory they had achieved. Reverend Morrell had escaped the day's battle without injury. He reflected later.

> Men and boys of every variety of character composed that noisy crowd, that was busily engaged all night long talking of the transactions of the previous eventful days. Here were three Baptist preachers—R. E. B. Baylor, T. W. Cox and the writer, all in the fight, with doctors, lawyers, merchants and farmers.[87]

The most bizarre event of the day was the story of one Comanche chief who had been shot in the head. His head had been nearly severed at the base from the shot. Although he certainly died quickly, he gripped his saddle horn tightly and his body locked in that position. The horse raced across the battlefield with its rider still aboard. Several Texans reportedly struck at the corpse with their musket butts, attempting to knock the Indian off.[88]

Hall also claims that the Tonkawas had a cannibalistic nature.

> The Tonkawas brought in the dead body of a Comanche warrior, and they built a big fire not far from where I was lying. My wound had begun to pain me considerably, and I did not pay much attention to them for some time. After awhile, they began to sing and dance, and I thought that I detected the odor of burning flesh.
>
> I raised up and looked around, and, sure enough, our allies were cooking the Comanche warrior. They cut him into slices and broiled him on sticks. Curiously enough, the eating of the flesh acted upon them as liquor does upon other men. After a few mouthfuls, they began to act as if they were very drunk, and I don't think there was much pretense or sham about it. They danced, raved, howled, and sang, and invited me to get up and eat a slice of Comanche. They said it would make me brave. I was very hungry, but not sufficiently so to become a cannibal.[89]

Another Texan, Jim Nichols, later wrote that the friendly Indians "retired with the prisoners about a mile above us and had a big scalp dance that night."[90]

General Huston sent one of his aides, Captain Andrew Neill, to Austin the following morning with his original August 12 battle report. The *Austin Sentinel* reported several days later that Neill "brought in the first express from General Huston" after the Texans had finished chasing the Comanches.[91]

During the morning of August 13, the captured horses and mules were classified, numbered, and drawn by lot by the men who had fought at Plum Creek. For his part, John Henry Brown drew a horse, "a fine mule, $27 worth of silk," and he was given about $50 worth of "other goods fit for ladies' use." Brown chose to sell the mule on a promise to a stranger whose horse had died. An inexperienced youth, Brown would never see a dime for this "sale." He felt compelled to give his booty horse to a poor man to use as a plow horse.[92]

Jim Nichols selected a new saddle tree and "the best" saddle horse "that I ever rode." John Jenkins found that "a Comanche mule fell to my lot, and an odd specimen he was, with red ribbons on ears and tail."[93]

Goods that could be identified were later returned to their rightful owners, but that which could not be identified was divided among the battle victors. Among those arriving late to the battlefield with Colonel Moore were volunteers from the Victoria and Linnville area who had joined Owen, Tumlinson, and Zumwalt's companies. In his early Texas memoirs, John Linn from Linnville wrote that they could not even get their property returned to them.

> To the victors belong the spoils, and the Colorado men appropriated everything to themselves. Ewing recognized many of his goods in the captured property, but identification did him no good. Captain J. O. Wheeler, though 150 of the recaptured horses bore his brand, obtained with the greatest difficulty a horse to ride home.[94]

Hutch Reed, with six arrow wounds, was patched up by Dr. Brown but was unable to ride. Brown had drawn a strip of silk completely through his body where an arrow had passed through him. Reed's companions formed a litter and pulled him back to the settlements. Juliet Watts, suffering from her severe arrow wound, was the only other wounded person unable to ride back.[95]

The Texans retired with about thirty prisoners, mostly women and children, who were guarded by their Tonkawa allies. There was also one little boy found in a thicket about fifteen miles from Plum Creek. One man entered the wooded area, suspicious of a trap by the Indians, and found the boy. Judge Edmund Bellinger took him home and adopted the child. The boy, reportedly the child of the head chief of the Comanches, lived but a few months with Bellinger.[96]

The large-scale raid undertaken by the Comanches to avenge the treachery at San Antonio's Council House had been disastrous to them. The tribe had paid too high a price in dead for the plunder the war party managed to escape with and for so few Texans slain.[97]

General Huston's first battle estimate on August 12 had given the number killed as "upwards of forty." After returning to Austin, however, he would be hounded by others to change his report. By September 28, he was convinced to write another report to Secretary Archer.

> My report was written immediately after the return from the chase, when I was surrounded by all the confusion and bustle incident to a force so hastily collected together, engaged in gathering in several hundred horses and pack-mules.
>
> I am satisfied that our force was estimated too high, and the force of the Indians much too low; and also, that the number of slain was under stated. Our real force was a hundred and eighty-six.[98]

Felix Huston now reported that his men had killed more than forty Comanches. "When the report was [being written], Gen.

Burleson insisted that upwards of sixty were killed, and I ought to have yielded to his greater experience." In the day following the battle, Huston heard from scouts and others searching the area of more bodies found along the pursuit routes. He was later left with "no doubt that eighty were killed."

John Henry Brown estimated that 52 Indians died from their wounds in the days following the battle. This information he claimed came from prisoners reclaimed afterwards. He felt that at least 86 were killed in action or were lost in the mud of the boggy creek, bringing the day's total to 138 ultimately killed.[99]

Bodies were later found as high up country as the San Antonio Road. Still others were likely carried away by fellow Comanches. "A great many others must have died from their wounds, as they do not appear to have rendered each other much assistance, or to have collected in any large bodies after the battle," wrote Huston.

As for the Comanches, the persistent pursuit by the Texans and the resulting decisive engagement were a bitter lesson. They did manage to escape with a large number of stolen horses and cattle, but never again would they carry out such a major offensive raid that deeply into the Texas settlements. Depredations and horse stealing would continue for many years, but future battles with Texas Rangers and militiamen would be of much smaller scale.

CHAPTER 6

Moore's Comanche Village Raid

September–October 24, 1840

General Huston arrived back in Austin on Friday, August 14. Colonel Burleson's Bastrop volunteers returned home several days later, on August 17. Burleson brought in a "magnificent Comanche cap" from the fight, presenting it to his old San Jacinto buddy George W. Bonnell, the editor of the *Texas Sentinel* in Austin.[1]

The Gonzales volunteers also reached home several days after the Plum Creek fight. Henry McCulloch had postponed his own wedding to take part in the pursuit of the raiding Comanches. The battle won, he returned home to take up his vows, marrying Jane Isabella Ashby on August 20, 1840, at the home of his wife's brother-in-law, Bartlett D. McClure.[2]

Felix Huston, correctly perceiving that the Comanches were on the run, proposed to President Lamar that a militia expedition be dispatched into Comanche country immediately to finish the chastisement of the Indians. Lamar rejected this recommendation, likely because of his animosity toward Huston.

This decision was bitterly resented by West Texans, who had long been firm supporters of President Lamar. "The people here are much enraged at the course of Lamar in refusing command and men to Huston," wrote Bastrop citizen William F. Oliver on September 7. "Had he only done so promptly a perfect finish might have been made of the whole party."[3]

The day after returning home, Colonel Burleson wrote to Secretary of War Archer on August 18. For the second time in

129

the same year, Burleson resigned his commission as the senior commander of the First Regiment. He explained that the "late interruption of the Comanches upon our lower settlements, has prevented the march of my resignment."[4]

In conclusion, he explained that "My retirement from active service is the result of actual necessity in my family affairs. But whenever an enemy may appear, my services are at the command of my country."

In honor of Colonel Burleson's long service in leading the Texas Army, his men drew up a letter of praise for him. A large public dinner was held in Bastrop on August 21 to honor him, and another was held in Austin on September 3 to honor both Burleson and General Huston for their Comanche victory at Plum Creek. President Lamar, Vice President David Burnet, Dr. Anson Jones, and other dignitaries were among the attendees.[5]

The retirement of Colonel Burleson on August 18 was only one of many changes to the Frontier Regiment. While Burleson was out fighting the Comanches, his number two man was busy preparing to join General Antonio Canales of the Federalist Army. Lieutenant Colonel William Fisher had organized a force of some 200 men at Tenoxtitlán, on the west bank of the Brazos River. Fisher's men joined with Canales by August 19.[6]

Fisher's conduct in joining the forces fighting for control of the area of Texas between the Nueces and Rio Grande apparently did not sit well with President Lamar. On August 18, Fisher was removed. On the same date, Major Peyton Wyatt also resigned. General Order No. 39 on August 18 covered the resignation of Colonel Burleson and Major Wyatt. It stated that Lt. Col. Fisher had been "dropped from the rolls of the army." It further shows that Surgeon Shields Booker had resigned on July 31 to join General Canales' Federalists.[7]

Therefore, in a single day, the Frontier Regiment had lost its top two commanding officers and the major in charge of all of its cavalry. Their positions were quickly filled, however. Colonel William Gordon Cooke, a San Jacinto veteran and the army's commissary general, was promoted into senior command of the First Regiment. Captain Adam Clendenin, who had recently commanded Company B, was promoted to lieutenant colonel and second-in-command of the army. Captain George Howard was promoted into command of the detachment of troops at San Antonio and he took the rank of major. Captain William D. Houghton, the army's adjutant, was transferred to command of Company G by promotion on August 18. Second Lieutenant Theodore Sevey of Captain Lewis' Company E was promoted into the adjutant's spot.[8]

In replacement of chief surgeon Booker, the government appointed Surgeon Francis A. Whitaker from Company F and assistant surgeon Edmund Wiedeman. Assistant surgeon Charles Aake was later added on September 30, 1840. By August 22, Captain Benjamin Y. Gillen had assumed command of Company A.

The First Regiment companies, their commanders and their locations as of August 31, 1840, were as follows:

Co.	Commander	Location as of 8/31/40
A	Capt. Benjamin Y. Gillen	Camp Cooke
B	Capt. John Kennymore	San Antonio area
C	Capt. Duncan C. Ogden *	San Antonio area
D	Capt. John J. Holliday	Camp Chambers
E	Capt. Mark B. Lewis	Austin area
F	Capt. James B. January	Little River Fort
G	Capt. William D. Houghton	San Antonio area
H	Capt. Mark B. Skerrett	Austin area

* Promoted on August 21, 1840, to replace Major George Howard, who was promoted from Captain of Company C.

Adjutant General Hugh McLeod, who had missed the battle at Plum Creek, arrived in Austin in mid-August. Aside from the changes in the First Regiment, he also made changes to other companies. He ordered the disbanding of the Border Guards under Captain Cocke. In a letter to President Lamar from San Antonio on August 19, McLeod announced, "I was compelled to deprive them of their arms, as they were muskets issued by the government. They are the old arms, very indifferent in construction, and injured by long exposure. I have disarmed the Border Guards accordingly, and they are now out of service," wrote McLeod.[9]

Military papers for most members of the Border Guards show that they were disbanded on August 28 at Camp Cooke (named for Col. William Cooke) after only two months and ten days service of their original six month enlistments. The discharges were signed by Major George Howard and Captain James Cocke. In public debt papers, others would indicate their discharge date as that when they returned to the Houston area. Private C. F. Houston's discharge, for example, was signed by Charles F. Worcester on September 10, 1840.[10]

Captain Nichols' Pitkin Guards were similarly disbanded on August 27, 1840. In a follow-up note from Béxar on August 28, Colonel McLeod expressed his bitterness. "The Pitkin & Border Guards were worthless and complaining—and I have discharged them. They have done and would, *do nothing*."[11]

Erath's Expedition: August–September 1840

Despite President Lamar's refusal to allow him to gear up an expedition against the retreating Comanches, Major General Huston was determined to at least try something. Prior to Plum Creek, he had issued orders to surveyor George Erath on July 14, 1840, to raise a squad of spies to reconnoiter the upper Brazos River region.[12]

Captain Erath wrote that Huston

gave me an order to raise 12 men to proceed up the country and spy out the enemy homes, movements and positions and continue so to do until further orders. I only raised 8, as given on the roll. We furnished ourselves everything necessary for the scout.[13]

Erath left Nashville on August 20 with his eight men and proceeded up the Brazos River along the east side. He arrived at the Falls of the Brazos on August 22 and recrossed the river the following day. He ascended the Texas countryside along the river's western bank. He reached the Waco village on August 24, "where I found some Indian sign two months old."[14]

Erath's spies camped at the old Waco village and on August 25, they advanced up the Bosque River. In the evening, they came within the area of a party of Indians with about twenty horses.

> The Indians, having the advantage to discover us first, fled immediately, setting the grass on fire as they went. The ground being too hard and dry, it was impossible to trail them, and night soon brought them out of our reach.
> The 26th, while advancing up the Bosque, we surprised two foot Indians, apparently Keechies, in the act of skinning a buffalo. We killed one on the ground. The other escaped badly wounded, through the favor of a briar thicket, leaving us both their guns and apparels.

Erath's men continued to scout up the Bosque. The Indians he had encountered and fought managed to get the word out to other hunting parties in the area. Signal smokes could be seen rising from various streams and rivers about the area as Erath progressed. Thus alerted, the other Indian parties in the area abandoned their hunting grounds and set fire to the prairie grass as they fled towards their large village in the upper Texas territory.

On the evening of August 27, Erath's men reached a road with "very plain and fresh" tracks. The road led up country on a ridge between the Brazos and Little rivers. Erath followed this trail until late in the night before making camp. Following the trail

Austrian immigrant George Bernhard Erath (1813–1891) made his first Texas Ranger expedition in 1835. Captain Erath commanded a ranger company in 1839, a spy unit in 1840, and the Milam County Minutemen in 1841. *Texas State Library & Archives Commission, 1/102-149.*

again on August 28, his spies soon came to Comanche Peak near present Granbury.

At this point, Erath decided not to continue following this trail. The grass on either side of the road was dead or burned, leaving nothing for their worn-out horses to forage upon. The path ahead led through mountainous regions to the high country. Erath felt that the well-worn path could at anytime "be shown to an army in search of the savages."

His scouts then took a course down towards the Brazos River and crossed over it on August 28, finding no fresh signs of Indians. They also encountered a number of buffalo that appeared "gentle and little hunted." On August 29, Erath reached the Ioni village where Colonel John Neill had fought Indians a year previous in October 1839.

> On our approach, we discovered some Indians, with pack horses going through the old town, apparently crossing the river. In maneuvering to get a fair sight of them, I got into the bed of the river above them, when several Indians came down the opposite bank to drink, which caused me to suspect a larger camp there than my strength would allow me to attack. I ordered my men back on the eastern hill, but when arriving high enough to survey the opposite side of the river, we discovered, not to little surprise, the Indians in all haste making up the country; and only five in number, and four pack horses, already several miles distant.

Captain Erath decided that pursuit was without purpose. He descended the river and found several other evacuated Indian camps, which had also been hastily abandoned when the alarm signal had been given at the Bosque. His spy company reached the Falls of the Brazos on September 2nd and was in Nashville-on-the-Brazos by September 4.

Of his squad, four men were discharged on September 4. The other four men—Henry Kattenhorn, Dan McKay, Guy Stokes, and Thomas Spooner—remained with him. After making his scouting report, Captain Erath's reduced squad "remained on the Little River at the Three Forks at an old fort known as Little River Fort." Erath had overseen the building of this fort in 1837.[15]

Capt. Erath's Spy Company: July 14–September 20, 1840

Captain:
George Bernhard Erath

Privates:
John Dodd [1]
Henry Kattenhorn [2]
Daniel McKay [3]
Charles Sevier [4]
Thomas I. Smith [4]
Thomas H. Spooner [5]

Guy Stokes [6]
Joseph A. Tivy [1]

[1] Served August 15–Sept. 4, 1840.
[2] Served July 16–Sept. 20, 1840.
[3] Served August 12–Sept. 20, 1840.
[4] Served August 20–Sept. 4, 1840.
[5] Served July 14–Sept. 20, 1840.
[6] Served July 20–Sept. 20, 1840.

Source: George B. Erath PD, R 157, F 638–9.

Along with Erath's scouts were "a few soldiers of the regular army, left by Col. William G. Cooke at our post on his way to Red River." He and his scouts remained at Little River Fort until receiving new orders from General Huston. Huston related that his planned Indian expedition had failed "for the present and we might consider ourselves at liberty" from service. Erath dismissed his remaining scouts from service on September 20.

In his report to Huston, written the following day, Erath signed his title as "Spy Captain." He felt that the Indians had fled under the assumption that his spies were an advance scouting party for a large army force. His men had killed one Indian and seriously wounded another. He felt that a mounted expedition of two hundred Texans or less could sweep through their villages.

He reported that the Indians no longer inhabited the Brazos area where Colonel Neill had fought them in late 1839. He estimated that the new village he had found was "not more than twenty miles from the Comanche Peak." Erath had likely come upon the outer edges of the Indian villages, which by summer of 1840 had moved close to the present Fort Worth area.

The terrain had proven tough on his spies. "The Indians burnt the country everywhere," he wrote, "and the chance for horses is bad, water in some parts scarce, and on the Indian passing grounds no game."

Major General Felix Huston went before the Texas Congress to recommend compensation for Captain Erath's spy company. By November 1840, however, they still had not been paid for their valuable intelligence-gathering expedition.[16]

Armed with Erath's intelligence, General Huston approached President Lamar again, confident that he could not be unaware of the people's sentiments. The Indians continued to conduct sporadic attacks on Texas' outer settlements even after the Plum Creek battle. Bastrop carpenter Michael Nash was killed on Saturday, September 1, while out hunting. He had killed a deer and slung its body over his saddle. En route home, he was fired on and killed by Indians who scalped him, took his horse and venison, and left his badly mutilated body to be found by friends.[17]

Felix Huston now obtained Lamar's blessings to head up a major expedition into Indian territory. He was authorized to enroll a total of 1,600 men by calling for volunteers and by a draft on all the militia brigades. Huston instructed each man to bring half a bushel of "cold flour" for himself, as well as sacks to carry corn for the horses and a hundred rounds of ammunition. The militia brigades were ordered to assemble their men in early November. General Huston toured Texas in the meantime, attempting to rouse the people into favoring his expedition. In the more eastern parts of the country away from the Comanche frontier, Huston was not as warmly received.[18]

James Harper Starr, the former Texas secretary of treasury, wrote of numerous complaints against the planned expedition from Nacogdoches. He wrote to Lamar on October 9, 1840, stating that he doubted the quota for the third brigade could be raised, as there was no appropriation to buy supplies or to pay the men. He wrote that many believed that "Felix Huston will return without having slain twenty Indians." Another Montgomery County citizen reported on October 21 that General Huston had passed through the area the previous day "stirring up people on the subject of his 'expedition'—they are taking it very coolly."[19]

Huston was eventually forced to give up his expedition. His resignation from the task was likely more because he was persuaded that he would not be successful, not because of the expense it would cost his country. He obviously would not be able to raise the full 1,600 men, and Huston apparently objected to leading a smaller expedition.

Major Howard's Expedition to the Nueces

While Huston struggled to raise an expedition, the First Regiment conducted one. The secretary of war had ordered Major George Howard, newly promoted, to lead a party into Comanche country. The September 3, 1840, *Telegraph and Texas Register* noted that Major Howard had been ordered to march from San Antonio with men through the Canyon de Uvalde to the headwaters of the Colorado to "scout the country in that direction."[20]

Secretary of War Archer sent additional orders to Major Howard in San Antonio on September 11. He spread the word for volunteers. The ever-faithful ranger, Captain Paint Caldwell, was the first to raise a small group of men from Gonzales on September 25. No complete muster roll survives for the Gonzales company, although extant documents show that Caldwell's senior officers were twenty-eight-year-old First Lieutenant James Hughes Callahan and Second Lieutenant Christopher B. Acklin. Among the company were at least six who had recently fought at Plum Creek: Caldwell, Acklin, Alonzo Sweitzer, Wilson Randle, Darwin Stapp, and Creed Taylor.[21]

Although some public debt papers later referred to this unit as "Gonzales Volunteers," Captain Caldwell signed the discharges of his men on October 16, 1840, as "Captain, Gonzales Rangers."[22]

Soon after the Gonzales Rangers arrived in San Antonio to join Major Howard, two more small companies were formed from Béxar citizens. The "American" volunteers elected Captain John Cunningham into command. Cunningham, of course, had led another expedition of San Antonio volunteers in July. Captain Salvadore Flores, a Tejano who had served during the Texas Revolution and thereafter as a cavalry leader about the San Antonio area, took command of the fourteen San Antonio area Tejanos who also volunteered.[23]

Volunteers provided their own horses and ammunition, but were supplied with rations. Major Howard had two infantry companies available, Captain Duncan Ogden's Company C and Captain Benjamin Gillen's Company Gillen, promoted into command on August 22, had only recently moved to San Antonio from Camp Cooke. Howard estimated his "whole force effective, 180 men." After counting the regular army men, this would bring the total number of volunteers to just under 70 men.

Major Howard's Expedition: Sept. 29–Nov. 16, 1840

Major Commanding:
George Thomas Howard

Capt. Gillen's Company A, First Regiment of Infantry

Captain:
Benjamin Y. Gillen
First Lieutenant:
Daniel Lewis
Second Lieutenant:
Thomas Johnson
First Sergeant:
William D. Grimsby
Second Sergeant:
John Manson
Third Sergeant:
James Marlow
First Corporal:
James Chaplin
Second Corporal:
Joseph Kenah
Third Corporal:
H. W. Miller
Fourth Corporal:
J. C. Harleson
Musician:
Levi Spalding

Privates:
James Barrett
Michael Bradley
Francis V. Brossard
Timothy Buckley
Arthur Burns
Barney Cannon
Wilbur Cherry
George Chyler
Aaron Crawford
Elisha Dubois
William H. Dwiggins
Allen Eaton
Joseph Farley
Robert Foster

Thomas Gates
James Harrington
Henry Hartman
Frederick Jacob
William Judge
Milton M. Justice
Thomas Kane
Martin Kelly
William Kelly
George H. Kidd
John Layman
James B. Lee
Adolphus Lefebre
Thomas McDonough
Maxwell McGary
Francis McKay
John Ogle
Joseph Ray
Robert Ronaldson
C. A. Root [1]
Michael Sheehey
Frederick Showman
James Sloan
J. S. Smith
Michael Smith
Patrick Smith
Edward Stroll
Patrick Sullivan
William D. Town
Thomas Wreford
Joseph Zoaller

[1]   Deserted from Mission San Jose on October 30, 1840.

Source: Company A muster and payroll data for June 30–December 31, 1840, from DRT, *Defenders of the Republic of Texas*, 59–63.

Capt. Ogden's Company C, First Regiment of Infantry

Captain:
Duncan Campbell Ogden
First Lieutenant:
Michael H. Chevallie
Second Lieutenant:
John C. Howard
First Sergeant:
Washington Stephens
Second Sergeant:
Robert R. Germany
Third Sergeant:
Henry M. Kinsey
Fourth Sergeant:
Samuel K. Nelson
First Corporal:
Chandler L. Wing
Second Corporal:
James Wyatt
Third Corporal:
John McElroy
Fourth Corporal:
Urse Guilleman [1]

Privates:
Charles L. Anderson
John G. Asher
Alexander Bell
James Bird
Abraham Bradley
Benjamin S. Brown
Augustus Cameron
Robert Cameron
Michael Castillo
Abel A. Chapman [2]
Julius Coquet
Peter F. Craft
Michael Dunn
Modesta Duschene [1]
Edward Fitzgerald [3]
Andrew Glenn

Thomas Harding
John Hare
John Harper
Jacob Hoodle
Zephelin Islin
Arthur Itchingham
Augustus Kemper
James Kimberly
William P. Laddy
John Lewis
John Martin
John McDonald
Charles McLaughlin
John McLaughlin
Henry Mundell
Patrick O'Donnell
William H. Ottawall
Basily Pyant
Thomas Roach
Adolphus Rosette
William Scott
William Shelmico
Frederick Shepherd
Alvin Smith
Alonzo Story
Christopher Trouts
George Tuttle
Swen Viemark
John R. Welch
Samuel Young

[1] Deserted from Mission San Jose.
[2] Deserted on unknown date.
[3] Deserted while on detached service to Austin on unknown date.

Source: Company C muster and payroll data for June 30–December 31, 1840, from DRT, *Defenders of the Republic of Texas*, 116–20.

Capt. Caldwell's Gonzales Rangers: Sept. 25–Nov. 16, 1840

Captain:
Mathew Caldwell
First Lieutenant:
James Hughes Callahan
Second Lieutenant:
Christopher B. Acklin
First Sergeant:
W. W. Warren
Second Sergeant:
William Mitchell
Third Sergeant:
George D. Miller

Privates:
Tillman Berry
Green Cunningham
Mark W. Dikes
Bryant Donley
Patrick Donnelly
Daniel Grady
William N. Henry

Nathaniel G. Hudson
J. W. Hunt
William J. Kellett
William H. Killen
William R. Lockhart
Green McCoy
Benjamin McCulloch
John D. Perenfold
Wilson Randle
Jeremiah Roberts
J. R. Smith
Darwin M. Stapp
Philip Stiffey
Alonzo B. Sweitzer
Creed Taylor
Josiah Taylor
Rufus Taylor
Nathan Trotter
William Tumlinson
Calvin S. Turner
Francis Williams

Capt. Cunningham's Béxar Volunteers: Oct. 1–Nov. 11, 1840

Captain:
John R. Cunningham

Privates:
Thomas H. Addicks
Horatio Alex Alsbury
George Blow
James H. Brown
Damon Coats
Archibald Fitzgerald
James W. Gray
John Hancock
Thomas Hancock

Nathaniel Harbert
John Hemphill
John James
James Matthew Jett
George Lillie
Samuel H. Luckie
John McClanahan
John Dabney Morris
Franklin L. Paschal
James L. Trueheart
Cornelius Van Ness
Dr. Edmund Weideman

Capt. Flores' Béxar Volunteers: Oct. 1–Nov. 11, 1840

Captain:
Salvadore Flores

Privates:
Antonio Benites
Antonio Coy
Martin Delgado
José Maria Espinosa
Damacio Galvan

Leandro Garza
Antonio Hernandez
Jesus Hernandez
Manuel Hernandez
Antonio Lockmar
Francisco Longavilla
Manuel Montalvo
Jil Salas

Key sources: George T. Howard UN, R 252, F 313–4; Mathew Caldwell PD, R 142, F 111–2, and other republic claims public debt files. See also Sowell, *Texas Indian Fighters*, 808–9.

Howard's expedition moved out from San Antonio about the first of October and would spend the next six weeks on vigilant patrol. His party would move north and west of Béxar, touching the headwaters of the Nueces, Frio, Pedernales, Llano, and San Saba rivers.[24]

Major Howard had information from his spies that indicated that recent depredations committed around San Antonio had been carried out by parties of Indians to the west of San Antonio. Following his spies, he moved his expedition from Béxar in a northwestern course for the first two weeks.

"Upon reaching the head waters of the Nueces, the spies reported fresh sign," wrote Howard, "and it was evident we were in the vicinity of a considerable encampment of Indians."

They moved past to the Pisanne, a tributary of the Nueces, and on to the Las Nuras, a tributary of the Rio Grande, before turning back again. Finally, on Turkey Creek, beyond the Uvalde, they found fresh signs of a band of Comanches.[25]

On the afternoon of October 12, Howard decided to lighten the load being carried by his command. They would dump their heavy supplies and make a forced march through the night on the Indian trail, hoping to reach the Indian camp before daylight the following morning. He left a detail with some of the baggage that afternoon and marched quickly until midnight, when the guides lost the trail. Howard wrote:

> The men were halted, ready to move on at any moment. The guides, however, could not discover the trail during the night. At daybreak [of October 13], it was found on our right, and I despatched Capt. Caldwell, Mr. McCulloch, and a Mexican to examine it. They soon returned and reported to have seen Indians, and that we were discovered.[26]

Howard immediately ordered his men to mount up and they rode in rapid pursuit of the fleeing Indians. They covered the ten miles to the area of the Comanche camp, which was located at the head of the Las Moras Springs. The Comanches were obviously alert, and had fled on their best horses.

As the soldiers and frontiersmen raced through the large Comanche village, they found few inhabitants. The town con-

sisted of three main divisions or encampments. Those on the
faster horses were able to kill three Comanches. During the early
part of the chase, the Texans overtook one Indian woman and a
captive Mexican child of about twelve years of age.

During the chase, Irishman volunteer Pat Donnelly captured
the young Indian woman and managed to tie her up, despite her
violent thrashing. After wrestling mightily with the fighting
woman, he snapped, "I'll carry you home for our housekeeper!"[27]

Donnelly then continued in the pursuit of fleeing Comanches.
Upon his return to the Indian camp, he was upset to find that
someone had killed the bound woman. Thus deprived of his
future "housekeeper," Donnelly soon became the source of many
jokes from his comrades.

According to George Howard, his command "continued the
chase for about five miles, in which four Indians were overtaken
and killed." He considered further pursuit "useless," as the horses
of his men were "almost completely tired down."

The Texans returned to the large Comanche village on Las
Moras Springs in the late afternoon of October 13. Finding it
to be a large town "of well constructed tents, with a good supply of provisions," Howard ordered the Indian provisions and
winter quarters destroyed. Among the wigwams, the men found
immense quantities of food, horses, mules, and even a kind of
fruit cake to eat.[28]

Major Howard moved out from the Comanche camp on
October 14, taking several Indian rifles and "about 125 mules
and horses" from their village. He did not allow his men to over-
burden their horses with loot. One party of men did, however,
load a pack mule high with buffalo robes. On top, they fastened
a large brass kettle. The mule suddenly stampeded off, the brass
kettle banging loudly as it ran. The noise frightened the horses
and many stampeded off. "The race which followed formed a
queer and comical scene," as the kettle-banging mule sent horses
fleeing in all directions.[29]

His command proceeded on a march along the edge of the
foot hills to the head of the Frio River. They moved on to the head
of the Guadalupe River, scouring the countryside along the way.
"From the Guadalupe, I proceeded to the head of the Llano, and
despatched a party to the San Saba, under Capt. Cunningham,"
wrote Howard.[30]

While Cunningham's scouts were out, Major Howard's main party marched "some 30 miles" down that river to the Pedernales River. On November 5, a detachment of soldiers under First Lieutenant Mike Chevallie of Company C encountered a party of twenty Indians. Chevallie immediately gave pursuit, and an extended chase was made through western Texas. He was unable to overtake them, but the Indians were forced to dump some of their baggage to escape. Several of their horses were left dead from wounds and physical exhaustion during the chase.

While on the march, and while awaiting the return of scouts, Howard demanded that his troops maintain silence, to enhance the chance of surprising any more Indians that might be encountered. No guns were to be fired unless against an enemy. The sight of deer present within gunshot range ultimately proved too tempting for some of the volunteers.

Nine men, including Creed Taylor, Dan Grady, and William H. Killen, slipped away from their forces to attempt to bring down tastier game. They killed deer and made camp, roasting their supper. During the night, a party of Indians attacked their camp. The Indians attempted to stampede the Texans' horses, and drove off three. The Texan volunteers fought bravely against superior numbers and Taylor claimed to have killed one Indian.[31]

John Cunningham's scout detachment returned from the San Saba on November 6. They had found no fresh Indian signs in that section of the country. The signs that Major Howard could find indicated that a large body of Comanches had been in the area in the past month. "The old trails all lead to the west."

Howard knew that Colonel John Henry Moore was also out in the area with an expedition. Near the San Saba, he found the trail of Moore's American horses. With hopes that his fellow Texan would have a more successful campaign, Major Howard opted to end his own on November 7, "being destitute of provisions."[32]

He headed from the Pedernales directly to San Antonio, his men arriving November 11. Captain Cunningham's "Béxar Volunteers" were discharged on November 11, 1840, following forty-two days of service. Paint Caldwell's Gonzales Rangers did not reach their hometown until November 16, on which date he disbanded his company.[33]

Major Howard would continue to operate from the San Antonio area during the fall of 1840. Sometime after returning

from this expedition, he led another small force out in December
to pursue Indian raiders. A party of Comanches made an appearance near San Antonio and killed two Mexican citizens.[34]

Howard immediately rounded up a pursuit party of about ten
to fifteen men. Among his men was Captain Salvadore Flores,
who had commanded men on his previous expedition. Howard's
party pursued the Comanches and came upon them at their campground.

"The Indians were cooking, and not expect[ing] an attack,"
wrote Howard. He immediately ordered an attack and his men
charged into their camp. Flores and Major Howard had the ablest
horses, and found themselves far ahead of their comrades as
they raced into their camp with weapons drawn. The Comanches
were

> disconcerted at finding themselves thus suddenly charged
> upon, but perceiving the assailants to be only two in num-
> ber, they immediately wheeled and fired upon them.
>
> Captain Howard's horse was wounded; he himself was
> severely wounded by an arrow in the abdomen. He had
> thus been thrown among the enemy from his horse. While
> thus wounded, his antagonist attempted to take the horse
> from him. A scuffle ensued in which the Capt. however
> was victorious. He had a revolving pistol. One cap busted.
> He tried another barrel, and his foe fell dead.

Major Howard was thus saved by his new cavalry-issue Colt
revolving pistol. Remounting his horse, he joined the other members of his volunteer party in pursuing the fleeing Comanches.
"Disgorging much blood" from his arrow wound, Howard was at
last forced to halt the chase.

Salvadore Flores closed the gap rapidly on his fleet horse. One
of the volunteers managed to shoot and kill a horse being ridden
by a fleeing Comanche woman. Several of the Comanches, however, quickly turned and fired upon Flores. "Flores' horse was
shot dead, and in falling, fell upon the rider."

While pinned under his dead horse, Flores suddenly found
himself under attack by the Comanche woman who had also been
thrown from her horse. "She seized Flores' empty gun and was
laying it heavily over the prostrate warrior's head." Knowing the

gun was empty, Flores managed to shoot two other Comanches who had approached with their weapons to help finish off the fallen Tejano.

Seeing the Indian woman holding the pistol at Flores, another Texan fired and killed her. "It was unavoidable," wrote Howard.

His party, being small in number, and suffering two wounded men, gave up the pursuit. They had killed at least three Comanches and succeeded in sending the survivors to flight from the San Antonio area.

John Moore's Comanche Raid: October 24, 1840

Major Howard had noted the tracks of another Texian expedition force during early November, that of Colonel John Henry Moore. Moore had led one of the first ranger expeditions back in 1835 and another in February 1839, during which his men lost all of their horses to the Comanches. Moore's new group had left for the country north of Austin just a few days after Howard's army and volunteer force had left San Antonio.

Moore's expedition had its origin in a public meeting held in La Grange just five days after the Plum Creek engagement of August. The citizens of Fayette County had passed resolutions calling for a 300-man expedition to go into Indian country for 90 days to follow up on the preceding week's battle.[35]

The dates for the expedition would change periodically, but the townspeople of La Grange originally hoped to have more than 300 people ready to leave by September 10. These Fayette County citizens planned to serve for three months and had sent their petition to President Lamar for approval.[36]

Lamar, at the same time that he was denying Felix Huston permission to lead a militia campaign, quickly authorized veteran Indian fighter John Moore to undertake the proposed expedition, which was to operate under Texas War Department orders.[37]

Moore sent out circulars calling for volunteers who would go to the upper waters of the Colorado River to attack the Comanches. One such circular, written by Colonel Moore on August 28, advised all volunteers that the date of rendezvous at La Grange had moved from September 10 to September 20, due to orders from President Lamar.[38]

The town of Gonzales had also put out the call for volunteers. Leading men Andrew Neill and Ben McCulloch worked on organizing recruits. In a letter they wrote on September 9, they encouraged residents of Victoria and Texana to also organize themselves to join the expedition. Gonzales citizens were hoped to "turn out *en masse* against the Indians."[39]

September 19 had been the date fixed where a rendezvous would occur in Gonzales in order for men to join the expedition into the rugged, hilly terrain of Texas. The Gonzales volunteers would then join Colonel Moore's volunteers on the Guadalupe. Time was of the essence, Neill and McCulloch stated. "The first who go will surely get a fight."

Moore called for volunteers to rendezvous at La Grange on September 20 and began making arrangements for the expedition. Beef cattle were purchased to feed the men. Chief Castro of the Lipans was invited to come along with a number of his warriors. The people's interest in punishing the Comanches, even on the edge of the western frontier, did not include volunteering for such expeditions. Due to low turnout, Moore was forced to announce in mid-September that he was calling off the expedition. Near the end of the month, he reconsidered and decided to proceed with a hundred volunteers—one third of what was originally planned—and perhaps a dozen of Castro's Lipans.[40]

Moore's volunteers gathered at Walnut Creek near Austin during the first days of October 1841. Smallwood S. B. Fields, a La Grange lawyer who had fought with Moore in his 1839 Comanche expedition, was selected to serve as adjutant. Dr. Henry Weidner Baylor supplied his own medical gear and joined as the expedition's surgeon. There were ninety men in all from Fayette and Bastrop counties, commanded by captains Thomas J. Rabb and Nicholas Mosby Dawson.[41]

Captain Dawson, a battle of San Jacinto veteran, was thirty-two years old. He was in Deaf Smith's 1837 Laredo fight and had thereafter taken command of Smith's cavalry unit. Captain Rabb, thirty-nine, was equally experienced in frontier wars. One of Austin's Old Three Hundred Settlers, Rabb had served as first lieutenant in one of Stephen F. Austin's 1824 militia battalions and had commanded a company during the Texas Revolution.

Thomas Rabb had been a volunteer in both John Henry Moore's 1835 and 1839 Indian expeditions. First Lieutenant

Clark L. Owen of Texana had just recently commanded one of the volunteer companies which narrowly missed the battle at Plum Creek. Most of Moore's men were from the Fayette and Bastrop Colorado River communities, although Owen had brought a number of his men from the Lavaca and Texana areas, including: Isaac N. Mitchell, Mason B. Foley, Joseph Simons, Nicolas J. Ryan, Peter Rockefeller, and John Henry Brown. Brown started with these men, his neighbors, "but was compelled to halt, on account of my horse being crippled at the head of the Navidad."[42]

Captains Rabb and Dawson's volunteer companies are generally accepted by Texas Ranger historians as having served as ad hoc ranging units. These men elected their own leaders and were not called up by the regional militia generals.[43]

Historian John Henry Brown wrote in 1883 that ninety Anglos accompanied Colonel Moore on this expedition. This author's best attempt to re-create Rabb's and Dawson's muster rolls indicate that this number is exactly right. Colonel Moore also had with him a detachment of Lipan braves under Colonel Castro, their principal chief, with young Flacco as his lieutenant. Moore wrote that Castro's men were "seventeen in number, who acted as spies during the campaign." This would put the total expedition size at 107 men.[44]

Moore's volunteers left Walnut Creek near Austin on Monday, October 5, and set a course through the hilly countryside up the Colorado River. Once they had passed the Llano River and the headwaters of the San Gabriel River, they moved north toward the San Saba River. They rediscovered an old Spanish presidio on the San Saba and Moore carved his name in one of the door frames. Chief Castro kept his Lipan scouts continually on alert to either side of the main force, looking for Indian signs.[45]

As the men moved toward the Concho River, they encountered a bitter Texas norther complete with icy winds and bitterly cold rain. Some soon became sick. Moore's expedition was at Camp Rabb on October 16. Camp Rabb was located along the Concho River, somewhere in present Concho County or possibly a little west in present Tom Green County.[46]

Garrett Harrell of Fayette County died in camp this day. Harrell, a young son of early Austin-area settler Jacob Harrell, had developed a sore throat which led to a fatal choking spell. Colonel Moore read the burial service for Harrell in camp.[47]

Colonel Moore's Comanche Expedition
September 20–November 7, 1840

Colonel Commanding:
John Henry Moore
Adjutant:
Smallwood S. B. Fields

Surgeon:
Dr. Henry Weidner Baylor

Lipan Apache Scout Company

Captain:
Chief Castro
Lieutenant:
Flacco
Fifteen other unnamed Lipan

Apaches accompanied Colonel Moore's expedition.

Captain Dawson's Colorado County Company

Captain:
Nicholas Mosby Dawson
First Lieutenant:
Robert Addison Gillespie
Second Lieutenant:
William G. Hunt

Privates:
Darwin S. Alexander
John Robert Baylor
Andrew J. Blackburn
Julian C. Calhoun
Burton M. Daughtery
John H. Day
John Dodd
Henry Earthman
Nicholas W. Eastland
Gustav Elly *
A. A. Gardiner
Matthew M. Gillespie
George Habermill
Gerard Hayden
James M. Hill

Erwin Holcomb
Thomas D. James *
David S. Kornegay
Joseph Lawrence *
William Long *
James P. Longly
John F. McGuffin *
William Mitchell
A. L. D. Moore
Lewis M. Nail
William A. Nail
Gouvenor H. Nelson
Thomas M. Penick
Charles Shuff
James A. J. Smith
John O. Snelling
William Spencer
Jasper Newton M. Thompson
Frederick Vogle

* Service per Donaly Brice of the Texas State Archives. Company of service not confirmed.

Captain Rabb's Fayette County Company

Captain:
Thomas J. Rabb
First Lieutenant:
Clark L. Owen
Second Lieutenant:
William M. Robinson
Orderly Sergeant:
Reddin Andrews

Privates:
Micah Andrews
Benjamin W. Breeding
John Breeding
John Henry Brown [1]
Lionel Browne
Jesse Burnam [2]
John H. Burnham
Arter Crownover
Elijah V. Dale [2]
John W. Dancy
Socrates Darling
Lewis W. Dickerson
Jacob Elliott
William N. Evans
Nathaniel W. Faison
Mason B. Foley
Garrett Harrell [3]
Leander Harrell
William Jones Elliott Heard [2]

John T. Holman
David Hudson
James P. Hudson
Griffith H. Jones
Myers F. Jones
Richard H. Keene
Thomas S. Lubbock
DeWitt C. Lyons
Pleasant McAnelly
Thomas Sutherland Menefee
Elijah G. Mercer
Isaac N. Mitchell
Pendleton Rector [2]
Peter Rockefeller
Nicholas James Ryan
Newton Scallorn
Josiah Shaw
Peter V. Shaw
Joseph Simons
John A. Wells [2]
Charles Williams
Henry Gonzalvo Woods
Charles Wright [2]

[1] Did not finish campaign.
[2] Service per Donaly Brice of the Texas State Archives. Company of service not confirmed.
[3] Died in camp October 16, 1840.

The Moore expedition followed the valley of the Colorado River without encountering Indians. It became very apparent to the men that they were in "Indian territory." Along the river, they found curious Indian pictographs painted on the rocks.[48]

On the morning of October 23, Castro and Flacco's Lipan scouts found signs along the trail where the Comanches had been cutting pecan trees for fruit. Moore then sent two of his best

Colonel John Henry Moore (1800–1880) of La Grange led his third, and most deadly, ranger expedition against the Comanches in October 1840. *Prints and Photographs Collection, The Center for American History, University of Texas at Austin, CN Number 03821.*

Clark L. Owen (1808–1862), a former 1837 Texas Army captain, was placed in command of fifteen cavalrymen during Moore's Colorado River Comanche village raid. *Prints and Photographs Division, The Center for American History, The University of Texas at Austin.*

Lipan scouts out that day while his men tried to stay warm. They took shelter underneath a hill, trying to duck the howling bitter north wind.[49]

The scouts departed at 10:30 a.m. and remained gone all day. As evening approached, Chief Castro grew very concerned over the safety of his scouts. He climbed a high nearby hill to stand as a lookout for his men. He soon informed the Texans that they were returning at a distance of about two or three miles. Castro read their shield signal and relayed that their mission had been successful in finding the Comanches.[50]

The Lipans reported a large Comanche encampment about fifteen or twenty miles distant, leading up the Red Fork of the Colorado. It was located on the east bank and in a small horseshoe bend of the Colorado, near present Colorado City. The site was over 250 miles northwest of Austin in a straight line. This bend had a high and somewhat steep bluff on the opposite side of the river.[51]

The Lipans' news was enough to warm the spirits of the cold frontiersmen. After eating supper, Moore's men packed up camp and prepared to attack the Indian camp. They rode about ten miles to the Colorado River and then another four miles upriver.

Here, Moore ordered his men to secure their commissary of beef cattle on a mesquite flat near the river for safekeeping. They continued their ride up the Colorado another four miles until reaching a hollow near the river at midnight.[52]

The Texans dismounted and Moore sent two Lipan spies ahead to the Comanche camp to scout it out. It was clear and cold and the ground was white with frost at this location deep into western Texas. The Indians were better prepared for such weather. They wore heavy buffalo robes and slept in their warm tepees. In contrast, the Texans wore only what they had brought along two weeks prior and most were shivering from the cold. No fires were allowed this night to warm the men and their wet clothing.[53]

The Lipans returned about 3:00 a.m. on October 24, with the news that the Indian encampment was located on the south bank of the river. The spies estimated by counting tents that there were approximately 60 families and 125 warriors. Colonel Moore had his men silently advance closer to the Comanche village. He had their pack mules secured in a hollow, located within two miles of the camp. The experience of his 1839 Comanche village attack—after which his men had been forced to walk after all of their mounts were stolen—had taught Moore never to leave his horses unprotected again.

Whispering words of encouragement to his men, John Henry Moore led on his steed. He moved silently and with determination during the pre-dawn hours of October 24 toward the large village. In his report, Moore relates the final approach just after daybreak.

> I soon ascended the hill, and ordered Lieut. Clark L. Owen to take command of fifteen men taken from the companies, to act as cavalry, to cut off any retreat of the enemy. I ordered Capt. Thomas J. Rabb, with his command, up the right, Lieut. Owen in the center, and Capt. Nicholas M. Dawson, with his command, upon the left.
>
> Just before reaching the village I had to descend the hill, which brought us within two hundred paces of the enemy. I then ordered Lieut. Owen with his command to the right of Capt. Rabb's command.[54]

Within two hundred yards of camp, John Henry Moore's men were detected. A Comanche watchman caught the sound of their horse hoofs approaching and let loose a shrill yell of alarm.

"Charge!" Moore shouted, and his Texans and Lipans rushed forward, directly into the Comanche camp.

Even as quickly as his men raced into camp, many of the Comanche men and even their women had strung their bows and were ready to fight. The Texans raced through their camp, firing rifles, shotguns, and pistols. The surprised Comanches shot back, but largely without effect due to the excitement of the moment. "A general, effective fire was opened upon the enemy," wrote Moore, "who soon commenced falling upon the right and left."[55]

During the charge, Isaac Mitchell's bridle bit parted and his mule rushed wildly headlong into the midst of the Indians. It then halted and sulked, refusing to move. An angry Comanche woman with a log of firewood smashed Mitchell in the head, knocking him from his mule to the ground.[56]

Dazed, Mitchell sprang to his feet, and saw the Indian woman rushing at him with a knife. "Kill her, Mitchell!" his buddies shouted.

"On no, boys, I can't kill a woman!" he protested.

Mitchell was forced to knock her down and snatch the knife from her hands to save himself.

After charging most of the way through the Comanche village, many of the Texans abandoned their horses and continued to fire upon the Indians from the ground.

Seeing their fate, a large number of the Comanche fled for the river, which was in the shape of a half moon, encircling the entire village. They leaped into the Colorado and swam to the other shore. Those first across fled across the prairies.

Lieutenant Owen, leading the fifteen cavalrymen, crossed over the river and began cutting off the retreat of the fleeing Indians. "In this, the gallant lieutenant succeeded admirably," wrote Colonel Moore.[57]

The Comanches began climbing the cliff on the far bank, only to have Owen's men appear and open fire on them. Some were shot and tumbled backward into the river. For the Texan riflemen, it was a shooting contest. Each shot was deliberate and the crack of the rifle almost flawlessly sent another crawling Indian back into the river.[58]

Commanding two ad hoc ranging companies and a small unit of friendly Lipan scouts, Colonel John Henry Moore led a bloody assault on a large Comanche village on October 24, 1840. This early illustration was originally printed in DeShields' *Border Wars of Texas*.

The shooting along the riverbanks lasted about thirty minutes according to John Henry Moore's post-action report.

> The river and its banks now presented every evidence of a total defeat of our savage foes. The bodies of men, women, and children were to be seen on every hand, wounded, dying, and dead. Having found that the work of death and destruction had been fully consummated here, I accordingly ordered my troops to cross the river, and a portion to act in concert with Lieut. Owen.
>
> With the residue, I ordered a general charge in pursuit of the Indians who were attempting to effect their escape. My men were soon seen flying in every direction through the prairie, and their valor told that the enemy was entirely defeated. The pursuit ceased at the distance of four miles from the point of attack, and finding that the enemy was entirely overthrown, I ordered my men to the encampment.[59]

At the onset of the camp raid, two horses were tied up in the camp. On these animals, two Comanches escaped. Except for these two, Moore's men believed that they had killed every

Comanche warrior with the exception of a few old men and one or two younger men, who surrendered and were thus spared.

Some of the Indian women had fought just as bravely as their men. Some of them had been killed, despite the efforts of some Texans to prevent such killing.

One of the captives was an Indian boy of about fourteen years. Nicholas Eastland and Charles Shuff of Captain Dawson's company happened upon him. Instead of fleeing, the boy grabbed a mesquite branch and swung it to keep the Texans at a safe distance. Eastland stopped another man from shooting the Indian boy, sparing him for his bravery.[60]

Thirty-four Comanches, mainly women and children, were captured in small parties and brought into the Texan camp. Moore's men also took roughly five hundred horses and any camp goods the men felt compelled to haul off.[61]

Micah Andrews, a former ranger captain, had used a new Colt Paterson five-shot repeating rifle in Moore's Comanche fight. He reported that he was able to fire the Colt ten times while his companions were able to fire their rifles only twice.[62]

The attack lasted little more than a half hour. Colonel Moore inspected the battle ground during the daylight. "From the best information, there were 48 killed upon the ground and 80 killed and drowned in the river." He considered this number to be conservative compared to the number he believed he had actually killed. One early historian who interviewed some of the participants estimated that 130 Indians were left dead on the field. A more modern evaluation of this Comanche village attack states that about 140 Indians were killed and perhaps as many more perished while attempting to swim the cold Colorado River under rifle fire.[63]

Moore wrote that he left three Indians behind, possibly because they were too old or feeble to travel. Among the thirty-four captives taken were two "sprightly Mexican youths, between the ages of fourteen and sixteen." These youths had been made captives of the Comanches in the vicinity of Camargo on the Rio Grande about three months prior.[64]

Among the spoils taken by the Texans were goods that were recognized as those stolen by the Indians during the Victoria and Linnville raids of August. John Henry Moore's men thus had no doubts that the Comanches they had killed had been involved in the coastal raids that had killed numerous Texans months before.[65]

Only two Texans were slightly wounded in the attack, Myers F. Jones of Captain Rabb's Fayette County company and Burton Daughtery of Captain Dawson's Colorado County company. Moore also reported that two horses were wounded in the fight.

By 10 a.m., Moore's pursuit forces had all returned to the Colorado River village. He then ordered the remnants of the village to be burned. All of the Indians' property, including more animal skins than could be carried off, were fed to the flames. Some of the more desperately wounded Comanches were left with one wigwam, in which they were left in the care of a few Indian women, while the other prisoners were taken on.[66]

The journey home was only as quick as the men could drive the 500-horse *caballado* taken from the Comanches. The Texans moved back down the Colorado to the spot where Colonel Moore had ordered their beef cattle to be secured the previous night.

> I then ordered the troops to march, assigning a sufficient guard to herd and drive the immense caballado of horses which had been captured from the enemy, in number about five hundred, and then turned my course for this place [Austin], marching by the position where I had left my beef cattle.
>
> After herding my cattle, I marched about six miles and encamped for the night. The weather on my return was unfavorable—had to lie in camp two days on account of the north winds and rain.[67]

Moore estimated the distance to be about 300 miles from the town of Austin to the Colorado River battleground. Once the foul weather had passed late on August 26, his men resumed their trek back toward Austin. During the latter days of October, he passed near the old Mission San Saba. There his troops met with a fifteen-man tribe of Seratic Indians. Lipan Chief Castro held a consultation with them and found their interests to be much the same.

"I concluded to bring in two of their captains," wrote Moore, "as they appeared friendly and desirous to treat with us, and to aid in our wars with the Comanches, with whom they are also hostile." He found these Seratics to be representatives of their 800-person tribe, which lived in the vicinity of the Rio Grande, between Santa Fe and Chihuahua.[68]

During the return home, the Texans were followed by some of the Indian survivors, possibly joined by other Comanches. On the Pedernales River, the Indians slipped past the guards and stole four animals, including Colonel Moore's mule. At the time of this stampede, "on a very dark night," Moore wrote that seven of his thirty-four prisoners also managed to escape.

Noah Smithwick properly likened Moore's retaliatory raid to that of the Comanches upon Victoria and Linnville in August. The after effects of Moore's raid were quite different this time. The Comanches did not become roused to commit further violence on the Texans. Apparently this raid and the losses they had taken at Plum Creek were enough to convince the senior Comanche chiefs to leave the Texan settlements alone as much as possible. During the remaining years of the Republic of Texas, the Comanche raids were largely against Mexican settlers.[69]

Colonel Moore's men arrived in Austin on November 7 with twenty-four Comanche prisoners, several hundred horses, and other plunder. In his report, published in the November 11 *Austin City Gazette*, he wrote that "My men have returned in good health and fine spirits, though much fatigued."

Moore and Captain Rabb discharged Rabb's men in Austin on November 7, 1840, allowing them an additional twelve days' pay to return home.[70]

The *Gazette* also carried a note showing that a number of the leading citizens invited Colonel Moore's men to attend a barbecue given in their honor on Monday, November 16. Moore sent back a thank-you note, stating that his men appreciated the invitation. Most, however, had been away from their families a long time and were more anxious to return home than to stay in town for another week.

According to one early source, some of Moore's men did stick around town long enough for the celebration. Those attending the party secured their horses in a field surrounded by a ditch below Waller's Creek. The Texans posted a guard near the gate of the field. During the party, a number of Indians crept around to the back side of the field. They filled a section of the ditch so that the horses could cross the water and managed to steal thirty or forty of the Texan horses. Some of the men of Moore's recent expedition were forced to walk home the day following the big party.[71]

Some of the Comanche women and children prisoners were taken into individual homes in Austin to work as domestic servants. The young Comanche boy who had threatened approaching Texans with a stick was taken into the home of the French minister to the Republic of Texas, Monsieur Alphonse de Saligny. The boy remained under Saligny's care for some time, until he escaped on one of the French minister's best horses.

The other young Indian boy taken on the Colorado River was taken home by Nicholas Eastland, who nicknamed the youth "Sam Houston." He remained with Eastland for several years, becoming very attached to the family. Later returned to his tribe in an exchange of prisoners, "Sam Houston" was still living many years later. He was recognized by Colonel John Robert Baylor, a government agent among the Comanches who had first encountered the Indian while a member of Moore's 1840 Comanche expedition.

John Henry Moore and his men were not paid for their Comanche expedition. In January 1842, he was still trying to get a bill past the Texas Congress, but President Houston returned the bill unsigned. He felt that Moore's men had been well compensated by their captured animals. The five hundred horses they collected were easily valued at $15,000, or about $140 per man on the expedition.[72]

Moore's Indian village attack and the battle of Plum Creek brought back-to-back defeats for the Comanches. These two engagements offered revenge to the Texans for the deadly raids against Victoria and Linnville. For the Comanches, Plum Creek and Moore's attack may represent the most severe punishment ever inflicted upon the Comanches in Texas.

Future Texas Rangers tactics were shaped during these two decisive battles. The Texan frontier leaders had learned once again that vigorous spirit and a determined charge went a long way in breaking an opponent's fighting resolve. The use of mounted cavalry forces, in conjunction with dismounted fighters, and the new repeating firearms had also offered positive results that could not be ignored by future leaders of the Texas frontier wars.[73]

CHAPTER 7

The Great
Military Road

October 25–December 31, 1840

On the night following John Henry Moore's assault on the Colorado River Comanche camp, the settlement of Franklin in Robertson County endured its first ever Indian depredation. Although Indians had passed through this community, the November 7, 1840, edition of the *Austin Sentinel* noted this to be Franklin's first serious encounter with native Americans.

On the night of October 25, 1840, a party of five or six Indians—who were believed to be Kichais or Caddos—came into Franklin and stole six horses. A small party of citizens immediately took up the pursuit. Six to seven miles from town, the Indians were overtaken.[1]

During the chase, two Indians fell from their horses and were overtaken. One of them was immediately shot down by Andrew C. Love. The other was charged upon by J. L. Hill, but his gun failed to fire, and he was severely wounded by the Indian. Two other settlers fired at the Indian, but missed him. Love next charged and killed the Indian with his Bowie knife. The settlers then resumed pursuit of the others and killed two more before they had fled the area of the settlements.

Ranger Units of Fall 1840

Andrew Neill, a former lawyer who had teamed with Ben McCulloch in September 1840 to call for volunteers to campaign

---

Capt. Askins' Mounted Gunmen: October 1–November 20, 1840

Captain:	Benton B. Davis
Wesley Askins	Harvey B. Davis
First Lieutenant:	Isaac Gillaspie
Zachariah B. Miller	James Hardin
Orderly Sergeant:	James Leach
J. J. Norvell	V. Leach
Second Sergeant:	Leven V. Moore
Sherrod Roland	B. G. Norvell
Third Sergeant:	David K. Pace
Warren Williams	William B. Pallon
Fourth Sergeant:	Z. M. Paul
Augustus J. Butts	Sydney Smith
	William Smith
Privates:	George W. Still Sr.
Charles S. Askins	George W. Still Jr.
Thomas Askins	James Ward
Henry Bingham	Stephen T. Wethers
Joseph Brannon	Sterling E. Williams
James S. Bridger	George L. Wynn
William Campbell	
Davis Case	Source: Texas State Archives.
Lewis Crook	

---

against the frontier Indians, continued his recruiting efforts into October. Alexander Somervell, a land office inspector and former army officer, wrote to Captain Neill on October 21, regarding a proposed grand expedition against the Indians in November. Somervell had been informed that Neill intended to raise a company. He requested that Neill muster and organize it and report with the command by November 10, at Fort Dunnington (ex-Fort Kenney), on Brushy Creek, the rendezvous designated by Major General Felix Huston.

There is little evidence on what Captain Neill's company might have done, if it was indeed properly formed. There is more extensive evidence that the Fourth Militia Brigade under General Edward Tarrant maintained at least two ranging units in the field during late 1840.

Captain Wesley Askins commanded one short-lived ranger company which he mustered into service on October 1 by orders of Tarrant. Sherrod Roland served as second sergeant in "my

Capt. Wilson's Rangers: October 24, 1840–January 25, 1841

Captain:	William H. Kimball
Jason Wilson	William Kizer
First Lieutenant:	A. W. McDonald
John M. Watson	Henry G. McDonald
Second Lieutenant:	John Nidiver
Thomas J. Birdwell	John Onstot
Orderly Sergeant:	Elijah Piland
L. L. Owens	Jesse Piland
	E. W. Pollett
Privates:	John Robertson
George Birdwell	John Simmons
William B. Birdwell	Benjamin Tyler
Zachariah Birdwell	J. D. Webb
Merritt Brannon	
Samuel Burke	Source: Author's search of audited military claims and public debt papers, Texas State Archives.
John Dawdle	
William Finley	
Martin Harvick	

company of mounted riflemen," wrote Captain Askins. Sergeant Roland served from October 1–November 20, 1840, and was discharged in Red River County.[2]

From his headquarters in Clarksville, General Tarrant appointed Captain John R. Craddock as Quartermaster, Fourth Brigade, Texas Militia, on October 10, 1840. Craddock was to provide for Askins' gunmen and a second ranger company which was beginning to organize. Captain Askins' men took on eight pounds of powder, five bushels of corn, and 450 pounds of beef from Craddock between October 13 and 15, as they prepared for scouting expeditions.[3]

Captain Jason Wilson's company was mustered into service for a three-month period, beginning on October 24. His audited papers show him to have been paid as a "Captain of a volunteer ranging company for the counties of Red River and Fannin." William B. Stout later wrote that "one Indian in a stealing party was killed on the Sulphur [River] in December by Jason Wilson." In the discharge papers for his men, Captain Wilson gave the tenure of his "mounted ranging company from the 24th of October 1840 to the 25th of Jany. 1841."[4]

Texas Ranger Companies of 1840
listed in order of formation

Captain	No. of Men	Service Period
John William Lane	25*	Aug. 15, 1839–Feb. 28, 1840
George K. Black	46	Oct. 22, 1839–Jan. 29, 1840
Mark R. Roberts	43	Sept. 16, 1839–Mar. 16, 1840
Thomas N. B. Greer	37	Feb. 23–May 23, 1840
Constantius Pierce [1]	48	March 13–June 7, 1840
Daniel R. Jackson	21	March 28–Sept. 28, 1840
Moses Wells, Lieut.	18	April 9–July 9, 1840
William B. Stout	36	May 2–August 2, 1840
Ebenezer B. Nichols	38	June 8–August 27, 1840
Henry Stout	20*	June 11–September 10, 1840
James Decatur Cocke [2]	41	June 18–Sept. 10, 1840
Robert Barkley	44	July 4–October 4, 1840
Adolphus Sterne	53	July 8–Oct. 16, 1840
George B. Erath	9	July 14–Sept. 20, 1840
Thomas J. Rabb	45	September 20–Nov. 7, 1840
Nicholas M. Dawson	38	September 20–Nov. 7, 1840
Wesley Askins	33	October 1–Nov. 20, 1840
Jason Wilson	25*	Oct. 24, 1840–Jan. 25, 1841

* Approximate number of men who served.

[1] Operated under the Second Brigade, Texas Militia. Ebenezer Nichols took command of revamped unit in June. Disbanded by Col. McLeod in August. Pay records indicate Nichols may also have reorganized a small unit which served from Sept. 25–Nov. 16, 1840.
[2] Disbanded by Col. McLeod in August.

By mid-October, Captains Barkley and Sterne had disbanded their East Texas ranging units. Colonel Moore's two ad hoc ranger companies disbanded in early November in Austin, following their bold offensive into the Comanche camp. Captain Askins' Red River gunmen were disbanded on November 20, leaving a single company of Texas Rangers during December 1840.

★ ★ ★ ★ ★

The Comanche conflicts of 1840 had been fought with much less help from the Frontier Regiment than President Lamar might have expected. Most of the decisive fights of 1840 were conducted by largely volunteer forces, friendly Lipans, and Tonkawa Indians.

The First Regiment had made only one expedition, in which four Comanches were killed. Their only other significant showing was in March during the massacre at the courthouse in San Antonio. Political opponents of Lamar could point out apparent defects in the management of the regular army and the large amount of money it took to fund it. The army had also, just as in 1839, failed to come up to full strength in 1840. Albert Sidney Johnston abandoned the recruiting campaign and had resigned in March 1840.[5]

The Frontier Regiment's recruiting officers had focused on New Orleans, where men were willing to enroll in the Texas army. They were accepted before being sent on to Galveston for their formal enlistments. The progressive decline in the value of government promissory notes during 1840 to almost 16¢ on the dollar played a part in forcing the new Secretary of War, Branch Archer, to abandon recruiting efforts later in the year. At its maximum strength—reached near the middle of 1840—the regular army had ten full companies, totalling 560 men. After that time, the army slowly declined in size. By the end of September 1840, its strength was approximately 540 men; at the end of 1840, there were only 465 men still in service.[6]

In his ordnance memorandum of September 1840, Colonel George Hockley reported that the Frontier Regiment had its ordnance stores and shops in Austin. Among the cannon he had in battery at the Austin garrison were the brass pair known as the "Twin Sisters," which had helped defeat Santa Anna at the battle of San Jacinto.[7]

Colonel Hugh McLeod reported on October 1 that he was unable to give any details of militia companies that had been properly organized thus far in 1840. He only had lists of the election of the generals and their staff officers. McLeod wrote in disgust, "Some radical change in our military laws is necessary to enforce responsibility and discipline."[8]

The Great Military Road: August–November 1840

Lamar's Frontier Regiment did not succeed in establishing frontier posts and the military road called for by the general plan of defense envisioned at the start of Lamar's term. In the new army's first year, it had established detachments at San Antonio, Austin, Galveston, and Houston. Smaller detachments had been posted at Fort Burleson (formerly Fort Milam) near the Falls of the Brazos and at Gonzales. Secretary of War Johnston's plan in December 1839 of locating twelve posts for the line of frontier protection did not fully materialize for several reasons. One, he had believed twenty-four companies would be needed instead of the budgeted fifteen. The inability of the army to even fill out these fifteen companies had compromised his ability to fulfill this plan. While the army struggled to attain its capacity, Johnston had allowed the military road from Corpus Christi to the Red River and the new forts to go unbuilt, waiting on further resources.[9]

Following Johnston's resignation, the matter was brought to President Lamar's attention again by Senator James S. Lester in July 1840. Lester wrote to Lamar that it was desirable to at least build the road from Red River to Austin. According to him, at least one hundred families were waiting along the Red River in hopes of moving into the country, which would be opened for settlement by the completion of this road. Lester felt that at least a few posts built along this road would suffice to protect the new settlements as well as the northwestern frontier.[10]

Lamar gave his approval to this plan, and in August, Colonel Burleson was given the task of surveying and constructing the road from Red River to Austin. Two companies of regulars were detailed to do the preliminary work. This project came under further delay, however, when Burleson resigned from the First Regiment in late August. The great Comanche raid further put this project on hold in August.

Colonel William Cooke and Lieutenant Colonel Adam Clendenin had stepped into the two senior command roles in the First Regiment following Burleson's resignation. As work on the road project prepared to commence, Cooke arrived September 3 at the camp on Little River—where the expedition was preparing for mobilization.

Colonel Cooke's first big expedition got off to a slow start. He impatiently waited five days at the Little River Fort for promised

Colonel William Gordon Cooke (1808–1847) took command of the First Regiment of Infantry in August 1840, following the resignation of Colonel Edward Burleson. He had served as the army's commissary general since January 30, 1839. Cooke was the former captain of the New Orleans Greys company which fell at the Alamo. He also served on General Sam Houston's staff during the San Jacinto campaign. *Texas State Library & Archives Commission.*

pack mules which never arrived. The camp guards then negligently allowed the beef cattle intended to feed the men to escape and more valuable time was lost in rounding them up.[11]

The troops massed with Cooke included companies B, D, E, F, and H. Colonel McLeod, who joined the army troops briefly while they were gathered awaiting the start of their expedition, noted: "Their arms, accoutrements, and clothing (except the undress cap, which is not adapted to our climate) are good; the men were healthy, and their subsistence abundant."[12]

Before Colonel Cooke marched out, he detached one company eastward to handle supplies. Another, Company H—under the new command of Captain Joseph Wiehl—was sent to the head of the San Marcos River "to establish a permanent post to cover the passes through the mountains at that point." Wiehl's men arrived there on October 18, 1840, and worked on building this fort through February 1841. Designated Post San Marcos, the fort was near San Marcos Springs in Hays County. The assignment was obviously trying and unpopular, as Captain Wiehl suffered at least twenty-one desertions during November and December.[13]

Cooke decided to get his expedition underway in mid-September. He ordered the quartermaster to find more beef for the men and detached Captain John Holliday's Company D with some of his command to drive the cattle toward the main army. At least five of Holliday's men—Privates Daniel Burns, John Morell, William Messer, William Wallace, and Jacob Werking–

Frontier Regiment Unit Assignments: Fall 1840

Company/Commander	*Fall 1840 Post Assignment*
A Capt. Benjamin Gillen	Alamo, San Antonio
B Capt. John Kennymore [1]	Military road expedition
C Capt. Duncan Ogden	Alamo, San Antonio
D Capt. John J. Holliday	Military road expedition
E Capt. Martin Moran	Military road; building forts
F Capt. James January [2]	Military road expedition
G Capt. William Houghton	Military road expedition
H Capt. Joseph Wiehl [3]	Camp San Marcos
I Lt. J. Beverly Martin	Military road; Little River Fort

[1] Capt. Kennymore was arrested on October 9, and replaced by Lt. Robert R. Scott.
[2] Capt. Mark Skerrett assumed command in October.
[3] Capt. Wiehl assumed command on October 6, 1840, from Capt. Skerrett.

—were too sick to travel and were left behind at Beden Stroud's plantation on September 13.

Cooke left the majority of Captain Benjamin Gillen's Company A and Captain Duncan Ogden's Company C to operate from the Alamo in San Antonio during the latter months of 1840. The First Regiment moved from the Little River Fort up to the Waco village on September 17 and camped there long enough for the quartermaster to catch up with the cattle.

From the Brazos area, Cooke's men moved eastward toward the Trinity River. The expedition was slowed, however, by the difficulty of getting the heavy supply wagons across the creek bottoms between the Brazos and Trinity rivers. Fortunately, the season was dry and the grounds beyond the creeks were navigable with wagons. There was little water for the horses and two or three camps were made without water. By the first of October, camp had been made at Chambers Creek, some forty-five miles south of present Dallas.

Camp Chambers Creek had been established several months earlier by Captain John Holliday's Company D after Fort Burleson had been abandoned in June. This camp would be used into the early months of 1841. Camp Chambers Creek was located on the east side of the Brazos about two miles north of the State Highway 7 bridge over the river west of Marlin in present Falls County.[14]

Camp was again dry, so a small party of soldiers was sent back upon the trail to fetch water. Contrary to orders, they did not bother to carry their muskets with them. A party of ten to fifteen Indians attacked the unarmed Texas soldiers and killed five of them. During the same night, a severe norther blew in, and the cattle again escaped. Although "every exertion was made to recover them," wrote Cooke, "they were probably driven away by the Indians, who were prowling about our camp."[15]

Moving from the Brazos to the Trinity, Cooke figured that his soldiers averaged "about six or eight miles per day, both on account of the difficulty of getting through the bottoms, and the bad condition of our mules." Once the cattle had stampeded during the storm, his men were left entirely without provisions. No corn had been brought for the expedition. The only thing left to enjoy around the campfires was coffee and sugar. On October 9, Captain John Kennymore was arrested on charges unspecified and command of Company B passed to Lieutenant Robert R. Scott for the duration of the expedition and the year.

Buffalo had been seen between the Little River and the Brazos, but game became scarce as Colonel Cooke's expedition neared the Trinity River. Before they had reached the Trinity bottoms, the starved Texian soldiers were forced to kill dogs, mules, and horses for food.[16]

Seeing that it was impossible to reach the settlements with the cumbersome wagons, and with the number of sick men in his ranks, Cooke questioned his pilot on the distance. The pilot stated that it was still another two days' journey to reach the settlements on the Sulphur Fork of the Red River. Cooke therefore decided to leave a portion of his command behind on October 11. He would march on ahead to get supplies.

"Lieut. Col. Clendenin, at his own request, was left on the west side of the Trinity, with the wagons, sick [men], and forty men as a body guard," wrote Cooke. Clendenin's group consisted of First Lieutenant J. Beverly Martin and fifteen men from Company D, Third Sergeant Edward Smith and ten others from Company E, and ten men from Captain Houghton's Company G. Muster rolls show that these men were sent on detached duty with Clendenin as of October 11.[17]

Colonel Cooke's men had more difficulty than he imagined in reaching the settlements. Five days after leaving the Trinity

River, they encountered a dense thicket which their guide believed to be the headwaters of the Sabine River. "We were five days in cutting through," wrote Cooke. By October 21, they finally struck the trail used by Chihuahua traders, which led them on to the settlement on the Bois d'Arc, a fork of the Red River. There, "we were received very hospitably by Mr. Bailey Inglish, and furnished with supplies, after having been without beef for twenty-two days." Cooke's detachment had reached the fortified house called Fort Inglish, at the site of present Bonham.

Lieutenant Colonel Clendenin's men spent three miserable weeks at the Trinity River waiting for Cooke's return. His men were literally starved and were forced to kill and eat their own twenty horses and pack mules. By November 3, Clendenin elected to moved on down the Trinity before his men literally expired. He then buried his ammunition and heavy equipment and marched his men 120 miles south to the Falls of the Brazos.[18]

From Bois d'Arc, Colonel Cooke detailed a company of men to go back to the Trinity with cattle for food and oxen to draw the wagons. These men reached the campground but found that Clendenin's men had departed. They did find a forty-man party under Captain Mark Skerrett and Captain William Houghton's Company G. Skerrett had been detached from his command of Company H on September 12 to lead men to Colonel Cooke. Houghton's command was three detachments known as 13, 7, and 9.

The new recruits found only a note from Adam Clendenin, dated November 3, which stated that his men had been starved out. They had eaten most of their mules and horses and they had been obliged to leave. Clendenin wrote in the note that he expected to return within ten days.

Four messengers were sent back to Bois d'Arc to report to Colonel Cooke, while the remainder of the new recruits took up station on the Trinity to await the return of Clendenin. By November 14, 1840, Colonel Cooke had a firmly established camp on Bois D'Arc. He had found a fine area for his first outpost on the Red River at a spot ten miles above Holland Coffee's station. He was satisfied that supplies were plentiful at Coffee's and "it will afford the most protection against the Indians."

Coffee's Station was located in Fannin County (in an area that later became the extreme northern part of Grayson County). The site later became the settlement of Preston, about ten miles north-west of Denison, in an area along the Red River which is now flooded by Lake Texoma. The First Regiment's soldiers regularly found provisions and tools for the use of their detachments from Coffee's Station.[19]

Cooke's remaining soldiers were in fine health by mid-November. He found that Holland Coffee and some of the other settlers were nearly to the point of abandoning their post before the First Regiment arrived. Cooke wrote to Secretary of War Archer on November 14, "Upon the arrival of Capt. Skerrett with his command, I shall proceed to obey my orders respecting the military road."

During December, Cooke's men worked on establishing military posts in North Texas. The first post was east of the Cross Timbers, near the junction of Mineral Creek with Red River in present Grayson County northwest of Shermantown (Sherman). It was named Fort Johnston. Another post was started on the east bank of the west branch of the Trinity River. Cooke's men also worked on establishing Fort Preston, a supply station located above Coffee's Station.[20]

Fort Johnston was built by companies D and E by a con-struction detail under Captain John Holliday. The regulars would be stationed at this fort through April 1841. The fort was located between Little Mineral Creek and Red River in what is now extreme northern Grayson County, about four miles north of Pottsboro. The creek and river are now flooded by Lake Texoma.[21]

During his early surveying for the great military road, Cooke decided that it should be moved slightly from its originally desig-nated course. He hoped to establish military posts along the edges of the Cross Timbers, extending from Mineral Creek to the Waco village on the Brazos and crossing the Trinity River at the Cedar Springs.

Cooke's revised plan called for the road to strike the Brazos River near the Towash village, above the mouth of Aquilla Creek. From this path, he felt that the road could be extended easily directly to the mouth of the Llano River, where the road would likely end for the near future. The distance from Austin to Coffee's Station was an estimated 270 miles. The area along this road was filled with numerous small streams flowing from

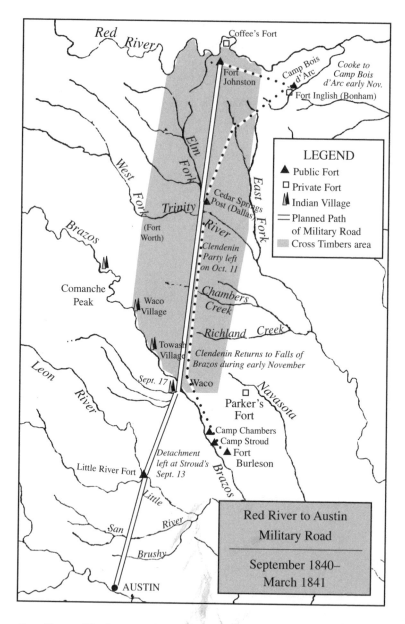

LEGEND
▲ Public Fort
◻ Private Fort
⚲ Indian Village
═ Planned Path
   of Military Road
▨ Cross Timbers area

Red River to Austin
Military Road

September 1840–
March 1841

the Cross Timbers and the countryside was diversified with
pockets of heavy trees. Near the mouth of the West Fork on the
west bank of the Trinity, a remarkable high hill could be seen
for miles. There were no marshes or swamps along the planned

military road and it contained good soil. The *Telegraph and Texas Register* reported on January 16, 1841, that the road "in one or two years will become the main highway from the northeastern settlements to the capitol."[22]

The path of the Texas Frontier Regiment's new military road roughly follows the path of modern IH-35, which passes from the Red River border through Dallas and Waco down to Austin.

A bill was put before the Texas Congress in January to encourage settlement along this road. Anyone who would reside for five years along this road—within 12 miles of the actual path—would be eligible for 640 acres of land for a family and 320 for a single man.

Colonel Cooke's military road expedition was also important in mapping out the northern areas of Texas. Mr. Hunt, the military road engineer, worked with a man named Randel to create a map of the Cross Timbers. The *Telegraph* on January 16 gave a definition of the Cross Timbers area, based on Hunt's surveys.

> This curious belt of woods extends from the east bank of the Brazos near the Towash village above the Aquilla, almost due north to Red River, about forty miles above the mouth of the false Washita . . .
>
> The trees composing it are chiefly post oak; and it resembles in many respects the high post oak ridges extending between the Brazos and Colorado, above Bastrop. Numerous small streams rise in the Cross Timbers, and flow into the Trinity and Brazos.

By Hunt's information, the Cross Timbers thus started at the Towash village (slightly northwest up the Brazos from present Waco). This band of timber extended due north past present Fort Worth and Denton all the way to the present Texas border with Oklahoma.

Cooke's men continued to work on the road from their base of operations at the newly established Fort Johnston, in Preston Bend of Red River, during the remainder of 1840 and into early 1841. By the time the project was complete, the soldiers had blazed a trail from Little River to Red River, a small part of the road in the north had been opened to traffic, and all of it had been surveyed and mapped by an engineer.

Although plagued by problems, the army had managed in its survey expedition to pull off its greatest accomplishment for the Republic. As a result of Cooke's men, this road was soon opened for traffic between Austin and Preston Bend, further extending the line of settlements. Expulsion of the Indians in the Three Forks area of the Trinity later in 1841 would help to further establish growth and settlement into the north-central Texas area surrounding present Dallas and Fort Worth.[23]

Financial problems plagued the Fifth Congress as it sat between November 2, 1840, and February 5, 1841. In his message to Congress in November, President Lamar warned that the issue of declining paper money value must be addressed. He hinted that budget cuts were in order, but did not yet specify where. He did make it clear that he did not intend to disband the regular army. He contended that citizen soldiers would not endure extended garrison duty or build forts and roads. The regular army's lack of significant fighting did not faze Lamar. "It was not its actual fighting," he said in November, "but its existence in the field that was serviceable."[24]

A report by Colonel Hugh McLeod, adjutant and inspector general of the Texas Army, made on December 17, 1840, gives

---

State of the Frontier Regiment, Jan. 1839–Dec. 1840
First Regiment of Infantry:

Soldiers Recruited	640
Deserted	169
Apprehended	61
Not apprehended	108
Honorably discharged	48
Dishonorably discharged	7
Died	24
Killed during duty	24
Shot by order of court martial	3
Promoted	6
In service at last return	465

Source: McLeod to Archer, December 17, 1840, in *Appendix to the Journals of the House of Representatives: Fifth Congress*, 376.

an indication of the kind of discipline problems that the Frontier Regiment had encountered during the year. The number of desertions was appalling. In two years of existence, the Frontier Regiment had recruited 674 men but had lost more than one-quarter to desertion. While in service, twenty-four soldiers had died, thirteen had been killed, and three had been executed by order of a court martial board.[25]

McLeod's report also showed that the First Regiment had purchased 396 horses and 90 mules for the army's use. Fifty-seven horses and mules had been sent with Colonel Cooke on his road expedition for transporting wagons and packs. "Upwards of one hundred have died and been lost in service," stated McLeod. The balance of the mules and horses had been distributed to the troops stationed at San Antonio, Post San Marcos, and to the detachment under Lieutenant Colonel Clendenin.[26]

Murder of James Childers: December 13, 1840

Even the near presence of the Frontier Regiment did not prevent the Texas Indians from continuing to attack settlers close to where army troops were stationed. Such was the case with an Indian depredation which occurred near the Little River Fort in December 1840.

In 1836, Texas Rangers had built Fort Smith, also known at times as Little River Fort and Fort Griffin, near the property of settler Goldsby Childers, just below the three forks of the Little River. This early pioneer was no stranger to Indian violence. Near the Little River Fort in June 1836, Childers had led a party of settlers from their homes toward safety, but had lost two men to Indian attacks before reaching Nashville. Childers' son Frank had been killed in 1837 in the Elm Creek Fight while under command of Captain George Erath. Determined to remain on his land, Goldsby Childers had lent out his wagon and oxen later that year to help support the local rangers. Once the rangers had departed the area, Childers had been forced to move his family back downriver to Nashville-on-the-Brazos for safety.[27]

In the summer of 1840, he went back up to his land to tend to a corn crop he had planted. He wanted to move his family back, but the evacuated post there offered no protection. Childers complained in a letter to President Lamar on August 11, 1840, that at least twenty other Nashville families had been unable to return to their land to make corn because of their fear for their lives. The help would not come soon enough, and Childers would move up to his land on his own later in the year.

A detachment of the First Regiment under Second Lieutenant Hiram A. Allen was still manning the Little River Fort post as of December. Captain Goldsby Childers was acting commander of the settlers who lived around this post. Indians were discovered in the area early in the month, and a courier was dispatched to Branch Archer.[28]

Shortly after the courier was dispatched, the Indians attacked the Childers home and killed James Childers, another son of Captain Childers, on December 13. James was shot down and mutilated while working near the fort. In a letter to Secretary of War Archer, written the following day, Lieutenant Allen gave details of the depredation.

> We visited the remains, yesterday, of a young man, named James Childers, who was cowardly shot down, and mutilated in the most horrible manner, while engaged at work. Near Little River Fort, three of his companions succeeded in making their escape; they state that they were attacked and surprised by fifteen in number, who, from their appearance, they judged to be Northern Indians.[29]

Allen's letter was also signed by Captain Childers, Robert Childers, John Marlin, Benjamin Bryant, Charles Wagoner, Francis Hughes, and Henry Kattenhorn, the latter having served recently as a spy under Captain Erath. They advised Secretary Archer that a large smoke signal had be seen in the distance and that "a party of mounted Indians were just seen within five miles of this place."

They requested that assistance be sent to them quickly, lest they be further attacked by the Indians. "If we are not furnished aid, we will be obliged to abandon our homes and our improvements, to give up the idea forever of earning a subsistence on the frontier, and leaving our desolated homes standing witnesses of the neglect of the Government to protect us."

In December 1840, Edward Burleson gathered a large group of Tonkawas and Lipans in Austin. He planned to carry out an expedition to drive the Comanches from the San Saba area and build blockhouses. The *Telegraph and Texas Register* of December 19 says that the men gathered on December 11, but the expedition never departed.

There is record that former ranger commander Sterling Clack Robertson was commissioned as a first lieutenant of Beat No. 1, Second Regiment, First Brigade, Militia on December 22, 1840, to serve against the Mexicans and Indians. There is no record that he actually carried out service in the field, however.[30]

Major George Howard wrote to the secretary of war in December 1840 from San Antonio. Howard was acting as commander of the forces in this area and had also been commissioned in May 1840 to serve as sheriff of Béxar County. Howard said that he expected a Mexican army from the Rio Grande to attack San Antonio. Various reports he had received showed some troops to be on the march, while others were gathering and awaiting orders from General Mariano Arista.[31]

Secretary of War Archer received Howard's dispatch on December 10 and sent orders for the sheriff to maintain scouts to the west of San Antonio to keep the War Department informed. Howard shot back a reply on December 11 that he could only partially obey this order. "Our horses are in such poor condition that my instructions can be but slowly executed," he claimed. From his Alamo headquarters, Post San Antonio only had one keg of powder on hand and his horses were in poor condition. Howard wrote on December 16 that he expected his condition to improve somewhat the next day, as he was expecting a detachment under Lieutenant Daniel Lewis to arrive in San Antonio.

Major Howard recommended that all communications between San Antonio and the Rio Grande by traders be intercepted. He felt that most of the traders were sympathizers with the Centralist Army. Two nights before, on December 14, Howard reported that a courier "had arrived in town in great haste." Since his arrival, it was rumored that Captain Leandro Arriola, Captain Antonio Pérez, and Colonel Juan Seguín, all veteran ranger and cavalry leaders from Béxar, had accepted commissions in the Centralist service. Seguín, who had the led the only all-Tejano company to fight at San Jacinto in 1836, was elected mayor of San Antonio in late 1840.[32]

This noble Tejano frontiersman was unjustly accused by his enemies of supporting Mexico's Centralist government. He had actually resigned his seat in the Texas Congress earlier in the year to help support General Antonio Canales' Federalist troops in driving out the Centralists. Throughout the latter part of the year, Seguín remained in communication with President Lamar, informing the Texas leader of his efforts to support Canales. Seguín would write that Lamar "not only authorized me to raise volunteers but ordered that I should be supplied with arms from the armories of Texas." In order to help him raise funds, Major Howard and Captain Duncan Ogden approved a $3,000 mortgage against Mayor Seguín's property.[33]

Seguín had ventured to the Rio Grande with Captain Samuel W. Jordan and some 110 men to help aid Canales' cause. Seguín was disappointed, however, to reach Mier in time for General Canales' signing of an armistice with Centralist General Isidro Reyes on November 5, 1840. The war was thus ended, and Centralists and Federalists of Mexico alike were now united to help protect Mexico from Comanches and Texans. Seguín and Captain Jordan's men were ordered to disband and return home. The Texans returned home in mid-December, frustrated and unpaid for their efforts.[34]

The Texas–Mexico border lands thus became even more of a political hotbed during 1841, and new efforts would have to be established to protect against Mexican military forces. Back home in San Antonio, Juan Seguín advised President Lamar on December 26, "The campaign against Texas is most certain and I am sure we shall be attacked very soon. I have never witnessed such enthusiasm as that which exists amongst all classes of Mexicans against Texas."[35]

In his warning to Branch Archer about the border unrest, Major Howard requested the funds to purchase three or four good American horses for his spies. The War Department, however, was completely out of money. Secretary Archer informed the acting president, David Burnet, on December 19 that he was unable to provide the Béxar troops with "the munitions of war necessary for their defence."[36]

Vice President Burnet had become the acting President of the Republic of Texas when President Lamar was granted a leave of absence from Texas on December 12 to go the United States for treatment of an intestinal disorder. Burnet would continue in this interim role until Lamar's return to Austin on March 5, 1841.[37]

Major Howard's request for horses and ammunition was approved by acting President Burnet on December 24. Congress also approved Colonel Samuel Jordan to raise three hundred volunteers to be stationed on the western frontier to watch General Mariano Arista's movements on the Rio Grande. Jordan and Captain John T. Price raised companies of men which they stationed on the frontier near Victoria during late 1840 and early 1841. There is no record that Jordan's battalion saw any action. In fact, they were more harmful than good to the Victoria County settlers. Local farmer John F. Kemper petitioned the Sixth Congress in 1841 for reimbursement for all the loss of stock he had suffered "by the company of men raised by Col. Jordan."[38]

Philip Dimmitt reported on January 9, 1841, on the movement of General Arista's troops, saying that they had visited Colonel Henry Kinney's ranch and had given Kinney an offer of protection. Dimmitt also advised of a planned Mexican attack, and pled with the executive department, "I hope to see the government act without delay, and not suffer the whole frontier to fall a victim to the Mexican guillotine and expose your country to emminent danger."[39]

Secretary of War Archer received a report on Christmas Day advising him of new plans to use volunteers and militia as supplements to the regular army. Farmers could be used more when crops were not in need of harvesting. Although this plan was not used in its entirety, the Texas Congress authorized the president to appoint three men to raise fifteen men each to act as spies on the western and northwestern frontier for the space of four months, or less if the president thought their services could be dispensed with quicker.

This resolution was passed on December 26, 1840. It would give the power for three new ranger companies to be created. President Lamar was authorized to appoint and commission three captains who could "raise fifteen men each, to act as spies upon the Western and North Western Frontier of this Republic, for the space of four months."[40]

Captain John T. Price was instructed on December 26 to raise a small company to scout toward Corpus Christi. He was to keep an eye on the movements of Federalist leader Antonio Canales, and Centralist leaders Rafael Vasquez and Enrique Villareal, who were operating in the area below the Nueces River. Captain Price was a veteran cowboy who had commanded a company during Colonel Reuben Ross' 1839 Federalist army episode. During the spring of 1840, Price had actively recruited for the Federalist army until joining Colonel Jordan's troops in December.[41]

Another of these newly designated companies would be headed by a surveyor and Indian fighter whose name was becoming well known. He was, in fact, destined to be considered the model of a Texas Ranger—Jack Hays.

CHAPTER 8

The New Frontier
"Minute Men"

January 1–April 7, 1841

The 1841 Texas Rangers

The December 26, 1840, legislation to raise three small companies of rangers was one of the acts most quickly followed up on. Within six days, Captain John Coffee Hays had been elected to command a company that would operate out of San Antonio.

Although already a veteran frontiersman, Hays had never officially commanded his own ranger company until 1841. He had served under Deaf Smith in 1837 and had led scouts on Colonel Henry Karnes' June 1839 expedition from San Antonio. He had also fought at Plum Creek in August 1840. In between his Indian fights, Hays was frequently leading surveying expeditions out of San Antonio to locate headright claims.

On February 15, 1840, Hays had been recommended to President Lamar to be assigned to run the northwestern boundary line of Travis County. During March 1840's Council House Fight, he had been below town on the San Antonio River surveying a tract of land. He was busy in the field throughout the year, locating eighty-nine land certificates in 1840. Twenty-three of these were as far as sixty miles from Béxar, on the Pedernales River.[1]

During his frequent service as a surveyor, scout, and spy, Jack Hays had gained "an enviable reputation for bravery, daring, endurance, and skill in commanding men." Such reputation certainly played into his being appointed as a captain of spies over other Texan frontiersmen many years his senior. He would celebrate his twenty-

Captain John Coffee "Jack" Hays (1817–1883) is the most legendary of all early Republic-era Texas Ranger leaders. A frequent scout, spy, and surveyor from the San Antonio area, he took command of his first government-authorized ranger unit in January 1841. His company was almost constantly in the field during the year, fighting bandits, hostile Indian tribes, and Mexican troops. *UTSA's Institute of Texan Cultures, No. 073-0641. Courtesy of Library of Congress.*

fourth birthday on January 28, while in command of his new ranger company.[2]

Many accounts of the service of Hays mistakenly report that he took command of this first ranger company in early 1840. A thorough examination of his action reports, his personal audited claims, and the military papers of his various companies clearly shows that Captain Hays did not command these rangers in 1840. Hays was often in the field as the head of surveying teams, which could have been mistaken for ranging units.

Much of the confusion as to the date that he took command of a Texas Rangers company is due to the errant memory of Captain Hays himself. In 1844, he provided information of his involvement in the early Indian wars to Mirabeau Lamar. In this letter, he described his first ranger command and the various expeditions and battles fought by his men as having taken place in 1840. The events of these expeditions match up exactly with Hays' own action reports that were written in 1841, following each encounter with hostile forces. Hays was consistent in his errant dates, providing details of his exploits as a ranger to a man named John Caperton who later served under him. Caperton's sketch of Hays also erroneously states that his first company authorized by the Texas government was raised in 1840.[3]

Capt. Price's Company of Spies: January 3–May 2, 1841

Captain:
John T. Price

Privates:
Ezekiel Ballard
John Blackwell [1]
William J. Cairnes
Ewen Cameron
Stephen Dincans
Jacob Elliott [2]
N. Estrevon
A. García [3]
George W. Guthrie
Silas W. Jenkins
Thomas Lane
George Lees

Adam Mozier [4]
Ary Pieratt
Joseph Rogers
Peter (Pierre) Rouche
William Rupley
William Snodgrass
Isaac Phillip Stem [5]
J. Louis Tresten

[1] "O. M." Blackwell on muster roll.
[2] Joined on February 5.
[3] Joined on March 3.
[4] Joined on February 4.
[5] Erroneously shown on muster roll as "W. Stemm." See Isaac P. Stem PR, R 257, F 25–6.
Source: Texas State Archives.

Capt. Hays' Rangers: January 10–May 10, 1841

Captain:
John Coffee Hays

Privates:
William H. Attwell
Pasqual Leo Buquor [1]
Michael H. Chevallie [1]
E. H. Davis
Archibald Fitzgerald
Peter Fohr
Thomas Hancock

Nathaniel Harbert
William Alexander Hesskew [2]
James Matthew Jett
Stephen Jett
William B. Small
James L. Trueheart

[1] Joined on March 10 at San Antonio.
[2] Spelled phoenetically as "Escew" on rolls.
Source: Texas State Archives.

Capt. Pérez's Rangers: January 20–May 20, 1841

Captain:
Antonio Pérez

Privates:
Cristano Casanavo
Luis Castano
Antonio Coy
Ensano Farías
Francisco García
Matias García
Raphael García

Leandro Garza
Francisco Granado
Canato Perez
Pablo Perez
Martin Salinas
Antonio Sánchez
Melchor Travieso
John O. Trueheart

Source: Texas State Archives.

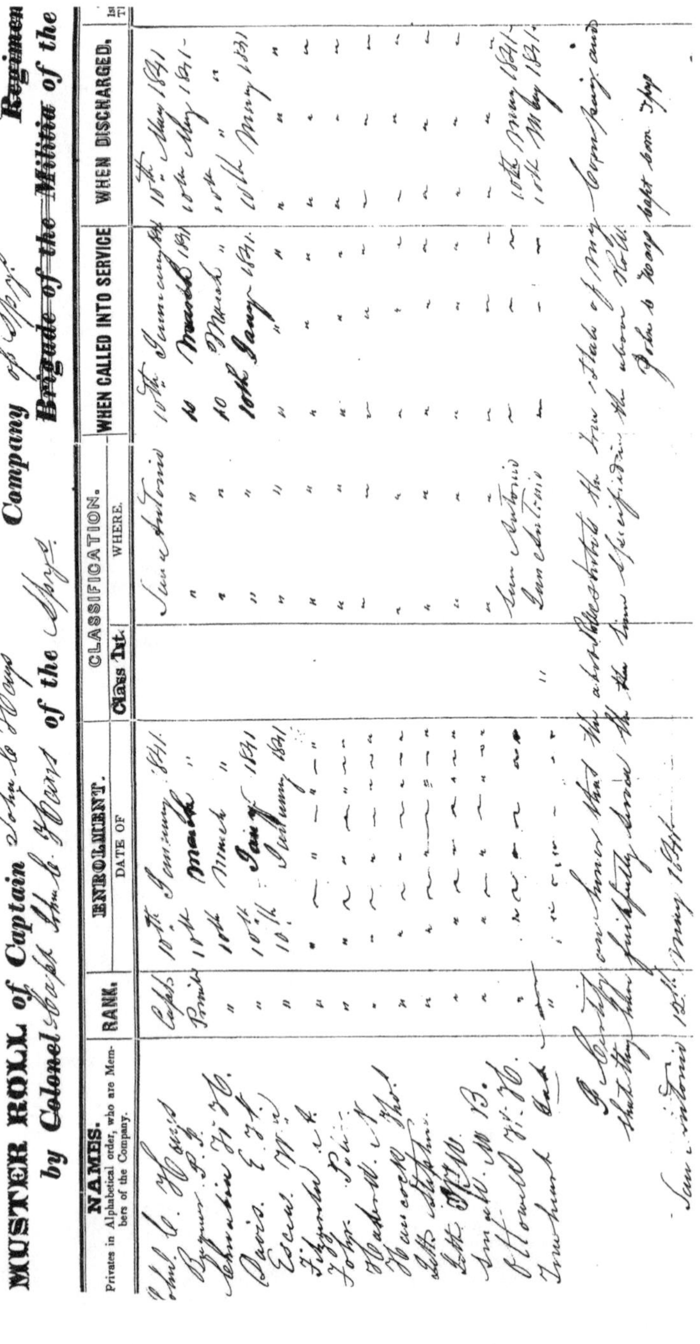
MUSTER ROLL of Captain John C. Hays Company of Spys
by ~~Colonel~~ of the Spys ~~Brigade of the Militia~~ of the Regimen

NAMES. Privates in Alphabetical order, who are Members of the Company.	RANK.	ENROLLMENT. DATE OF	CLASSIFICATION. Class 1st.	WHERE.	WHEN CALLED INTO SERVICE	WHEN DISCHARGED.

San Antonio ... May 1841

Among his original twelve-man unit that mustered into service on January 10, 1841, were James Matthew and Stephen Jett, whose service for Texas dated back to the Texas Revolution. They had served in ranger and cavalry companies continually, including the 1835 ranger company of Captain Daniel Friar. Another experienced fighter with Hays' new spy unit was William Alexander Hesskew, a thirty-year-old from South Carolina who had fought in the Texas Revolution during 1835. Twenty-five-year-old former Virginian James L. Trueheart had settled in San Antonio in 1838. Following his first stint with Captain Hays, Trueheart would serve as clerk of the district court during 1841.

Each of Captain Hays' rangers were required to furnish their own arms, equipment, and horses. The government supplied the ammunition for these men with the additional promise of three dollars per day for payment for captains and privates alike. Although food rations could be obtained from San Antonio for extended expeditions, these men frequently relied upon their guns to bring down game while in the field.[4]

Jack Hays' men were well-armed. At least a few of the new Colt Patent arms .34-caliber five-shooter pistols had found their way into the hands of Hays and his rangers. These weapons were not yet common on the frontier, having been originally purchased only by the Texas Navy and the First Regiment's cavalrymen. They could fetch $200 in price.[5]

In addition to their pistols, most of Hays' rangers were also each equipped with a rifle, a knife, and a small provisions wallet. Within this wallet, the men frequently carried some panola (parched corn), ammunition, and tobacco. Using a Mexican saddle, the rangers' horses were equipped with a rawhide Mexican *riata* (form of a lariat), a hair rope *cabrista,* and a lariat for roping horses. Lightly equipped, the Texan frontiersmen moved as nimbly over the frontier as the Indians did.[6]

During the month of January 1841, the first two ranger companies were originally formed. Captain Hays wrote in 1844,

(Facing page) Muster roll for the original Texas Ranger company of Captain Jack Hays, who signed as "Captain, Commanding Spys." Some sources have listed him commanding ranger companies in battles in 1840, but muster rolls clearly show that his formal ranger company commands began in 1841. *Texas State Library & Archives Commission.*

"Two spy companies were organized, Captain Price commanding the company at Victoria; and Capt. Hays, that at Béxar."[7]

A third new ranger unit went into service on January 20, 1841, under command of Captain Antonio Pérez, who had served on Henry Karnes' fall 1839 Comanche expedition. Pérez mustered in a full fifteen men by January 20. The names of his men appear to all be of San Antonio Tejano descent, with the lone Anglo exception being John O. Trueheart, whose brother had joined Captain Hays' unit.

Two of these units, those of Hays and Pérez, were placed in San Antonio, which indicates that there was a growing awareness of Comanche danger and the fear of a possible Mexican invasion. Each of the three captains labeled their unit as "Company of Spies," filling out their muster rolls on Texas Militia muster forms. Price commanded from January 3–May 2, 1841, and Pérez from January 20–May 20, 1841.[8]

Captain John Price's Victoria rangers were actually the first new unit to organize, mustering in on January 3, with twenty-one men, six more than his authorized level of fifteen. Price's men were recruited in San Patricio County and included William J. Cairnes and Ewen Cameron, both former Scotsmen who had become notorious as cattle-rustlers in 1839 through the area below the Nueces River which was claimed by both Texas and Mexico.

Isaac Stem, one of Price's new rangers, gives some insight into the provisions needed for an 1841 spy.

> When we equipped ourselves, the Capt. [Price] recommended the members of each company to furnish themselves with three horses if they could do so, and if they could not procure three horses to take two. Each one was for a travelling horse, one of brighter mettle or of a finer kind to reconnoiter upon, and one for a baggage or pack horse.[9]

Another of Price's men, William Rupley, later stated, "The expedition originated at Victoria. The service performed was that of a spy company." Formed and equipped, Price's spies proceeded westward from Victoria on January 4. His company reached the Nueces River and on January 9 met Captain Jack

Hays, who had been scouting from the mouth of the Frio along the Nueces. Hays reported that he had found no signs of enemy above.[10]

Captain Benjamin Gillen of the First Regiment, commanding Company A at the Alamo while Colonel Cooke was working on the military road to the north, sent a letter to Hugh McLeod on January 10. He wrote that Captain Jack Hays and his spy company were on a scout toward the Nueces and Rio Grande, and a report was expected from him any day.[11]

Gillen also informed McLeod that Phillip Howard had arrived at the Alamo with news of a party of forty Mexicans under Centralist leader Rafael Vasquez's command. These men had driven "from one hundred to two hundred head of cattle" from the ranchos of Juan Seguín and other locals. Accompanied by Seguín and a party of San Antonio citizens, Major George Howard set out in pursuit toward "a small stream between the San Antonio and Nueces rivers" where Vasquez's troops had reportedly taken the cattle.

Following his meeting with Captain Price, Jack Hays took his rangers in the direction of Laredo to ascertain information on the Mexican troops who were reportedly assembling for an invasion. He found only a few soldiers in Laredo. "There were but few soldiers there and the inhabitants were not disposed to offer resistance," he wrote. The soldiers instead crossed to the other side of the river as Captain Hays boldly entered town.[12]

Hays' men appropriated a number of horses from town and drove them back to their camp. The following morning, these horses were returned to the Laredo citizens with a note that the Texans were willing to fight enemy troops but not to rob peaceful citizens. Hays reported in January that this move was "merely to let the Mexicans know that if we chose to retaliate the robbing which had been committed on the Americans," his men were fully capable of so doing.

Following their rendezvous, Captain Price's company proceeded to Henry L. Kinney's rancho on Corpus Christi Bay, some forty miles below San Patricio. He learned that Kinney, a land speculator originally from Pennsylvania, had been visited by Colonel Enrique Villareal's Mexican troops. Price wrote to Secretary of War Branch Archer on January 23, that he felt Kinney was acting in conjunction with Villareal's men. "I also have assurance that Kinney has promised his assistance to the enemy."[13]

Kinney's ranch was found to have a twelve-pound iron cannon mounted on wheels, which had been left by General Canales the previous summer. Price recommended that the cannon be removed and that "some means be adopted by the Government to render ineffectual, if possible, the treasonable designs of Mr. Kinney."

Captain Price returned with his company from Corpus Christi to Victoria on Saturday morning, January 23, due to "weather and the muddy and almost impassable state of the prairies." He found that his hastily selected horses were rendered almost useless by the weather. He asked Secretary Archer for three or four good horses, "suited for extraordinary service."[14]

Price wrote that he planned to remain at Victoria for eight to ten days while recruiting horses. He would then proceed west "as far as practicable." He requested information from Archer on how long his company was to remain enrolled and the means by which he should secure ammunition, supplies, and provisions.

While in Victoria, Captain Price received two new men into his small spy company: Adam Mozier on February 4 and Jacob Elliott on February 5. These men replaced three who had left the company on February 4. This left Price with himself and fifteen other rangers as of February 5. Price's company was still in Victoria on February 15, on which date he drew lead, powder, soap, coffee, rice, sugar, salt, pepper, and tobacco from local merchant Frederic Giroud. Price signed for his provisions as "Capt. of Spyes."[15]

In January 1840, General Canales had organized the "Republic of the Río Grande." This area comprised the Mexican states of Tamaulipas, Nuevo León, Coahuila, and the portion of Texas lying west of the Nueces River. Political leader Jesús Cárdenas was elected president of the Republic of the Rio Grande. Canales kept his seat of government in Guerrero, Mexico, but in late February moved his seat of government into Texas to Laredo, which fell within his republic's claimed territory.[16]

On March 1, Cárdenas commissioned Captain John Price to solicit volunteers to form a six or nine-month company. Leaving three men in the field, Price was back in Victoria by March 24 and to begin his recruiting drive. He hoped to be en route to the Rio Grande by about April 7.

The Morehouse Campaign: February 1841

While Colonel Cooke's First Regiment worked on the military road, the Red River settlers were anxious to settle. As the road progressed from Preston toward the Three Forks of the Trinity, the settlers began calling on the government to expel the Indians from the present Dallas–Fort Worth areas.

The white inhabitants of Fannin County on Red River were among those most adamant in moving the largely Caddoan tribes from this area. Settlers along the Red River were plagued by raids from marauding Indians.[17]

In December 1840, Congress had authorized a large force of volunteers to ascend the Brazos River to hunt for these hostile Indians. General Edwin Morehouse, commanding the Second Militia Brigade, was to draw volunteer companies from the counties of Montgomery, Milam, Washington, and Robertson. Morehouse, at age forty, had raised troops from New York to join the Texas Revolution and had subsequently served his republic as a senator in the First Congress and as an adjutant general of the army. His volunteers forces were ordered to rendezvous at Nashville-on-the-Brazos by January 25, 1841, for a campaign expected to last about three weeks.[18]

Morehouse arrived at Yellow Prairie in late December to help with troop organization. On December 31, he informed Secretary of War Archer that he was proceeding into Robertson and Montgomery counties to recruit.[19]

Chief Plácido of the friendly Tonkawa tribe came into Houston and volunteered for the expedition. He reported that he had just come from the village on the upper Brazos where 400–600 Indians were congregated. Plácido offered the services of his forty-seven warriors, who were then camped on a tributary of the Brazos, between Houston and Austin. He asked for his men to be paid as the white soldiers would, to receive a share of the plunder, and to have exclusive disposal of all Caddos and Kichais who might be taken in battle. He said that the Anglos could have the Cherokees.[20]

Chief Plácido and his Tonkawa Indians were frequently employed as scouts on ranger and militia expeditions during the Republic of Texas era. The Tonkawas had agreed in 1838 to act in coordination with Texan forces to help punish hostile Indian tribes. Plácido's tribe had previously fought with Colonel Burleson's volunteers at Plum Creek in 1840 before joining the early 1841 Morehouse Expedition. From Wilbarger's 1889 *Indian Depredations in Texas.*

Chief Plácido met with Judge Isaac Moreland, an aide to General Morehouse of the Second Militia Brigade. Plácido was sent to Nashville to find Morehouse to offer his Tonkawas as scouts. The expedition, known during its time as the "Morehouse Campaign" did organize at Nashville on Monday, January 25, with the Tonkawa Indians, several Lipans and whites, collectively numbering more than 125.[21]

Captain George Erath, "at the call for volunteers to proceed against the Indians on the upper Brazos," was authorized by the government to take command of a spy company. The friendly Tonkawa Indians were authorized to join this expedition, and they fell under the authority of Erath. General Morehouse later approved payment to Erath as "Captain of Spies," commencing with January 1, 1841, through March 2nd, at the Falls of the Brazos.[22]

Erath later wrote that the Morehouse expedition "went up the Brazos above Comanche Peak, from there to the Trinity, and then back to the Brazos. There were about one hundred and twenty-five whites in the party, a hundred Tonks and fifteen Lipans. I had charge of the Indians and about twenty white men for spies."[23]

The expedition was still at Nashville on January 28 and 29, on which date Colonel Morehouse and commissary Lewis H. M. Washington signed a promissory note for John C. Pool for furnishing pork for the expedition and another for Neil McLennan on January 29 for furnishing corn. Washington, who had come to Texas from Georgia during the revolution, was appointed as commissary on January 1, 1841, by Morehouse.[24]

Aside from Erath's spies, recruited largely from existing companies, Morehouse's expedition included three other companies of the "Robertson Battalion" from Robertson County under Major Thomas Jefferson Smith. Captain Albert Edward Gallatin, thirty-one, commanded one of these companies. A veteran of San Jacinto who had been slightly wounded in that battle, Gallatin had come to Texas in November 1833 and settled in what became Washington County. His company became Company C, Third Regiment, Texas Militia under General Morehouse. Gallatin—who was paid $75 per month for his service—also furnished provisions for his men for their march to the Falls of the Brazos.[25]

A second company under Major Smith was that of Captain Wilson L. Murry. His men were veteran frontiersmen, and it appears that a number of Murry's men were selected to serve under Captain Erath as scouts and spies. Captain Murry had previously commanded a militia company from Milam County during the summer of 1840. Another Robertson County spy company was placed under Captain Samuel B. Killough. This "volunteer mounted gunman" company was mustered into service on January 25 and served through March 5, 1836. Among Killough's scouts was land empresario Sterling Clack Robertson, who had previously commanded his own ranger companies in 1836. At age fifty-six, Robertson likely felt more compelled to offer his experience as a scout and to let a younger man deal with the strains of command.

The privates of Captain Killough's company received $33.33 for their total service period. Killough was paid $50 per month, or $66.66 for his 40 days service.[26]

General Morehouse's Third Militia Brigade Expedition:
January 20–March 5, 1841

Commanding General:
Edwin Morehouse
Major:
Thomas J. Smith
Commissary:
Lewis H. M. Washington

Quartermaster General:
Henry Reed
Doctor:
George H. Sneed

Capt. Murry's Company: January 25–March 5, 1841

Captain:
Wilson L. Murry
Second Lieutenant:
William S. Holmes
Orderly Sergeant:
Frederic Niebling
Third Sergeant:
E. R. Van Horne

Privates:
Joseph J. Addison
John H. Anderson
G. B. Bowen
George W. Chapman
Robert Childers [1]
John R. Craddock
Samuel W. Davis
Thomas Dillard
William Eichelberger
John S. Fokes
George Green
Jacob Gross
Robert E. Harvey
George W. Humphreys [2]
Enoch M. Jones
Wiley Jones
Nathaniel C. Killough
William H. King [3]
Henry Lakey
Neill McLennan
William H. Moore [4]
David Mumford
A. L. Murry

William Oldham
James Overton
J. J. Owen
Jerome B. Porter
Nathaniel C. Raymond
Daniel Robinson
Joseph T. Robinson
Shapley P. Ross
Montgomery B. Shackleford
Nathaniel Shields
George W. Smith
James H. Smith
Guy S. Stokes [5]
John C. Sullivan
John Thompson
Pleasant Thorp
Charles S. Walden
John M. Wilkinson
M. Wilkinson
William Wilkinson
Edward J. Wortham

[1] Substitute for Prior Childers.
[2] Substitute for Joseph A. McMurry.
[3] Substitute for S. D. Smith.
[4] Substitute for Berry L. Ham.
[5] Substitute for John C. Pool.

Source: Incomplete muster rolls for Morehouse Expedition based on author's research of audited military claims.

Capt. Killough's Mounted Gunmen: January 20 - March 5, 1841

Captain:
Samuel B. Killough
First Lieutenant:
Andrew Smith
Second Lieutenant:
Charles H. Raymond
Third Sergeant:
Roll Tyus
Privates:
John Adams [1]
Joseph J. Addison
William Anglin
David A. Barton
G. B. Bowen
John R. Burriss
John Carner
Volney Cavitt
Joseph A. Clayton
George W. Crawford
James Dunn
William F. Flint
Reuben Flippert
H. R. Henry
J. D. Henry
Absolom Henson
John Hutchinson
Charles Kilgore
Samuel G. Killough

John Lynn
Bailey Martin [2]
J. P. McCanless
John C. McCustion
Andrew McMahan
J. W. Masten [3]
Samuel A. Nutt
William H. Odom
L. Baker Pendergrast
Elijah Reed
W. P. Rice
Haziel Robertson
Sterling Clack Robertson
Joseph Rogers
George W. Smith [4]
Ethan A. Stroud
Mandrid Stroud
M. Tivus
James Vanzant
Skeaugh Walker
Jesse J. Webb
Charles Welch
John Welch
Clinton M. Winkler

[1] Substitute for A. Owen.
[2] Substitute for Randal Robertson.
[3] Substitute for William Morgan.
[4] Substitute for Logan A. Stroud.

Capt. Gallatin's Company C: January 20 - March 5, 1841

Captain:
Albert Gallatin
Orderly Sergeant:
Dickerson Garrett
Privates:
William Elkins
Samuel Lindley
Alvin Perkins [1]

Thomas S. Pinckney [2]
James Spillers
Nelson Spillers
William Tankersly
Anderson Worlady [3]

[1] Substitute for J. Sauls.
[2] Substitute for John Darwin.
[3] Substitute for John Montgomery.

Capt. Erath's Spies: January 1–March 2, 1841

Captain:
George Bernhard Erath

Note: Erath claims this spy company included one hundred Tonkawa Indians, fifteen Lipans and "about twenty" Texans, although no roster is available. Many of the men who later served under Erath in March as rangers were among Captain Murry's unit.

The Morehouse Campaign did not see significant action while traveling up the Brazos River and to the Trinity, but did serve notice to the Indians of the area that the settlers were prone to take to the field. The Morehouse expedition had made camp at "Camp Stroud" as of March 1, 1841. Some of the volunteers who lived in the upper settlements of Robertson and Milam counties were discharged from Camp Stroud this day, including Captain Erath. The site of this camp was in the central part of present Falls County, near the Falls of the Brazos.[27]

Several of Captain Gallatin's men, such as Orderly Sergeant Dickerson Garrett, were given furlough to return home from Camp Stroud on March 1, although the company was not formally disbanded until March 5. Some of the Morehouse expedition volunteers were disbanded on March 5, 1841, at Camp Franklin. The town of Old Franklin had a blockhouse fortification which often served as a rendezvous site for surveyors and militia units. The site of the camp was in present Robertson County, on Touchstone Creek—a tributary of Muddy Creek—approximately two miles southwest of present Franklin (just north of U.S. Highway 79).[28]

Captain Gallatin's Company C was disbanded on March 5 at "camp near Stroud's" by General Edwin Morehouse and Captain Gallatin. Captain Killough's company and that of Captain Murry were also discharged at headquarters, Camp Franklin on March 5.[29]

According to George Erath, the Indian scouts who participated in the Morehouse Campaign killed two Indians— "all that were seen on the whole trip; no one on our side was hurt." Erath's evaluation of the offensive:

> The expedition was the mistake of military characters, newly arrived in Texas. They were of the opinion that Indians could be exterminated by carrying the war into their own country in the winter season, by finding their winter villages, destroying their provisions, and starving them out.
>
> Experience had already taught the Texas rangers that the Indians were quartered in their villages in the summer time only, eating what little agricultural produce they made, and that in cold weather they scattered to hunt and feast on bear and other wild animals.[30]

Military Funding Cutbacks

Some Texas Hill Country families had more than their fair share of hostile Indian encounters. On January 9, 1841, Judge James Smith of Austin was pursued by Indians near the capital. His young son was riding behind him on the same horse. Smith made a desperate dash with the Indians in pursuit, but the pair were knocked from their horse by a limb during the chase. Judge Smith was killed and scalped, and his son was taken captive. Judge Smith's brother narrowly escaped Indians on the same day in a separate incident, only by the speed of his horse. On January 19, Judge Smith's father-in-law was cutting bee trees four miles south of Austin when he was killed and scalped by Indians.[31]

The Texas frontier system was not fully supported by the Fifth Congress and the days of the Frontier Regiment were numbered. Acting President David Burnet had, however, approved a law on January 18 concerning the organization of the Texas Militia. Brigadier generals were to be appointed, but the militia of each "beat" could chose their own company commanders.[32]

Unlike previous years, when the militia sported five brigades, the 1841 Texas Militia system would only have four brigades. Burnet designated the First Militia Brigade to comprise the area west of the Brazos River, including the counties of Brazoria, Fort Bend, Austin, and Washington, east of the Brazos. The Second Brigade covered all counties lying between the Trinity River and the Brazos Rivers—excepting the counties mentioned specifically in the First Brigade's area. The Second Brigade, under General Edwin Morehouse, also specifically included Liberty County. The Third Militia Brigade, under General James Smith, included Nacogdoches and Houston counties and much of East Texas. General Edward H. Tarrant's Fourth Militia Brigade included the North Texas counties of Harrison, Bowie, Red River, Lamar, and Fannin.[33]

Congress stipulated that the President was not to allow militia or volunteer companies to carry out offensive warfare. He was allowed to call out such forces only "to suppress insurrection or repel invasion."

Congress passed an act on January 23, 1841, allowing a uniformed company to be raised for the protection of the Travis

County area. The Travis Guards, of course, had already been in service since their incorporation on March 1, 1840. Captain Matthew Woodhouse had commanded the company during 1840. In a regular meeting held on March 2, 1841, Woodhouse resigned from the company, having completed a year of service. Captain Joseph Daniels, the former commander of the Milam Guards, was elected to take charge of the Austin volunteers. Thomas Forster, who had served with the Travis Guards since its creation, became his first lieutenant.

Another uniformed company, the Galveston Artillery Company, was incorporated by an act of Congress on January 30, 1841.[34]

Such smaller, regional companies were easier for Congress to approve than was maintaining the funding needed for Mirabeau Lamar's Frontier Regiment. In 1839, the Republic of Texas' Congress had pledged $2,400,000 for the military. In 1840, appropriations were cut by seventy percent to just under $700,000. On January 28, 1841, the House pushed a measure to disband the regular army. The Senate refused to approve this measure. The House then refused to accept any appropriation for the support of the army, thereby making sure that the system would find its end shortly. As the Congress adjourned on February 5, 1841, the Frontier Regiment was without funds and living on borrowed time.[35]

For 1841, funding was cut much more sharply to just over $100,000. For the military road, $5,000 was appropriated to the engineer who would run the road from Red River. Most of this money was to support the war department, which had been reduced in size, and to support the ranger companies which would replace the regular army.

On its final day on February 5, the Fifth Congress did resolve to provide $75,000 "for the payment of spies and volunteers for frontier service."[36]

The County Minutemen

On the day before the Congress of the Republic of Texas adjourned, an act was passed on February 4, 1841, to "encourage frontier protection." The residents of each of twenty frontier counties were authorized to raise a company of "minutemen" who would operate under the supervision of the county's chief justice.[37]

The twenty counties were: Fannin, Lamar, Red River, Bowie, Paschal, Panola, Harrison, Nacogdoches, Houston, Robertson, Milam, Travis, Béxar, Gonzales, Goliad, Victoria, Refugio, San Patricio, Montgomery, and Bastrop. Only one company could be raised in each county, with rank and file no fewer than twenty and no more than fifty-six. Each county minuteman company would have a convenient assembling place. The men would elect their own officers, a gesture which always brought the most respect to commands.

Members of these companies were expected to hold themselves "in readiness as minute men, for the purpose of affording a ready and active protection to the frontier settlements." As such, they must be constantly able to take the field on short notice. Each man was required to provide himself with a good horse, a gun, one hundred rounds of ammunition, and rations, just as all previous ranger companies had required. The captain could also delegate up to five of his company to serve as spies, to range over neighboring counties. These minutemen were also exempt from militia duty, public roads work, and were exempt from state, county, and corporation poll taxes and the tax due on one horse.

The minutemen were to be deployed only in true emergencies, and their members were to be paid only for the days they were actually in service. In an effort to reduce unnecessary pay and abuse of the system, the county's chief justice was required to endorse all muster rolls submitted to the War Department for pay. No one would be paid for more than an aggregate of four months' service in a single year. Payment was specified at one dollar per day per minuteman.

Each expedition was not to exceed fifteen days at a time. Within the year, a four-month total payment maximum was imposed on the rangers, regardless of the number of days that they had actually spent on expedition. The only exception to this rule was that each county minuteman company could employ five spies, who could be paid to be in the field for extended service periods during the year.

These minute companies were organized in spring 1841 in most of the counties where they were allowed. Five Texas counties—Bastrop, Panola, Bowie, Goliad, and Harrison—however, did not form minutemen companies. If they did, their existence has escaped surviving records.

Bastrop County, frequently an area of Indian depredations in early Texas, appears to have been tranquil enough in 1841 to have not placed its designated company into the field.[38] Harrison County had been established in 1839, but was not properly organized until 1842. Therefore, if a company did operate in the area of Harrison County in 1841, there was no proper chief justice who signed off on any muster rolls for expeditions.

It also appears that no true ranging company operated in Panola County during 1841. The so-called Regulator-Moderator War would continue for years over the border of the United States and Texas on its eastern side, preventing Panola County from being officially established until 1846.

Bowie County was another county established by the Fifth Congress in December 1840. Its county seat was the new town of Boston. In the absence of county records indicating that a minuteman company was formed for Bowie County, it must be assumed that this area was protected in 1841 by Captain William Becknell's Red River County Minutemen and Captain Mansell W. Matthews' Lamar County Minutemen.

While some of the twenty counties formed minutemen companies for which ample records do exist, others have only spotty evidence that such ranging companies operated. Within Victoria County, Captain Adam Zumwalt—who had commanded volunteers during 1840—raised a new company of Minutemen in May 1841 at the home of John Alexander Clark. Arthur Sherrill was elected first lieutenant. Nearly every able-bodied man of the Lavaca River settlement belonged to this company. The company made two short scouts in 1841 when rumors of danger reached the settlement. No Indians were found or attacked, which gave the settlers much peace. No audited military claims or muster rolls, however, appear to exist for this unit. Zumwalt's men lived in present Lavaca County, which was originally created as a judicial county known as La Baca County in 1842 from portions of its neighboring counties of Victoria, Fayette, Jackson, Colorado, and Gonzales.[39]

At least fourteen other of the twenty approved counties did operate minutemen companies who went on recorded Indian expeditions during 1841. Following the passage of the new law in February, word quickly spread to the county officials.

From available records, it appears that Captain George Erath's Milam County Minutemen were the first new county rangers in service after the passage of this new frontier law. "Five men were to serve as scouts, the balance to remain at home and serve when called out on occasion of Indian invasion, getting paid accordingly," he recalled. On March 9, six of Erath's men—Daniel Robinson, Shapley P. Ross, Guy Stokes, Daniel Sullivan, Josiah Thompson, and Henry Kattenhorn—went into the field for a ten-day scout. Several other spies went out during the next few weeks before Captain Erath found enough Indian activity to warrant calling up his entire company.[40]

During 1841, Nashville-on-the-Brazos was the central community of the vast territory of Texas which originally comprised Milam County. George Erath mustered fifty men of his county ranging unit into service there on April 11, 1841, for his first full-fledged expedition with the new company. Among his seasoned frontiersmen were: Benjamin Bryant, company commander at San Jacinto and leader of the ill-fated 1839 settlers fight with Chief Jose María's Anadarkos; 1837 ranger captain Daniel Monroe; and newcomer Shapley Ross, destined to be a ranger leader and Indian commissioner of Texas. Many of Erath's men had originally served under Captain Wilson Murry during the Morehouse Expedition, which ended on March 5.

During its initial expedition, Erath's company was in service for fifteen days, the maximum number for a pay period, from April 11–26. He designated five men to serve as the company spies—Second Sergeant Daniel McKay, Fourth Sergeant J. S. Thompson, and privates John Anderson, Benjamin Bryant, and Jesse Bryant.

The first full expedition returned without any major conflicts. Erath's rangers would make two more expeditions during the late spring and summer of 1841, their third expedition ending on July 4, independence day for the United States. Their presence on the Milam County frontier likely helped prevent Indian uprisings during the spring and summer months, but Erath's minutemen would not pass the year without their share of action.

Captain Thomas N. B. Greer—a native of Tennessee who had served in the Texas Army's artillery at San Jacinto in 1836—took

---

Capt. Greer's Montgomery Co. Minutemen: April 10–Oct. 7, 1841

Captain:
Thomas N. B. Greer
First Lieutenant:
John Robbins
Second Lieutenant:
A. G. Rogers

Privates:
Edward Ariola
Eli Blackburn
Eli Blackwell [1]
James C. Bloodworth [1]
William Bolten [1]
John E. Buchannon [1]
William W. Byers [1]
Duncan C. Carrington [1]
W. D. Carrington [2]
Clay Cobb [2]
David Cobb
Martin Copeland [2]
Richard Copeland
John S. Downs
Andrew Greer
George W. Grimes [1]
John Harris [1]
Hugh Henderson [3]
Charles Hill
Samuel Hill
Samuel Hunter

Baxter A. King [1]
Samuel C. King
W. G. Landford [1]
John Longbotham
A. Maximillian
Joseph McLaughlin
Thomas J. Middleton [2]
Edward Mitchell
James Mitchell [2]
Joseph P. Philpot
R. J. Rayburn
James Reily [1]
William Robbins
John L. Robinson [1]
Robert Rogers [2]
Stephen N. Rogers [1]
C. C. Smith
M. B. Smith
Thomas C. Snalum
Jesse Young [1]

[1] Joined by June 20, 1841.
[2] Joined by September 24, 1841.
[3] Joined by April 20, 1841 as a spy.

Source: Minute Man Pay and Muster Rolls, Texas State Library and Archives Division.

---

command of the Montgomery County Minute Men on April 10, 1841. He had previously commanded the Boggy and Trinity Mounted Rangers for three months in 1840.

Greer's company made its first expedition from April 10-18. The company did not make another expedition until June 20. Thirty-two rangers were paid for the June 20–July 2, 1841 expedition. Between April and June, Hugh Henderson, Charles Hill, David Cobb, Martin Copeland, and Edward Ariola were paid

---

Capt. Gage's Nacogdoches Co. Minutemen: 16 April–25 June, 1841

Captain:
David Gage
First Lieutenant:
Alston Ferguson [2, 8]
Second Lieutenant:
John P. Grigsby [4]

Privates:
John Allen [4, 5]
William Anderson [1, 3, 7]
Matthew R. Birdwell [4, 8]
Thomas Chandler [9]
Zekekiah Chavety [3, 7, 8]
Wilson W. Cochran [2, 5, 8]
John W. Crunk [4, 9]
Kalib Farmer [10]
Stephen C. George [9]
Jackson Grayson [2, 5]
Berry Green [2, 8]
Thomas M. Hawkins [1, 6, 8]
Fletcher Howith [3, 5, 8]
Tandy Howith [5]
Robert S. Hulme [1,3,4,5,6,7,8]
James M. Johnson [5]
James F. Lane [10]
John C. Lane [5, 6, 7, 8]
Robert L. Lane [10]
Thomas Maxwell [3, 5, 8]
James Moore [8]

Peter Moore [10]
John M. Page [6, 9]
Isaac G. Parker [5, 8]
Thomas W. Ramsay [2, 3, 5, 8]
A. H. Reed [8]
James B. Reid [1,3,7,8]
Henry Madison Smith [10]
J. P. Smith [10]
James Smith [10]
Josiah Thomas [6]
John Vandyke [4]
S. W. Vardeman [2, 6, 8]
William H. Vardeman [1, 5, 8]
Hiram Walker [9]
William Wells

[1] April 6–10 expedition.
[2] April 12–18 expedition.
[3] April 21–27 expedition.
[4] April 30–May 6 expedition.
[5] May 7–10 expedition.
[6] May 13–19 expedition.
[7] April 30–June 3 expedition.
[8] June 4–14 expedition.
[9] June 18–25 expedition.
[10] On muster roll, but did not make an expedition into the field.

Source: Transcribed from Major David Gage muster roll, Texas State Archives.

---

as spies. Second Lieutenant A. G. Rogers and Private Duncan Carrington also served as spies during the June–July expedition.

Captain Greer kept his spies active from April through October. His company activated for the third time in September, making an expedition from September 24–October 7, 1841. Greer turned in his muster rolls to Montgomery County Chief Justice Hugh McGriffin on November 14, 1841. The company does not appear to have made any further expeditions.

In Houston County, Captain William Charles Brookfield was placed in command of the county rangers. Brookfield, a cavalryman at San Jacinto, had previously commanded a small ranger company during the 1838 Kickapoo War. Little is recorded of the Houston County Minutemen, as encounters in the area were limited in 1841. Captain Brookfield did take three men—Selden L. B. Jasper, E. A. Burrell, and Benjamin Warmel—out on one two-week campaign.

He presented his muster roll to Houston County Chief Justice Elijah Gossett on September 3 for payment. Brookfield affirmed that he and his three men had "served as minutemen in expedition against the Indians on the frontier of Houston County" from June 19 to July 1, 1841.[41]

In neighboring Nacogdoches County, forty-five-year-old Captain David Gage was elected into command of the local minutemen. Watching his time and payroll restrictions closely, Gage sent small groups of scouts into the field for either five or seven-day missions. By mid–May 1841, his minutemen had conducted six separate, small expeditions, easily making them the most active of the new county ranging companies.

The Yeary and Rowland Depredations: March 14, 1841

Some settlers survived Indian attacks only by their own brute strength and fighting abilities. Such was the case during an attack on the Fannin County home of John Yeary, which occurred on March 14, 1841, by the statements of neighbor William H. Bourland—a thirty-year-old who had moved to Texas from Kentucky just three months prior.

Forty-four-year-old John Yeary had held command under Andrew Jackson during the Florida Indian Wars. He later commanded forces moving captive Cherokee Indians from the states of Florida, Georgia, and Alabama to the reservations west of the Mississippi River in Indian Territory that later became Oklahoma.[42]

As of 1836, John Yeary was in Y Company, Arkansas Mounted Gunmen, of the First Batallion, Second Regiment. His company was called out in 1836 by General Edmond Gaines for the protection of the Sabine frontier. Muster rolls show that Yeary was stationed at Fort Coffee at various points in 1836 and 1837, thereby making him very familiar with the Texas land that he would later come to settle upon. John Yeary reportedly reached the rank of Captain by 1839—although archival records do not show his service after 1837—at which time he resigned his commission. He led a party of six families to present Fannin County, Texas, that year and settled northeast of present Ladonia across North Sulphur River.[43]

Yeary's family settled in a valley of the North Fork of the Sulphur River, near the present town of Honey Grove in Fannin County. On March 14, 1841, their cabin was attacked by a party of about fifteen Indians. John Yeary, his son David, and the family servant Anderson were working on the garden with their hoes at the time of the raid.

Yeary's thirty-seven-year-old wife, Mary Elizabeth Chinault Yeary, was in the early months of pregnancy with the couple's tenth child. The smaller children were at home with her and nineteen-year-old daughter Melvinia at the time of the attack. Melvinia spotted the approaching Indians and Mrs. Yeary bolted the door as she saw the Indians approach. The Indians attempted to break down the door, but to no avail before John and David Yeary and their servant Anderson arrived.

The Indians noticed the three men approaching them and ceased pounding on the cabin door. The Indians moved to greet the settlers at the Yeary fence, located some thirty feet from the cabin.

Several arrows were shot toward Yeary, but he managed to avoid being hit. Wielding only a hoe, he swung mightily at the Indians, and the muscular man knocked down several Indians. After finally breaking the hoe, he struck at his assailants with his fists. David Yeary and Anderson also joined the hand-to-hand fighting. John Yeary took a number of blows, as the Indians struck him about the face with their unstrung bows.

Mary Yeary and her daughter Melvinia finally threw open the cabin door and rushed into the fight with loaded rifles. Mrs. Yeary was shot in the thigh with an arrow, but managed to offer a rifle to her husband, who leaped the fence to retrieve it from her. Melvinia passed the other rifle to her brother David.

John Yeary, bleeding about the face and enraged, now strongly challenged the Indians with his son. The sight of the two rifles was enough to send the Indians fleeing. Yeary sent Anderson to the home of neighbor Elbert Early, who lived five miles to the east. William Bourland, visiting Early from his own Red River home, was present when Anderson raced up.

> Myself and [Early] were standing in his porch, about 2 o'clock, p.m., when we discovered a negro man belonging to Capt. John Yeary, of Fannin County, who lived about 5 miles from Early's, approaching the house in full speed. . . We at length succeeded in allaying his excitement, when he informed us that the Indians had attacked his master's house, had shot his master and mistress, and he verily believed some of the family was or would be killed.[44]

Bourland immediately mounted his horse and raced toward the Yeary's home with Anderson. The Indians had fled prior to their arrival. Bourland found Mary Yeary had been shot with an arrow, which was buried about five inches deep into her hip. "She had bled until she was much exhausted. She had a slight wound also in the arm."

John Yeary's face "was completely scored," where he had been beaten while fighting the Indians with only a hoe. Yeary felt that his family had been assailed by fifteen Indians. The ground about his home was "lying thick" with spent arrows.

A small pursuit party went after the Indians, but lost their trail, due to "a very severe rain falling that evening." Bourland was impressed with the determination of Yeary in maintaining his frontier Fannin County residence.

> Captain Yeary was strongly solicited by his family and friends to leave the frontier, but he refused, and said he felt as though he could succeed every time. Even if double the number should attack him, he has kept his ground, and is now living in peace, not dreading the approach of Indians.

Another Indian depredation happened in Robertson County near Tenoxtitlán in late May 1841, when Indians attacked the home of Joseph Rowland, located some distance from Tenoxtitlán.

Young R. Y. King, son of the Milam County Judge Hugh B. King
—who held court at Nashville-on-the-Brazos—sent his young son,
Rufus Y. King, and his black servant Jim to fetch a new spinning
wheel from Benjamin Bryant at Tenoxtitlán. As it got dark on the
way home, Jim and young Rufus King stopped for the night at the
neighborhood home of Joseph Rowland for safety.[45]

Close to sunset, Rowland's children encountered two Indians
skinning one of the family's calves near the pen. The alarm was
shouted and the settlers took cover in their homes and sat through
the night armed. Rufus King and a Mr. Campbell, a workman of
Rowland's, stood the late watch. King drifted off to sleep, only
to awaken to a calamity as Indians stormed the Rowland house
to steal horses.

> The noise of startled horses, their tramping feet and
> wild, scared snorting, betrayed the near vicinity of the
> Indians. They had slipped up, cut loose the horses, shot
> Mr. Campbell as he attempted to rise, with an arrow clear
> through his body. . . The poor fellow in mortal agony
> struggled to his feet and endeavored to reach the door,
> at which he fell stone dead before he could effect an
> entrance.
>
> In a moment all was wildest alarm, but to no avail. The
> Indians had gotten off with the horses and no pursuit could
> be attempted until morning. But there was no more sleep
> for that night.

Young King and his family servant Jim headed for home
after daylight the following morning. Campbell was buried and a
pursuit party from the Tenoxtitlán area made preparations during
the predawn hours. "Powder horns were looked up and carefully
filled," recalled King. "Bullets were molded. Rations for a couple
of days were cooked and put up by the women, and all made
ready for an early departure."

Although the local settlers pursued these Indians, there is no
record of any serious encounter that may have occurred. Joseph
Rowland's son Ezekiel—perhaps motivated by this depredation
against his family—would later serve as a Texas Ranger.

Captain Dolson's Fight: March 31, 1841

Although George Erath's Milam County company was the first to send spies into the field, Travis County was the first to put a full company of minutemen on expedition in 1841. These rangers, under Captain George M. Dolson, were also the first new county minutemen to find battle.

Dolson had previously served as a second lieutenant in Henry Karnes' 1837 cavalry and as a first lieutenant of Captain Louis Franks' 1839 volunteer company under Colonel Karnes. Dolson's Travis County Minute Man company was organized on March 28, 1841. It was the second smallest such unit (next to Brookfield's Houston County Minute Men) which operated in 1841, being only eleven men at its organization and generally comprising only five spies in service at a given time.

Captain Dolson's number two man was First Lieutenant James W. Newcomb. His second lieutenant was the veteran James O. Rice, who had been in the 1837 Stone Houses fight and had served ably as a scout for Captain Paint Caldwell's rangers.

At the time his Travis County rangers were organized at Austin on March 28, Captain Dolson immediately sent men into the field in response to a horse theft by Comanche Indians. Lieutenant Newcomb, in company with privates Henry Rinehart and John W. Ladd, departed on March 29 to reconnoiter Brushy Creek for signs of these Comanche. In his report written on April 2, Captain Dolson details:

> [They] returned the following day and reported a fresh trail of Indians leading towards Austin. A portion of my men were soon mounted, and accompanied by some volunteers, were in immediate pursuit. We were unsuccessful in finding these Indians; but discovered the trail of the party who had stolen Capt. Brown's horses a few nights previous.[46]

When Captain Dolson departed Austin on March 30 to follow this fresh intelligence, he had only eleven other men in his company. He was accompanied by four volunteers, Captain Joseph Daniels, and Lieutenant Thomas Forster of the local Travis Guards company. By late day, this group of eighteen men had succeeded in approaching the vicinity of the Comanche camp without having been discovered. This location was a few miles above the Pedernales River, likely in present Blanco County west of Austin.

Captain Dolson ordered his men to halt for the day to rest their horses. He noted that they had "travelled about sixty miles in twenty-four hours over a mountainous country."[47]

Dolson sent out his spies that evening, Lieutenant Newcomb with Rinehart and Ladd. Each was mounted upon the best horse available. Newcomb's men returned to camp with three of the Indians' horses, and they reported fresh signs in the Colorado River bottomlands.

> At midnight we were in our saddles, and again on their trail, with the hope of discovering their camp, and attacking them at dawn; but the darkness of the night prevented. Having halted again for a short time, we continued our route.
>
> At day break, we discovered their horses, and a few minutes afterwards, found ourselves upon their camp. The action commenced on the part of the Indians, by a rapid report of rifles.

Captain Dolson immediately brought his men and the volunteers to a charge. The Indians were driven from their camp. Their chief was seen to act with "considerable bravery." Twice he rallied his men to charge the Texans. "Nothing could stop the impetuosity of my men, and the Indians broke in every direction, leaving us in possession of the camp."

Captain Dolson was shot in the chest during the commencement of the charge into the Indian camp. Dolson soon took another painful shot through his thigh and his horse was shot through the neck.

Due to the rugged ground surrounding the camp, the men found it impossible to pursue the Indians on horseback. Dolson instead led his men in pursuit on foot. "After being shot," wrote Dolson, "I continued the chase on foot, until so completely exhausted, I could neither proceed farther, or command my men."

Captain Daniels came to Dolson's aid, but the wounded captain was not wanting assistance. "For God's sake," he yelled, "Do not permit the charge to end!"

Capt. Dolson's Travis Co. Minutemen: March 28 - Dec. 28, 1841

Captain:
George M. Dolson *
First Lieutenant:
James W. Newcomb *
Second Lieutenant:
James Ogden Rice *

Privates:
Henry W. Clark *
William Coltrin (join 6/15)
W. Gibbons *
William Gibson *
John W. Harrison
Joshua Holden
John W. Ladd *
David Patterson *
George W. Ricks
Henry Rinehart *
C. R. Sassaman *
J. M. Shockley *

John Tibble (joins 11/19)
Nathaniel H. Watrous
David R. Webb

* Indicates original company.

Volunteers on March Expedition:
Brig. Gen. Edwin Morehouse
Col. Louis P. Cooke
Powhattan Archer
Mr. Gates

Travis Guards on Expedition:
Capt. Joseph Daniels
Lt. Thomas G. Forster

Source: Report of Captain Dolson, from *Journals of the Sixth Congress, Republic of Texas*, III: 409–10. Minute Man Muster Rolls from Texas State Library.

Daniels assumed acting command of the Texans and they continued the charge against the Indians. The Comanches suffered heavy losses before they could retreat. The brave chief and seven other of his warriors were left dead on the battlefield. A number of other wounded Indians were escorted away rapidly.

Aside from Captain Dolson, no other Texan was wounded. The Texans gave up on the chase and returned to the Indian camp. They proceeded to destroy and burn the items which they could not use, including the Indians' bows and arrows. The twelve rangers and six volunteers arrived back in Austin on the night of April 1 with the stolen horses of Captain Brown.

George Dolson's wounds from this Indian battle were serious enough to keep him from the saddle for some time. His rangers continued to cover the Austin area throughout 1841, however. Muster rolls for the Travis County Minute Men show First Lieutenant Newcomb and Second Lieutenant James Rice to be regularly out on scouting missions. Captain Dolson continued to sign each roll for the "spies detached from my company."

Newcomb led one scouting mission of fifty-four days, spanning the period from May 22 to July 14, 1841, with his trusted spies Henry Rinehart and John Ladd. Private David Patterson was paid for a sixty-nine-day patrol period which overlapped that of Lieutenant Newcomb. Interestingly, the daily pay rates for the spies under Captain Dolson vary between $5.50, $6.00, and $7.00 per day on the various company pay rolls. Legally, they were only sanctioned for one dollar per day in pay.

Dolson submitted his final muster roll on December 29, 1841, which was authorized and approved by Travis County Chief Justice Joseph Lee.

★ ★ ★ ★ ★

End of the Frontier Regiment: January–March, 1841

Major Clendenin arrived in Austin in early February from the Falls of the Brazos. He reported that the regular troops in that area numbered about sixty men. They had recently returned from the Waco village, where they had remained about four weeks. They had not, however, erected any blockhouses or pickets.[48]

Some of the First Regiment soldiers remained on duty at the Little River Fort and another detachment remained on duty at the Falls of the Brazos. Desertion became more widespread. First Lieutenant Robert R. Scott had lost seven men from Company B on January 26 and January 27 from his camp on Timber Creek. Only one of these men was apprehended. Private Michael Dunn of Company C in San Antonio was court-martialed and shot.

Another soldier was accidentally killed on February 14, 1841. While on a surveying expedition under command of Lieutenant Scott, Private Leonard Taylor of Company E was shot and killed when another soldier mistook him for an Indian. Taylor, however was "dressed at the time in the Grey undress of the 1st Rt of Infantry," and was shot at midday at a distance of only thirty paces, as measured by surveying chain. This apparently led to some speculation as to whether his death was accidental.[49]

Captain James Goodall experienced his fair share of troubles at Fort Johnston during the winter. On February 3, 1841, Corporal George Taylor and five privates deserted their post. Goodall wrote on his muster roll of May 8:

The company has been stationed at Fort Johnston, the building of which has progressed rapidly. There has been many desertions and none caught, for want of horses and money to pursue them.[50]

At least one of these men, Private Michael Riley, was apprehended after deserting the army. He was tried before Colonel William Cazneau, who wrote to President Lamar on March 4. He recommended a mitigation of the sentence on Riley, following the same method that the deserters of Company G had been given the previous year.[51]

Colonel William Cooke wrote a new report to Secretary of War Archer from Austin on February 17, 1841, outlining his successes of command thus far.

He had established two permanent military posts after laying out the military road. The first post was on the Red River above Coffee's Station, on the east side of the Cross Timbers. The other was on the cedar bluffs, on the Trinity River, "about due south from the post on Red River." Cooke also noted that "emigrants are ready at this time to settle near the Trinity post."[52]

The second post was one established by Captain William Houghton with a detachment of men from companies B, F, and G. In Colonel Cooke's vision, he planned to construct a chain of forts from the Red River to the Nueces River. The first fort established had been Fort Johnston on Preston Bend of the Red River.[53]

Cedar Springs Post, the second outpost, was built approximately three miles northwest of downtown Dallas. The site is near Cedar Springs Place and Maple Park in North Dallas. The state has erected related markers five miles south of the old post in Marsalis Park.

During February, Captain Houghton's soldiers marked off the military road from the Red River and made it passable from Camp Jordan to Cedar Springs. Camp Jordan was the camp of Captain Houghton's detachment. This camp, likely named for former First Regiment leader Samuel Jordan, was located six miles north of Pilot Grove and perhaps two miles west of present Whitewright in Grayson County. The army regulars used this camp from February to at least late March 1841, during construction of the great military road.[54]

Final Locations of Frontier Regiment Units in 1841

Company/Commander	_Location and Date of Final Muster Roll:_	
A Lt. Daniel Lewis [1]	Austin	March 25, 1841
B Lt. Robert R. Scott	Camp Jordan	May 8, 1841
C Lt. John B. Reavis	Austin	March 20, 1841
D Capt. John Holliday	-	May 8, 1841
E Capt. James Goodall	Fort Johnston	May 8, 1841
F Lt. Collier Hornsby	-	May 8, 1841
G Lt. Roswell W. Lee	Camp Jordan	May 8, 1841
H Lt. John S. Sutton	Austin	March 15, 1841

I *Company was decommissioned and men were spread throughout other companies after February 28, 1841.*

Other detachments:

Capt. Palmer J. Pillans	Post Galveston	April 11, 1841
Lt. J. Beverly Martin [2]	Austin Arsenal	April 30, 1841

[1]   Capt. Benjamin Y. Gillen deceased on March 9, 1841.

[2]   Commanding artillery arsenal at Austin.

Some temporary buildings were likely erected at the Cedar Springs Post during the spring of 1841, but a permanent fort was not constructed before events in April would cause the First Regiment to move on. Whatever structures that Houghton's men did erect were certainly the first structures ever built by white men at what would become Dallas, Texas.[55]

Captain Holliday, with a detail from companies D and E, had built Fort Johnston during December 1840. Fort Johnston was located between Little Mineral Creek and Red River in present extreme northern Grayson County, approximately four miles north of Pottsboro. The site is marked by a State of Texas stone marker, although the creek and river have since been flooded by Lake Texoma.[56]

In spite of the progress of the military road and these new frontier outposts, the Frontier Regiment was on its last legs. "I regret that after all the labor and expense has been incurred," wrote Cooke, "Congress should have deemed it politic to destroy our military force." He asked for the continuance of his regiment,

at least just the officers still in the field, to help settle and cultivate the frontier.

Colonel Cooke proposed to use Major George Howard's
troops at San Antonio to fill out the company now stationed at
the head of the San Marcos River. He also proposed to establish
a post on the Brazos River, "which will make communication
practicable and safe from this city to both extremes of the frontier."[57]

Cooke also gave a status report on the Texas Indians. He
claimed that the Cherokees, Shawnees, and Kickapoos who had
been expelled from Texas had since sought shelter in Choctaw
territory in Arkansas. He had heard, however, that the Choctaws
did not approve of these "vagabonds who have intruded upon
them" and planned to run them back down south into Texas in the
spring.

The squabble between the Fifth Congress' House and Senate
members ended in early February with no funding being appropriated for Colonel Cooke's army for 1841. Acting President
Burnet therefore instructed Secretary of War Archer on March 2,
1841, to order the First Regiment to disband. Colonel Cooke was
to disband all troops on the Red River, on the Trinity, those stationed between the Trinity and Austin, and those at San Marcos,
San Antonio, and Galveston. The troops at San Antonio, except
for those who used to live there, and those at San Marcos, were
to be marched to Austin before being disbanded.[58]

President Lamar, upon his return to office in March, ordered
the comptroller on March 24 to open an account on his books for
the disbanding of the army. At the time that Cooke's army was
discharged from service, enlistment had fallen to 540 officers and
men.

Just as the government was dismantling its regular army, a
new threat reached the capital. President Lamar in Austin was
warned by Dr. Shields Booker of the late Federal army, who
had just reached the capital from General Arista's headquarters. Shields warned that Arista was assembling thousands of
Centralist troops for a campaign against Texas. Arista's men were
reportedly furnished with heavy artillery and were expecting
thousands of reinforcement troops from deeper within Mexico.[59]

Lamar issued a letter to all of his militia colonels on March
22, 1841, which relayed some of the warnings brought to him by

Dr. Booker. "It is not my intention to create any alarm," Lamar cautioned, "or to call out the militia unless it becomes absolutely necessary to repel a direct invasion."

While there is no evidence that militia companies moved out, the chief justices of some counties were busy organizing their local militia. Chief Justice Thomas H. Poage of Victoria County knew the value of being prepared. He had lost slaves in the previous year's Comanche raid in his county. Poage reported to Lamar on April 28 that Victoria County had been laid off into three captain's beats. Colonel Abner S. McDonald proceeded with the organization of the county militia.

Like so many of the warnings of an imminent Mexican attack on the Republic of Texas, this one would pass without incident. Lamar did advise his militia colonels to bring their commands up to full quota to be ready to move out "at one hour's notice."[60]

By the time that the Mexican invasion threat had subsided, the Frontier Regiment was in its final days. The northernmost companies were stationed at Camp Jordan, located near Pilot Grove. Thomas Gales Forster reported to Colonel Cooke on April 9, 1841, on the resignations of captains Kennymore and Ogden and of lieutenants Hiram Allen, J. B. Martin, John Howard, A. C. Morgan, and Daniel Lewis.[61]

Jack Hays' Laredo Fight: April 7, 1841

During January 1841, Captain Hays' men had made their bold journey into Laredo to make their presence known among the Mexican soldiers. After stealing and returning local horses just to prove a point, his men had patrolled the western frontier some time before returning to San Antonio.

During early March, a band of about thirty freebooters under Agatón Quinoñes attacked a trader party. Quinoñes—whose marauders roamed the Nueces frontier, pillaging and robbing traders—attacked a party in early May which included Antonio Herrera and Francisco Ganado. These men hastily returned to San Antonio to report their losses. Several leading Béxar merchants sent a request to the government in Austin for permission to raise a company of rangers for the protection of frontier trade.[62]

Fortunately, Captain Jack Hays' men had recently returned from their first scout out to Laredo. Muster and pay roll records show that Hays added two men to his ranger unit on March 10. One was Michael H. "Mike" Chevallie, who was born in Richmond, Virginia, and had recently served as an officer with the First Regiment of Infantry in 1840. There was also twenty-year-old Pasqual Leo Buquor, who was destined to become a mayor of San Antonio. Born in New Orleans, Buquor was commonly known as "P. L." Like Chevallie, he had served in the Frontier Regiment. He joined Company E as second sergeant in Galveston on September 16, 1839, and had taken part in Edward Burleson's Christmas 1839 fight with Chief John Bowles' Cherokees. Buquor served with the army until 1841, before being given a furlough to join Hays' rangers.

When word reached Chief Justice John S. Simpson at Béxar, he notified Captain Hays, who was out on patrol, in response to orders he had received from the War Department. Hays immediately set out on March 15 with the thirteen other men of his command to pursue these marauders. He had received orders from Secretary of War Branch Archer to help deal with various robberies that were being committed between San Antonio and Laredo. Hays set out from San Antonio with his company and that of Captain Antonio Pérez, whose unit numbered one dozen Tejano volunteers. In his report, Hays stated: "Our force consisted of thirteen Americans, and twelve Mexicans."

They departed San Antonio on March 15 for Laredo, located on the Rio Grande at the border of Mexico, as Captain Hays reported.

> Shortly after leaving Béxar, I was informed of considerable robberies having been committed upon traders returning from Béxar with goods, by two parties which had been infesting our frontier, one under Agatone with thirty men and the other under Ignacio García with twenty five men.
>
> I endeavored to intercept these parties before they could return to Laredo, but they reached that place one day before I arrived in the vicinity. In the mean time, two men were dispatched from Béxar, giving information of my company being out.[63]

The two raiding parties mentioned by Hays were those of Agatón Quinoñes, who had been in action since the fall of 1839, and a more recently formed gang of about twenty-five men under Ignacio García. En route to Laredo, Hays and Pérez stopped at the ranch of Antonio Navarro to bury two Mexicans who had been killed by the Comanches a day or two prior.[64]

Although Hays had tried to keep his pursuit concealed, word soon leaked out that his rangers were moving out against the bandits. Soon after the rangers departed San Antonio, Francisco Flores, a local whose loyalty to Texas was questionable, sent an express under two men to his son, Eduardo Flores, at Laredo. These couriers raced toward Laredo with news that Hays was heading for Laredo. On the third night out from Navarro's ranch, Hays' camp was passed in haste by the riders from San Antonio.

Garcia's bandits thus received a one-day advance warning of the approaching rangers. Hays and Pérez soon found that their approach had been broadcast, and they pushed forward with resolve. About ten miles from Laredo on April 7, they were first intercepted by Garcia's forces. Two Texan spies, Pascal Buquor and Martias Díaz, were riding in advance of the rangers and were first to spot the approaching Mexican riders. The Texans halted, as did the Mexican forces.[65]

"They rode up to us, sounding a bugle, and made an immediate attack, firing upon us and ordering us to surrender, saying they had a large force," wrote Hays.

Hays did not believe the story of reinforcements. He told the young man with him to fire at the Mexican alcalde who had ordered them to surrender. "He did so and the Mexican fell," wrote Hays. "A general fight then ensued."[66]

The Mexican force then charged on the Texans, but the Mexican escopetas (shotguns) did no damage. The Texans returned fire with their longer range rifles, killing one of the Mexicans and wounding another. Garcia's men then rode off a short distance and tried to surround the rangers. Hoping to deceive and discourage the rangers as to their actual numbers, Garcia's men slipped past a small knoll and through the brush to circle the hill near Hays' men.[67]

Private Buqour, one of the two new members of Hays' ranger unit, later wrote of this encounter.

> While our command halted to consider the situation, the enemy performed a bit of strategy which was far from encouraging. They filed off to the left at the foot of a small knob and seemingly disappeared in the brush, but going around the hill repassed on their trail, making their number appear double what it really was.[68]

Some of Garcia's men took a position on the hill to cut off a possible retreat. The other bandits circled about and opened fire on the rangers. Some of Captain Pérez's Tejano rangers were unnerved, but Pérez gave a hasty pep talk to his men. He stated that he knew Garcia's men were not too plentiful and that ten well-armed rangers on the charge would send the entire enemy force to flight.

Hays then crossed a deep ravine to their left, and he ordered his men to dismount. They were within two hundred yards of the Mexican riders. The rangers tied their horses to a grove of Spanish persimmon trees, leaving five men as guards. The other twenty rangers moved right and left through the thick underbrush toward their opponents. Private Buquor later related the action that ensued.

> Being favored with a thick underbrush, we deployed right and left, right and left, from brush to brush until about 60 yards from the enemy, when we commenced firing. Being nearly all provided with Kentucky and Tennessee rifles, our shots were unerring.
>
> On the first fire, we killed two and wounded several, loading as we advanced. Upon nearing them, the cavalry and lancers, who were on foot and firing from behind their horses, got demoralized and commenced retreating, being soon followed by their citizen allies.[69]

Seizing their own horses, Hays and Pérez gave pursuit to the fleeing bandits. Mike Chevallie, one of the two new men of Hays' company, was reportedly thrown from his horse during the fight. Several of Garcia's rebels advanced upon him. Captain Hays and Nat Harbert charged forward and Hays shot the foremost Mexican who was preparing to kill Chevallie. The others fled, leaving Chevallie to scramble to safety.[70]

After running several hundred yards, Garcia's men made another attempt to rally. Hays' report relates this portion of the fight.

> We made a charge, and the enemy gave way; we mounted and pursued for a few hundred yards, when the enemy rallied, posted themselves, and again dismounted; we also dismounted at the distance of about one hundred yards, the enemy firing upon us continually; we instantly charged on foot.[71]

Bullets whizzed past Hays' men as they tied off their horses. The rangers charged hard into their midst, killing two more Mexicans in this advance. The balance of the men were forced to flee on foot. Only Captain Garcia and three of his men made their escape on horseback. Garcia, according to P. L. Buquor, "carried a bullet in the left cheek from my rifle. This man is still alive in Laredo."[72]

The Mexicans were in disarray. While Garcia fled with his three men, the others were encircled by Captain Hays' rangers. The Texans fired warning shots as the exhausted bandits decided on their next course of action. Garcia's other men apparently decided that enough was enough. They threw down their weapons, raised their hands, and began to call out for surrender terms in their best broken English.

Hays made no effort to slaughter these men, chosing to accept their surrender. His rangers moved about, collecting the Mexican weapons. "We took twenty-five prisoners with all their arms, ammunition," he wrote. His men also seized twenty-eight horses with their saddles, bridles, and other gear.

None of Hays and Pérez's rangers had been wounded. In return, Hays reported that they had killed three of Garcia's rebels and left another three severely wounded. "Several others were wounded early in the action and taken off." Buquor, later a mayor of San Antonio with a pulse on the Tejano community, would write that Garcia's rebels had ultimately suffered nine dead or wounded.

Captain Pérez's men were used to interrogate the prisoners as to the whereabouts of General Arista. One of the more intelligent prisoners, Eduardo Flores, whose father had sent the couriers to warn of the approach of Jack Hays, stated that Arista was near Matamoros with some 2,000 troops. "They were drying beef all over the country for a campaign," reported Hays, "said to be to operate against the Indians."[73]

Captain Garcia retreated to Laredo and excited the locals greatly with his news of death and terror from the rangers. The local alcalde rounded up several deputies and rode out to Hays' camp under a white flag. They asked that Laredo be spared from destruction. Hays informed the party that all he sought was for marauder leaders Agatón Quinoñes and Manuel Leal to be delivered to him. He also asked that traders going to and from San Antonio be offered protection.[74]

The alcalde assured Captain Hays that these conditions would be met, whereupon the rangers headed back for San Antonio. Hays left the alcalde (the town's chief administrator) with several of the prisoners, and took the remaining prisoners back to San Antonio. They arrived at Béxar on or before April 14, on which date Hays penned his official report of the Laredo fight to Secretary of War Archer. Their Mexican prisoners, including Eduardo Flores, were questioned and ultimately released.

Hays' tireless rangers would not go long without another challenge from the western banditos. By early May 1841, a Mexican force was reported to be within sixty miles of San Antonio, at the point where the Presidio del Rio Grande road crossed the Nueces River. This force was under frontier commander Calixto Bravo, whose force had reportedly been dispatched to pursue Captain Pérez's rangers on the western frontier. Bravo succeeded in uniting his forces with other small groups under Captain Menchaca, Captain Rodríquez, and Agatón Quinoñes, the latter being one of the two bandit leaders promised to be handed over by Laredo's alcalde.

Word of this Mexican force reached Captain Hays in San Antonio via a man dispatched by the Mexican command. This man portrayed himself as a poor trader who was afraid of being robbed. He went to Hays and explained that he knew of a large Mexican force lying in wait beyond San Antonio which would attack him. Hays later wrote that this man had been sent "for the purpose of luring" his rangers into an ambush.[75]

The combined Mexican force numbered between one and two hundred men. The local San Antonio merchants felt that this force must be attacked. They furnished supplies to the rangers who prepared to head out. Undaunted by the possibility of an ambush, Jack Hays mobilized his forces and rode out west from San Antonio to meet this force.

Before leaving the city, however, a young Mexican came to him and expressed his suspicions that this trader was nothing more than a spy, and he endeavored to dissuade Hays from proceeding. The young man, perceiving however that the Capt. was determined to go, went to the pretended trader and told him that he had nothing to fear—that Hays would soon be joined by one hundred men from Gonzales, which would enable him to extend all the protection he sought.

According to Hays' account, the Mexican "trader" then departed "in great haste" to spread the word that the rangers were mobilizing. This messenger was followed closely by Hays and a party of forty men, likely including Captain Pérez's rangers.

The Mexican forces under Bravo had attacked a small party of traders bound for the Rio Grande days before. Tailing the trader who had visited San Antonio, Captain Hays' party suddenly came upon the superior Mexican force. With tired horses and little chance of winning a heated fight, Hays ordered his men to charge upon the Mexicans as though he was leading an army.

The ruse worked in sending the Mexican robbers to flight. The Mexican leaders had been warned by their informant that Hays was leading "a hundred and forty men," although the Gonzales company had, of course, never joined Hays' forty men. The Mexicans fled toward the Rio Grande, with Hays' rangers dogging them in their steps "nearly to the Rio Grande."

It may be well that his forty men did not catch up with the Mexicans for a real fight, for they would have been outnumbered by at least three or four-to-one. The rangers returned to San Antonio by May 10, on which date Captain Hays disbanded his "company of spies." He filled out his unit's muster roll in San Antonio on May 12. He was gratified that the townspeople "rejoiced" the safe return of his men.[76]

Antonio Pérez disbanded his company on May 20, 1841, exactly four months after they had commenced service. The

Telegraph and Texas Register of May 22 reported that the Mexican bandits pursued by Hays and Pérez may have numbered as many as three hundred.[77]

CHAPTER 9

The Lewis Expedition

April 8–May, 1841

Captain Chandler's Minutemen

Although George Dolson's Travis County Minutemen had been the first new county rangers to find a fight, it was the Robertson County Minutemen who would most consistently find action during 1841. The commander, Captain Eli Chandler, was an old-timer in the ranging system. He had served with Captain Sterling Robertson's January 1836 ranging company in Robertson's Colony and had briefly served with Captain John Pierson's cavalry company that same summer.

Chandler's rangers were based out of the old settlement of Franklin, which was the original county seat of Robertson County. This was the northernmost town between the Brazos and Trinity rivers during its early existence. The town's blockhouse, Fort Franklin, was fortified with a brass, four-pound cannon supplied by the Lamar administration in March 1839.[1]

The Robertson County Minute Men were organized on March 29, one day after Captain Dolson had organized his minutemen in Travis County. Captain Chandler could proudly count some of the ablest rangers of Texas among his minutemen. His first lieutenant, William M. Love, had fought with Captain Harrison's mounted riflemen in the 1839 Cherokee War and had narrowly missed the deadly Surveyors Fight of 1838 when he returned to fix a faulty compass. Chandler's second lieutenant, John Marlin, was a trusted scout who had been involved with the Texas Rangers since Major Williamson's 1836 battalion.

Capt. Chandler's Robertson County Minutemen: April 4–18, 1841

Captain:	Joseph Leal
Eli Chandler	Hugh Lockemy
First Lieutenant:	Andrew C. Love
William M. Love	Samuel Wilson Marlin
Second Lieutenant:	Joseph Mather
John Marlin	James D. Matthews
Orderly Sergeant:	Robert E. Matthews
John F. Adams	Hardin R. McGrew
	James L. McMaury
Privates:	Edward McMullin
Charles Beasley	Memnon A. Mitchell
Daniel Boone Jr.	Charles W. Nanny
Mordecai Boone	William W. Patrick
A. G. Braden	L. Baker Pendergrast
William Buttrell	Robert H. Porter
Harvey Capps	Elijah Powers
John Casey	Charles H. Raymond
John Chandler	William W. Reed
William Cox	William W. Roberts
Green B. Duncan	Eli Seale
Thomas Duncan	David Sealy
Jesse Ellison	Charles Sevier
John A. Gilbreath	Robert Steele
John Graham	John L. Strother
Moses Griffin	Thomas Sypert
John Hardisty	Neri Vanzant *
James A. Head	Charles Welsh
George W. Heard	Harrison York
George W. Hill	
James W. Hill	* Joined April 14.
John Kerner	Source: Minuteman Pay and Muster
Miles King	Rolls, Texas State Library and Archives
Aaron Kitchell	Division.
James Lane	

Three other members, James A. Head, Eli Seale, and James D. Matthews, had previously commanded their own ranger companies. Also among Chandler's muster roll were Daniel Boone Jr. and Mordecai Boone, relatives of the famous frontiersman Daniel Boone.

On the evening of April 1, Captain Chandler received intelligence that Indians had attacked and killed Stephen Rogers Jr.

and stolen eight of his horses. Rogers was a resident who lived on the east side of the Navasota River.

Chandler immediately collected twenty-five of his men and set out on "a forced march" in pursuit of the depredating Indians. The Franklin-based rangers moved east of the Navasota and spotted the Indians about 11:00 a.m. on April 11. They were about two miles ahead of Chandler's men, driving the stolen horses.

In his official report to Branch Archer of April 16, Eli Chandler details his expedition.

> I immediately gave chase at full speed for the distance of seven miles, and was enabled to recover all of the horses back, and take one from the enemy.
>
> I am sorry to say that, from the jaded situation of our horses, and the start which they had, they were able to elude us. While we must regret their escape, it affords me pleasure, that from the perseverance manifested on the march, and in the chase, by every man under my command, to believe that nothing is wanting, on the part of this command, but a fair opportunity, to sustain that character for chivalry, which is always anticipated from Texan citizens.[2]

Captain Chandler's minutemen were back in Franklin by April 16 with the recovered horses.

By nature of the minutemen, his company could not be paid for more than 15 straight days of service, so his first expedition was officially ended on April 18 on his muster roll. Captain Chandler's pay roll, however, shows that his rangers were only paid from April 10 through April 16, the day they returned to Franklin. Each man, from the lowest private to the captain in command, was paid $7 per day for protecting Robertson County.

Ben McCulloch's Fights: Early May 1841

Late in April 1841, a party of twenty-two Indians made a night raid into and around Gonzales. They captured a considerable number of horses and were en route back to their mountain homes before daylight.

Capt. McCulloch's Volunteers: Early May 1841	
Captain: Benjamin McCulloch	Henry Eustace McCulloch Alsey Silvanus Miller William Morrison
Privates: James Hughes Callahan Archibald Gibson William Anderson Hall Eli T. Hankins Clement Hinds William P. Kincannon Green McCoy	Thomas R. Nichols Wilson Randle James B. Roberts Jeremiah Roberts Arthur Swift William Tumlinson Source: Brown, *Indian Wars and Pioneers of Texas*, 84.

Ben McCulloch called for volunteers to help him. Instead of rapidly pursuing the fleeing force, he preferred to wait a few days for them to drop their guard. He hoped to follow their trail after waiting for the Indians' own scouts to feel more relaxed that the weak Texans were not following them.[3]

Among his sixteen volunteers was his brother Henry, ever-present at his side for battles. There was Green McCoy, who as a teenager had fought with George Erath at Elm Creek in 1837. There was also James Hughes Callahan, who often commanded the Gonzales area minutemen. Callahan had already been made captain of the Gonzales County Minutemen, based out of Seguin, on April 7. It is possible he was in Gonzales recruiting for his company at the time that McCulloch pulled together his party of men.

Along with Callahan, the pursuit group led by Ben McCulloch included five other Gonzales County Minutemen. McCulloch's men found the Indian trail where it crossed the San Marcos River at the mouth of Mule Creek. They followed it northwestwardly up and to the head of York's Creek. The trail then led the seventeen men through the hill country to the Guadalupe and then up that river to what is now known in Kerr County as "Johnson's Fork," the principal mountain tributary to the Guadalupe on the north side. The trail was followed along this fork to its source, and thence northwestwardly to the head of another "Johnson's Fork"—this one of the Llano (located in present Kimble County)—and down this to its junction with the Llano River.[4]

Before reaching the junction with the Llano, Captain McCulloch halted his men in a secluded area. He was confident that he was near the Indians' encampment. Leaving his company, he made a reconnaissance of their position. McCulloch scouted out the Indians and then silently led his men back to their camp, with plans to surprise them at daylight.

At first light, the Texans took the Indians under fire and achieved total surprise. They killed five Indians, who were left dead on the ground. Half of those remaining were wounded. Of twenty-two Indians, only about eight escaped unhurt. The original party of twenty-two may well have been joined by others since their raid on Gonzales, so the total number was uncertain.

In their flight, the Indians left everything except for their firearms. McCulloch's men found horses, saddles, camp equipage, blankets, robes, and even the Indians' moccasins. This bold raid certainly came as a warning to the Comanches to not let down their guard, even in their own territory.[5]

The fact that McCulloch led this hasty offensive is supported by several historians. Why Captain Callahan did not take command is a little perplexing. Again, perhaps he was recruiting for his new company and time did not allow him to rush back to Gonzales to gather all of his men. In any event, muster rolls for the new Gonzales County Minutemen show the unit to have organized on April 7, 1841. They did not, however, make their first expedition until May 7.

It is very likely that Callahan returned to Gonzales, gathered his complete company of minutemen, and then began scouting for more hostile Indians.

Chandler's Wise County Expedition: May 21, 1841

Eli Chandler's Robertson County Minutemen were vigilant in pursuing reports of hostile Indians. In mid-April, they had successfully recovered stolen horses from one band east of the Navasota. Things were relatively quiet around their post at Fort Franklin until news came in on May 16.

The main company had not been active since April 16. By law, Chandler could employ up to five spies on patrol while the regular company sat idle. On April 28, he had sent out William

Cox, John Graham, Charles Sevier, Neri Vanzant, and Harrison York as his spies.

On May 16, several of Captain Chandler's spies brought in intelligence of a large Indian camp near the present Dallas–Fort Worth area. A large surveying expedition under Capt. Thomas I. Smith and Barzillai J. Chambers, who had settled in Robertson County in 1837, was working the northern areas of Texas and had happened upon a large body of Indians on Pecan Creek, a tributary of the Trinity River. This location was more than one hundred miles north of Chandler's ranger station at Franklin in Robertson County. Pecan Creek is located in present Wise County, just west of present Decatur and north of Fort Worth.[6]

Smith and Chambers dispatched two of their surveyors, John Hardisty and Robert Porter, to inform Chandler (the nearest ranger commander) of the Indians' location. These two men were members of the Robertson County Minutemen.

According to his pay roll, Chandler immediately set out from Franklin on May 17 with forty-nine men of his command to make their second expedition. The rangers were joined by eight volunteers: Thomas I. Smith, Mr. Branch (of Milam County), Barzillai Chambers, Clinton M. Winkler, John Copeland, Fountain Flint, and M. M. Ferguson. With these Franklin-area surveyors as volunteers, Chandler's posse numbered fifty-seven.

The unit moved northward toward present Fort Worth over the next few days. By travelling all night on May 19, Captain Chandler was able to reach the area on Pecan Creek by morning of May 20 where the Indians had been reported.

> Believing we had not been discovered, I concealed my men, and dispatched reconnoitering parties, which resulted in Lt. Love's reporting his having found, down the creek a few miles, a deserted village, which had been visited within a few days by the enemy. But the lateness of the hour induced me to remain until the dawn of the next morning; at which time we took up the line of march for the deserted village.

The Texans moved toward the deserted village on May 21. After having proceeded about five miles through Wise County, Chandler's rangers suddenly spotted about eight to ten Indians (believed to be largely Wacos) some three hundred yards ahead. These Indians were pursued for three miles. Captain Chandler later discovered that they wisely led him away from their own village during the chase. "By their superior knowledge of the woods, they evaded us," wrote Chandler.

The rangers returned to the deserted village that had been discovered the previous day. They counted twenty-eight Indian lodges. More importantly, they found a good trail, which they could track. At the distance of one mile from the deserted camp, Chandler's men struck the Indian party again, on the same trail.

Chandler immediately ordered all of his men to charge at full speed. The path the Indians were following was treacherous in this area. It ran up on a ridge, which was no more than four hundred yards wide. The ridge was elevated and along each of its edges ran a creek, both running almost parallel to each other. On the opposite side of each creek ran extended bottomlands which were so densely packed with underbrush that Captain Chandler deemed them impossible for horsemen to penetrate.

The only chance was to give the Indians a fight on the open ridge before they could flee into the thickets. The rangers pursued them for five miles, but were unable to overtake the Indians before they had run right upon yet another Indian village.

The wild chase continued right on through the Indian camp, where frightened women and children scattered for safety. The Indians ahead fled before the rangers could get within gunshot range. Chandler found that they fled into "almost impenetrable thickets, abandoning every vestige of their property."

Chandler ordered Lieutenant William Love to stay with a detachment of seven men at the Indian village to watch the baggage and pack mules. Lieutenant Love's detail included volunteer Thomas Smith and rangers John L. Strother, Aaron Kitchell, and Neri Vanzant.[7]

During Chandler's absence, Love's men had a brush with Indians. They were approached by a large body of Indians and were forced to fall back to a ravine for protection. They could only hope to defend themselves, as the nearby terrain made escape impossible. The Indians surrounded the baggage and supplies, where their chief spoke before his men. Watching from their ravine, Vanzant "carried the largest rifle of any of the men" and determined that he would shoot the chief. With Strother helping him to steady his rifle against a small bush, Vanzant fired and dropped the chief.

In the ensuing fighting, Captain Thomas Smith, leader of the former surveying expedition, was slightly wounded in the hand. In return, Lieutenant Love's party claimed to have killed three and wounded several of the Indians who fired upon them.[8]

Captain Chandler and another detachment of his men had dismounted and left their horses with Love's men. Chandler took his men to search into the bottomlands across the creek from the hastily abandoned village. They succeeded in collecting some property. In the course of his scouting, Chandler's party traded shots with Indians several times. He claimed that his men returned the shots "with effect."

The rangers plundered the Indian village and took all that they could, including nine mules, twenty-three horses, powder, lead, axes, peltry—all of which Chandler estimated at $3,000 value. The rangers then destroyed anything that was deemed useful to the Indians and set fire to the lodges of the village.

The volunteers and rangers moved out for home with all that they could haul. The return trip was four days, but proved uneventful. The men reached Fort Franklin on the night of May 25, 1841, with only Thomas Smith being slightly injured from the whole expedition. In his report, Captain Chandler complimented his rangers on their performance. As for the surveyors who had sent him the intelligence and who had volunteered to go out on the expedition with him: "Too much praise cannot be given to those gentlemen."

Captain Lewis' Expedition: Late May 1841

While Eli Chandler's busy Robertson County Minutemen were chasing Wacos in Wise County, the veteran Captain Mark Lewis—a former Frontier Regiment captain and veteran of the 1839 Cherokee War—was leading a volunteer expedition from the Austin area. They were pursuing raiding Indians toward Mexico.

More than 130 Texans, including Major George T. Howard, went on this six-week foray. Lewis' expedition included two volunteer Texan companies, as well as Chief Flacco and twenty of his Lipan Indians. Captain James Dunn headed the small Victoria

Captain Thomas Green (1814–1862), a San Jacinto artillery veteran, commanded a volunteer company on Major Lewis' 1841 Indian expedition. Killed while serving as a general in the Civil War, he is the namesake of Tom Green County, Texas. *Texas State Library & Archives Commission, 1905/9-1.*

Cicero Rufus Perry (1822–1898) was a member of Green's unit. Perry was a veteran of the 1835 Béxar seige, Captain William Hill's 1836 ranger company, and had been wounded while on Colonel John Henry Moore's 1839 ranger expedition. *Author's collection.*

Company. His second-in-command, Lieutenant Anson G. Neal, had previously served as a second lieutenant and assistant quartermaster for the Texas Army during 1836-1837. Private Joseph Sovereign, a native of Portugal, was a veteran of the battle of San Jacinto. Serving as adjutant of the expedition was Captain William Bugg, who had briefly commanded the Victoria area company for two days.[9]

The other volunteer company, known as the "Fayette Volunteers," was headed by Captain Thomas Green, another San Jacinto veteran who had helped man the Twin Sisters cannon. Green, for whom Tom Green County would later be named, was second in command under Major Lewis.

Green's company included such veteran rangers as Rufus Perry and Dewitt C. Lyons, who had made his first ranger expedition in 1835. Captain Green recorded that Lyons "was enrolled on the 20th day of March last to serve in a campaign against the Indians." In the service papers of First Sergeant James P. Longly, Green recorded that his company was "on the campaign of 1841 against the hostile Indians up the Colorado and Concho."[10]

Major Lewis' Expedition
March 20–June 4, 1841

Expedition Field and Staff

Mark L. Lewis	Major, Commanding
George Thomas Howard	Major
Capt. William Bugg	Adjutant
Joseph H. Rogers	Quartermaster

Capt. Green's Mounted Riflemen: March 20–June 4, 1841

Captain:
Thomas Green
First Lieutenant:
Robert Addison Gillespie
Second Lieutenant:
Griffith H. Jones
Orderly Sergeant:
James P. Longly

Privates:
Isaac Allen
Truman B. Beck
Claudius Buster
William Custard
Campbell Davis
Harvey Hall
Milvern Harrell

Stephen A. J. Haynie
Thomas H. Hord
E. P. Howland
Richard H. Keene
James Morrow
Cicero Rufus Perry
Alexander G. Peyton
Andrew J. Peyton
William F. Powell
Marcus L. B. Raper
Wilson Simpson
Francis R. Tannehill
Frederick Vogle

Source: Author's research of audited military claims.

Capt. Dunn's Victoria Company: March 14–June 5, 1841

Captain:
James Dunn
First Lieutenant:
Anson G. Neal

Privates:
J. W. Brown
L. J. Irwin
William W. Moore

M. Parker
Micajah Puckett
Joseph Sovereign
Thomas J. Wheeler
Jacob Zingerle

Source: Partial roster based on author's research of audited military claims.

Chief Flacco's Lipan Scouts: March 20–June 4, 1841

Twenty of Flacco's Lipan Apaches accompanied Major Lewis' expedition to serve as scouts, although no muster roll of their names has survived.

Lieutenant Newcomb's Travis County Minutemen

First Lieutenant:
James W. Newcomb [1]
Second Lieutenant:
James Ogden Rice

Privates:
Colden Denman [2]
John W. Ladd
David Patterson
Henry Rinehart

[1] Newcomb led the company after Captain Dolson was wounded on March 31. His spies operated from Austin continually through September 6, 1841.
[2] Volunteer who served under Newcomb for this expedition per Colden Denman PD, R 149, F 85.

Source: Service dates from Minutemen Muster Rolls and Pay Rolls, Texas State Archives.

Captain Green and his second lieutenant, Griffith H. Jones, later testified that Colden Denman served under "Captain James Newcomb" on Lewis' 1841 expedition. Newcomb was, of course, the first lieutenant and acting commander of Captain Dolson's Travis County Minutemen at this time. "Colden Denman was a soldier in the spy company commanded by Capt. James Newcomb in the year 1841, in an expedition against the Indians under the command of Maj. Mark Lewis," Green and Jones affirmed.[11]

Denman was assigned to Lieutenant Newcomb's spy unit from Captain Murry's company for this expedition. Pay rolls and muster rolls for the Travis County Minutemen show James Newcomb and four of his spies to have been in continual operation in the field from late March through September 6, 1841, although little idea of their specific actions is given.

The expedition prepared itself at Austin, the capital town which had grown to more than 1,200 citizens by early 1841. *Texas Sentinel* editor George W. Bonnell wrote in the March 25 edition that leader Mark Lewis "has the right sort of boys—real buck-skin hawk-eyed fellows, who would as soon sleep in a creek as not."[12]

Major Lewis moved out from Austin in the direction of Chihuahua, following the Colorado River far beyond its settlements. They continued to the San Saba River, where he sent his first report to Secretary of War Archer.[13]

After that time in late May, Captain Lewis was undecided whether to leave the Nueces River area and Rio Frio entirely (south of San Antonio in present McMullen County) and to move in "the direction of the Moras." Las Moras Creek is a tributary of the San Saba River. His other dilemma was whether to instead occupy the passes between the headwaters of the San Saba River and its intersecting streams, while detaching his volunteers into small pursuit parties.

The Indians, by all evidence, had broken up their camps and scattered. Lewis figured this was "either for the purpose of finding game more plentifully, or of eluding pursuit."

Veteran ranger Cicero Rufus Perry was among Mark Lewis' volunteers on this expedition into far western Texas. "We started to Chihuahua but did not get farther than the head of the Colorado," he wrote. "We then turned back by the head of the Concho thence to San Saba, Llano, then to the Nueces."[14]

Lewis decided to occupy the main passes between the headwaters of the San Saba and its adjoining streams. He noted that there were smoke signals and trails from many hunting parties "passing through the country in various directions." He felt that it would be impossible to intercept a significant force of the scattered Indian bands. It would therefore be a waste of his men to keep them all gathered together to attack each small band of Indians at one point. Lewis thus split his forces about May 18.

The Lipan scouts accompanying Captain Lewis' force were sent to the head of the Llano River (spelled phonetically as "Yano" by Lewis) to search for fresh Indian trails in that direction. The Lipans returned with intelligence that they had found a small party of Comanches near "the Road."

Captain William Bugg was ordered on May 20 to take twenty men and go in pursuit of these Comanches. His force soon came upon this band and killed three of them. Among those going out with Bugg was Rufus Perry, who was acting as an interpreter for Major Lewis.

> We struck one party of Indians between San Saba to Llano. We killed all the bunch there was. The first Indian I ever scalped and the last, I promised Miss Elisor Haynie to bring her a scalp. Her brother Jack [Haynie] was with me when I shot the buck down. He fell as though he was dead, and we thought he was, but when I went to raise his top knot, he raised with me. I tell [you] we had a lively time for a while until old Butch got the best of him.[15]

On the same day, May 20, Lieutenant Gillespie was detached with ten men in pursuit of another Indian party. He came upon them, but these Indians hastily abandoned their horses and fled into the cedar brakes and mountains. Gillespie's party returned without killing any Indians.

Captain Green took twenty men and four Lipan scouts on the following day, May 21, and commenced pursuit of a party of Indians whose trail Green's men had discovered. They followed this trail for an estimated sixty miles. Forty of these miles were over rugged mountainous area where the volunteers had no water. Green's force overtook the Indians in the valley of the Nueces River. The Indians discovered Green's men in time to make good on their escape. One Indian was killed by the Texans before he could flee.[16]

Captain Lewis "lost no time in examining the country for other parties, and in the evening of the same day, killed another Indian and captured a prisoner." Lewis' group was led by young Flacco, the Lipan guide. Rufus Perry later stated that Lewis' command "struck a trail and followed them to the Nueces." In addition to capturing the Indians' camp equipage, they also "took one squaw." According to Perry, the Lipans took liberties with their female prisoner and even offered two of the Texan volunteers a turn, which was declined.

> The way the friendly Indians did to keep her was to sleep with her, each one every night as their time. Young Flacco told me to tell Colonel Lewis that he and me could sleep with her when they all went around, as he was commander and I interpreter, but we did not, but let them have her to themselves.[17]

Reporters of the Republic era often speculated that female captives of the Comanches were raped, regardless of whether the victims made such reports. In this instance, the Lipans were obviously more barbaric than the Comanches.[18]

Lewis and his fellow commanders found the pursuit impossible to wipe out an entire band of Indians. Those who escaped from each encounter with the Texan volunteers quickly had smoke signals "rising in every direction." With such alarm spread through the area, Lewis found further pursuit of the Indians to be fruitless. On May 21, Lewis' volunteer expedition thus turned to march back for San Antonio from the Nueces River.

About twenty miles above the Presidio Road on the Nueces, a trail was found by the Lipans. It appeared to have been made by three or four hundred horses, and was judged by the scouts to be about fifteen days old. Captain Lewis wrote:

> It was my impression, from the size of the trail, and its course when first discovered, that a large body of Comanches had concentrated for the purpose of attacking the settlements on the San Antonio, but upon following it to their first camp on the river, it was ascertained to be a body of Cherokees.
>
> Their route continuing down the east bank of the river, induced the impression that it was their intention, either to unite with a party of marauding Mexicans, which have for some months past infested the main road from the Rio Grande to San Antonio, or make a descent upon the frontier, at some point least protected.[19]

Lewis' party decided to make a forced march to try and catch up. Upon moving a short distance down the trail, however, the Lipan guides reported the Indians to have crossed over the San Antonio River and to have gone in the direction of Presidio. From some Mexicans residing around San Antonio, Captain Lewis learned that this Indian force had reached Presidio about mid-May. "From the size of their camp, there must have been about two hundred & fifty men, women and children," wrote Lewis.

Lewis' men returned to San Antonio, where they heard numerous reports of Indians being in that vicinity. His men spent the next few days following up on these various reports before moving against anyone in particular. John Twohig, an Irish store-keeper and 1835 Béxar siege veteran, furnished flour, salt, coffee, and sugar for the men under Major Lewis when they appeared "out of provisions on his arrival at San Antonio."[20]

On the evening of May 28, a force of sixty to eighty Indians appeared near San Antonio and killed a Mexican citizen and drove off some cattle. "As little time as possible was lost in collecting volunteers," Lewis related. Mark Lewis apparently did not join this pursuit party from the style of his writing. He was in Austin on June 2, where he wrote a report of his most recent expedition to Branch Archer. According to Rufus Perry, the volunteer pursuit party was organized by Edward Burleson during June 1841 to chase after these raiders.

> I then as soon as I got home started with Ed Burleson on an expedition against Indians, found but one party, ran them thirty miles, but could not catch up with them. We was out [for] one month.[21]

Major George Howard joined Burleson with his own company of citizen volunteers and the forces moved out from San Antonio. Captain Tom Green had immediately gone out with his company to the Leon River to check the movement of this band until the others could arrive. Major Howard and Captain Green pursued these Indian raiders with a fury.

They moved in so close that the Indians finally killed most of their own horses and fled into the bottomlands of the nearby creeks, thus eluding further pursuit. "We got after them and ran them about twenty miles and made them drop the cattle, but did not get close enough to kill any of them," recalled Rufus Perry.[22]

Ranger and Minuteman Companies of 1841

County Minuteman Companies

County	Captain	Service Period
Béxar	John Coffee Hays	June 1–October 1, 1841
Fannin	Joseph Sowell	July 6–Sept. 26, 1841
Gonzales	James H. Callahan	May 7–Dec. 20, 1841
Houston	William C. Brookfield	June 19–July 1, 1841
Lamar	Mansell W. Matthews	June 1–Sept. 27, 1841
Milam	George B. Erath	March 9–Dec. 24, 1841
Montgomery	Thomas N. B. Greer	April 10–Oct. 7, 1841
Nacogdoches	David Gage	April 12–Oct. 19, 1841
Paschal	Joseph D. Lilly	June 12–Nov. 31, 1841
Red River	William Becknell	June 25, '41–June 25, '42
Refugio	John R. Baker	Oct. 25–Dec. 12, 1841
	John McDaniel	Dec. 16, '41–Feb. 24, '42
Robertson	Eli Chandler	March 29–Nov. 5, 1841
San Patricio	Alanson T. Miles	May 14–Aug. 25, 1841
	William J. Cairnes	Aug. 29–Nov. 12, 1841
Travis	George M. Dolson	March 28–Dec. 28, 1841
Victoria	Adam Zumwalt	May–December, 1841
	Charles N. Creaner	July–August, 1841

Note: Five other Texas counties (Bastrop, Bowie, Goliad, Harrison, and Panola) were approved to organize minutemen companies in 1841, but there are no records to indicate that formed a company.

Ranger and Spy Companies

Base	Captain	Service Period
San Antonio	John Coffee Hays	Jan. 10–May 10, 1841
San Antonio	Antonio Pérez	Jan. 10–May 20, 1841
Victoria	John T. Price	Jan. 3–May 2, 1841
Travis Guards	Joseph Daniels	Jan. 23–December, 1841
Robertson Co.	Samuel B. Killough	Jan. 25–March 5, 1841
San Patricio	James P. Ownby	May 18–June 6, 1841
Bird's Fort	Alexander W. Webb	Sept. 9, '41–Mar. 19, '42
Western Spies	William J. Cairnes	Nov. 12, '41–Feb. 12, '42

CHAPTER 10

The Village Creek Expedition

May 4–30, 1841

Tarrant's Expedition: May–June 1841

The present Dallas-Fort Worth metroplex area was a hotbed of Indian expeditions conducted by militia and ranger forces during 1841. General Morehouse's early spring expedition to the Trinity was soon followed up by another large militia force from the Red River settlements under General Edward H. Tarrant.

A noted lawyer who had settled in the present Bowie County area, Tarrant had replaced General John Dyer as the northern Texas commander of the Fourth Militia Brigade of the Texas Militia. His regional headquarters was in Clarksville in Red River County. He was eager to take to the field to counter depredations against the settlers by the northern Indians living in the area of present Fort Worth. In March, John Yeary's home in Fannin County had been attacked. He had been badly beaten, but had fought off his attackers.

Shortly after the attack on the Yeary family, General Tarrant received word of another Indian depredation in his district. This occurred on April 10, 1841, against the Ambrose Ripley family, who had settled in 1837 on Ripley Creek in what later became Titus County, northwest of Mt. Pleasant near the Red River. Ripley had furnished corn to General Dyer's Fourth Brigade militiamen who operated in the field during 1839.[1]

While Ambrose Ripley was absent on April 10, his family was attacked during the daytime by a band of hostile Indians. His

235

twenty-year-old son was killed first while plowing in the field. Ripley's wife, Rachel Wood Ripley, his older daughter, and four small children were shot and killed. After plundering the house, the Indians set it afire and burned an infant child to death. Only two daughters managed to escaped into the cane fields to tell the horrible story to other settlers.[2]

Captain William Stout, often in command of ranger forces in the Red River area during the Republic years, later wrote of the Ripley depredation.

> Two of the family only escaped, a girl about 15, and one 10 years. They were pursued by the Indians, but outrunning them, they reached a neighbor's house, when their pursuer stopped. He had fired at them at the commencement of the chase, which was about 2 miles.
>
> The youngest girl was so stiffened up by the great effort she made in running that she was not able to walk for several days.[3]

Charles Black and Charles S. Stewart, who heard the word from the surviving Ripley daughters, led a hastily gathered group of volunteer citizens in pursuit of this band of Indians. They met a group of Indians near the Sulphur River and attacked them, killing several.[4]

News of the Ripley family murders spread throughout the Red River settlements and General Tarrant's Fourth Militia Brigade. Tarrant, according to acting brigade inspector William N. Porter, "determined, with the small number of 69 men, if possible, to find the Indians and attack them."[5]

Although the northern Texas settlements along the Red River area were thinly populated, the citizens determined to put together a retaliatory expedition. According to the notes of John M. Watson, the volunteers rendezvoused on May 4, 1841, on Choctaw Bayou, eight miles west of what became known as Old Warren. This settlement was located on the western fringe of settlement in Fannin County near the Red River. On the following morning, they elected Captain James Bourland, who had led a group of Red River volunteers in an 1838 Indian fight. The other key officers elected were First Lieutenant William C. Young, Second Lieutenant Samuel Johnson, and Orderly Sergeant

Lemuel M. Cochran. Veteran Indian fighters John B. Denton and Henry Stout were each placed in charge of a few men who would serve as scouts.[6]

The rate of pay was $75 per month for Captain Bourland, $60 per month for Lieutenant Young, $40 per month for Sergeant Cochran, and $35 per month for the privates.[7]

According to Fannin County chronicler J.P. Simpson, Tarrant gathered volunteers from Red River, Bowie, Lamar, and Fannin counties. Henry Stout claimed that the expedition was because of recent depredations. Stout said that Tarrant did not order the men out, but that they volunteered, and Tarrant joined their number as a private.

> We met among ourselves and elected Bo[urland] our Captain. Tarrant felt slighted, but wanted to come along, and offered to serve under anyone we would elect . . .We met eight miles north of Clarksville and formed our company.[8]

By Stout's count, there were about seventy men. Dr. Cochran later stated that there were eighty men. The higher number is likely correct, as some men would later leave the expedition. A combination of those men who reportedly joined the expedition only during its early days and those whose service was later affirmed through public debt papers brings the initial volunteer count to ninety-three men.[9]

Many of the men were from near Fulton's Ferry on the Red River and from Coffee's trading post. Among the volunteers was the muscular John Yeary, who had fought Indians hand-to-hand in March when they had attacked his Fannin County homestead. Many of Bourland's men were veterans of previous Indian battles, including the Cherokee War of 1839. Garrett Pangburn and George Dugan were veterans of Lieutenant Colonel Daniel Montague's 1838 Sloan-Journey ranger battalion.

Captain Bourland's company moved to the vacant barracks of Fort Johnston in Fannin County to further organize. This fort had been built by Colonel Cooke's First Regiment during December 1840 and abandoned in April 1841. It was located four miles north of present Pottsboro in Grayson County, but the location is now below the waters of Lake Texoma.[10]

Village Creek Expedition
General Edward H. Tarrant, Commanding

Captain:
James Bourland [1]
First Lieutenant:
William C. Young
Second Lieutenant:
Samuel Johnson
First Sergeant:
Lemuel M. Cochran
Second Sergeant:
McQuery H. Wright

Privates:
Daniel Adams
Josiah Ashley
Hiram Baker [1]
William R. Baker
John Baldwin
James Beatty
Jonathan Bird
John Mack Bourland
William H. Bourland
Thomas Wade Box
Wiley B. Brigham
Samuel Burke
William C. Chisum
Andrew Clark
Jimmy Clifton
Cal Coffee
Holland Coffee [3]
John H. Collum [1]
Silas C. Colville [3]
Thomas Cousins
Alfonzo Crowder
James Crowder
Andrew Davis [2]
John Bunyan Denton [4]
James Dillingham
John C. "Jack" Dolby
J.N. Dornstein
George Dugan

Elbert Early
Alsey Fuller
Mabel Gilbert
José María Gonzáles
John Griffin
William G. Grinder [1]
Joseph C. Guest
William Hemphill
Richard Hopkins [2]
Henry Hunt
Edward Hunter [1]
John Hunter
James Isham
John Ivey
Lindley Johnson
John Kimbell
Lee Langford
John L. Lovejoy [2]
Jackson McFarland
Albert Madden
Robert L. Matthews
Wiley B. Merrell
Daniel Montague
Samuel Moss
John D. Nelson [1]
William J. Norris
James R. O'Neal
Garrett Pangburn [1]
Nathan Parker
William Patton
Nathan Petty
John D. Pickens
William N. Porter
William Pulliam
Littleton Rattan
John Rattan
W. Hampton Rattan
Caswell Russwell
Randolph Scott
Frank Sharp

Joshua B. Sharpless [1]
Eli J. Shelton
C. C. Simmons
Samuel Sims
Phillip Smith
William Snider
Joseph Spence
Ira Stanley
James G. Stevens
Henry B. Stout
Calvin Sullivan
Edward H. Tarrant
David Waggoner [1]
Ansen Walden
Green Walden [1]
William Walden
Jefferson Wallace
William A. Wallace [3]
John M. Watson
Alexander W. Webb
Thomas Westback
Thomas B. Westbrook
Daniel Williams
David Williams
Lewis Williams
John D. Wilson [1]
John Yeary

[1] Service affirmed by William C. Young and Captain James Bourland in Samuel Burk PD, R 141, F 334–362.
[2] Per Andrew Davis' account.
[3] Departed expedition prior to Village Creek battle.
[4] John Bunard Denton per some sources.

Key source: James Bourland PD, R 138, F 560–709.

The company remained posted at Fort Johnston for several days as volunteers returned from various assignments. Finally, the expedition departed Fort Johnston on May 14, 1841.[10]

When the expedition departed, they had been joined by Jack Ivey, a man of mixed Indian and African descent, who would serve as their pilot. Ivey led the men out on the old Chihuahua trail, which led on toward Natchitoches, Louisiana, to the east. Bearing west, they were also accompanied for some time by Holland Coffee, William A. A. "Big Foot" Wallace, Silas C. Colvile, and seven other men. At some point in the march, however, Coffee, Wallace, and the other eight men left the expedition and returned to Coffee's trading post north of Fort Johnston. This group of men detaching likely led to the disparity in expedition numbers later given by Dr. Cochran and Henry Stout.[11]

The company marched westward for five days, bearing to the south toward the West Fork of the Trinity. From the Denison area of present Grayson County, they moved southwesterly into present Cooke County, passing where Gainesville now stands. They passed through the lower Cross Timbers in a southwesterly direction that progressed them toward present Wise County.

On May 18, "we entered the upper Cross Timbers and changed our direction a little more south," wrote William Porter. "On the 19th, we discovered tolerable fresh sign—we had every reason to believe there were Indians in the vicinity."[12]

On the main West Fork of the Trinity, the expedition discovered two Indian villages, "which we found to be deserted." According to Porter, "The Indians at some previous time had cultivated corn at these villages. There were some sixty or seventy lodges in these two villages." Henry Stout recalled, "We went where the old Keechi village was in Wise County, and went in the night to Bridgeport on the Trinity, and found that the village had been deserted."[13]

According to Porter:

> General Tarrant deemed it imprudent to burn the villages, for fear of giving alarm to the Indians. From such elevated positions, the smoke could have been seen for many miles. But they were, in a great measure, destroyed with our axes.[14]

From the present Bridgeport area of Wise County, Bourland's men moved south and east from near the Jack County line following the West Fork of the Trinity for some distance through Wise County. On May 21, they crossed the high divide and camped that night on the most eastern branch of the Brazos River. Little did Tarrant's men know that Captain Eli Chandler's Robertson County Minutemen were also in the Wise County area on May 21 engaging Indians.

Having discovered no sign of Indians, Tarrant changed his course to the east. His men marched until they again struck the Trinity River, "intending to scour the western branch to its mouth."[15]

Henry Stout says that the Texans encamped on the night of May 22 "at the upper edge of the Cross Timbers at a big spring, where we stayed all night." On the next day, May 23, Stout says that "we rode down towards Birdville [present Haltom City] and over the Trinity and Fossil and camped again. This was the night before the fight and there was not a sign of an Indian around."[16]

★ ★ ★ ★ ★

Battle of Village Creek: May 24, 1841

On May 24, they came to the ford of the Trinity where Colonel Rusk and General Dyer had charged a Kickapoo camp in 1838, within sight of the lower Cross Timbers. "Here we recrossed the Trinity from the eastern side to the western, and upon the high prairies one mile from the ford, we found very rich sign of Indians," wrote William Porter.[17]

Henry Stout claimed that on the morning of May 24, Tarrant was about ready to "give up the chase. He said he wanted to get back before [the] Trinity raised, but it did not look like rain and we would not agree."[18]

As the men were not yet ready to turn for home, Tarrant agreed to continue the search a little further. Stout had been sent out with seven other men to scout for signs during the night of May 23–24.

> We followed a buffalo trail down to Fossil [Creek] and as soon as we crossed, discovered two pony tracks. We noticed, too, that the brush alongside the trail had been

pulled out tufts of oats and rye, and we knew we were close to them. We sent back word to the main part of our little army—I have seven or eight men as a scouting party, the rest were behind under Tarrant—and we received word from Tarrant to watch out behind and before. One of my little party was Early of Ladonia. Denton, [Randolph] Scott, and Bourland were others.

We passed over a little knoll and around close to where there were a whole tribe of Indians, but they did not see us nor we them. We turned further on to the left, there saw two ponies and soon after two squaws. One of the squaws had a brass kettle, preparing something. The o[ther] was an Anadarko squaw and had a baby in her arms.

Stout's men remained concealed behind a brush-covered rise in the ground, watching the Indian women. According to Andrew Davis, Stout's spies reported back early in the morning of May 24 of their discovery of the Indian village. By daylight, Tarrant's camp had broken and was on the move forward. By about 9:00 a.m., his men were within three or four hundred yards of this village and took up a position behind a thicket.[19]

"The men were ordered to divest themselves of their blankets, packs, and all manner of incumbrance, after which, the line was formed," recorded brigade inspector Porter. According to Andrew Davis, Tarrant gave the men five minutes to be ready to charge.[20]

As his men approached the village, one of the Indian women discovered the Texans and gave a loud scream. Tarrant then gave the word for his men to charge into the Indian village on horseback. The Indian woman charged into a creekbed as the Texans raced forward. She was shot and killed by Alsey Fuller, who did not notice that she was a woman as she ascended the opposite creek bank.[21]

The Indians were caught off guard and the village was "taken in an instant," said Porter. The Indians scarcely had time to flee their lodges before the Texans were upon them. Several were shot while attempting to escape. Andrew Davis later gave his account of charging this village.

In a moment, the sound of firearms, with a voice of thunder, rang out over the alarmed and terror-stricken

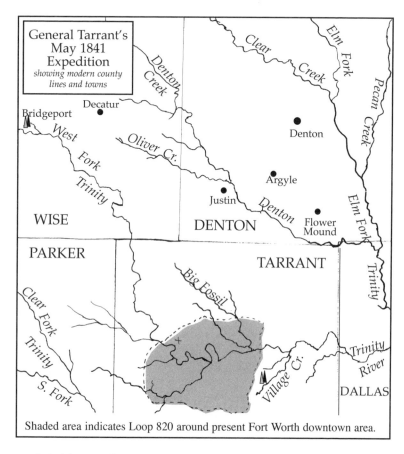

General Tarrant's
May 1841
Expedition
*showing modern county
lines and towns*

Bridgeport

Decatur

Denton

Oliver Cr.

Argyle

Justin

WISE

DENTON

Flower
Mound

PARKER

TARRANT

Big Fossil

Clear Fork

Trinity

S. Fork

Village Cr.

Trinity
River

DALLAS

Shaded area indicates Loop 820 around present Fort Worth downtown area.

inhabitants of that rude city of the wilderness. Tarrant and James Bourland, with Denton, led the charge, while every other man followed with the best speed his horse could make.

I was riding a mule furnished me by Aunt Gordon. She was my friend in orphanage and helplessness. That mule was a mule, and just like its kind, was slow, and made me among the last to reach the enemy. As I passed the first huts, I saw to my right a number of Indians. I fired into the crowd with the best aim my excited nerves would allow.[22]

Henry Stout did not have the inclination to kill a woman. The Anadarko woman and her baby ran straight toward him as the

Texans charged the village. "I could have killed both of them and, thinking of the eight people killed in one of my neighbor's [Ripley's] families, I wonder I did not." This woman and her child were instead taken prisoner by Tarrant's men.[23]

The Indian villages were thrown into terrible confusion. As the Texans advanced down Village Creek, the families fled from their lodges. If the Indian leaders knew that only about eighty Texans were rushing down upon them, a serious defensive stand could have been much more deadly for Tarrant's men. Fortunately for him, the element of surprise and the continued offensive charge worked well in driving his opponents onward.

Following the sweep against the first village, the Texans became scattered as they pursued fleeing Indians in multiple directions. Captain Bourland took about twenty men, including John Denton, Sergeant Cochran, and Lindley Johnson, with him. They crossed Village Creek and found a road along its valley. They galloped along the road beside the creek for about a mile.

Through the timber ahead, they soon noticed what appeared to be the second village, even larger than any of the ones they had already charged through. Captain Bourland, with about half of the men, bore to the right of the creek, and Sergeant Cochran, with the other men, bore to the left in order to flank the Indian position. The Indians, however, were seen to retreat into the thickets on the far side of the creek. Cochran and Elbert Early both attempted to fire at retreating Indians, but their guns snapped. Upon reaching the creek, one Indian fired a shot at Early which missed.[24]

The Texan command was further split and badly confused by this point. Eight men again crossed Village Creek and came upon a third Indian camp which had just been deserted. Porter wrote:

> Discovering a large trail, leading down the creek, and some of the Indians having gone in that direction, a few men were left at that village, and the rest at full speed took their course down the creek, upon which the village was situated.
> Two miles from the first village, we burst suddenly upon another village; this was taken like the first—there was another village in sight below. Many of the horses having failed, the men ran towards this village on foot; but the Indians having heard the firing at the second village,

had time to take off the guns and ammunition, and commenced occasionally to return our fire.[25]

Having selected the second Indian camp as a rallying point, General Tarrant now passed the order for all of his men to rendezvous at this point to recollect themselves, as Porter recorded.

> From the time, there was no distinction of villages, but one continued village for the distance of one mile and a half, only separated by the creek upon which it was situated. We had now become so scattered that Gen. Tarrant deemed it advisable to establish some rallying point to which smaller parties should be expected to rally.

The rearguard had by this time advanced from the first village with the company's baggage and supplies. Tarrant soon had about forty of his men gathered together, with another thirty men still out pursuing Indians. Remarkably, no Texans had been killed or wounded in the sweep through the first two Indian villages. Andrew Davis, the young volunteer riding his aunt's mule, had his old mule shot out from under him. "On roll call, it was found that not a man had been killed," recalled Davis. "A dozen, perhaps, had been unhorsed. Quite a number were hatless."[26]

While waiting for the other men to return, John Denton asked for permission to take another party of men down the creek. Tarrant reluctantly allowed Denton to take command of ten men, but only under the promise the scouting captain would avoid an ambush by exercising extreme caution.

Ambush and Death of Captain Denton

Shortly after Captain Denton's scouting party departed the second village, Captain Bourland also tired of waiting. He took another ten men and started out in a different direction.

At a point about a mile below Tarrant's rendezvous spot, Denton and Bourland's parties joined back together again. After moving only a short distance ahead, Bourland and Calvin Sullivan crossed a boggy branch to capture some Indian horses, one of which wore a tell-tale bell.

Indian villages once ran along this area of Village Creek, which is located in Arlington in present Tarrant County. The area of the heaviest fighting during the battle of May 24, 1841, now lies beneath Lake Arlington just east of Fort Worth. *Author's photo.*

The other scouts rode farther down the creek into a cornfield, which they crossed through. On the other side of the cornfield, they found a well used road which led into the bottomlands. William Porter found it to be "much larger than any we had seen, one end of which led over a mountain west, the other east, towards the main Trinity, crossing the creek upon which the villages were situated."[27]

At the edge of the bottom thicket, they halted. Denton was intent on fulfilling his promise to not needlessly endanger his men. Captain Stout then rode to the front, saying, "If you are afraid to go in there, I am not."[28]

John Denton then replied strongly that he would follow Stout to hell and shouted, "Move on!"

At a point about three hundred yards ahead, the small group of men came to the creek bank and descended with their horses into the water. Henry Stout led the riders down the embankment, followed by Captain Denton, John Griffin, and the other scouts. Splashing through the creek bed, the party moved upstream.

The three foremost riders had only traveled about thirty paces up the creek when the group was unexpectedly taken under fire

Captain Henry B. Stout (1799–?) was a veteran frontier scout who had previously commanded a company of Texas Rangers during 1840. He was wounded in the same ambush that killed Captain John Denton on May 24, 1841. Originally published in 1912 in DeShields' *Border Wars of Texas*.

Andrew Davis (1827–1906) was only thirteen at the time of General Tarrant's Village Creek battle. Later a Methodist minister in the 1840s, Davis claimed to have ridden as a volunteer with this expedition. Originally published in 1912 in DeShields' *Border Wars of Texas*.

by Indians. The ambushing party was well hidden in a thicket on Village Creek's west bluff. Although Stout was leading the procession and was in front of the other Texans, he had the good fortune to have his body partially obscured by a small tree at this exact instant.[29]

Captain Stout was shot through his left arm. He wheeled his horse to his right and raised his gun to fire. In that instant, five more bullets pierced Stout's clothing around his neck and shoulders. Another ball passed through the butt of his gun, causing the barrel to strike him violently on the head. "I received a severe wound in the arm and another bullet struck the lock of my Dutch gun; tore off the spring and knocked the stock against the side of my head with such force as to stun me," recalled Stout.[30]

The eruption of rifle shots startled all as the rifle balls tore violently through the Texan force. "When the company reached the point opposite and under the Indians, they opened a deadly fire upon us," recalled young volunteer Andrew Davis, "it being

Captain John Bunyan Denton was shot from his horse during the Village Creek expedition on May 24, 1841, in present Tarrant County. Denton, the namesake of Denton County, Texas, was an early Methodist preacher who had previously commanded volunteers during the 1839 Cherokee War. During the Village Creek expedition, he was a leader of a company of spies. This early artist's depiction of the death of Captain Denton—who is following the horse of Henry Stout—was originally published in DeShields' *Border Wars of Texas* in 1912.

mainly directed on our men in front." William Porter claimed that the men "were fired on from every direction, by an enemy that could not be seen."[31]

Following immediately behind Stout, Denton was shot at the same instant. Wheeling to the right, he rode back up the bank and fell dead from his horse. Denton was struck by three balls, one through his right breast, one in his shoulder, and another in his arm. "I heard the shots and looked at Denton," stated Captain Stout. "He had raised his gun to shoot, but dropped it and fell dead." Another of Denton's men, fourteen-year-old John D. Pickens, saw Denton slump over and fall from his horse.[32]

The third man in line, John Griffin, was grazed in the cheek by a rifle ball. Several other shots passed through his clothing without injury. Musket balls ripped through the clothes of many of the other Texans without tearing their flesh. In other close Indian fights, such as the 1838 battle at the Kickapoo village in East Texas, lucky survivors would report their clothing being ripped by shots. The other men, following in the single file line, were screened by a projection of the creek's bank and were not harmed. The trailing men had not quite reached the creek bed.[33]

The Indians fired a single volley upon Denton's party before
running for cover into the surrounding thickets. The surviving
scouts hastily retreated to the field, where they met Captain
Bourland's men. Randolph Scott cried out that Denton had been
killed and that Captain Stout was seriously wounded.

The loss of Captain Denton demoralized the Texans. Bourland
managed to rally all of his men at the first point of attack. He
then led twenty-four volunteers back to retrieve the body of their
fallen comrade. Although they fully expected to find a scalped
and mutilated corpse, the Indians had retreated after the encounter. "The body of Captain Denton was securely tied upon a gentle
horse," recalled volunteer Andrew Davis.[34]

The yells and firing having ceased, both parties retired from
the scene. The fighting had left one Texan dead and two wounded.
For their part, the Texans felt that they had killed twelve Indians
that could be counted. "A great many more must have been killed
and wounded, from the quantity of blood we saw on their trails
and in the thickets where they had ran," wrote Porter.[35]

General Tarrant had not planned on taking prisoners, although
his men had taken some. William Porter's report continues:

> From the prisoners who we had taken, we learned
> that at those villages there were upwards of one thousand
> warriors, not more than half of whom were then at home.
> The other half were hunting buffalo, and stealing on the
> frontier. Here is the depot for the stolen horses from our
> frontier, and the home of the horrible savages who have
> murdered our families.
>
> They were portions of a good many tribes—princi-
> pally the Cherokees who were driven from Nacogdoches
> County—some Creeks and Seminoles, Wacos, Caddoes,
> Kickapoos, Anadarkos [etc.]. We counted 225 lodges, all
> in occupation, beside those that they could see the glimpse
> of through the trees, in the main village. They had about
> three hundred acres in corn that we saw; and were abun-
> dantly provided with ammunition of every kind. Each
> lodge had two or three little bags of powder and lead tied
> up in equal portions; and at one lodge (a sort of black
> smith shop where we found a set of blacksmith's tools),
> we found over a half bushel of moulded bullets.

We also found some sergeants' swords, musket flints, rifle and musket powder, pig lead, and musket balls, which we supposed they must have taken from the place when the Regular Army buried a portion of their ammunition. They had all manner of farming utensils of the best quality, except ploughs. In some of the lodges we found feather beds and bedsteads.[36]

While some men searched the abandoned upper villages and gathered goods, others helped move the dead and wounded back to General Tarrant's second village. Stout later recalled:

I was bleeding profusely and was weak, and Bourland said we had better go to camp. We went to where Tarrant's command was, and on the way Bourland reached down and picked up a brass kettle that the Indians had left, and dipping up water from the branch poured it on my head. I think that saved my life.[37]

Tarrant decided it was most prudent to depart the area now. "If the Indians could ascertain the smallness of our numbers," wrote Porter, it would prove deadly for their men. The Indians could easily take advantage of the heavy woods to lay more ambush at the creek and river crossings where they knew the Texans would be most likely to cross. If not completed defeated, a good number of the Texans could likely be cut off and the main body could have been prevented from crossing a body of water as large as the Trinity without severe loss. "It was deemed advisable therefore, to take up the line of march and cross the Trinity that night."[38]

Captain Denton's body was tied across a horse. At 5:00 p.m. on May 24, Tarrant's men departed the second village and marched twelve miles back up the trail they had followed down. They crossed the Trinity without attack and camped in an open prairie for the night. The men retraced their steps to the Fossil Creek camp of the previous night, arriving there about midnight. Much of the spoils of war, including many of the eighty horses originally rounded up, were lost in the retreat to this camp.[39]

The next morning, May 25, Tarrant's men crossed Fossil Creek bottom to its north side. At a point stated by Porter to be

Located along Spur 303 in Arlington, Texas, is one of the two markers (above left) which commemorate the Village Creek Fight of May 24, 1841. The remains of Captain John Denton—who was killed in this battle—were reburied in 1901 in the courtyard of the Denton County Courthouse. This marker (above right) commemorates his service to Texas.
Author's photos.

"25 miles from the village," they buried Captain Denton. The actual location was apparently just north of Fossil Creek, although at least one account would later claim that the men were as far north as Oliver Creek in Denton County. Historian John Henry Brown interviewed a half dozen veterans of this expedition and in 1886 determined that Denton was buried near Birdville (later Haltom City) under the bank of a ravine, at the point of a rocky ridge. Within twelve feet of the grave stood a large post oak tree. Henry Stout would later tell a Fort Worth newspaper reporter, "We buried Denton in the forks of Fossil and I marked the place and recollected it and found it thirty-eight years after."[40]

The tools taken from one of the Indian villages were used to dig a grave for John Denton. According to Andrew Davis:

> His grave was dug a good depth. A thin rock was cut so as to fit in the bottom of the grave. Similar rocks were

placed at the sides and also at the head and foot. Another rock was placed over the body and the grave filled up. Thus was buried one of God's noble men.[41]

The bones of John Denton would lie in the spot long, although not permanently. In later years, Fort Worth leaders deemed it noble to exhume Denton's bones and offer him a proper hero's burial. Many efforts were made unsuccessfully until one of the battle veterans, Henry Stout, was called to find the spot of the burial.

Major Jarvis of Fort Worth offered to help with giving Captain Denton a proper burial. He sent for Stout—part of the seven-man party who had helped to bury Denton—to help locate the spot of the burial. Borrowing a horse from Jarvis, he and a man named Peter Smith rode north of Fort Worth. "I struck the trail and could tell by the timber and the hills that it was the same one I had rode over thirty-eight years before." They proceeded up the forks of the Fossil Creek and Trinity River to around where Haltom City is. They reached a spot where "the country was too broken for farming, and it was left in its primeval condition." Stout pointed out a leaning tree, where they dug down and soon found Denton's bones.[42]

His body was reburied on the ranch of one of his friends, John Chisum, on Clear Creek near Bolivar in Denton County. In later years, Denton's body was exhumed a second and final time. The Old Settlers' Association of Denton County began a movement to locate the remains of the old hero and offer him a public burial in his namesake town and county. By this time, the old Chisum property had changed hands and Captain Denton's grave was now in the yard of Mr. J. H. Waide on Clear Creek.[43]

In 1901, his bones were buried for the third and final time in the courthouse yard in Denton, Texas, the county seat of Denton County, Texas. The Reverend William Allen presided over the ceremonies at the courthouse. Among those gathered were two of Denton's sons and a grandson.

Much of the area of the heaviest fighting of the Village Creek battle now lies beneath the waters of Lake Arlington. Two historical markers have been placed along Village Creek just north of the lake. One is located on the Lake Arlington Golf Course near Village Creek and the other, more easily accessible, marker is located near the creek along Spur 303 in Arlington close to the intersection of Green Oaks Boulevard.

Following the burial of John Denton, Captain Bourland's company set out for home on May 25. During the return trip the captive Indian woman escaped and fled. General Tarrant kept her child, but it was returned to its mother some two years later, at a council in the Indian territory.

The expedition proceeded up the country on the west side of the Cross Timbers and Elm Fork, until they struck their trail outward at the site of present Gainesville. Then they followed the trails back to the empty barracks at Fort Johnston, where they disbanded on May 30 after a division of the captured property.[44]

"We brought in six head of cattle, 37 horses, 300 lbs. of lead, 30 lbs. powder, 20 brass kettles, 21 axes, 73 buffalo robes, 15 guns, 13 pack saddles, 2 ladies' saddles, and 3 swords, plus diverse other things not recollected," recorded brigade inspector Porter. Stout recalled that "We also found powder and lead and more salt than a mule could pack. A Dutchman in our party got ten head of horses that were stolen from him previously and we were rich in plunder and spoils."[45]

Although General Tarrant's men did not know it, their little battle on Village Creek proved to be a decisive one. Prior to this engagement, the Indians of the Three Forks region had begun to discuss the possibility of making peace with the relentless Texans in order to end the harassing attacks and the burning of their crops and villages. This information was obtained by Captain Eli Chandler from a Mexican who had travelled with Choctaw traders among the Indians on the Trinity and Brazos.

Had the Texans been able to keep unified after charging the first village, they might have been able to provoke a more decisive battle farther down Village Creek.

The Indians' reaction to this minor offensive by the Texans was to abandon the area of the Three Forks—around present Dallas and Fort Worth—and to move farther westward up the Trinity and Brazos rivers.

CHAPTER 11

"Active and Energetic Measures"

June 1841

Edward Tarrant was not satisfied with the result of the Village Creek expedition. Immediately upon returning to the settlements, he began working to raise another, larger force to return to the area of the Cross Timbers near present Fort Worth.

General James Smith, a gallant warrior of the Creek War under General Andrew Jackson, was commander of the Third Brigade of the Texas Militia in the Nacogdoches area. He had previously commanded ranger battalions in 1836 and in 1839. By early June 1841, Smith was also busily organizing volunteers from the Nacogdoches area for an expedition into the Cross Timbers area.

As he was writing a report to President Lamar on June 13 in Nacogdoches, Smith was handed intelligence from Captain David Gage out in the field. Gage had taken his Nacogdoches County Minutemen out to pursue Indians near Nacogdoches.[1]

Captain Gage's Nacogdoches County Minutemen had been organized in early April. When the unit formed on April 4, Gage's muster roll shows that he initially recruited thirty minutemen. During the next week, he would pick up another dozen men, and would only increase his company size significantly when his unit actually went out on campaign in July.

David Gage had initially taken some of his men—Robert Hulme, James B. Reid, Thomas M. Hawkins, William Vardeman, and William Anderson—out on a three-day scout from April 6–10,

1841. Another small group—First Lieutenant Alston Ferguson, S. W. Vardeman, Berry Green, Thomas Ramsay, Wilson W. Cochran, and Jackson Grayson—made a weeklong scout from April 12–18. Between April and October 1841, Captain Gage's company made eleven recorded scouts or expeditions for Indians varying between just a few days to nearly a month in duration. Seven men—Kalib Farmer, James F. Lane, Robert L. Lane, Peter Moore, James Smith, J. P. Smith, and H. M. Smith—were enrolled with the Nacogdoches County Minutemen, but made no recorded scouting missions.

Without any depredations during the next month, he maintained only small forces of scouts. Service papers for scout Hezekiah Charty show that he served nineteen days in the field between April 6 and April 27, as compared to his captain's three days of service.

After nearly a month off duty, Gage took out some of his men from May 7–10. The majority of the Nacogdoches rangers were then off duty until renewed Indian activity in the county compelled Captain Gage to call his men into service on June 4, 1841.[2]

In his report to General Smith, Gage wrote that he believed that there were fifteen Indians in the raiding party, which moved out toward the Trinity River. Gage set out with seventeen of his minutemen—Lt. Ferguson, Robert Hulme, James Reid, George Vardeman, Thomas Maxwell, Berry Green, James Moore, Thomas Ramsay, Wilson Cochran, Thomas Hawkins, Hezekiah Charty, Matthew R. Birdwell, William Vardeman, Fletcher Howith, John L. Lane, Isaac G. Parker, and A. H. Reed. Shortly into the pursuit, Captain Gage's spies discovered the Indians and fired on them. They later believed that they had killed seven of the fifteen Indians, "as they could not discover the trail of but eight, from that place."[3]

General Smith reported that Gage followed the Indians closely until his horses gave out. He then pursued them on foot. Eight to ten miles east of the Trinity River, Gage discovered another eight Indians. His men followed them to the river and set up an ambush. Smith wrote:

> When the Indians attempted to cross the river, he charged upon them, killing seven out of eight of the Indians, without the loss of a man, killed or wounded.

They were making their way directly in the course of the village discovered by General Tarrant. The fight took place about fifty or sixty miles north of Fort Houston.

General Smith sent his second dispatch on to President Lamar via his aide, P. S. Hollingsworth.

Chandler's Cross Timbers Fight: June 9, 1841

Captain Eli Chandler's busy Robertson County Minutemen had returned to Franklin on the night of May 25 from their most recent expedition. They were in town only a few days before gearing up to go out again. Chandler departed Franklin on Friday, June 4, 1841, with 41 men of his company. "Being convinced of the necessity of active and energetic measures, on my part, to prevent a descent of Indians upon the frontier settlements," Chandler was thus motivated to keep his rangers active.[4]

They moved up the Brazos River to the Cross Timbers, which they entered and marched through under cover of its heavy woodlands. They marched to the divide between the Brazos and Trinity rivers and then proceeded up this divide in a northerly direction, to near the northwest boundary of the Cross Timbers.

Captain Chandler's men then made camp at this area on the night of June 8. During the three previous days of marching up into the Cross Timbers area, he had "discovered considerable Indian trails."[5]

On the morning of June 9, the line of march was resumed about 7:00 a.m. Newton C. Duncan, brother of one of the Robertson County Minutemen, wrote that Captain Chandler's rangers were led by Dr. George Washington Hill—Milam County's twenty-seven-year-old House representative in the Texas Congress—as pilot. At about 9:00 a.m., the rangers heard the firing of a gun. Knowing how far they were away from any white settlement, they instantly realized that Indians must be near. They proceeded in the direction of the shot.[6]

With Hill in the lead, they soon discovered a man on horseback. Assuming him to be an Indian, the minutemen gave chase. The fleeing man's horse stumbled over a fallen log and threw the rider. With guns drawn, the rangers took the man prisoner and found him to be a Mexican man who had been kept prisoner by the Indians. Captain Chandler wrote:

> After being disarmed, he informed me that we were [with]in about four or five miles of an Indian encampment, which he would take us immediately to. Believing that I had been discovered at that place by a hunting party of Indians, and having some heavy packs, I ordered them left with a guard of seven men, and proceeded with all possible speed to the encampment, capturing two women before reaching it.[7]

The minutemen bound the Mexican man's feet under his horse, fastening a rope to his bridle rein to prevent him from fleeing. Riding quickly through "excessive heat" and "unparalleled thickness of the woodlands," Chandler's thirty-four rangers reached the Indian camp but found it to be deserted. He pursued their trail until 3:00 p.m., capturing eleven more prisoners. His total now stood at fourteen prisoners, including one Mexican, seven Indian women, and six Indian children. "At this time I was informed by one of the prisoners, that on that day a party of sixty warriors were to meet at that place for a large hunt."[8]

The Mexican prisoner spoke good English and offered quite a bit of intelligence. He stated that he had been living among the Choctaws as a trader and had been trading principally with Ionies, Shawnees, and a few Wacos. He also gave Captain Chandler useful intelligence on the location of Indians in northern Texas:

> The Wacos and Cherokees live not far distant. The Tawakonis, Caddoes, Kickapoos &c. are all making corn between the Brazos and Trinity rivers. That many of them live at what is called the Big Bend Village on the Brazos, which he says is about twenty miles above where the Americans were last winter. That all the different tribes talk of getting together, and living at one place. That there is some talk among them of making peace with the Americans.[9]

The Mexican prisoner also told Chandler that the Indians kept their lead buried in large quantities in the upper country. He knew of several encampments where he could take the rangers. Chandler's men immediately proceeded back to the empty Indian village and took possession of all of their camp equipage. This included axes, hoes, powder, lead, and sixteen horses.

At this point, Chandler decided to release the oldest Ioni female prisoner. The aged woman was given instructions "to tell her people that we wished them to come in, and bring with them the Americans they had with them, with a white flag." Chandler promised that he would exchange his Indian prisoners for their prisoners and that peace talks would be held. "We took off little of their camp equipage, and burned none," wrote Chandler, "to show them that we only wanted peace."

Captain Chandler then proceeded to where he had left his baggage with the seven rangers. He arrived there about 6:00 p.m. only to find that the sixty-Indian party he had been tracking had attacked his baggage guard early in the day. The guards had retreated to a ravine and taken position. "By their union and valor, [they] succeeded in driving back the enemy, with the loss of their chief and one other killed," wrote Chandler.

All told, Chandler reported killing four Indians and wounding three or four others during the day. "None of my command received the slightest injury from the enemy."

Having few men to guard fourteen prisoners, Chandler abandoned pursuing the Indians any farther and turned for home. He arrived at Fort Franklin on June 18 with all of his men and prisoners. He narrowly missed recovering a young hostage.

> I am informed that there was a white boy at the encampment, nine or ten years old, but being put on a good horse, he succeeded in making his escape without being discovered by any of my command.

Chandler retained his prisoners under guard, awaiting further direction from President Lamar. He wrote his campaign report on June 19, asking for quick direction from the government on how to handle the prisoners. He had two Shawnee women, two Ioni women who had Shawnee husbands, and two other Ioni women. "One of the Shawnee women has four sons, who were at the encampment, and, from all the circumstances, I am of opinion that some of the Indians will be in, in a short time."

Captain Chandler asked Lamar for guidance on how to handle the Indians he expected to come seeking their mother. He also reported on the intelligence of the northern Texas Indians which he had received from his Mexican prisoner. This man was willing to take Chandler's rangers back into the Indian territory and point out various encampments. "I expect to make another expedition," Chandler vowed, "so soon as my horses [can be] recruit[ed]."

Tarrant's Trinity Campaign

The intelligence from Eli Chandler's Robertson County Minutemen could not be ignored. Word was in President Lamar's hands by late June, and he wasted no time in mobilizing other forces to move against the Indians of the Cross Timbers. He put out orders for both General Jim Smith's Third Militia Brigade and General Edward Tarrant's Fourth Militia Brigade to mobilize and sweep into the Cross Timbers.

General Tarrant began organizing his volunteers during the early days of July. He had an understanding with General Smith that their Third and Fourth Brigade forces would rendezvous, if possible, somewhere in the Cross Timbers during late July. When all of Tarrant's Red River volunteer mounted gunman companies were organized within two weeks, his force was sufficient to carry out a strong sweep. Although one historian claims that Tarrant's brigade numbered between 400 and 500 men for this expedition, another contemporary source more accurately wrote that Tarrant departed "with 250 troops."[10]

In confirmation of this latter figure, William B. Stout, who was frequently in command of rangers in the Red River settlements during the Republic years, wrote: "Tarrant after returning [from the Village Creek expedition] raised another force [of] 300 men, made another expedition."[11]

Captains David P. Key and John William Lane's first two companies were mustered into service on July 5, 1841, at Fort DeKalb. Formerly known as Fort Lyday, this blockhouse had been constructed by Captain William Stout's rangers in late 1838 in present extreme southwestern Lamar County, north of the old Lyday crossing of the North Sulphur River. Captain Lane had commanded rangers in the Red River area through early 1840.[12]

GENERAL TARRANT'S TRINITY EXPEDITION
JULY 5–AUGUST 11, 1841

Expedition Field and Staff, Fourth Militia Brigade

Edward H. Tarrant	General
Robert S. Hamilton	Colonel
William C. Young	Lieutenant Colonel
Ballard C. Bagby	Major
John H. Smithers	Adjutant
Jonathan Bird	Sergeant Major
George W. Basin	Surgeon
Samuel Smith	Judge Advocate
McQuery H. Wright	Quartermaster

Source: William C. Young PD, R 199, F 97–106.

Capt. Johnson's Spy Company

Captain:
Samuel Johnson

Privates:
Hugh Cox
Thomas Glascock
John W. Lupton

Note: Johnson's small spy company was apparently recruited from the existing companies. John Lupton, for example, was pulled from Captain Orton's company.

Capt. Key's Mounted Gunmen (Co. A): July 5–Aug. 11, 1841

Captain:
David P. Key
First Lieutenant:
William J. Blythe
Second Lieutenant:
Andrew D. Wilson
Orderly Sergeant:
John A. Booth

Privates:
Thomas J. Bassett
James J. Beeman
Stephen S. Booth
Calvin C. Breeding
John A. Browning
Robert H. Browning
John H. Cox
John C. Dolby
James Frazier

Frederick A. Gerdes
George Gerdes
James M. Holloway
William Holloway
Albert G. Kimbell
John M. Kimbell
James W. Merrill
John T. Miller
Sidney W. Neal
James Parkham
Napoleon B. Patton
Benjamin Ratcliff
Edmund J. Smith
Lewis Y. Smith
Henry Stallings
Matthew Titus

Author's compilation from audited military claims and public debt files.

Capt. Orton's Mounted Gunmen (Co. B): July 15–Oct. 15, 1841

Captain:
Samuel B. Orton
First Lieutenant:
John P. Lincecum
Second Lieutenant:
Elias D. Barnett
Orderly Sergeant:
Robert H. Graham
Second Sergeant:
Alfred Allen
Third Sergeant:
Henry C. Ritchey
Fourth Sergeant:
Samuel Wheat

Privates:
Hiram Baker
Barkley M. Ballard
N. G. Ballard
William Cole
John H. Cullum
William N. Fleming
Thomas S. Hamilton
Green M. Langford
John W. Lupton [1]

William C. Martin
James Matthews
William H. McBee
Wiley B. Merrill
Cyrus A. Moore
Samuel Pew
William M. Priest
John Reed
Ambrose Ripley [2]
Madison Rolls
Caleb Smith
Adam Sullivan
Preston Taylor
John Terry
Richard Tomlinson
Montgomery Vaught
Nicholas Voyles
Robert Wheat

[1] Joined Capt. Johnson's spies.
[2] Substitute for D. N. Barney.
Author's compilation from audited
military claims and public debt files.

Capt. Lane's Mounted Riflemen (Co. C): July 5–Oct. 5, 1841

Captain:
John William Lane
First Lieutenant:
Alfred H. Hulme
Orderly Sergeant:
Gibson Myers

Privates:
Thomas C. Baker
William C. Baker
George Brinlee
James M. Capps
Harvey M. Derryberry
Joseph W. Ellett
Jacob W. Fleming
William Gaylor
James M. Goff
J. N. B. Jones
William Knight
David Lane
Thomas Mahan

Samuel H. McFarland
John D. McGahey
James B. McWhirter
Anderson R. Moores
Eli H. Moores
James C. Moores
Thomas B. Moores
David Morgan
James H. Moss
William B. Poor
Absolom Sherwood
John W. Sherwood
William D. Shocklee
John A. Talbot
John Watson
William B. Williams
William D. Wootten
James D. Wright
Pinckney Wright
Author's compilation from audited
military claims and public debt files.

Capt. Williams' Volunteers (Co. D): July 12–October 12, 1841

Captain:
William M. Williams
First Lieutenant:
Bennett T. Logan
Second Lieutenant:
George Kennedy
Orderly Sergeant:
John A. Dillingham

Privates:
Charles Adams
Isaac Bailey
Henry Baker
Lucien Barney
Henry Barney
Robert E. Beasley
Jesse M. Boyd
William Brown
James Dalton
Mark Dalton
James Davenport
John Davis
William Davis
James C. Dillingham
Thomas C. Doss
James Ferrill
William Gamble
William Gaston
Epsom Hamilton
William H. Hobbs
Jesse Kuykendall
James M. Lindsey
Pleasant Logan

George Mabin
Joseph Mabin
Albert Madden
Robert S. McFarland
John McMinn
Morgan Meeks [1]
Abram Miltower
Benson Montgomery
Peter Morgan
Hardin Moss [2]
William B. Pace
Andrew J. Perryman
Benjamin Pettit
David L. Pettit
Robert Price
John Roberts
Felix G. Sadler
Daniel Slack
Robert Sloan
Joseph P. Spence
John W. Stephens
John W. Stephens Jr.
Littleton Stephens
Jefferson Wallace
Hiram Willbanks
David Williams
Pleasant Wilson

[1] Substitute for Squire Mays.
[2] Substitute for Thomas Martin.

Source: William M. Williams PD, R 197, F 195–329 and other military claims and public debt files.

Capt. Fowler's Mounted Gunmen (Co. E): July 12–Aug. 11, 1841

Captain:
Andrew Jackson Fowler
First Lieutenant:
Turner B. Edmondson
Second Lieutenant:
William Chisum
Orderly Sergeant:
Lewis Harmon

Privates:
Josiah Ashley
Wesley Askins
Henry Bingham
William Bledsoe
Benjamin F. Bourland
William Brackeen
John Calvin
John Carter
William Chadwell
Andrew Jackson Click
Calvin M. Click
William C. Click
William G. Gavin
James B. Harland
Nathan R. Harland
John Hart
A. McGee Jeffries
John Jones
Wilson Maddon
John W. Mark

Wiley B. Merrill
John Nicholson
Benjamin Nix
David Pevler
Garrett Pevlor
Cary Ragan
Nathan H. Ragsdale
John Rattan
Wade Hampton Rattan
James Reily
Z. B. Rice
George Richardson
Caswell Russell
Joseph Salmon
Abraham Skidmore
William Skidmore
J. S. Smith
William D. Smith
Edward Thompson
James Tumlinson
Andrew Vaught
Hiram Williams
Lewis Williams
Sterling E. Williams
George Wilson
George M. Wright
George Wynn

Key source: Turner B. Edmondson PD, R 151, F 111.

Capt. Blair's Mounted Gunmen (Comp. F): July 15- Oct. 15, 1841

Captain:
James Blair
First Lieutenant:
Josiah J. Brantley
Second Lieutenant:
Marvin Setzer
Orderly Sergeant:
Hiram C. McKinney
Sergeant:
Joseph T. Kimbro

Privates:
Adrian Baker
Hiram Baker *
Elias D. Barnett *

John Daniels
William N. Dillard
Wadson E. Duke
Major Farice
William Gibbard
Thomas S. Hamilton
B. B. Hayney
Daniel Mason
Lewis Richardson
Abraham Stalions
Jesse Tate
Joseph Wagley
J. W. Walker

* Also served with Capt. Orton's unit.

Capt. Stout's Mounted Gunmen: July 15–Oct. 15, 1841

Captain:
Henry B. Stout
Second Lieutenant:
James H. King
First Sergeant:
William Cole

Privates:
Nelson Askins
James Bourland
William H. Bourland
James H. Crowder
Charles C. Dale
Edward M. Dean
David Doak
Lorenzo Downing
Isham Farris
John Farris
A. J. Frially
Garland Gear
John C. Guest
William Harkins
Nathaniel Harris
William Harris
Martin Harvick *
A. N. Johnston

Robert Jones
John Levins
Daniel Matthews
William Mays Jr.
Andrew J. McAnier
John McCarty
G. C. Miles
Jeremiah Monk
Isaac Moore
Lanson Moore
Zachariah W. Moore
George A. Patillo
Samuel Perkins
William H. Pulliam
John S. Richey
John B. Simmons
Tilman Smith
Charles E. Spence
Martin W. Still
R. P. Trimble
Jordan P. Ward
Alexander W. Webb

* Also served under Capt. Orton.
Source: Author's search of public
debt papers, including William Cole
PD, R 144, F 601–733.

General Tarrant ordered the Fourth Brigade companies to assemble at Fort Inglish, the home of Bailey Inglish. On July 12, captains Andrew Jackson Fowler and William M. "Buckskin" Williams each mustered a mounted gunman company into service. Captain Williams had previously served as quartermaster and commissary in 1840. Tarrant assembled and organized his force between July 15 and July 20, 1841, at Fort Inglish.[13]

Tarrant's newly elected staff was experienced with frontier fighting. Quartermaster McQuery Wright had served as orderly sergeant of Captain William Stout's 1840 ranger unit. Colonel Robert S. Hamilton had commanded a company of mounted riflemen during Rusk and Dyer's late 1838–early 1839 Indian expedition. Lieutenant Colonel William C. Young had just completed service as first lieutenant of Captain Bourland's Village Creek company under Tarrant. Colonel John H. Smithers was elected regimental adjutant.

Colonel Hamilton designated Captain David Key's unit as Company A and Captain Orton's as Company B. Captain Lane's company became Company C, and other units were so assigned as they arrived at Fort Inglish. Hamilton also created a small scout unit under Captain Samuel Johnson, his men pulled from the ranks of the other riflemen companies.[14]

General Tarrant and Colonel Young's troops departed Fort Inglish in late July and moved southwest. They encamped on the west bank of the Trinity River, probably in present Wise County. They sent out a scouting party, but made no discoveries. Tarrant would later find that the Indians had discovered his movements in time to remain unseen by his men. The Indians would also stay just out of harm's reach when General James Smith led his troops through the same area. Tarrant visited the camp of General Smith briefly on July 26 and informed Smith that his own intelligence pointed to signs that the Indians had moved on to the Brazos River.[15]

After his quick visit with General Smith, Edward Tarrant kept his Fourth Brigade in the field for two more weeks in search of hostile Indians. His men saw no action during this time and ultimately returned home with provisions nearly exhausted.[16]

General Tarrant and his troops were back in the area of Fort Inglish by August 6. Tarrant hoped to move out the next morning to drive hostile Indians from the Fannin County area. Upon his return, Tarrant learned of another Indian attack that had occurred in Fannin County at the time his troops were assembling in July.

William Cox, who lived about four miles north of Bonham, had sent his son Isaac and his twelve-year-old nephew—son of his brother Jesse Cox—to drive up his milk cows. The boys did not return and the family was in great distress, fearing that their children had been killed by the Indians. They soon found that the boys had been kidnapped. According to William Cox, "My son, Isaac, was taken by the Keechi Indians on the 12th of July from near my residence in Fannin County."[17]

A runner was sent to General Tarrant to alert him. Tarrant sent scouts out in every direction in search of the children and to alert other settlements to be on the alert. "The scouts sent to me, delivered the message and wheeled their horses to go in search of the captured boys," recalled John P. Simpson, who lived in the Fort Inglish settlement.[18]

The spies did run across a group of Indians and pursue them as they left Simpson. The Indians reportedly made a charge on Fort Inglish with the two captured boys behind them on their horses. One of the fort's picket guards fired at the charging Indians, striking an Indian woman. She died that night and was buried by the Indians near where Orangeville now stands. This was according to one of the two boys who was later returned.[19]

The public debt papers of Henry Stallings, a member of Captain David Key's mounted gunmen, show that he lost a horse while in service. Calvin Breeding and William Poor—the latter of Captain Lane's unit—affirmed that Stallings had a horse stolen from him at Fort Inglish by Indians while in service.[20]

Upon the return of General Tarrant's troops to Fort Inglish, an effort was made to send a mounted company in search of the Kichais who had taken the Cox cousins. Colonel Lindley Johnson, in charge of the militia regiment of Lamar County, ordered up a company under Captain John Emberson, which he placed under the supervision of Major Robert Price. Lindley reported to Tarrant that he had ordered Captain Emberson "with his company of minutemen" on expedition with Major Price in command.[21]

Capt. Emberson's Mounted Gunmen: August 7–29, 1841	
Captain:	Martin D. Hart
John Emberson	Meredith Hart
First Lieutenant:	Silas Hart
Thomas Dennis	James Isham
Second Lieutenant:	John Isham
Nicholas Maddox	Elijah Jackson
Orderly Sergeant:	Josiah Jackson
Thomas Chisum	Martin Johnson
	Mitchell Keller
Privates:	J. J. Morrison
David Allen	Urias D. Pace
Christopher Baker	Willard Stowell
Joseph Baker	James Wharton
William H. Brown	Gardner Wilbanks
Hiram B. Bush	Isaac Wilbanks
John Cornelison	J. E. Williams
William Davis	A. J. Wood
Charles Erwin	
William G. Gavin	Source: Author's search of public
Free L. Hart	debt and audited claims papers.
Hardin Hart	
John Hart	

Emberson was a seasoned frontiersman. He had taken part in General Thomas Rusk's late 1838 Three Forks Expedition and had commanded rangers in Red River and Fannin counties during 1839 from the Fort Inglish area. His new company of roughly three dozen men was mustered in on August 7, 1841, and set out immediately to track the Kichais. Emberson later affirmed that his men "furnished their own equipage and rations" while serving as mounted gunmen.[22]

Captain Emberson's men were unable to catch up with them, as the Indians had crossed out of Texas. His company was discharged at Fort Inglish on August 29, after twenty-two days of service. Jesse Chisum, a noted frontiersman of the Red River, utilized a friendly Delaware Indian named Jack to help negotiate a ransom for the Cox boys. William Cox managed to borrow $306 from friends and neighbors for Jack to retrieve Isaac Cox and his cousin from the Canadian River in present Oklahoma on September 12, 1841, two months after their capture.[23]

During the time that Emberson's gunmen were searching for the Cox boys, General Tarrant allowed some of his expedition companies to disband. Captain A. J. Fowler's gunmen were discharged from service on August 11, as were Captain Key's men. A large number of Captain William Lane's Company C was discharged on August 11, after serving thirty-six days. Lane and a portion of his company continued to range the Fourth Brigade until being discharged on October 5, 1841, at headquarters.[24]

Some of Colonel Hamilton's company served on into October. Many of these militiamen were discharged on October 5, while Captain Stout's company was discharged on October 15. Captain William Williams' rangers completed three months of service. They were discharged on October 12, 1841, at the "Headquarters, Volunteer Regiment, Fourth Brigade, Texas Militia" by Captain Williams and Colonel Hamilton.[25]

Captain Orton's company was discharged on October 15 at headquarters by Orton and Colonel Hamilton. Captain Blair's men were also discharged on October 15 as Tarrant's Fourth Militia Brigade regrouped.

The Texas Militia's Third Regiment, Fourth Brigade remained active through the end of 1841, with Colonel Lindley presiding over it—although little action seems to have taken place.[26]

★ ★ ★ ★ ★

General Smith's Trinity Campaign: July 1841

General James Smith's Third Regiment saw some action in the summer of 1841. He moved out of the Nacogdoches area in July with his volunteers. Henry B. Elliott had served as quartermaster for the "Nacogdoches Volunteers" for seventeen days. On July 11, 1841, as he mobilized his expedition, General Smith promoted Elliott to lieutenant colonel to help lead the foray.[27]

Captain David Gage's Nacogdoches County Minutemen were also along on this expedition, as evidenced by pay roll receipts for privates Thomas W. Ramsay and Robert Wyatt.[28]

Among the companies was that of Captain John L. Hall of Houston County. Captain William M. Burton, who had previously fought under Captain Bob Smith during the 1839 Cherokee War, took command of another Nacogdoches company. Private Robert J. Gwinn affirmed in his public debt papers that he had served "as a ranger, or mounted rifleman, in the company commanded by Capt. William Burton, in the campaign against the Indians on the upper Trinity."[29]

Troops from Burnet and Houston counties rendezvoused at Fort Houston in present Anderson County. Pay roll information for Captain Daniel Murry Crist's Burnet and Houston County Volunteers company shows that the private soldiers were paid $25 per month. Captains were paid $75 per month, first lieutenants $60 per month, and second lieutenants $50 per month. One of his volunteers, Isaac Powers, later dubbed their mission the "Trinity Campaign."[30]

General Smith's expedition departed Fort Houston on July 11 and moved toward the present Dallas area. They reached the settlement of Kingsborough, which included blockhouses known as King's Fort, at the present town of Kaufman in Kaufman County, on July 18 and 19.

This private fort had been built about August 1840, by a group of civilians headed by Dr. William P. King of Mississippi. Surrounded by ten-foot log picket fences, the fort was one of the most remote settlements of East Texas, and was only a few hours' ride from the Indian villages at the forks of the Trinity.[31]

Captain Crist, Lieutenant Thomas Berry, James Carr, and Frank Burk had arrived at King's Fort ahead of the troops on July 17.[32]

General James Smith (1792–1855) of Nacogdoches led his Third Militia Brigade into the area of present Dallas on an Indian expedition in July 1841. The namesake of Smith County, Texas, he had previously commanded a ranger battalion in 1836 and was a lieutenant colonel during the 1839 Cherokee War in East Texas. *Archives & Information Services Division, Texas State Archives.*

Upon reaching King's Fort, Captain Crist "found ten men in the fort, most of them sick. The fort is composed of four log cabins, picketed round, enclosing about three fourths of an acre, in a poor condition for defense." These few militiamen and the sick men at the fort were assaulted during the early hours of July 18 by a force of Indians. Crist wrote:

> At 5 o'clock, when the men were lying down, the alarm of Indians was heard. We ran for our guns, and on sallying out saw about 25 Indians coming from an adjoining wood. They raised the war-whoop, and swept by close to the fort, on full gallop, driving all our horses with them. We exchanged a few shots, and killed one of their horses, and wounded some of them.
>
> After reconnoitering and making a grand display, they left us in possession of three of their mules, a quiver of arrows, a Comanche saddle, and some skins. They were well mounted, and had the appearance of Comanches and Ionies.

Other Third Brigade militiamen, including the Houston County company under Captain Hall, arrived at King's Fort the following two days. They found that the few men there had valiantly fought off the Indians. General James Smith arrived on July 20 and organized the volunteers at King's Fort into four companies under Captains Crist, Gage, Hall, and Burton.

They fell upon the Indian trail, crossing Cedar Creek in present Kaufman County. The men followed "the fresh trail of the Indians north west, across the Bois de Arc and Whiterock River, fifty-three miles to the main Trinity, a few miles below the mouth of West Fork," wrote Crist.[33]

Smith's expedition thus passed over the present Dallas area just months before John Neely Bryan, the first permanent settler of Dallas, first camped on this same spot. Smith's men crossed the Trinity River on July 21 by swimming their horses and baggage across.

A mile or so on the west side of the river, Smith's command halted at a cold spring on the edge of an extensive prairie. The springs around the area of Smith's camp were known as Honey Springs due to an abundance of honey in the area. Captain Crist wrote:

> Here the trail, increasing in size, had the appearance of large droves of buffalo and Indians going S. W. Sent out the spy company to reconnoiter and find the Indian town and corn fields. Also sent out three men on express, north, to look out for Gen. Tarrant's troops.[34]

From this camp, Smith dispatched a scout of twelve men under Captain John Hall to seek out and report the location of the Indian village attacked by General Tarrant in May. Among Hall's scouts was John H. Reagan, one of the negotiators of the 1839 Cherokee War. The other men serving as scouts were: Samuel Bean, Isaac Bean, John I. Burton, Hughes Burton, George Lacey, Warren A. Ferris, a Creek Indian named Charty, and three others.[35]

While Hall's men scouted, the remainder of General Smith's men passed July 22 in camp with no word from the spies all day. The men in camp killed a cow, and cut "lots of bee trees." Buffalo were in sight during the day.[36]

July 23 was another quiet day in camp without word from the spies. "Killed another beef; cut more bee trees," wrote Daniel Crist. "Camp overflowing with meat and honey." The men not on duty guarding the cattle and horses lounged about. Some hunted bees while others amused themselves with stories "and all the minutia usual in camp."

Expedition Field and Staff, Third Militia Brigade
General James Smith
Lt. Col. Henry B. Elliott
Major J. J. Hollingsworth, adjutant

Capt. Crist's Burnet/Houston Co. Volunteers: July 10–Aug. 10, 1841

Captain:
Daniel Murry Crist
First Lieutenant:
Thomas Berry
Second Lieutenant:
Francis B. Falkner
First Sergeant:
Eli Mead

Privates:
Frank Burk
James Carr
Alexander Wist Dunagan
Ludwick Fry
Robert Fry
Thomas Hughley
Allen Killough

Calvin Longstreet
W. W. Munson
John B. Nash
Peyton Parker
Thomas Payne
Isaac Powers
David Roberts
James R. Rowe
John Rowen
Calvin Rucker
J. H. Skanks
Nathaniel Smith
P. W. Smith
Jacob Snider
John W. Thomas
John B. Williams
Source: Daniel M. Crist PD, R 146, F 674.

Capt. Hall's Houston County Volunteers: July 10–Aug. 10, 1841

Captain:
John L. Hall
First Lieutenant:
Eldridge G. Sevier
Second Lieutenant:
Ira M. Freeman
First Sergeant:
Riley B. Wallace

Privates:
John Adams
____ Arnold
Isaac T. Bean
Samuel M. Bean
E. Bonner
Andrew Boyer
Benjamin Burton
John I. Burton
William Hughes L. Burton
James Carr
John Coats
John Cooper
John Silas Edens

Ludwick Fry
Robert Fry
John Garner
James S. Ghormley
Joseph Hackett
William Haney
George B. Lacey
Pendleton Luckett
Eli Mead
Marcus P. Mead
Steward Alexander Miller
J. S. Moore
Isaac Parker
Isaac D. Parker
Isaac Powers *
John Henninger Reagan
Peter F. Rodden
Clayton D. Skidmore
Calvin Wilcox
Erwin Witt

* On muster roll, but actually member of
Captain Crist's company.

Capt. Gage's Nacogdoches Co. Minutemen: July 10–Aug. 8, 1841

Captain:
David Gage
First Lieutenant:
Alston Ferguson
Second Lieutenant:
John P. Grigsby

Privates:
John Casey
William Cason
William Chair
Thomas Chandler
Henry L. Chapman
Hezekiah Charty
Wilson W. Cochran
Henry P. Corkey
John W. Crunk
John Davis
George W. Dunlap
Warrick Ferguson
Robert Ferrill
Warren A. Ferris
Berry Green
Thomas M. Hawkins
Thomas J. Heath
Tandy Howith
James M. Hughs
Robert S. Hulme
James M. Johnson
C. A. Lovejoy
Thomas Maxwell
A. J. Miller

John C. Miller
John Mitchell
James Moody
James Moore
E. G. Page
John M. Page
Isaac G. Parker
William Parmer
William Ragan
Thomas W. Ramsay
O. W. Randall
A. H. Reed
James B. Reid
Richard Robertson
Edward C. Simmons
Berry A. Stone
Jacob Taylor
Josiah Thomas
Thomas Timmons
S. W. Vardeman
William H. Vardeman
Hiram Walker
William Wells
W. Williams
C. L. Wood
Robert Wyatt

Source: Transcribed from Major David Gage muster roll, Texas State Archives.

Capt. Burton's Mounted Riflemen: July 10–August 10, 1841

Captain:
William M. Burton
First Lieutenant:
John N. Sullivan
Orderly Sergeant:
Henry J. Stockman

Privates:
Henderson Birdwell
Robert J. Gwinn
Hardy F. Stockman
John Williams
John L. Williams

Source: Partial roster based on author's search of audited military claims and public debt papers.

Captain Hall's men crossed Mountain Creek above or south of the Texas and Pacific railroad of present day, then passed over the prairie into the Cross Timbers to within a short distance of Village Creek. From the number of fresh trails, apparently converging to a common center, it became evident they were in the vicinity of an Indian town. Hiding his party in a low and well-hidden spot, Captain Hall sent John Reagan and Isaac Bean on foot to reconnoiter the exact location of the village and the best means of approaching it and surprising it.[37]

These two young men spent more than half a day on July 23 in spying out the land ahead, finding the Indians in quiet possession of their campground. They found that it was approachable at both the upper and lower ends of the village. With this intelligence, they returned to Captain Hall. As soon as night fell, Hall cautiously emerged from his hiding place with his scouting party and hurried with this information to General Smith.

The spies reached Smith's camp on July 24. Daniel Crist felt that the scouts brought:

> news of the town being about thirty miles west. Orders were immediately given to march, and the troops took up the line of march, in double column, over rolling prairie, for thirty miles, and camped in an edge of timber, near a creek of clear water. Indian signs plenty, and the remains of a large camp to be seen.[38]

Smith's men moved out soon after the arrival of Hall. Camp was made that night on Mountain Creek, just west of present Dallas. The following morning, July 25, Smith sent out his spies again. They quickly returned with news of Indian corn being found in the trail ahead.

At noon, Smith took up the line of march, after first addressing the troops. The command was divided into two battalions, respectively commanded by General Smith and Lieutenant Colonel Henry Elliott.

John Reagan acted as guide in conducting Smith to the upper end of the village, while Isaac Bean performed the same service in guiding Elliott to the lower. Both moves were successfully made; but when the enthusiastic men moved to sweep into the village, it was found that the Indians had already quickly fled the scene, leaving some supplies and camp fixtures. "We hove in sight of a corn field, when a general charge was made through cornfields, thickets, and ravines," wrote Captain Crist. "After a fatiguing rush, not an Indian was found."

The troops soon found that General Edward Tarrant's men had arrived in the same area only three days prior and were now in camp only nine miles away from General Smith's men. Crist relates a brief conference between the militia brigade generals on July 26.

> Gen. Tarrant visited our camp, and informed us that from a trader from the Red River, they had received information that the Indians with their families had all removed to the Brazos, where they were fortifying; they have about three hundred warriors of all the tribes.

After this brief meeting, General Smith's Nacogdoches area troops set about destroying the corn and Indian village they had found. Smith and his Nacogdoches troops returned home by the head waters of the Sabine, Angelina, and Neches rivers. The Fort Houston and Crockett volunteers returned on the west side of the Trinity to Fort Houston. Captain Crist wrote on August 3 from Fort Houston: "Thus, scouring the whole country east of the head waters of the Brazos; and it may now be said, that not an Indian can be found east of the Brazos to molest the settlers or prevent emigration, for the future."

Crist further stated that General Tarrant, "with 250 troops," continued to follow the trail of the Indians. With a larger force gathered from Robertson County, Tarrant hoped to "route and break them up on the Brazos."

Both Smith's and Tarrant's commands returned home independently in August. The two brigades had scoured the present Dallas–Fort Worth metroplex. According to the public debt papers of Private James S. Ghormsley, a member of Captain Hall's company, the men were disbanded without pay. Captain Hall filed his muster roll in Houston County in 1853 before the county court as best he could from memory. Captain Daniel Crist's company was discharged at Fort Houston on August 10, 1841, in what was then Houston County. Although bloodless, this offensive into "Indian territory" in such strong force made a deep impression upon Indian leaders. They would be more open to the peace treaty that was later entered into in September, 1843, with smaller bands.[39]

There was talk of sending out another group of volunteers under Edward Burleson, but this plan was abandoned after General Tarrant and his men returned to the settlements to report their failure in finding the Indians.[40]

June: Hays' Uvalde Canyon Fight: June 29, 1841

Captain Jack Hays had returned to San Antonio in May and disbanded his rangers. He was allowed to reactivate his unit on June 1, 1841, although he was the only member mustered for a while. He signed up five men on June 12 and another nine men on June 23.

During this time in early June, President Lamar and his entourage visited San Antonio, looking to recruit volunteers for his expedition. A grand ball was held at the large home of Mrs. Yturri, which had a long room for receptions. The room was decorated with evergreens and flags. President Lamar wore wide, white pants which were short enough to show the tops of his shoes.[41]

Lamar and Mrs. María Gertrudis Flores de Abrego Seguín, wife of the new San Antonio mayor Juan Seguín, opened the ball with a waltz. One of the guests, Mary Ann Maverick, later commented on the scene:

> Mrs. Seguín was so fat that the General had great difficulty in getting a firm hold on her waist, and they cut such a figure that we were forced to smile. The General was a poet, a polite and brave gentleman and first rate conversationalist—but he did not dance well.

Mrs. Maverick also noted John Howard and some of the town's Texas Rangers present. Howard, Captain Jack Hays, and ranger Mike Chevallie "had but one dress coat between them, and they agreed to use the coat and dance in turn." The two not dancing would wait at the door to the grand room, watching the one who was dancing. "Great fun it was watching them and listening to their wit and mischief as they made faces and shook their fists at the dancing one."[42]

The resulting expedition put together by Lamar became known as the Santa Fe Expedition, which was a disaster. President Lamar sought to help the sagging Texas economy by claiming the town of Santa Fe, which lay in the western extremes of Republic territory. He hoped to cash in on the trade value of the profits now going to St. Louis and Mexican towns. Claiming this territory would add to the international prestige of Texas.[43]

Establishing a trade route between the Texas Gulf Coast and Santa Fe had long been suggested. Stephen F. Austin had even supported the idea in 1829. Major William Jefferson Jones had pushed the proposal to Lamar in February 1839, and Lamar had addressed the Texas Congress on the subject again in November 1839, pointing out all of the advantages the Republic could reap from such a trade road. This plan came to the spotlight again in April 1840, when an American trader resident of Santa Fe, William G. Dryden, came to Austin with a letter of introduction to President Lamar.[44]

With the collapse of the Texas Army, Lamar now had a good number of men to volunteer for the Santa Fe Expedition. Colonel William Cooke, discharged from the army on April 30, joined. On May 8, Major George Howard and captains William Houghton, John Holliday, John Kennymore, and Collier Hornsby were all discharged, and they would also join up. John S. Sutton took command of one of the Santa Fe companies. Famed ranger commander Mathew "Paint" Caldwell took command of another company.[45]

Commanded by Hugh McLeod and George Howard, the Santa Fe Expedition numbered 321 men as it set out on June 19, 1841, from Kenney's Fort on Brushy Creek, twenty miles north of Austin. McLeod's expedition struggled through the southwest, often lost and ultimately split in its search for Santa Fe. Mexican authorities learned of the expedition and sent troops to intercept it. One of the Texans contacted the senior Mexican officials and arranged to surrender the Texan forces. With the promise that they would soon be released, the Texans surrendered. They were instead treated as prisoners of war and marched on foot into Mexico. Men died along the march. Many others were held in Mexican prisons until released in April 1842.[46]

Just as the Santa Fe Expedition was preparing to depart the Austin area in mid-June, Captain Jack Hays was forming up his unit of Béxar County Minutemen in San Antonio for another patrol into Indian territory. Hays had been originally commissioned to command a company of rangers during early 1841. The December 26, 1840, resolution, however, had only provided that these ranger companies could exist for four months. Béxar County, however, had been authorized on February 4, 1841, to operate a company of minutemen who would range as needed for short periods of duration.

In her memoirs, San Antonio resident Mary Maverick refers to Captain Hays' company as "Minutemen." The public debt service papers of men serving under Hays in late 1841 show that the government considered them to be minutemen, as well. The men who served under him as of July 1841 were issued claims for their "services in Captain Hays' company of minute men in 1841."[47]

Hays had exactly twelve other rangers under his command by late June and made preparations to go out on expedition again in response to renewed depredations. A party of Indians had driven off cattle from settlements around San Antonio. Only one man, Private John Carroll, departed his command on June 21 after only serving ten days.

He set out on June 27 from San Antonio with his thirteen-man company. He was joined by a twenty-man Tejano unit under Captain Flores. They "took the trail, which led us in the direction of the Canyon de Ubalde."[48]

Uvalde Canyon was some fifty miles west of San Antonio at the headwaters of the Frio River. Although referred to as Canyon de Uvalde by early frontiersmen, this area in present Real and Uvalde counties is now known as the Frio Canyon. Near the canyon, Hays found that the Comanches had a main camp. Being too small in number to attack the main camp, he hid "his men in a place of concealment, and taking with him a Mexican, went forth to spy out the strength and situation of the enemy."[49]

At a point within two miles of the entrance to the canyon, he and his companion discovered a party of about ten Comanches who appeared to be traveling down from their main camp, heading toward the vicinity of San Antonio. Gathering his company, Hays wrote, "I immediately attacked them."[50]

Among those foremost in the charge were Hays, Joseph Miller, and John Slein, a man new to the company. Slein had recently joined Hays' command at San Antonio to see the action, but had not been with him on his previous missions. As recalled by Hays in his later years, only one of the fleeing Indians was shot down by Slein before they retreated into a thicket.

> He was shot by a man who did not belong to the company, a man who was connected with some mercantile house in New York who went out to Texas to sell goods, and while there he fell in with the Rangers, and went along with this little party just to see the fun. He had a double-barrel shot gun, and killed this Indian.[51]

In an account he wrote of this battle in 1844, Hays offered more details.

> Charging them fiercely, the Indians retreated into a small thicket, fighting, however, in their retreat, disputing every inch of ground. The thicket being too dense to charge, Hays had it surrounded by his men, whilst he and two of his men entered the thicket and commenced a contest which was one of a most daring and trying nature.
>
> Hays and his two companions were soon . . . joined by another soldier [Slein]; these four kept up the fight until every Indian was killed. The Indians had but one gun, and the thicket being too dense to admit their using their arrows well, they fought under great disadvantage, but continued to struggle to the last, keeping up their war songs until all were hushed in death.
>
> Being surrounded by horsemen, ready to cut them down if they left the thicket, and unable to use their arrows with much effect in their situation, their fate was inevitable—they saw it and met it like heroes.[52]

In his 1844 recounting of the battle, Hays claimed that his rangers killed ten of twelve Indians. In his report immediately following the expedition, however, he listed that eight of the ten Comanches encountered were killed and the other two were taken as prisoners.

Capt. Hays' Rangers: June 1–July 1, 1841	
Captain: John Coffee Hays *Privates:* S. P. Ball [1] John M. Carroll [2] Antonio Coy [3] Addison Drinkwater [1] Peter Fohr [3] Francisco Granado [1] G. H. Grubbs [1] William Isbell [1]	Joseph Miller [3] Robert Pollett [1] Benjamin Prior [1] Benjamin Prior Jr. [1] John Slein [1] Note: Captain Hays paid from June 1, 1841. [1] Enlisted June 23, 1841. [2] Served June 12–21, 1841 only. [3] Enlisted June 12, 1841. Source: Texas State Archives muster rolls.

One of his rangers, Joseph Miller, was wounded but "not severely." The captured Comanches were a "squaw" and another Indian "desperately wounded." It was rare for the Comanches to leave an able fighting man behind to be taken. "This is the only instance on record of a Comanche's surrendering to the whites under any circumstances," noted Hays in 1844.

Hays' men took all of the Comanches' horses and property. He hoped to continue on to their main camp, but he found the distance to be much greater than his "much jaded" horses could bear. He was also concerned with coping with their main body, which greatly outnumbered his own forces.

"Although within two miles of their encampment," Hays reluctantly decided to withdraw to Béxar to tend to the injuries suffered by Private Miller. His thirty-six-man party reached San Antonio on the morning of July 1, 1841. Once he could successfully recruit a larger unit, Hays vowed to soon "proceed to the encampment, the situation of which I have now ascertained."

CHAPTER 12

The Gulf Coast Minutemen

July 1841

West Texas Rangers Captured

Stephen Dincans and his two fellow rangers found themselves on a very lonely vigil in a remote area of Texas. Members of Captain John Price's Victoria rangers had gone into service on January 3, 1841, just days ahead of Jack Hays' San Antonio rangers. His small ranger unit had scouted continually between the Guadalupe and Rio Grande rivers. During April, Price had established his ranging area around a good watering hole west of the Nueces River.

Captain Price had asked that each of his rangers equip themselves with three good horses while out in service. Dincans had done so, but he had since been forced to leave one of his horses just west of the Nueces, about thirty miles above Corpus Christi. With his two remaining horses, Dincans and fellow rangers John Blackwell and Thomas Lane were ordered to remain in camp in late April as the company rode back east for more provisions.

During the time that they were gone, however, the four-month service period which Price's rangers had been authorized by the Texas government to fulfill, was completed. According to Private Isaac Stem, the balance of the company was disbanded on May 2, 1841. "Captain Price merely returned the muster roll and never gave us any written discharge."[1]

Before word could be sent to the three rangers still on duty far west of the Nueces, they ran into trouble with Mexican forces.

Private Stem related:

> Part of the company came into the settlements for pro-
> visions, by order of Capt. Price. Stephen Dincans and two
> others, who I think were John Blackwell and a man by the
> name of Lane, were left behind on duty by the Capt. at the
> place called the water hole, or Palo Oaks, some 30 or 40
> miles west of the Nueces. Before we could return there
> again, we learned these men were all taken prisoners by
> the Mexicans.

Dincans, Blackwell, and Lane must have been in the field
for some period of time after the disbanding of Captain Price's
ranger company. By the time these men learned that their own
company had been discharged, they had joined up with another
ranging unit under Captain James P. Ownby.

Ownby's men had been mustered into service on May 18,
1841, as a result of attacks by Mexican forces in the area. The
southern settlements along the Texas Gulf Coast were especially
vulnerable to attacks by bandits and rogue Mexican military
forces during 1841. In the southwestern areas of Texas, Mexican
marauders sporadically attacked traders, stealing their goods
and livestock. In May 1841, a small group of Mexican soldiers
entered Refugio, where they killed a few men, robbed the town,
and carried off several citizens as hostages.[2]

A small party of volunteers was immediately organized by
Refugio's sheriff, thirty-two-year-old John Reagan Baker. A
former Tennessean who had settled in Texas in 1839, Baker had
served as a member of the Texan auxiliary corps of the Federalist
Army. His unit had fought a battle on October 23, 1840, at Ojo
de Agua, near Saltillo, and narrowly escaped back to Texas.[3]

Elected into command of his impromptu company, Captain
Baker pursued the Refugio attackers all the way to the Rio
Grande, but failed to overtake them. On his return, Baker's com-
pany encountered a *caballado* of horses that had been stolen in
Texas. Baker's men attacked the small Mexican party, recovered
the horses, and drove them to Carlos' Rancho, located in Refugio
County, twenty miles below Goliad.

Using Colonel Henry Kinney, President Lamar sent word to
General Arista that his soldiers had taken innocent citizens from

---

Capt. Miles' San Patricio Minutemen: May 14–June 30, 1841

Captain:
Alanson T. Miles

Privates:
George Anderson
James Bennett
John M. Black
John Bosharn
William J. Cairnes
Joseph Dolan
Alanson Ferguson
George M. Geary
Christopher Gonzales
James W. Hackett
John James
James W. Lenard
James McPhearson

Lawson F. Mills
Thomas W. Murray
Joseph B. Parks
Patrick Quinn
Peter Rouche
A. P. D. Sapp
Charles Sherman
William Snodgrass
William H. Van Horn
Thomas Walker *
Henry D. Weeks
James Wilson

* Served through June 15, 1841.

Source: Muster rolls of the Texas State Archives.

Refugio during this raid. Arista, learning that his men had not taken soldiers prisoner, ordered them released to maintain his peace with Texas.

In nearby San Patricio County, two new ranging units were organized as a result of the Mexican raid on Refugio County. San Patricio County was one of the twenty Texas counties approved to operate a company of minutemen. Captain Alanson T. Miles was elected into command of twenty-five minutemen, who mustered into service on May 14. Miles had served in Colonel Robert Coleman's 1836 ranger battalion and had thereafter become one of the southwestern Texas cowboys. The band he had ridden with was accused of rustling cattle at times, making Captain Miles seem ironic to now be leading rangers out against such rustlers. Three of his new rangers—William J. Cairns, Peter Rouche, and William Snodgrass—had just completed four months of service in Captain Price's Victoria ranger company as of May 2.

Captain Miles' San Patricio County Minutemen stayed active patrolling for bandits through the end of June 1841, although the company does not appear to have engaged in any serious conflicts.

The second company formed as a result of the Refugio attack was known as the "San Patricio Rangers." It was created for the "mutual protection of our persons, property, and civil and religious liberties." It formed at Camp Independence, west of the Nueces River, on May 18, 1841. Captain James Ownby, veteran of the 1839 Cherokee War, took command of two dozen men.[4]

Ownby's company included John H. Yerby, a former Travis Guard member, and Ewen Cameron, a pro-Federalist. Both were cowboys who had originally lived in the Austin area. Cameron was named after an early hero of his native country Scotland, from which he had traveled to join the Texas Revolution at age twenty-five. He served two terms in the Texas Army and then decided to make Texas his permanent home.[5]

Yerby, Cameron, and Captain Ownby's other "rangers" agreed that any spoils collected from a fight would be held jointly until equally divided. A company member was liable to the forfeiture of one-eighth to one-fourth of his share of the booty for breach of discipline or neglect of duty.

The "San Patricio Rangers" appear to have operated more for their own gain than in defending the county's citizens. From its inception on May 18, Captain Ownby's company took on other men as it moved out on expedition. One of his San Patricio Rangers was William M. Rozier, who had come to Texas in 1837 and had served as a cowboy under Ewen Cameron and William Cairnes on the southwestern frontier during 1839. In his pension papers, Rozier left good detail of his company's actions.

> James P. Ownby was commissioned to raise a company of rangers in 1841 by Mirabeau B. Lamar, then President of Texas. I joined his company on the 2nd day of April 1841. It numbered 62 men, 32 white men and 30 Lipan Indians.
>
> We proceed from Goliad west with the promise of $25 per month and all that we could take from the enemy. We beat up and down the Nueces River and west of that river until the Indians became indignant and left us.[6]

Captain Ownby's company made its first attack not against Mexican bandits, but against a party of traders in early June. Ownby's men took the traders without a fight and then proceeded to kill them. His company captured all of their goods, cash, and horses, valued at one thousand dollars.[7]

Capt. Ownby's San Patricio Rangers: Muster Roll May 18, 1841

Captain:
James P. Ownby *
Lieutenant:
David B. Fowler *
Orderly Sergeant:
H. M. Pratt *
Sergeant:
Daniel Davis *

Privates:
William Badgett
Ezekiel Ballard *
R. W. Basil *
John Blackwell *
Ewen Burgess
John Cameron
Stephen Dincans *
James G. Fowler *
G. L. Fruster
James Gaze *
Marvin Hastings
John G. Jamison *

Dennis Kennedy
Thomas Lane *
John Legman
F. H. Makinster
Joseph S. Marsh
Francis McCafferty *
E. M. McDonnell *
William H. Pate
William M. Rozier *
William Smith *
Berryman Oliver Stout *
Charles Todd
John H. Yerby

* Captured by Mexican troops June 14, 1841. Ballard, Blackwell, Dincans, and Lane had served as rangers under Capt. John T. Price until his unit was disbanded on May 2, 1841.

Key sources: Chabot, *Texas Expeditions of 1842, Vol. I: Corpus Christi and Lipantitlan*, 31–2. Nance, *After San Jacinto*, 424–5, 466.

Shortly after killing the traders, Ownby's company began bickering over the booty. One man withdrew from the unit. The remaining twenty-three "rangers" were so badly divided that they chose sides, some continuing to follow Captain Ownby and the remaining nine men choosing to be led by John Yerby, who had served in the Texas Army during 1836 and 1837.[8]

"Contention got up in the company and it split up," recalled ranger William Rozier. John Yerby led "the mutineers off on their own hook. There was only 14 men, Captain and all, left." Ownby, according to Rozier, decided he "would not go to the settlements just then, for fear those fellows [under Yerby] would charge us with cowardice. So we ventured further west."[9]

Captain Yerby's nine mutineers from the San Patricio Rangers soon became victims of their own greed. General Pedro de Ampudia, commanding the First Division of the Second Brigade of the Army Corps of the North, made his headquarters in Matamoros, Mexico. He dispatched a Mexican force of two hundred rancheros under Captain Enrique Villareal toward Kinney's ranch to break up "the Texan gangs who boldly advance to hostilize the frontier."[10]

Villareal's men came upon Captain Yerby and his nine former rangers at daylight on June 13 at Leonistos, near the Nueces River. A division of Villareal's men attacked Yerby's party. Nine out of ten former rangers were killed, with only a Mexican guide named Thomas Cabasos escaping through the woods. Mexican losses were two killed and two wounded, one gravely. One report listed that some of Yerby's men were captured and hanged.

Soon after Yerby and Ownby's rangers had split from each other, Captain Ownby's men had come upon Captain Price's three rangers, who had been left in the field in early May when their company disbanded. John Blackwell, Thomas Lane, and Stephen Dincans joined up with Ownby's company.

Captain Price did send Ezekiel Ballard back out from Victoria "to tell Dincans and two other members of the company who were on the west side of the Nueces River to come in and be discharged." According to Ballard, he was to "hunt up and bring in the three men left encamped on the Nueces." Ballard did deliver the news, but, according to Dincans, they never made it back to Victoria.

> During the captain's absence, the term of service expired. [I] received word from Capt. Price to come in and be discharged. [I] started in, in company with some twelve other persons with [I] had joined company after the captain's departure. On the way in [we] the whole of [this] party were taken prisoner by the Mexicans, about 400 in number, at the Palo Blanco Oaks.[11]

Captain Ownby's twelve rangers, plus the four former Price rangers, encountered the force of Mexican soldiers on June 14. According to Corpus Christi's Henry Kinney, Ownby's rangers "met 60 or 70 Mexicans" under a Captain Ramírez at a place called "the Para" north of Matamoros while en route from the Rio Grande. Ezekiel Ballard felt that they "were surrounded by the Mexicans, two hundred and fifty strong." Although the exact location is unclear, the Palo Blanco reference by Rozier could be to Palo Blanco Creek, which runs through Brooks County, well south of the Nueces.[12]

The rangers were so vastly outnumbered that fighting would only have brought on death for all. According to William Rozier, Captain Ownby elected to surrender his men and take his chances on survival.

> On the 14th day of June 1841, we fell in with Colonel [Villareal]'s volunteer Mexican dragoons at the Santa Rosa water holes on the Matamoros Road. They so greatly outnumbered us, [we] were captured on the conditions that we would be treated as prisoners of war and ride our own horses to the city of Matamoros.[13]

Rozier and sixteen other Texans were taken prisoner, including Captain Ownby, Lieutenant David B. Fowler, and Sergeant Daniel Davis. The former rangers immediately found that the Mexican soldiers had no intentions of honoring their surrender conditions. Ownby's men were "put on a ditch to labor on scant rations until our shirts gave out and we could not stand the sun no longer."[14]

Captain Ownby's men were then marched toward Mexico's interior by way of Camargo and Monterrey. While in Monterrey, the rangers were arrested. The Mexican officials "had us put in handcuffs and [we] were ordered to be marched so to the city of Mexico," recalled Rozier. The captain of the guard was lenient enough to remove the prisoners' handcuffs during the march, but conditions were trying, nonetheless.

From Monterrey, Ownby's rangers were marched to Saltillo. Before finally being marched to Mexico City, the San Patricio Rangers and some of the Santa Fe Expedition prisoners collaborated on an escape plan with other prisoners while being held at Saltillo.

William Rozier describes the Saltillo jailbreak.

> We there met foreign friends who planned our escape and furnished us with morphine to put in mescal to dose the soldiers. We did so, but we overdone the thing and they would not sleep. So we had to fight and we did fight on the night of 14th of September.
>
> We jumped the guards and killed eight of them dead on the ground. We then fled to the mountains but was

followed the next day by the infantry and cavalry. We there lost Dan Davis killed, Stephen Farrow [another Texan prisoner who had been captured separately] wounded and retaken, David Fowler wounded and retaken [and] Ballard retaken. The balance scattered in the mountains but finally was retaken, except Capt. Ownby and one Cissel.

The Capt. went to San Luis Obispo and was sent [to] New Orleans by one Mr. Davis, an English merchant-man living there at that time. The balance of us were finally gathered in Saltillo and started again to the city of Mexico.

According to Stephen Dincans, they "fell in with a number of the Santa Fe [Expedition] prisoners and was marched with them to the city of Mexico." The former San Patricio Rangers were kept imprisoned in Mexico City for months until being liberated from prison on June 14, 1842. They and the other surviving Santa Fe prisoners were returned by ship to New Orleans and to the Texas Gulf Coast during August 1842.[15]

One of the hot spots during the summer of 1841 was Kinney's trading post, located near Corpus Christi. Trading between Kinney's trading post and Matamoros attracted the attention of border outlaws. Although Captain Ownby's San Patricio Rangers had been formed to combat the frontier thieving that had become prevalent in western Texas, rumors had begun to circulate that his men were nothing more than common horse thieves them-selves. Following a requisition from the Victoria County sheriff, Jeremiah Findley, Captain John Price organized a company of minutemen in late June to patrol this area. He recruited some forty men from Victoria and neighboring San Patricio and Refugio counties.[16]

Prior to Price's company marching out, Captain Enrique Villareal's men had slaughtered most of John Yerby's thieving San Patricio men on June 13. Villareal's men had also captured the balance of Captain Ownby's rangers and hauled them into Matamoros.

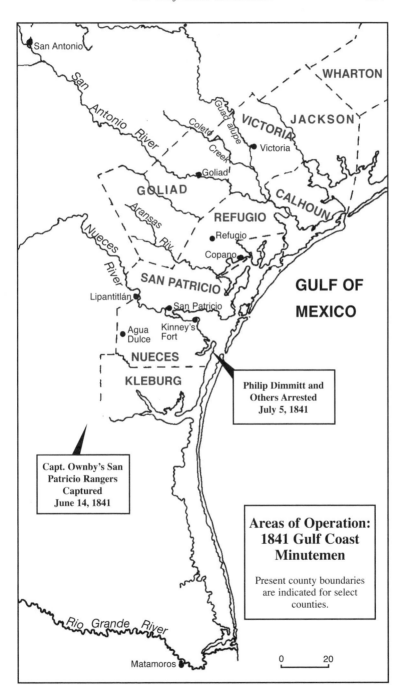

San Antonio

WHARTON

San Antonio River

Coleto

Guadalupe

VICTORIA

JACKSON

Victoria

Goliad

GOLIAD

Creek

CALHOUN

Aransas Riv.

REFUGIO

Refugio

Nueces River

Copano

SAN PATRICIO

GULF OF
MEXICO

Lipantitlán

San Patricio

Agua
Dulce

Kinney's
Fort

NUECES

KLEBURG

**Philip Dimmitt and
Others Arrested
July 5, 1841**

**Capt. Ownby's San
Patricio Rangers
Captured
June 14, 1841**

**Areas of Operation:
1841 Gulf Coast
Minutemen**

Present county boundaries
are indicated for select
counties.

Rio Grande River

Matamoros

0   20

Captain Price's rangers departed Victoria about June 20. They rode west of the Nueces River "for the purpose of arresting the marauders, who have for some time past infested our frontier," wrote Price.

> Our party was composed of citizens of this county, Refugio, and San Patricio. We reached the Nueces on the 23rd ulto., and there learned, that a short time previous, a Mexican had been to Kenney's Ranch, and stated that a party of three hundred soldiers were within thirty-five miles of that place, under the command of Col. [Villareal]. He stated that the troops were in search of robbers and had succeeded in surprising a party of ten, and had killed them all but one.
>
> The bodies of these men were found by our party. It appears that they (the robbers) had, a short time before, killed a party of traders and robbed them of several hundred dollars, a lot of blankets, [and] pelonceas [sic; sugar]. This party of Americans were led by a Mr. Yerby, who formerly resided at Austin.

Captain Price's company also encountered some Mexicans who had come from Camargo. They learned that the other half of the San Patricio company had fared little better. Captain Ownby "with about fifteen men, had been surrounded by two or three hundred Mexicans." Price was told that most of Ownby's men had been killed or captured. Having disposed of the San Patricio "cow-thieves," Captain Villareal's command had then returned to the Rio Grande before Captain Price's arrival at the Nueces.

From intelligence he had gathered from the various Mexican traders, Price felt that the Mexican authorities were very determined. He felt that they wished "not only to assert, but to *maintain* the control of the territory between the Nueces and the Rio Grande." Price learned from "a credible source that the Mexican mail passes weekly between Kenney's Ranch and Matamoros."

Mexican authorities continued to flex their strength in the dangerous area between the Rio Grande and Nueces. By July 14, 1841, the *Telegraph and Texas Register* reported that forty-seven cow thieves—including Ownby and Yerby's men—had been killed by Mexican troops in the space of a few weeks.[17]

Back in Victoria on July 2, Captain Price wrote to Branch Archer to report that his pursuit party had been unable to overtake Villareal's men. The citizens of San Patricio commenced building a fort at their town to give protection to the trade. San Patricio was closer to the Rio Grande settlements than any other Texas community and this area would remain a territorial hotbed for years.

Dimmitt's Capture and the Corpus Christi Minutemen

The trade wars in southwestern Texas grew more intense during the summer of 1841. By June, the trading post of Henry Kinney and William P. Aubrey was reportedly doing excellent business with the Mexican traders. Proprietor Kinney had paid a visit to General Mariano Arista's headquarters and on June 9 was reported to have been assured that his post would not be molested by Mexican troops.[18]

The backing of the Mexican army worked in the favor of Kinney and Aubrey's post when competition moved into their area. In May 1841, Texas Revolution veteran Philip Dimmitt began the establishment of a new trading post with his partner James Gourlay Jr., John Sutherland, and employees James C. Boyd and William Thompson. Dimmitt had first traveled to Texas from Kentucky in 1823 with a letter of introduction from Stephen F. Austin. He began operating trading posts on the Guadalupe River near Victoria, at Goliad, and at Dimmitt's Landing on Lavaca Bay, where he established his wharf and warehouse. He married a Tejano girl who was kin to Texas empresario Martín de León, and Dimmitt's trading business had flourished.[19]

Philip Dimmitt helped supply the Texas Army during the Texas Revolution and designed two different flags that were flown during the revolution. He had served in the Alamo until shortly before its fall to General Santa Anna's troops. After the 1836 war, Dimmitt had settled in Refugio. He built his newest trading post with his partners in May 1841, on the Laguna Madre, near the present site of Calallen, in the Corpus Christi area. Dimmitt's post was located near the head of Padre Island and, being only about fifteen miles below Aubrey and Kinney's rancho, he cut into their business.

On July 1, 1841, the Mexican government declared the ports of Texas and Yucatán to be in a state of blockade, prohibiting the introduction of products from either of these two "republics" to be brought into Mexico. Lieutenant (Brevet Captain) Vicente Sánchez was given orders to apprehend any Texian contrabandistas. He was also given specific orders to apprehend Philip Dimmitt.

Captain Sánchez set out with fourteen cavalry men under orders of General Ampudia. They travelled with Blas Falcón, a man known by locals to be "Aubrey and Kinney's spy, travelling agent or courier." On Sunday, July 4, 1841, Captain Sánchez and his detachment arrived at Dimmitt's Island and captured a small boat manned by William Thompson. He was taken prisoner, while a Mexican detail used his boat to cross Corpus Christi Bay to the island.[20]

There, the soldiers plundered the trading post of all its merchandise and robbed the locals of everything. The loss was estimated at nearly $6,000. The soldiers also seized Dimmitt and three more of his employees: James Boyd, Henry Graham, and Stephen W. Farrow. During the afternoon, a party of Sánchez's soldiers also captured a party of Texans working on a salt deposit.

That evening, Captain Sánchez and his Lieutenant Chipita visited the Kinney and Aubrey rancho. They did not attack the inhabitants, but came away with whiskey, bread, and supplies. The Mexicans then waited until the afternoon of July 5 for James Gourlay to return to Corpus Christi from his visit to President Lamar. Fortunately, Gourlay did not return before Captain Sánchez's soldiers moved out for Matamoros that day. Dimmitt argued his arrest, saying that he did not deal in stolen cattle. Sánchez informed him that his arrest had been ordered because Dimmitt was believed to be a spy for the Texas government.[21]

The most disturbing thing about this seizure was that James W. Byrne, a citizen of Lamar in Refugio County, felt the Mexican officers of this party "appeared to be on intimate terms" with the nearby trading post of Kinney and Aubry. Located a short distance from Dimmitt's, Kinney and Aubry's post "remained unmolested" although the cavalry officers visited that post just before raiding Dimmitt's.[22]

When Captain Sánchez's party withdrew, they left behind four of those taken at the salt lake and William Thompson, who was too sick to travel. Thompson later declared that the salt workers released were ones who declared that they worked for Colonel Kinney. Dimmitt, Boyd, Farrow, Graham, and two other hostages were taken to Matamoros for detainment.[23]

Byrne complained to Secretary of War Archer about this seizure and demanded "prompt and energetic action on the part of the government." He estimated that the Mexican army that was in Texas amounted to around 300 soldiers. Byrne and James Gourlay both wrote letters to Archer, which were sent via courier Thompson, recently released by the Mexicans. Thompson planned on denouncing some traitors, "who were the cause of the late transaction," according to Gourlay.[24]

The local citizens of the Victoria and Corpus Christi area did not sit around and wait for the government to respond to this seizure. Former Texas congressman James Wright wrote Archer on July 10 saying that the "citizens here take great interest in favor of Capt. Dimmitt, and would like to have the sanction of the government to go to his rescue." Should it not be given, Wright vowed that the citizens "will go on their own responsibility." He added that "I have no doubt that Kinney is acting a double part."

A public meeting was held on July 10 in Victoria at the house of Charles Vincent. Accounts of the raid written by James Gourlay and William Thompson were read and then Richard Roman—a former company commander at the battle of San Jacinto—read the citizens' resolutions. The Victorians resolved that such acts "should not be tolerated by a Texan possessing the feelings of a patriot." The townspeople thereby decided to aid the government "in the maintainance of her jurisdiction over the territory between the Nueces & Rio Grande."

The committee forwarded its strong recommendations to Secretary Archer, who sent his reply on July 14. The local militia district was the Fifth Regiment, First Brigade and was under Colonel Abner McDonald, based out of Victoria. At the request of the Victoria committee, and in response to Archer's reply, Colonel McDonald ordered out the sheriff to execute a warrant against the post of Aubry and Kinney.[25]

Aubrey and Kinney were arraigned on July 17 by the Victoria committee for having committed treason by conspiring with Mexican soldiers for Dimmitt's capture. They were also accused of being in cooperation with General Arista's forces.[26]

With orders for the arrest of William Aubrey and Henry Kinney, the Victoria County sheriff was to be accompanied by Captain Charles M. Creaner and his Victoria County Minutemen. Colonel McDonald of the Fifth Regiment issued orders to Captain Creaner on July 28, 1841. He was to proceed to Corpus Christi, serve the warrants, and to seize any enemy goods and traders he might find.[27]

Captain Creaner's rangers, numbering twenty-three, rode into Kinney's rancho on July 23, as Captain Creaner described in his report:

> We arrived at their establishment on the 23rd and found there ten Mexican traders, with a small cavayard of horses, recently from the Rio Grande.
>
> We made prisoners of the traders and have brought them, with their horses to this place [Victoria].
>
> On my return, I learned that a party of seven traders had just passed the Mission [Refugio], going eastward, with a number of mules and a few horses. I immediately detached a party from my command, for their capture, which was accordingly this day effected.

Creaner's minutemen hauled these other traders back into Victoria, where they protested that they were protected by fair trade agreements between Mexico and Texas. Among these July 28 captives were José María Cantú, Francisco María Cantú, Francisco Guzmán, and Valentin Gutiérrez. Cantú and his men were held as prisoners by the rangers for eleven days. During this time, they were stripped of their horses, mules, bridles, rifles, pistols, and other personal property. Cantú and his men later filed a claim that they had lost $2,348 during their detainment.[28]

Captain Creaner made his report to the government from Victoria on July 28, stating that he had both groups of Mexican prisoners in town. Colonel McDonald, the mayor of Victoria, warned the secretary of war that if the government determined that the traders should be released with their property, "some assurance from you would be necessary that the captors should be properly compensated." This was especially important, as the "minute men" worked with the knowledge that they split the booty from their captures.

Within days of Captain Creaner's captures, another group of Texan volunteers under Captain Richard Roman moved to Corpus Christi. Roman's men captured about ten Mexican traders, whom they herded back toward Victoria. En route, they stopped to divide the traders' effects, and then turned the men loose on foot.

When President Lamar returned in the fall from government business in Galveston, he sent orders that the innocent traders be released. They had not been involved with the capture of Philip Dimmitt and his men. Lamar also ordered that their property be returned, "so long as they demeaned themselves as peaceful traders." When he found that the captors had already distributed the traders' goods, Lamar recommended that Congress consider making reparation for the seized property. This was, after all, property "which the Government had pledged itself to protect."[29]

For his disobedience in hauling in innocent traders, Captain Creaner and his rangers were dismissed from service. They remained in operation until Colonel Peter Bell, adjutant general of the Republic, was sent to the frontier to replace them with other troops.

Henry Kinney and William Aubrey were brought to trial in Austin for their charges. They appeared on July 30 before Judge Anderson Hutchinson, a forty-three-year-old former Virginian who was considered by some to be one of the most scholarly lawyers and legal writers to ever sit on the bench. Before arriving in Austin in 1840 and subsequently becoming judge of the Fourth District of Texas, he had coauthored *A Digest of the Laws of Mississippi*, where he had also practiced. The Kinney/Aubrey case was heard before Judge Anderson on August 2, 1841. Several respected citizens spoke in the defense of Aubrey and Kinney, reporting that they had seen no treasonable activity between them and the Mexican military. When no one appeared to testify against them, Judge Hutchinson found them not guilty and dismissed the men with their freedom.[30]

Judge Alanson Ferguson, the fifty-year-old chief justice of San Patricio, was accused of receiving money from Henry Kinney to influence the case. Ferguson had been given money to pay Kinney's expenses to Austin to explain the circumstances around the abduction of Dimmitt and other citizens. Feeling that Judge Ferguson had been bribed to present Kinney's side of the

---

Capt. Miles' San Patricio Minutemen: July 12–August 25, 1841

Captain:
Alanson T. Miles

Privates:
George Anderson
John M. Black
John Botham
John W. Brown [1]
William J. Cairnes
Ewen Cameron [1]
Joseph Dolan [2]
Michael Duggan [1]
F. Gerard [1]
James W. Hackett [3]
Lindsay S. Hagler [1]
John Hefferon [1]
Patrick Mahan [1]
Seth P. Marvin [1]
Patrick McEvoy [1]
James McPherson
Lawson F. Mills
John C. Neill [1]

Joseph B. Parks
Patrick Quinn
William Rupley [1]
James W. Senan [1]
Thomas Senan [1]
French Smith [1]
William Snodgrass
Franklin R. Taylor [1]
Henry D. Weeks
William Wells [1]
Henry Whalen [1]
Thomas J. Wheeler [1]
John B. White [1]
John Wilson [1]

[1] Enlisted into company on July 27, 1841.
[2] Served 7/12–26 and 8/11–25, 1841.
[3] Served July 12–26, 1841.

Source: Muster rolls of the Texas State Archives.

---

case, friends of Dimmitt held a public meeting at San Patricio and petitioned President Lamar to have the judge removed from his position as chief justice of San Patricio County.

Operating under the eye of Judge Ferguson was the San Patricio Minuteman company of Captain Alanson Miles, under whose command Ferguson had ranged in June. Miles had first taken out the twenty-six-man San Patricio Minuteman company from May 20 to June 30, 1841. When he brought this unit back into service on July 12, he patrolled with just a dozen other men.

Two of his men, Joseph Dolan and James Hackett, completed the fifteen-day patrol and were replaced. Miles, in fact, added a total of twenty new men to his muster on July 27, bringing the company size up to thirty-one. The strengthening of the San Patricio Minutemen on July 27 occurred at about the time that Kinney and Aubrey were being sent to Austin for trial.

The petitioners who had wanted Lamar to remove Judge Ferguson from power soon found that the president did not have the authority to dismiss him. Ferguson later explained to Congress that he had heard the circumstances surrounding the Dimmitt abduction. When he prepared to go to Austin to present these facts, he found his own horses too broken down to make the trip. He therefore had borrowed twenty dollars from Kinney to buy himself a horse and one-for-one of the members of the San Patricio rangers.

When Ferguson had prepared to go to Austin, several members of the San Patricio Minutemen gave him a power of attorney to draw pay due for their services. When Judge Ferguson was able to successfully draw pay for these rangers, he came under further scrutiny. In Austin, he drew pay for twenty-five rangers who had served thirty-six days, including Captain Miles. For Private James Bennett, he drew pay for twenty-eight days.

Charges were made against Ferguson that only fourteen men of Captain Miles' company had actually served as much as thirty-six days. Judge Ferguson also, reportedly, drew pay for men who had not authorized him to do so and he also drew pay for men who had not been on active duty.

Lindsay S. Hagler, one of the San Patricio Minutemen, was among those who protested against the chief justice. He had immigrated to Texas in 1836 and served as a captain in the Texas Army who spent much of his time recruiting in the United States. In 1840, Hagler had served San Patricio County in the House of Representatives of the Fifth Congress of the Republic of Texas. On October 5, in a bit of political maneuvering, Hagler wrote that Judge Ferguson had "violated the oath of office for the purpose of swindling the Govt. and has retained the money which he received and defrauded the members of the company."[31]

While Aubrey and Kinney defended themselves in Austin in early August, Captain Alanson Miles' San Patricio Minutemen continued to range the western frontier. Upon his return to Corpus Christi on August 13, Kinney found that Miles' men were "robbing indiscriminantly." He and Aubrey wrote to President Lamar that the government should station mounted men "near the Nueces under a responsible officer," calling the current minute men "robber Texians."

Simeon L. Jones, a new trader orginally from Wales working the area, wrote on August 18 that the volunteer companies organized by Branch Archer were not doing their duty. Ironically,

---

Capt. January's "Company of Volunteers": August 3–31, 1841

Captain:
James B. P. January
Lieutenant:
George Lees
Orderly Sergeant:
George W. Guthrie

Privates:
Daniel Allen
Archibald W. Bass [1]
Joseph Berry
Lyn Bobo [1]
_____ Brewer
James H. Brown
_____ Brymer
_____ Carnalles
James Caruthers [1]
_____ Cheshier
Henry Clark [1]
_____ Davis [1]
John T. Dillon [1]
John Divine [1]
Joseph Dolan [1]
William H. Emory [1]
John James

B. S. Jenkins
_____ Licett
_____ Long
James B. Martin [2]
John McKenzie [1]
James McMilkin [1]
A. W. Morris
Richard Owens
James Peacock [1]
_____ Robinson
Richard Roman
_____ Ross
_____ Sanderson
_____ Smith [1]
_____ Smith
Robert Trimble
R. W. Turner [1]
James Vanbibber [1]
_____ Walker [1]
Jesse Youngblood

[1] Joined on August 9.
[2] Joined on August 6.

Source: George Lees PD, R 168, F 83–169.

Jones would end up taking the position as San Patricio's representative in the House of Representatives for the Sixth Congress after Lindsay Hagler successfully contested the election of Alanson Ferguson. Jones wrote of the volunteer companies:

> I fear they are transgressing all authority vested in them, as a company came to this place a few days since and carried off several horses, amongst them some belonging to Aubrey & Kinney. This act was committed under the pretence that the horses were Mexican property.[32]

Another of these volunteer companies mentioned by Jones was that of Captain James January, who was elected to head a forty-man company organized in Victoria County. His "company of volunteers" was acting under orders of the secretary of war, dated July 14, 1841. January mustered his company into service on August 3, with more men joining on August 9, possibly as he headed out.

Jones related to Archer that Captain Miles' company was at San Patricio during August, "and they continue apprehending all traders." Around mid-August, his men apprehended thirty-three Mexican traders and held them as prisoners. These men subsequently made their escape "and were followed by a party of Capt. January's company." January's company had returned to the settlements and disbanded by August 31.

Captain Miles' San Patricio Minutemen had made an excursion to the southern extremity of Padre Island, in company with several volunteers from Gonzales. The Texian group consisted of about fifty men, according to Lindsay Hagler, one of the rangers. On the afternoon of August 17, Miles' men had surprised a Mexican captain named Corsco and his nine soldiers.[33]

Captain Corsco and his soldiers were taken with their horses to San Patricio and turned over to Chief Justice Ferguson. According to Hagler, Captain Corsco wrote to General Ampudia at Matamoros to suggest that his men be exchanged for Philip Dimmitt and other Texans being held prisoner. Ranger William Snodgrass boarded the Mexican prisoners through September 14, at the cost of ten dollars per day for twenty-eight days.

From Corsco, the rangers learned that the entire Mexican force on the Rio Grande did not exceed three hundred troops. Forty rancheros under Colonel Villareal operated on the Arroyo Colorado. Further north of the Rio Grande, Colonel Ramírez reportedly had another fifty to one hundred men who robbed traders of either nationality. The intelligence also revealed that there were about one hundred regular infantry troops at Matamoros and another fifty men under Colonel Fernández at Camargo, although these latter troops had few horses strong enough to walk at all.

Colonel Peter Bell, the Texas Militia's adjutant general who was on a tour of the Texas military ordered by President Lamar, soon learned of the poor conduct of Captain Miles and his men. Bell had found Captain Miles to be so "odious" that he replaced him from command of his own company. In his place, he promoted ranger William J. Cairnes to captain.[34]

Cairnes was a Scotsman who had been taken prisoner by Mexican cattle rustlers in late 1837 near San Patricio. He was tied to a cannon and dragged along behind the marauders. Cairnes would spend months in prison in Matamoros before making his escape in October 1838. Cairnes had later served as one of Captain Price's spies during the early months of 1841. Now in command of his own ranging company, Captain Cairnes was certainly believed by Colonel Bell to be a man more likely to seek his vengeance on the Mexican bandit parties.[35]

Muster roll and pay roll records show that Captain Miles served through August 25, 1841, as commander of the San Patricio Minutemen. When the company went back into the field on expedition on August 29, it was commanded by Captain Cairnes, with Alanson Miles serving as one of his enlisted rangers. The only incident of note during Captain Cairnes' first few weeks of command was that ranger James McPherson drowned in the Nueces River on September 8.

Henry Kinney later wrote that

A force was now stationed at San Patricio (east side of the river) under this said Miles, in the ranging service. Miles, becoming odious, was displaced and join[ed] the company as a private; was succeeded by Capt. Cairnes (a Scotchman).[36]

At the very time that Colonel Bell was surveying the situation of the coastal Texas settlements, some of the captured Texans were trying to escape from their Mexican captors. As of August 1841, General Arista had held twenty-two Texans at Monterrey, including those captured with Philip Dimmitt and Captain James Ownby. Charged with such crimes as cattle stealing, robbery, murder, and spying, these Texan prisoners had then been marched from Monterrey to Saltillo.[37]

As related, a number of the Texans attempted to escape by spiking their guards' mescal with morphine. Eighteen attempted an escape, although most were either recaptured or killed in the process. Philip Dimmitt and several others were being held separately and were unable to escape. One of the Mexican captains sent out word that if the few remaining escapees did not return, Dimmitt would be executed. This news was apparently too much for poor Dimmitt. In an unobserved moment, he took a large dose of laudanum (opium) and committed suicide.[38]

The Refugio Attack and Cairnes' Rangers

Aside from dealing with the rogue nature of Captain Miles' ranger command, Colonel Peter Bell learned a great deal about the troubles being faced by south Texas coastal settlers in 1841. Shortly after dealing with Miles' rangers, Bell found that Mexican banditos had made another raid upon the Texas settlements at Refugio before dawn on Saturday, September 18.

This attack came in spite of recent assurances from General Arista that his Mexican troops would no longer molest the Texas frontier. The assault against the Mission of Refugio was carried out by a force of sixty mounted men under Captain Agatón Quinoñes.[39]

The marauders attacked just before daybreak, and the settlers offered a brief skirmish. Refugio County Justice of the Peace Henry Ryals fought desperately, reportedly killing one Mexican soldier and wounding at least one more. Benjamin F. Neal, John W. B. McFarland, and John R. Talley escaped to Victoria to spread the word of the assault. The other non-Spanish speaking men of Refugio, numbering about ten, were taken prisoner. They were stripped of their clothing, had their hands tied before them, and were tied to the tails of the Mexicans' horses and forced to follow at a brisk trot. After plundering Refugio of its valuables, Captain Quinoñes and his men departed at 8:00 a.m. with their prisoners.

Shortly after the Mexicans withdrew from the mission, five men were found murdered on the Aransas. Six miles south of the Mission Refugio, Quinoñes' men paused briefly. There, they killed and hanged the rebellious Justice of the Peace Ryals by his ankles. The wife of captive Michael Fox appeared in this camp and pleaded for the release of her husband. One of the soldiers struck her in the head with his pistol. Enraged, Captain Quinoñes ordered Fox released with his wife.[40]

Once the news of the raid reached the Victoria-area settlements, a pursuit party was quickly organized. Captain William Cairnes took the lead with his thirty-one-man San Patricio

Capt. Cairnes' San Patricio Minutemen: August 29–Nov. 12, 1841

Captain:
William J. Cairnes
First Sergeant:
William Snodgrass

Privates:
George Anderson
John M. Black
Lyn Bobo
John Botham
John W. Brown
Ewen Cameron
Michael Duggan
F. Gerard
John Hefferon
Thomas Lennon
James W. Linam
Patrick Mahan
Seth P. Marvin
Patrick McEvoy
John McKenzie
James McPherson [1]

Alanson T. Miles
Joseph Milford [3]
John Mills [2]
Lawson F. Mills
John C. Neill
Joseph B. Parks
Patrick Quinn
French Smith
Franklin R. Taylor
Henry D. Weeks
William Wells
Henry Whalen
Thomas J. Wheeler
John B. White
John Wilson

[1] Drowned in the Nueces River 9/8/41.
[2] Served from Sept. 21–27, 1841 only.
[3] Served from Oct. 13–27, 1841 only.

Sources: Muster rolls of the Texas State Archives and John Mills PD, R 197, F 687–706.

Minutemen from the San Antonio River and followed the Mexican attackers during late September. They failed to overtake them, however. Cairnes' company remained in the field from September 13 through November 12, making five consecutive fifteen-day expeditions.

Technically, the San Patricio Minutemen had already spent their maximum of four months in the field during 1841. Due to the current crisis caused by the Refugio raid, Colonel Bell made the call to keep the company of Captain Cairnes in service. "I reorganized it," wrote Bell, "and made arrangements with Messrs. Aubry and Kinney to supply them with subsistence and ammunition."[41]

On September 20, 1841, Bell issued written orders to Captain Cairnes to station his men on the east side of the Nueces River at or near San Patricio.

Colonel Peter Hansbrough Bell (1812–1898) was adjutant general of the Texas Militia in 1841. During an inspection tour of southern Texas coastal settlements, he reorganized the San Patricio Minutemen to combat Mexican marauders who operated along the Nueces Strip. Bell, a veteran of San Jacinto who later commanded Texas Rangers, was elected the third Governor of Texas in 1849. *Texas State Library & Archives Commission, 1981/57-6.*

The object of your command, being for defensive operations, you will be careful to do no act or make any movement calculated to induce attack from the Mexican enemy. You are strictly enjoined to give every facility and protection to any parties trading to and from the Rio Grande. You will be active and watchful in intercepting and breaking up all marauding parties, being careful to understand the true character of parties supposed to exist for marauding purposes.

At times when his company should be stationed near San Patricio, Cairnes was ordered to keep some of his scouts continually in the field. They should scout for "suspicious bodies of men lurking on the Nueces, Agua Dulce, San Fernandez, or any watering places adjacent."

Captain Cairnes' rangers were unable to overtake the Mexican marauders who had sacked Refugio in September. Captain Quinoñes' raiding party moved through Laredo and carried its prisoners to Lampazos, where General Rafael Vasquez ultimately ordered the Texans released. Quiñoñes was ordered to Arista's headquarters at Monterrey, where he was imprisoned for the outrage he had committed and was later wounded by a guard while trying to escape.[42]

A report on the sacking of Refugio reached Austin on Saturday, September 25. Colonel Bell was ordered by Branch Archer to investigate this affair and to "take whatever steps you deem necessary for the future protection of Refugio and the other exposed towns and settlements on the western frontier."[43]

Colonel Bell was to also report on the trade with Mexico that existed in this western area and what effect this had on creating the recent difficulties. He was to give his opinion on whether such trading should be closed down. Archer gave Colonel Bell authority to raise forces and quartermasters as necessary, but to not "prosecute and war beyond the limits of our own territory."

Peter Bell had been active in the field during September, visiting numerous points among the western Texas frontier to ascertain the problems between the trading posts, Mexican raiders, and the Matamoros military faction. He visited Victoria, Lamar, Live Oak Point, New Labahia, San Patricio, Lipantitlán, Corpus Christi, and other settlements.[44]

Bell gave his report to Secretary Archer on October 4. During Bell's travels in September, he found no bodies of hostile bandits or Indians at work on the western borders.

> The disbanding order of the 14th of August has been executed with reference to all bodies of armed men on the Western frontier; and there is at this time, no armed force of any character, other than the company commanded by Capt. Cairnes. All Mexican traders have been released, and furnished with the proper passports to the Rio Grande.

He did find that Mexican Colonel Villareal had stationed approximately 150 armed men on the Little Colorado River, "at the three principal crossings of that stream, for the double purpose of giving security to Varial's ranches, and of intercepting the trade between the two countries."

Bell also found that there were several parties of "mustangers" roaming chiefly on the Palo Blanco, Santa Rosa, and Las Ulmas streams, some 60–100 miles south of San Patricio. He estimated

---

Capt. Baker's Refugio County Minutemen: Oct. 25–Dec. 12, 1841

Captain:
John Reagan Baker
First Lieutenant:
Matthew W. Cody
Second Lieutenant:
James Wilson

Privates:
Jeremiah Findley
Edward Fitzgerald
Michael Fox
John McDaniel
John W. B. McFarland
Benjamin F. Neal
Willard Richardson
Charles Smith

Edward St. John
John R. Tally
John Wilson

Joined on November 25:
Michael Cahill
James B. Collinsworth
Edward Drew
Raphael Gonzales
Walter Lambert
Frances Plummer
Joseph E. Plummer
Michael Whelan

Source: Muster rolls of the Texas State Archives.

---

there to be some 150 mustangers in these parties. Although hostile by nature, these bandits did not pose immediate threats to the western settlements of Texas in Bell's opinion.

The bodies of men most dangerous to the western settlements were those commanded by "Agatone, Rimeras, and others," who were "of a different character." They were known to make frequent attacks on Texas citizens and were believed to be under orders of Mexico's frontier commander to break up trade along the Rio Grande. These men were not held responsible for their actions and were known to attack and kill both Texian and Mexican traders without regard.[45]

"Their object is plunder," wrote Colonel Bell, "no matter when, or where found; and there is no sacrifice that they will not make, but that of their own cowardly blood." Bell found that the west Texan citizens wanted the trade to remain open with Mexico, but that serious measures needed to be undertaken to alleviate the lawlessness that prevailed. Bell urged that future armed forces sent by Secretary of War Archer must carefully ascertain "the proper respect and distinction between friendly Rancheros, and suspicious and irresponsible Mexicans." The friendly ranch owners east of the Rio Grande were often mistaken for the marauding rebels.[46]

McDaniel's Refugio Co. Minutemen: Dec. 16, 1841–Feb. 24, 1842

Captain:
John McDaniel

Privates:
Bartlett Annibal [1]
Michael Cahill
Israel Canfield [1]
Matthew W. Cody
Jeremiah Findley [1]
Edward Fitzgerald [1]
James Fox
John Fox
Michael Fox
John W. B. McFarland
Benjamin F. Neal [1]

Willard Richardson
Charles Smith
Edmund St. John
Edmund St. John Jr.
James St. John
William St. John
Michael Whelan
James Wilson

[1] Paid as a spy.
[2] Served from Oct. 13–27, 1841 only.
[3] Served from Sept. 21–27, 1841 only.

Source: Muster rolls of the Texas State Archives.

On October 4, Colonel Bell called for a mounted force of 150–200 voluntarily enrolled men to serve on the western frontier of Texas. If such volunteers could not be had, he asked that Archer draft a three-month company. Bell felt that such men should be

> well armed, mounted and equipped; and in every manner
> provided, so as to make them efficient rangers between
> the Nueces and Rio Grande, and from the Agua Dulce, or
> even from the Coast, and as high up as the movements of
> an enemy may require. This would give confidence and
> repose from the much dreaded and formidable maraud-
> ers who are now roaming at will over the territory men-
> tioned.

To supply such rangers, Bell felt that Béxar and the trading post of Aubrey and Kinney would suffice for provisioning. Bell felt that the marauders who had recently attacked the Mission Refugio had fallen back to the Rio Grande, "but their respite will be short without the protection suggested."

★ ★ ★ ★ ★

Baker and McDaniel's Refugio Rangers

Prior to receiving this report from Adjutant General Peter Bell, President Lamar struggled to understand the true state of affairs on Texas' southern frontier. News of the September 18 attack on Refugio was still troubling. Lamar issued orders to Captain Jack Hays on October 2, 1841, to report as quickly as possible to the seat of government. Hays was ordered to raise one hundred volunteers and to report to Colonel Bell for direct orders in Austin.

Hays was ordered to clear the "entire Western country" of enemy marauders until the new government of Texas could be convened. President Lamar's administration was soon to depart office in favor of the inauguration of newly-elected President Sam Houston's administration. At that time, Lamar hoped that "some more efficient mode of giving security to that portion of the frontier, than can possibly be afforded by the operation of temporary volunteers or extended by the minutemen system," could be devised.[47]

While there is no evidence that Jack Hays rode to south Texas with the proposed volunteer force, there is evidence that another ranging company came into service to help protect the southern frontier. Captain John Reagan Baker mustered in the Refugio County Minutemen on October 25, 1841. Baker, thirty-two, had been elected the county's sheriff on February 1.

Among Captain Baker's original thirteen rangers was Refugio County Chief Justice Ben Neal, who had been present when Refugio was attacked, and Victoria County sheriff Jeremiah Findley. According to the company's first lieutenant, Matthew Cody, most of the rangers were in "destitute condition" by late 1841. Lieutenant Cody noted that his men were "sufferers at the late robbery at the Mission of Refugio."[48]

Findley, Neal, Edward Fitzgerald—a lawyer and the Refugio County representative in the House of Representatives of the Fourth Congress of the Republic of Texas—John McDaniel, and Michael Fox served as the company spies when the minutemen were not on expedition. The company went out on October 25 and served continually until December 12.

The minutemen were limited to only serve fifteen straight days. Lieutenant Cody resolved this by turning in three consecutive rolls, all of fifteen days' duration. They were all concurrent, but were approved by Ben Neal, a member of the company and also the chief justice.

Lieutenant Cody was acting commander of the Refugio Minutemen by this time. He completed a muster roll for each of the company's three expeditions, "the Capt. being absent and sick at Corpus Christi." Cody shows as "Lieut. Commanding" on November 9, indicating that Captain Baker became sick during the first expedition and never rejoined his company.

With Baker out sick, the company took on eight new rangers while in Victoria on November 25 prior to making its third expedition. When the third expedition returned from the field on December 12, Captain Baker relinquished his control of the Refugio County Minutemen. One of his spies, John McDaniel assumed command of the company from Lieutenant Cody. McDaniel organized twenty men and led his rangers back into the field on December 16.

They served back-to-back fifteen-day expeditions in southern Texas through January 15, 1842. After resting for five days, Captain McDaniel led his company back into the field for the period of January 20 to February 6. They returned to the settlements to rest and reprovision. The final recorded expedition made by McDaniel's Refugio County Minutemen spanned the period of February 10–24, 1842.

The only other ranging company operating during the last quarter of 1841 in extreme southern Texas was the San Patricio Minutemen of Captain William Cairnes. Authorized by Colonel Bell to remain active beyond the normal service limits, Cairnes' company completed five consecutive fifteen-day expeditions during the span of August 29–November 12, 1841. All muster rolls for these expeditions were presented by Captain Cairnes and were approved by San Patricio County Chief Justice William B. Goodman on December 17.

Cairnes' men operated in a defensive scouting mode and apparently did not have any major conflicts during October and November. Colonel Bell filed another report to Branch Archer on November 21, 1841. In it, he found that the desire for volunteer companies operating against Mexican marauders had failed, due largely to the inability of the local merchants to properly outfit such men. Bell found that the local citizens "have so long borne the brunt of frontier troubles that they are truly war worn, and in means worn out." Bell believed that the government must provide for such defensive companies by offering supplies and ammunition to rangers to operate on the western frontier. Colonel Bell turned his focus to organizing an efficient corps of spies to handle such operation. These men were to be enlisted for three months, unless discharged sooner.[49]

Bell placed command of this new spy group under Captain Cairnes, whose men were to act in the role previously conducted by his minuteman company. Cairnes was in Victoria as of November 12, where he began recruiting some new men to serve in his "Western Spy Company" for a three-month period.[50]

Operating along the Nueces River in late November, Cairnes' spies discovered a party of Mexicans organizing some thirty miles away. The Mexicans were observed during the early weeks of December by the Texan scouts. Word was finally passed that the Mexican force was advancing upon Corpus Christi. At Henry Kinney's post, the cannon was loaded and manned in front of the gate to the trading post.[51]

Captain Cairnes was ready with about twenty-eight rangers and twenty-five citizen volunteers. He ordered the Mexican riders into Kinney's post, where they were disarmed and their horses were placed under a strong guard for two days. Convinced that the Mexicans had come under peaceful terms, the Texans allowed them to trade and then leave the post.

Several days after the Mexican traders had departed, Captain Cairnes departed "with some volunteer citizens," wrote San Patricio Chief Justice William Goodman. This would have been about December 28, 1841. Hoping to rout Mexican marauders, Cairnes led twenty men in a charge upon a traders camp he had discovered. The traders fled as Cairnes' men charged them. After running for some distance, they halted and gave indications that they did not wish to fight. Cairnes, however, again charged and killed one of the traders. The Texans returned to the Mexican camp, took possession of their mules and other belongings, and then returned to their own post.[52]

Captain Cairnes' "Western Spy Company" remained in the field for its allotted three months, being discharged in San Patricio County on February 12, 1842.

Although some actions of Cairnes' men were questionable, the southern Texas Rangers of 1841, in general, performed much-needed service in protecting their frontier. The Indians who remained in the more northern and eastern settlements of Texas were small worry by comparison to the rogue Mexican bandits and cattle rustlers which prevailed in this area. Such would be the case along the famed "Nueces Strip" for many years to come.

CHAPTER 13

"Bravo Too Much"

August 1841

Chandler–Erath Expedition: August 1841

Captain George Erath apparently bought into the philosophy that the best defense is a good offense. Involved with the Texas Rangers since 1835, he had learned early the value of keeping mounted patrols in the field.

> My policy was to penetrate the Indian country and to keep a few men continually in the territory occupied by the Indians, by those means harassing them and compelling them to retire for fear of having the camps discovered and being attacked by larger numbers.[1]

Erath's Milam County Minutemen operated from Fort Bryant during the summer of 1841. Home of San Jacinto veteran Benjamin Franklin Bryant, Bryant's Station included the fortified blockhouse and was located on Little River in extreme western present Milam County. The site is designated by a marker six miles west of present Buckholts.[2]

Erath's minutemen had already made three expeditions since their organization on April 11, 1841. Making preparations to set out on his fourth expedition on July 16, Erath found plenty of volunteers. He allowed a number of them to volunteer into his company as temporary substitutes for some of his regulars. Each man would be paid six dollars per day for the expedition.

For this expedition, Captain Erath sought to rendezvous with the Robertson County rangers under Captain Eli Chandler. His Robertson County Minutemen had captured fourteen prisoners from an Indian village in the Cross Timbers near the forks of the Trinity River on June 9. Most were Shawnee or Ioni women and children, but Chandler also captured a Mexican man who had been kept prisoner by these Indians.

This Mexican captive proved to be quite informative on the locations and sizes of the various northern Texas Indian villages along the Trinity and Brazos rivers. After returning to Franklin on June 19, Captain Chandler had quickly sent out word of his prisoners and their intelligence.

Benjamin Bryant took the word from Nashville-on-the-Brazos to Austin, arriving there Sunday, July 4. Bryant informed the government that the Indians "are said to be several hundred strong" at the forks of the Trinity, with "some two or three thousand horses." An expedition was being prepared, and the news was published in the July 7, 1841, *Austin Centinel.*

> Captain Chandler collected a volunteer force of about two hundred settlers, residents of Milam and the upper part of Washington counties. With these he was to join Col. William G. Cooke, who would then proceed . . . in search of the enemy with a determination of breaking up the settlement.[3]

William Cooke, leading President Lamar's Santa Fe Expedition, departed the Austin area during late June and did not join Captain Chandler for the Indian expedition he was organizing. The Mexican prisoner had agreed to act as pilot, steering Chandler's expedition to the main Indian village in the Cross Timbers, which General Edward Tarrant's men had already found and attacked on May 24.

According to William Porter—the adjutant on Tarrant's May expedition—the Texas government sought to have this village destroyed. Secretary of War Branch Archer sent his fourteen-year-old son to take the Mexican prisoner to join Chandler.

> Powhatten Archer, a minor son of the honorable Secretary of War, volunteered and went alone over one

hundred miles through an Indian country in order to obtain this pilot. Young Mr. Archer arrived in town on yesterday from Robertson County for orders from the president to take said pilot. He leaves today with some spirited young friends to join his command.[4]

Captain George Erath's Milam County Minutemen departed Fort Bryant in late July to join the expedition. They rendezvoused with Captain Chandler's Robertson County Minutemen at the Ioni village on the Brazos River on July 26. The expedition was also joined by Captain Mark Lewis, Powhattan Archer, Hillequist Landers, and "several other gentlemen" volunteers from Austin, including a Mr. Murray.[5]

It is possible that some of these extra volunteers were under command of Captain John Tumlinson Jr., whose father had been instrumental in starting the first Texas Rangers years prior. Tumlinson was paid for command of a company from July 14–August 25, 1841.[6]

Eli Chandler's rangers had made four expeditions since their unit had been activated in April. Interestingly, their pay had increased from $5 per day to $7 per day by the time the Robertson County Minutemen started their fifth expedition on August 6, 1841. The men of his company were almost all the same as those that had served since April. One new face was Eleazor Louis Ripley Wheelock, a former ranger commander. Two other former ranger captains, Eli Seale and James Head, were among Chandler's minutemen for this expedition.

By the consent of all parties, Eli Chandler took command of the three parties. George Erath later wrote that, "In July, Captain Chandler and myself made a corporation [and] proceeded with 102 men in to the Cross Timber." Available muster rolls for this period show 55 men in service under Captain Erath, and 56 under Captain Chandler, for a total of 111 men. Adding in the small group of volunteers Mark Lewis brought from Austin, this expedition would have numbered roughly 120 men.[7]

The unified ranger commands moved slowly up the Brazos River past Comanche Peak, but were forced to contend with sickness daily. "We passed several evacuated towns of the enemy in the Cross Timbers," wrote Captain Erath, "and our spies used every exertion to ferret out the grand village."

Capt. Chandler's Robertson Co. Minutemen: July 20–Aug. 17, 1841

Captain:
Eli Chandler
First Lieutenant:
William M. Love
Second Lieutenant:
John Marlin

Privates:
John Adams
John F. Adams [1]
Charles Beasley
Mordecai Boone
Daniel Boone Jr.
A. G. Braden
William Buttrell
Harvey Capps
John Casey
John Chandler
William Cox
Thomas Drumgold [2]
Green B. Duncan
Thomas Duncan
Jesse Ellison
John A. Gilbreath
Moses Griffin
John Hardisty
James A. Head
George W. Heard [3]
George W. Hill
James W. Hill
Robert Hunt
John Kerner
Miles King
Aaron Kitchell
James Lane

Joseph Leal [1]
Hugh Lockemy
Andrew C. Love
Wilson Marlin
Joseph Mather
James D. Matthews
Robert E. Matthews
Hardin R. McGrew
Edward McMullin
M. C. McMurry
Memnon A. Mitchell
Charles W. Nanny
William W. Patrick
Robert H. Porter
Elijah Powers
Charles H. Raymond
William W. Roberts
Eli Seale
Joshua Seale
David Sealy
Charles Sevier
Robert Steele
John L. Strother
Thomas Sypert
Neri Vanzant
Charles Welch
E. L. Ripley Wheelock
Harrison York

[1] Served August 6–17 only.
[2] Served July 20–August 5 only.
[3] Killed by Indians on August 22, 1841.

Source: Minute Man Pay and Muster Rolls, Texas State Library and Archives Division.

By August 3, the expedition had made camp in the upper edge of the Cross Timbers, roughly sixty miles above Comanche Peak. They anxiously awaited word from spy patrols that they had sent out. The men would be forced to return to the settlements, due to lack of provisions, if the spies did not turn up any significant find. While the main body of the command waited, a few Indians appeared near camp.

Capt. Erath's Milam County Minutemen: July 16–August 14, 1841

Captain:
George Bernhard Erath
First Lieutenant:
Joseph A. Tivey
Second Lieutenant:
Neil McLennan
First Sergeant:
Nathaniel C. Raymond
Second Sergeant:
Daniel McKay
Third Sergeant:
William H. King
Fourth Sergeant:
John S. Thompson

Privates:
Oscar Addison
Joel Anderson
John Anderson
Sam Bass
Johnson Bell
Stephen Bell
Benjamin Bryant
Jesse Bryant
William Bryant
Sam Burns
William Carter
William Custard
C. M. Dixon
Ransom Eaton
Sterling Fitch
David P. Flint
John Gray
William Isaacs
Eli M. Jones
Jefferson Y. Jones
Wiley Jones
Henry Kattenhorn
Henry Lakey

Joseph Long
John B. McKeen
William H. McKeen
Z. McKeen
John McLennan
James Merritt
Daniel Monroe
Ross Morris
Alfred Murry
Daniel Robinson
Shapley P. Ross
A. T. Smith
James Smith
Tom T. Smith
Giles O. Sullivan
Price Standifer
Daniel Sullivan
John Sullivan
Guy Stokes
Richard S. Teal
M. D. Thompson
William G. Thompson
Joseph P. Turnham
James Wilkinson
John Wilkinson
R. S. Woolfolk

Note:
Other rangers who served under Captain Erath between April 11 and July 15 for varying lengths of service are: A. H. Boales, Nathan Campbell, Henry Chatock, Samuel W. Davis, Jacob Groce, George Green, Berry L. Ham, Robert Hogan, Charles Manning, William W. Moore, James Porter, Robert H. Porter, Robert Rayford, James Shaw, W. G. Thomas, Francis Thompson, Josiah Thompson, Thomas Thompson, William Wheeler, and William Wilkins.

George Erath was immediately dispatched with twenty men to pursue them. While in search of the trail, he divided his party, taking some of the men himself and sending the others with

Lieutenant William Love of the Robertson County Minutemen. Erath's men were first to find the Indians' trail and he "pushed hard" down it in pursuit.[8]

As his rangers followed the trail, they were suddenly fired upon by a party of Indians believed by Erath to be Kickapoos or Cherokees. The Indians had secured themselves behind a protective cliff of rocks, which hid them from view completely. Only on one side of the cliff was a rider able to ascend the hill, "with the utmost difficulty, which passage was defended bravely by the rifles of the enemy."

Erath unknowingly had fallen victim to the exact same type of ambush in a tight area that had so recently claimed the life of Captain John Denton. The first volley of shots hit A. T. Smith of Erath's Milam County rangers, who fell dead. Two rifle balls struck him from a distance of one hundred and fifty yards away, proof of the quality of the Indians' rifles. Smith was a brother of Colonel Thomas J. Smith. A number of other shots grazed other rangers and ripped through their clothing without causing injury.

"I formed in a little grove of timber and returned their fire," wrote Erath. The fighting was kept up for half an hour. During this time, Erath decided that his rangers had killed two Indians and "perhaps wounded others." During the late minutes of the fight, Lieutenant Love and his Robertson County detachment arrived on the scene, in company with other men from the main camp who had heard the firing.

"The celebrated chief José María was wounded and one Indian killed in an encounter with one of our parties," wrote Captain Erath in his memoirs. "Our side lost one man." Captain Chandler believed some of these Indians to be Cherokees, due to the fact that they spoke the English language well enough to dare the Texans to fight them.[9]

With reinforcements, Captain Erath then ordered a charge to be made against the Indians. The Indians were driven from the bluff and they fled, carrying their dead and wounded with them. "The mountainous situation of the country made pursuit impracticable."[10]

The expedition was not well prepared for a long time out. "No supplies except what could be carried on our horses had been taken along, and we were too many to live on game alone, so we soon returned," wrote Erath. The dead man, Smith, was buried and the expedition then immediately began its return for home, moving back down through the Cross Timbers.[11]

On August 7, Erath and Chandler's ranger units parted company. Erath returned toward Bryant's Station by way of the Bosque River, finding no signs of hostile Indians during his return. "We still feel convinced that a strong village exists on the Brazos, but that only a well fitted campaign can capture it," wrote Erath. His men had reached Bryant's Station by August 12, on which date he wrote his report to Archer.

The *Texas Centinel* of Austin reported on the Erath-Lewis-Chandler Expedition in its August 19 edition. Based on information from Captain Lewis, Powhattan Archer, and others, the editors felt that the rangers had come close to the main headquarters of all the northern Texas hostile Indians. According to the *Centinel*, five settlers had been killed and scalped by Indian bands during the first half of August 1841.[12]

Ironically, Erath, Lewis, and Chandler were searching for the major Indian encampment that had been located in May. Captain Chandler filed two concurrent fifteen-day expedition muster rolls to meet legal requirements, one spanning July 20–August 5 and the second one covering August 6–17, 1841.

The Robertson County Minutemen were only a week off duty before the killing of one of their own forced them back out into the field. Captain Chandler had ordered out a scouting patrol on August 21, shortly after his men had returned to Franklin on August 17. This eight-man patrol included John Kerner, Charles Sevier, Gilbert H. Love, John Hardisty, Thomas Sypert, William McGraw, and Thomas Drumgold. They were led by George W. Heard, who had made both of Chandler's first two Indian expeditions.[13]

Heard's scout patrol left on the rainy afternoon of August 21, and followed a trail leading up towards Parker's Fort on the Navasota River. On the morning of August 22, when about fourteen miles from Franklin, they were suddenly attacked by Indians.

The rangers were riding in single file while passing an area where two deep ravines joined together. About eighteen Indians suddenly rose from the deep ravine which paralleled the horse trail. From a distance of less than forty yards, the Indians fired on and completely surprised the minutemen.

George Heard, riding in the front of the procession, was hit by three rifle balls and immediately fell dead from his horse. Some of the men retreated a short distance and then halted. Others dismounted at the scene of the attack. Gilbert Love stood by the body of Heard to prevent the Indians from scalping and otherwise mutilating his fellow ranger.

Love was eventually forced to flee the scene. He lost his mule in the process, but did mount Heard's horse. The remaining seven rangers exchanged shots with the Indians for some time, but found themselves too outnumbered to charge. They instead opted to race back for Franklin and raise Captain Chandler's company.

Eli Chandler's company muster roll records show that his Robertson County Minutemen were mobilized on August 24, just one week after being discharged from their most recent expedition. Chandler and Lieutenant Love took a thirty-one-man pursuit party into the field, but were unable to overtake the band of Indians who had killed ranger George Heard. On Chandler's muster roll, the name "G. W. Hurd" has a single entry: "Killed by Indians the 22nd day of August." Captain Chandler's men found their comrade's body, which had been scalped and mutilated, with his head and hands being severed. Heard's remains were gathered and brought back to Franklin, where a proper burial was held after Chandler's men returned on September 2.[14]

George Erath's Milam County rangers continued to serve through 1841. Upon his return to the settlements on August 12, a number of his men continued to serve as scouts. Second Sergeant Dan McKay kept a five-man scouting party out from August 14 to August 28, with three of his rangers continuing into September. First Lieutenant Joseph Tivey took over scouting on September 13 with a fifteen-man patrol. Most of his men patrolled through September 27.

Captain Erath led fifty of his Milam County Minutemen out on expedition from October 25 to November 9. Upon return, he kept out a small number of spies to range the Milam County area. The final service of 1841 for his rangers was completed on December 24, 1841, when Lieutenant Tivey and Sergeant McKay returned from scouting with privates Henry Kattenhorn, Zebulon Porter, Jesse Bryant, Benjamin Bryant, and John Craddock. George Erath filled his final muster roll on December 30, 1841, with Milam County Chief Justice Hugh B. King.

Paschal, Red River, and Lamar County Rangers

At least three companies of county minutemen ranged the vast areas of northern Texas during mid 1841. Red River County had long been patrolled by various ranger and militia companies from the days of the Texas Revolution. By early 1840, two new counties had been carved from Red River County and each had its own mounted company.

Paschal County was almost as short-lived as the company bearing its name. It was created for judicial purposes on January 28, 1841, and included all of present Hopkins, Franklin, Titus, Morris, and Cass counties and most of present Marion County. This was all of the upper Red River settlement areas from present Sulphur Springs east to the current Louisiana border. However, Paschal County would be abolished by an 1842 Texas Supreme Court decision. When Paschal County was named as one of the twenty which could operate rangers, Captain Joseph D. Lilly was elected by the settlers to lead them. Lilly had served as first lieutenant of Captain Henry Stout's Red River Rangers for three months during the summer of 1840. Captain Lilly's two officers were veterans of militia and ranger service: First Lieutenant John King and Second Lieutenant Thomas Milligan.

According to his muster roll, Lilly's company had twenty-six privates. A. O. Hammack is listed as the first man and Thomas Jones as the twenty-sixth, possibly in the order in which they enlisted. Another twenty-seven names appear on the Paschal County Minutemen's original June 12 muster roll, but they apparently did not serve, perhaps because the unit was over capacity.

Little can be found in extant records for Captain Lilly's company other than dates of service. A second muster roll covers the period of July 23–August 4, 1841. A reduced-strength fourteen-man unit was sent out for this two-week period. This second muster roll was signed by Paschal County Chief Justice O. H. King and Chief Clerk D. C. Quinn. Finally, public debt papers confirm the fact that a dozen Paschal County Minutemen under Lieutenant Thomas Milligan made another expedition from August 24–September 12. Several of Captain Lilly's scouts remained out in the field two additional days, being paid through September 14.[15]

Capt. Lilly's Paschal County Minutemen: June 12–Aug. 4, 1841

Captain:	William Tankersley
Joseph D. Lilly	Elisha W. Turner
First Lieutenant:	
John N. King	*Also shown on original June 12,*
Second Lieutenant:	*1841 muster roll were:*
Thomas S. Milligan	John M. Bohannon
First Sergeant:	Isaac Bruton *
Robert C. Graves	John D. Bruton
Second Sergeant:	John E. Chisum
John P. Crownover	James T. Dove
Third Sergeant:	J. N. Gray *
W. S. Keith	Michael Grim
	William J. Hamilton
Privates:	Robert Hinson
Harvey Acres	Robert Hughes
Martin Binnion	Russ Hughes *
Robert Blair	W. V. Hughes
David Bruton	Martin Jones
James M. Burriss *	Marvel R. Jones
Henry H. Clifton *	Gabriel Keith
Andrew Coots	Nathaniel King
David Coots	Jonathan H. Kirkland *
A. O. Hammock	Harris B. Lilly *
Henry W. Jones *	J. J. McAdams
Hiram Jones *	William G. Milligan *
Thomas Jones	Mentor W. Northington
Levi Jordan	W. M. Pickett
John H. Milligan	E. C. Rogers
Reece P. Milligan *	James S. Stout
J. S. Sloan	Samuel Stewart
George W. Smith	William Truett
Aaron Starnes	James Wardlow
Titus Starnes *	
James Tankersly *	* Shown on separate muster roll for June
Richard Tankersly	23–August 4, 1841.
	Source: Texas State Archives.

Red River County was patrolled by Captain William Becknell's rangers during late 1841. Becknell had commanded militiamen and ranging units during 1836 and 1838 in his home area. Fellow ranger commander William Stout later described Becknell as "a brave backwoods man." Stout commented that Becknell commanded the only Red River Minuteman company. "Not a single Indian was killed," during their service per Stout.[16]

Capt. Becknell's Red River Minutemen: June 25, 1841–June 25, 1842

Captain:	Thomas C. Clark
William Becknell	Lovel Coffman
First Lieutenant:	H. F. Eskridge
Peter Ringo	Jesse Evans
Second Lieutenant:	William Evans
John C. Becknell	Isham Farris
First Sergeant:	William Gregg
H. B. Harris	Tim Griffin
Second Sergeant:	Benjamin Hall
William Dawson	Daniel Harris
Third Sergeant:	John Harris
David Clark	James M. Jones
Fourth Sergeant:	Samuel W. Jordan
William J. Pertle	John N. Kimball
First Corporal:	Isaac Langston
L. C. Jones	Sam McColler
Second Corporal:	Wilson McCrary
Tinsley Weaver	John Nugent
Third Corporal:	B. W. Osborne
Riley Jackson	Benjamin Pertle
Fourth Corporal:	Bartes Philey
James Hefflinger	Andrew J. Price
	John Price
Privates:	William Price
Aaron Bailey	James J. Ringo
Elisha Ball	John K. Rodgers
James L. S. Bevins	James Skinner
David Bishop	Isham Stevens
Joseph Bishop	William B. Stout
Jacob Blanton	Abner Weaver
William Brinton	Green Weaver
William Brown	Larkin Weaver
James Burkham	Isaac Wilson
James Cass	J. N. Wilson
Benjamin S. Clark	Source: Texas State Archives.

Captain Becknell's original fifty-six-man company was organized on June 25, 1841, and would serve the county for one full year. Very few of the Texas government-sanctioned county ranger companies actually operated into the following calendar year. With a term limit of four total months in service, most had surpassed their limits well before year's end.

Capt. Matthews' Lamar County Minutemen:

Captain:	Benjamin F. Gooch
Mansell Walter Matthews	Thomas Jordan
First Lieutenant:	Robert O. Lusk
George Birdwell	Barton W. Matthews
	Joseph J. Matthews
Privates:	Robert E. Matthews
John Anderson	William O. Matthews
Amos C. C. Bailey	William McCarty
James M. Bailey	Abner Netherly
Matthew R. Birdwell	John Nidiver
Zachariah Birdwell	John Oustal
Thomas Wade Box	L. S. Owens
William Young Box	_____ Ritchey
William T. Brackeen	John H. Rutherford
Merritt Brannon	Thomas M. Rutherford
Ezeriah Bredkin	John M. Watson
Wiley B. Brigham	John M. Woodson
Samuel Burke	Andrew S. Young
Joseph Cox	
Simon Derrick	Partial roster based on author's search of
William Finley	audited military claims and public debt
John C. Gahagen	papers, Texas State Library.

Becknell was a little more conservative, running his Red River unit more as it was intended. He would only call up the main body of men if truly needed. His first lieutenant, Peter Ringo, led a spy patrol out for eleven days in July.

The entire company was on patrol for fifteen days in August and went on expedition in September. When not out, Lieutenant Ringo led spy patrols. Finally, Captain Becknell and twenty-three of his minutemen ranged for a week in November. Becknell submitted his company's muster rolls on November 1840. If he patrolled in December, it is unrecorded. Captain Becknell's men remained the guardians of Red River County until June 25, 1842, one full year after their original mustering.

Lamar County was created in December 1840 from Red River County and it was also one of the Texas frontier counties designated to have a minuteman company. Captain Mansil Walter Matthews, thirty-five, was elected to command these men. Matthews, a large man of 275 pounds, was a preacher, doctor, and legislator born on Christmas Eve 1806 in Kentucky. He preached and taught in Tennessee and Alabama until 1835, then began a career as a physician and Disciples of Christ minister. He arrived in Red River County in January 1836 and served as a surgeon for the Texas Army during the Texas Revolution.

Bowie County and Lamar County in northern Texas were both established by acts of the Fifth Congress in December 1840. The county seat for Lamar County was originally the small settlement of Lafayette, located several miles northwest of the present county seat of Paris, Texas.

The exact expeditions of Captain Matthews' company are not all known. Pension papers, however, show that at least one expedition was made of twelve days' duration, from September 17–29, 1841.

While daily operations of these three northern Texas ranger companies are not well documented, their presence was certainly a comfort to the Red River area settlers who had long suffered random depredations.

Hays' Fight on the Llano: July 24, 1841

Captain Jack Hays was good on his word. On July 1, he had vowed to the Texas government that he would begin raising a large force of men to return to the scene of his June 29 Uvalde Canyon fight with the Comanches. With reinforcements, he fully expected to return and whip this band.

Mary Maverick later wrote of how Captain Hays had come to be feared and respected by many of his enemies.

> Hays displayed such rare military skills and daring, that very soon by consent of all, he was looked upon as the leader and his orders were obeyed and he himself loved by all. In a fight he was utterly fearless and invincible.[17]

Maverick wrote that Hays' rangers operated in the same fashion as the other counties' minutemen during 1841.

> Each volunteer kept a good horse, saddle, bridle, and arms, and a supply of coffee, salt, sugar, and other provi-

sions ready at any time to start on fifteen minutes warning, in pursuit of the marauding Indians. At a certain signal given by the Cathedral bell, the men were off, in buckskin clothes and blankets, responding promptly to the call.

For nearly two weeks in July, Captain Hays recruited and put out the word that he planned to make another expedition. He succeeded in raising 25 rangers, "some ten or fifteen from Gonzales." He also raised a like number of Lipans and Tonkawas, raising his total force to about fifty men. Hays' muster rolls show that the Indians were under Chief Flacco, the brave son of Lipan Chief Castro and a veteran of many a Texas Ranger expedition.[18]

Hays' core unit was truly functioning as the Béxar County Minutemen. In his reports and subsequent descriptions of his various Indian fights, he consistently wrote of the men under his command in a different manner. If someone was temporarily attached to his company—such as the Gonzales volunteers for this expedition—was wounded or killed, it would not necessarily even make his report. All, however, including Chief Flacco's Lipans, were listed on the muster roll that Hays filled out for this July expedition.

Hays' core unit of rangers included all twelve men who had made the Uvalde Canyon fight two weeks prior. During the first four months of 1841, when Hays had operated a specific ranger company, he had only been authorized to operate with fifteen men. By the subsequent February 4 law for the county minutemen, Hays could operate between twenty and fifty-six men for short periods of time, as conditions warranted their service.

His July expedition would consist of 43 men, including Flacco's seven Lipans and eight Tejanos not normally assigned to him. The balance of his company included San Antonio merchants and Gonzales volunteers who enrolled on July 12. Among the new recruits from San Antonio were six men who had served as rangers in Captain Antonio Pérez's company through May 20: Antonio Coy, Francisco Granado, Martin Salinas, Antonio Sánchez, Melchor Travieso, and John O. Trueheart.[19]

Hays' rangers and Flacco's Lipan Indians departed San Antonio on July 12 and proceeded to the point on the Frio River where he had recently engaged the Comanches. Hays had good intelligence that the Indians were still in the vicinity. In a report of his summer 1841 expedition, he wrote, "I had been informed they were still encamped in a considerable body."[20]

Hays found that these Indians had taken fright and had fled their campground, "after having murdered some prisoners then in their camp." His men doggedly pursued the fleeing Comanche forces for more than a week.

> I followed on their trail, which led me through the rugged passes at the head of the western branch of the Rio Frio [in present Real County]. We pursued at a great disadvantage, the Indians having designedly picked the worst road possible, and burned the whole country. Our horses and men were much starved and worn down by the time we had reached the head waters of the Llano, where we discovered from the freshness and extent of the trails, there was a large encampment.[21]

In a later account, Hays said that they had traveled "far into the mountains, where the white man had never before made a track."[22]

Some of his Indian spies became alarmed at the size of the trails they began discovering. Fearing that they were facing overwhelming odds, these spies on July 23 led Hays' rangers "from the main trail upon a smaller one, some eight miles below." The next morning, July 24, Hays' expedition was discovered by a party of Comanche hunters, who fled to sound the alarm.

"We pursued as fast as the condition of our horses would permit," wrote Hays. He rode ahead with two dozen of his men who were mounted on the best horses. About a mile short of the Comanche camp, the rangers were met by about fifty Comanche warriors, who came to cover the retreat of their families. "A running fight ensued between these and a few of our best horses; which lasted some two hours, over six miles of rugged country."

During this pursuit, Hays' rangers likely passed through present Real County into Edwards County, some twenty miles west of present Kerrville. Early Texas Ranger historian Walter Prescott Webb dubbed this Hays fight as "the Battle of the Llano."[23]

Hays felt that he had happened upon about two hundred Comanches, with about six hundred head of horses. The main body of the Comanches retreated slowly while they skirmished

Capt. Hays' Béxar County Minutemen: July 1–August 31, 1841

Captain:
John Coffee Hays

Privates:
John S. Adams [1]
S. P. Ball [2]
Antonio Coy [3]
Martin Delgado [4]
Addison Drinkwater [2]
Pedro Espeniso [5]
Archibald Fitzgerald [4]
J. A. Flores [5]
Peter Fohr [6]
Damacio Galvan [7]
Francisco Granado [8]
G. H. Grubbs [9]
Nathaniel Harbert [4]
Jacob Jackson Humphreys [4]
William Isbell [2]
Carlos Larso [4]
Samuel H. Luckie [4]
Joseph Miller [6]
John L. Milner [4]
William H. Moore [10]
John C. Morgan [4]
Robert Patton [4]
Samuel Pepes [4]
Pedro Pérez [5]
James Perry [4]
Robert Pollett [2]
Benjamin Prior [2]
Benjamin Prior Jr. [2]
Martin Salinas [11]

Antonio Sánchez [5]
John Slein [12]
John Trapnell [4]
Melchor Travieso [5]
John O. Truehart [4]
Florencio Vasquez [5]
John Young [4]

Lipan Apache Rangers:
Flacco [5]
Plasedonce [5]
Colquie [5]
Tom [5]
Juan [5]
Wash [5]
Antonio [5]

Note: Captain Hays paid from June 1, 1841.

[1] Served 7/5–8/31/1841.
[2] Served 6/23–8/31/1841.
[3] Served 6/12–8/10/1841.
[4] Served 7/12–8/31/1841.
[5] Served 7/12–8/2/1841.
[6] Served 6/12–8/31/1841.
[7] Served 7/4–8/31/1841.
[8] Served 6/23–7/20/1841.
[9] Served 6/23–8/4/1841.
[10] Served 7/5–8/31/1841.
[11] Served 8/2–8/31/1841.
[12] Enlisted 6/23/1841. Killed in action on July 24, 1841.

Source: Texas State Archives.

with the rangers, to allow their women and children to move away.

This long running fight completely exhausted the rangers' worn horses. In his papers, Mirabeau Lamar collected an account of this expedition written by Jack Hays. Following Hays' own testimony is an interesting anecdote of Hays and the gallant Lipan leader Flacco's action in the Llano battle.

This battle was fought on the extreme head of the Llano (pronounced Yano). In the fight, the Indians would retreat, form a line, and prepare for battle. On one occasion, Capt. Hays charged alone within a short distance of the enemy intending to discharge his piece, and retreat. But his horse, seizing the bit in his teeth, dashed off and ran entirely through the Indian ranks.

Flacco, perceiving this, followed his leader in rapid pursuit and broke thro' the lines and came off safely with his Captain. Their escape was a miracle.

After the fight, Flacco remarked that he never would be left behind by any one; but that his Capt. was "*Bravo too much.*"[24]

During his horse's wild run, Captain Hays shot one Comanche who had halted his horse to take aim at the "charging" Texan. Chief Flacco reportedly "tried to get his scalp, but the other Indians were too quick for him." Flacco instead raced on after Jack Hays, who amazingly survived his run through the midst of the Comanches and quickly circled back around them toward his own rangers.[25]

In his expedition report, written soon after returning to San Antonio, Hays specifically cited Chief Flacco and Demacio Galvan for their "service and bravery" in combat. "From the bloody saddles upon the trail," Hays estimated that that his company had killed or wounded eight to ten Comanches. "We fought at great disadvantage," he wrote. The Indians were plentiful enough that they were able to retrieve all of their dead and wounded on the run. In return, Hays' report states that "we had one man wounded in the hand & [another in the] breast."[26]

In relating his experiences as a Texas Ranger to a fellow ranger who later compiled his biography, "Captain Jack" offered more specific details on these wounds. "As they advanced, the Indians commenced upon them, and shot [John] Trueheart in the neck badly, also shot Hays in the finger, and killed the other man."[27]

The "other man" killed was Private John Slein, the merchant who had joined Hays' rangers on June 23, just in time to see some action in the June 29 Uvalde Canyon fight. One month later, he had found action with Jack Hays again on the Llano River, but this time it was too much. The ranger pay roll for Captain Hays which covers the period of June 1 to August 31, 1841, simply shows his service ending on July 24, with the notation "killed." Why Captain Hays did not mention the death of Slein in his brief action report is strange. Slein was a relatively new merchant volunteer, perhaps not considered by Hays to be one of his full-time rangers.

After turning back to the Comanche camp, they found a murdered prisoner. "We found a Mexican prisoner swinging by the heels, shot and lanced to death," wrote Hays. There appeared to be another large camp in the direction of the head of the San Saba River and one upon the head of the Guadalupe River. "In our plight," he wrote, "pursuit was useless."[28]

Hays' minutemen turned back toward San Antonio, "carrying Trueheart on a litter. He finally recovered." Flacco's Lipans left the rangers' company on August 2 and the remaining Béxar men reached town on August 4. Hays' payrolls show that his men were paid half their normal wages in August, distributed to the men by their captain.[29]

The whole countryside upon the Llano, Pedernales, and Guadalupe rivers had been burned by the Indians. Hays believed this was done to cut off grass supply for his rangers to prevent their expedition. Hays wrote his campaign report to Secretary Archer on August 13. His men had suffered from great "fatigue and deprivation," but he was very commendable of his rangers.[30]

Several years later, he claimed that this expedition had been successful in encouraging the Comanches to avoid raiding Béxar. "This was the last of the Indian difficulties about San Antonio. They never made their reappearance, except one or two small thieving parties who were run off without much difficulty."[31]

Burleson Recruits for Expedition

Upon the return of Captain Mark Lewis to Austin, the *Centinel* on August 19 reported that the town expected to soon hear from Edward Burleson, "that often tried Indian fighter." The editors felt that only Burleson "has sufficient popularity to get up a volunteer expedition of four or five hundred men, to exterminate those treacherous and inhuman Cherokees."[32]

Among those he could chose from there were several parties of men who had intended to join the Santa Fe Expedition but had failed to arrive in time to participate in this ill-fated expedition. These companies failed to find either the Santa Fe troops or any Indian villages, and had returned to Nashville-on-the-Brazos by August 24. The August 24 issue of *The Morning Star*, published in Houston, reported that Edward Burleson was still busy recruiting troops for another offensive to the Indian villages along the upper Brazos. His plans called for starting out from Nashville on September 15.[33]

The August 28 *Morning Star* called out from Houston for more volunteers to join Colonel Burleson, reporting the rendezvous date in Nashville had been pushed from September 15 to September 25, an indication that the recruiting of volunteers was not going as swiftly as had been hoped. The main Indian village was believed to be about eighty miles from Comanche Peak on the Brazos. The expedition was then expected to cross from the Brazos area to the sources of the Trinity. The editors of the *Morning Star* worked hard to call for volunteers. "Such a tour cannot fail to be exceedingly interesting and pleasant, notwithstanding the fatigues and privations that will necessarily be encountered."[34]

Burleson was requested by President Lamar to head the expedition into the Indian territory. The call had gone out to all central Texas counties to respond. Among the first to join him was Captain James R. Cook of Washington County. Other men were expected from Milam, Robertson, and Navasota counties. The September 2 *Texas Centinel* in Austin reported that the troop-raising efforts were still underway:

> We expect to hear a prompt response from the gallant Col. [John Henry] Moore and Capt. [Thomas J.] Rabb, of Fayette, and from Col. [William Jefferson] Jones, and many other good spirits and true, in this, Bastrop and the Colorado counties.
>
> Gen. Burleson, "Old Ned," as the boys call him, in answer to the President's request, says, "My services belong to Texas so long as she has an enemy to fight, and I will do all I can in raising the troops, but I wish them to select their own commander when they rendez[v]ous."

This meritorious modesty is worthy of the spirit which dictates it.[35]

Like the less experienced Felix Huston before him, Ned Burleson found it to be a frustrating effort to organize an Indian offensive at a time when bloody losses in that neighborhood were not fresh upon people's minds.

Sowell's Fannin County Minutemen

While Burleson and Hays pursued Comanches in central Texas, the new ranger company of Fannin County in northern Texas was challenged by Coushatta Indians along the Red River. Captain Joseph Sowell, commanding the Fannin County Minutemen, mustered in his "company of rangers" on July 17, 1841. They operated from Old Warren, a town on the present Grayson and Fannin county lines. Old Warren, sometimes called Fort Warren, was named for an Arkansas trader named Abel Warren and was located one mile below the mouth of Choctaw Creek.[36]

Their first expedition was in response to an attack on the Dugan family. A band of Coushattas had lived on the property of Dr. Daniel Rowlett for a short time during 1840. After accusations that they had killed at least one person in the area, the Coushattas moved across the Red River but continued to come back across the river to make raids on settlers.

These Coushattas were accused of the Dugan depredation in present Grayson County during early July 1841. A few miles southwest of the old town of Warren was the homestead of early pioneer Daniel V. Dugan Sr. His second son, Daniel Jr., and William Kitchens had gone out to get logs to build a house. When they did not return in two days, runners were sent to Warren for Captain Sowell's rangers stationed there. Early Fannin County pioneer and historian John P. Simpson recalled:

> Runners were sent to Warren for rangers and more help to search for the missing ones. The rangers were off in another direction, but friends and neighbors soon gathered together, and at the first glimmer of daylight a party started for the camp.[37]

The settlers found the badly mutilated bodies of Kitchens and Dugan. It appeared that Kitchens had died instantly but that Dugan had fought hard until his own death. The bodies were returned to Daniel Dugan Sr.'s homestead for burial. Captain Sowell's initial muster roll for the Fannin County Minutemen shows that they commenced service on July 6, 1841, apparently two days after Dugan and Kitchens had been killed. Sowell took out seventeen men, including Lieutenant William Bailey. They remained out only four days, returning to town on July 9 in an apparent effort to gather up more men.

Within a week of the burial of Kitchens and Dugan, the Coushattas made another raid, this time upon the homestead of John Kitchens, father of the boy slain just a week prior. The family and the friends who were staying with them were well armed, however, and put up a valiant fight. Kitchens and another man managed to kill one Indian and a freed slave who was working with the Indians to steal horses. The body of the black man was left lying on the ground, but the Indians fled with their own casualties.[38]

John Kitchens and his son Daniel were both wounded in the gun battle with the Indians, but they would survive. Young Dan Kitchens raced on horseback to the neighboring home of Daniel Dugan and raised support. A party of armed men maintained station at both the Dugan and Kitchens homes for several nights, but the Indians failed to return.

After suffering a defeat to the Kitchens family, the Indians pulled back from the Warren area of Fannin County for some time during the summer of 1841. Depredations occurred more on the nearby settlement of Choctaw during the fall months.

On July 17, Captain Sowell took out twenty-three of his Fannin County Minutemen to track these hostile Indians. They combed the upper Texas areas for eight days, but were unable to draw the Indians into combat. Sowell returned to Warren on July 25. For each of his expeditions, he submitted a muster roll to Fannin County Chief Justice Bailey Inglish for approval. Sowell's muster rolls were signed as him commanding the "Fannin Cty. Rangers."

Twenty-six of Captain Sowell's rangers made a third expedition of ten days which commenced on August 15. The last muster roll signed by Joseph Sowell covered September 8–20, 1841.

During this time, First Sergeant William Twitty and thirteen other rangers performed varying days of scouting for Fannin County. Military papers of Hugh Cox and Jesse Cox show that Captain Sowell's men were discharged on September 26, 1841, at Camp Warren. Captain Sowell submitted each of his first four muster rolls to Fannin County's Judge Inglish on November 2.[39]

Although Sowell would reorganize some of his rangers later in the fall to follow up on another Indian attack, there is no extant muster roll of the men who accompanied him. By early November, some of the settlers around the early communities of Warren and Choctaw were moving away from the area because of the constant raids made by the Coushattas. On occasion, some of the settlers would strike back, but some families chose to move on rather than to fight.[40]

Some of the settlers chose to stay long enough to attend the wedding of former ranger Daniel Montague to Mary Dugan on Sunday, November 13, 1841. On the following night, a group of Indians attacked the dogtrot home of Daniel Dugan, where a number of other settlers had chosen to stay for the winter. In one room was Dugan and his immediate family. The other main room held three young men named Green, Hoover, and Joseph Gordon, who were staying with the family. Occupying the stable loft to guard the horses were William and George C. Dugan.[41]

The young men staying in one room had retired for the night, although Dugan's family was still awake in their room. Indians suddenly forced open the door to the young men's room and fired a number of shots. Green was killed, and Hoover was wounded. Some of the Indians rushed into the house. Gordon seized the door-shutter and forcefully closed the door, throwing the Indians to the outside. The family dogs then attacked the Indians, who began shooting the dogs.

Across the dogtrot, Daniel Dugan's daughters heard the Indians attack the young men in the adjacent room. Kate Dugan later described the attack.

> Emily and I were talking in whispers about the wedding when we both started and listened to an unusual noise we heard in the men's room. The door pin fell on the floor and some one gave the door a kick. We were about to resume our work and conversation, thinking it was one

Capt. Sowell's Fannin County Minutemen: July 6–25, 1841

Captain:
Joseph Sowell
First Lieutenant:
L. B. Hill
Second Lieutenant
William Bailey
First Sergeant
William C. Twitty [1]

Privates:
Charles Adams [1]
John Adcock
David Albritz [2]
Spencer Asberry
William Costley
Hugh Cox [1]
Jesse Cox [1]
James M. Garner [1]
J. H. George [1]
Joseph H. Gordon
George W. Guthrie
T. H. Harrison [1]
James Jeffries
P. S. Lankford
William T. Lankford
T. S. Larimore [1]
Roswell W. Lee
C. Lockwood [1]
Peter Maroney
Silas Martin [1]

William Martin
C. T. McPherson [1]
Joseph Moody [1]
Calvin Moore [1]
James H. Moss
Henry Mouser [1]
Gibson Myers [1]
Jefferson C. Parish
James M. Patton
T. J. Pendergrast [1]
Elijah Powers
William Reeder
John T. Scott
James Seymore
Abram Shelly
Thomas F. Smith
Jesse Stiff
Joseph Strickland
J. P. Thruston [1]
Elias Underwood
Samuel Wychard

[1] Joined on August 15, 1841.
[2] Joined on September 8, 1841.

Expeditions: July 6–9, 1841; July 17–25, 1841; August 15–25, 1841; and September 8–20, 1841.
Source: Muster rolls of the Texas State Archives.

man, when like a thunderbolt two shots rang out, followed by another, and then all was confusion. Pandemonium let loose. In an instant the yard seemed full of Indians, all yelling and blowing whistles.[42]

Kate's old father Daniel Dugan grabbed his trusty flintlock and began shooting into the Indians as quickly as he could. Several shots were fired back into the house at Dugan. Back at the stables, George and William Dugan discovered an Indian trying to open the lock to the horse stalls. They could not manage a shot at first. Soon, the fighting died down near the house and the Dugan boys could see two Indians approach to work on the lock. They fired at once and one Indian fell dead. The other ran a short distance and fell, crying out with dying groans.[43]

The body of the dead Indian was found the next morning. He wore a calico hunting shirt that Dr. Rowlett had given him and he left behind a gun that had belonged to the Coushatta chief who had lived at Rowlett's. According to early settler John P. Simpson, youngest daughter Catherine Dugan took an axe and severed the head from the Indian's body. "I saw the skull about the house years after," he wrote. The sister had sworn vengeance for her brother Daniel, whom the Coushattas had recently killed, scalped, and tomahawked. Catherine's mother used the skull as a quill gourd for her sewing supplies.

Captain Joseph Sowell's minutemen went out in pursuit of the Coushattas to avenge the victims of the November 14 Dugan household attack. Numbering about a dozen, his men actually crossed the Red River at night and made a surprise attack on a camp of these Indians. They fired into their wigwams, killing ten or twelve of them. This act was kept secret for some time, as it was a violation of the international law with the United States.[44]

There is no extant muster roll of Sowell's final expedition with his rangers, as he did not live long enough to take another roll to Fannin County's chief justice for approval. The Indians his men had attacked followed them back to Old Warren.

Captain Sowell and one of his rangers, John Scott, operated a tavern at Old Warren. The spot was a frequent stay-over for visitors who were traveling in to Old Warren to tend to court business, such as serving on a jury. Shortly after the Dugan depredation in late November, and following the rangers' return from their own raid, district court was scheduled to begin in Warren on a Monday in late November 1841.[45]

Several men who were scheduled to serve as witnesses and jurymen stopped off at Sowell and Scott's tavern the night prior. While the men were engaged in drinking and swapping stories that Sunday night, the Coushattas made a retaliatory raid upon the tavern's stable. They seized the horses of the guests, including Captain Sowell's fine charger. As the horses were being gathered, their neighing alerted some of the men in the tavern. The men rushed out in alarm, many without their pistols and guns.

Fannin County Sheriff J. P. Simpson, who was in Warren at the time, felt that they were attacked by twelve Indians.

> Sowell and Scott ran to the gap, laid down by the Indians, Sowell armed with a pistol, Scott with a double barrel shot gun. Sowell discharged his pistol at them without effect, when they sent a volley of arrows at him, one passing through his stomach and out at his back. He fell at the Indians' feet, and called to Scott to shoot the Indian, and expired without a groan. Scott discharged his gun and one Coushatta fell dead with Captain Sowell. The other Indians left the horses and fled in every direction, and collected on the road near Brushy Creek.[46]

The Coushattas stayed hidden in the vicinity of Warren throughout the night, thus making travel for a lone courier potentially deadly. After Captain Sowell's murder, the Fannin County citizens were greatly alarmed. District Court in Warren met the next morning and organized for business. They had not proceeded far into the docket, however, when a scout raced in and announced that a large Indian trail had been discovered going in the direction of Fort Inglish.

The judge adjourned the court so that the men could protect their families in the outlying settlements. Sheriff Simpson, Major Jonathan Bird—who was in command of a ranger company that was building Bird's Fort—and several others headed out after dark to check on their homes. En route, Bird lost his hat and the group paused while he circled around to search for it. At that moment, a squad of Indians suddenly rushed upon the men.[47]

Simpson immediately fired his shotgun at the approaching Indians and shouted out, "Charge!"

The desired effect happened. The gun blast and the ruse that a company of men was charging upon them caused the Indians to scatter, giving the Texans time to escape the area.

Callahan's Gonzales County Minutemen

Fannin County was not alone in contending with horse thieves and Indian depredations. Gonzales County was defended in 1841

by the government-sanctioned minuteman company of Captain
James Hughes Callahan, whose men operated out of Seguín.
Callahan, twenty-nine, had come to Texas with a Georgia battalion in 1835 to fight in the Texas Revolution. Thereafter, he had
helped establish present Seguín and had served as first lieutenant
for Captain Paint Caldwell's company during Major Howards'
fall 1840 Indian expedition.[48]

Many of Captain Callahan's Gonzales County Minutemen
were veteran rangers and Indian fighters. Second Lieutenant
James Milford Day had been seriously wounded while serving
in Paint Caldwell's 1839 rangers. Very few military reports exist
to detail the exact actions of Callahan's company. As with other
1841 county ranging companies, his men were concerned with
maintaining scouts, conducting patrols, and in calling up the
entire company in times of crisis.

Callahan's company submitted numerous muster rolls to
Chief Justice Edmund Bellinger for 1841 service. The company
was first mustered in Seguín on May 7, 1841, and was discharged
on May 21 after its first fifteen-day expedition. Another fifteen-
day expedition was conducted in June. Various other expeditions
were called up throughout the summer and fall, some lasting as
few as two days. These shorter outings were no doubt just to
chase away horse thieves or to run down a reported danger.

While specific details are lacking for each of James Callahan's
ranger expeditions, several of his men left colorful memoirs of
their experiences that year. Early ranger chronicler Andrew J.
Sowell wrote the recollections of his father Asa Jarmon Lee
Sowell and two of his uncles, Andrew Jackson and John N.
Sowell, who all served in the Gonzales company. Another good
source is First Corporal Jim Nichols, a former member of Paint
Caldwell's rangers and a veteran of Plum Creek, who left detailed
memoirs.

Both the Nichols and Sowell memoirs seem to agree that
Captain Callahan's rangers were first called out to deal with
Mexican horse thieves. Among these was a Mexican citizen
named Christova Arouba, who was found to be stealing horses
and cattle around the San Antonio area. He would carry a bow
and a quiver full of arrows so that he could shoot an arrow or two
into a cow to be left behind as evidence that hostile Indians must
have effected the heist.[49]

A. J. Sowell later wrote of the scouting adventures of Callahan's company as told to him by his father and uncles.

> Mexican horse-thieves, as well as Indians, annoyed the settlers, and Captain James H. Callahan and his rangers used every exertion to catch them, but were for some time unsuccessful; but finally they were trailed to their hiding place by Milford Day, who was a splendid scout and trailer. Their location was in a large and very dense thicket, cut through by a deep and rugged gully. This place was about eight miles northeast from Seguín, on York's Creek.[50]

The horse rustlers had swooped in on a moonlit night and made their heist of six or eight horses, according to Jim Nichols. Among the stolen horses was "Captain Callahan's fine saddle horse. Of course, that riled the Cap's feeling." The following morning, Callahan searched the area for signs with Nichols and Lieutenant Milford Day.[51]

Day and Nichols found the thicket where the Mexican horse thieves had secreted their stolen livestock and rode back into Seguín to raise their company. With Captain Callahan at the lead, the rangers rode out to the thicket along the creek. Corporal Nichols later described their attack.

> We moved up cautiously and soon discovered a bunch of horses close hobbled and down the gully, at the edge of the brush, we discovered a smoke rising. We knew that was their camp.
>
> We alited, tied our horses, crawled up within thirty steps of the fire before we could get a fair view of them. There were five or six men sitting round the fire eating supper. The sun was just setting. We each picked out his man and Callahan was to give the word.
>
> Says he, "Take good aim, boys. Fire!"
>
> All fired about the same instant and five Mexicans fell dead. Two or three jumped to their feet and ran off. One of the men that ran off was Arouba, unhurt. The other two, one we never knew who he was or where he went. The other was a little Mexican we all knew well. His name was Sancho Cabines.[52]

Callahan's minutemen poked through the Mexican camp and examined the dead as darkness fell. "We rounded up the horses, 12 or 15 in number, including them stolen from Seguín the night before, and set out for home," wrote Nichols. In 1884, A. J. Sowell's published version was brief, but similar, to that of Jim Nichols. Sowell wrote that the Mexican thieves lost "some three or four of their number," and that "those who were not killed very easily made their escape after the defeat."[53]

After further scouting, some of Callahan's rangers later passed back through this Mexican camp and found it relatively undisturbed with bodies still lying about. Moving their horses to the spring some three hundred yards away, the minutemen were surprised to hear a voice call out to them. "We halted, looking round in the brush," wrote Nichols. "We saw Sancho, the little Mexican that had ran off but had been wounded."[54]

Per Nichols' account, Sancho was so badly wounded that the rangers honored his request and gave him a mercy shot to the head. Sowell's account has it that the wounded Mexican "hopped to Callahan's horse to get up, but was instantly shot dead with a pistol by the ranger captain." The dead horse thief was buried by a round rocky hill of live oaks near the spring. The gully where the attack on the thieves' camp had occurred became known as "Rogue's Hollow," and the gravesite as "Rogue's Grave."[55]

Seguín was also visited by Indian horse thieves during the summer of 1841. After another such raid, Captain Callahan called up the Gonzales County Minutemen for an extended twenty-day scout out west into Indian territory. "He said he did not want any man to go on a sorry horse, for he intended to follow them to their den," recalled Corporal Jim Nichols.[56]

Per Nichols' recollections, twenty-six men comprised the party that went on this long scout. They stopped over one night in San Antonio first to secure additional supplies before moving out on their expedition. Simon Cockrell, who had once been a prisoner of the Indians, served as the guide for the minutemen. Captain Callahan's rangers traveled up north to the Llano River and there they located an Indian trail. Cockrell, Jim Nichols, and Andrew Sowell were sent out ahead of the main force to scout the trail.

Capt. Callahan's Gonzales Co. Minutemen: May 7–Dec. 20, 1841

Captain:
James H. Callahan
First Lieutenant:
William P. Kinkannon
Second Lieutenant:
James Milford Day
First Sergeant:
John R. King
Second Sergeant:
Allen A. Crain [1]
Third Sergeant:
Isaac A. Faris [1]
Fourth Sergeant:
Asa Jarmon Lee Sowell [1]
First Corporal:
James Wilson Nichols [2]

Privates:
John Baker
William Baker
Tilman Berry
Ira Bisbee [2]
S. A. M. Boyd [3]
Jose Maria Cardinas [4]
Joseph D. Clements [5]
William Clinton
Simon M. Cockrell
Canah C. Colley [3]
Samuel J. Denyer
Mark W. Dikes [2]
Miles G. Dikes [6]
W. M. Dikes [2]
J. N. Faris
James Foster [7]
Robert Hall [2]
William A. Hall
Frederick W. Happell [2]
Hugh G. Henderson [2]
David Henson
Henry B. King [2]
Henry B. King Jr. [2]

William G. King [8]
Joseph S. Martain [9]
Benjamin McCulloch [2]
Andrew Neill [4]
George Washington Nichols
John W. Nichols [10]
Thomas R. Nichols
L. L. Peck [11]
George W. Price [12]
James B. Roberts
Jeremiah Roberts
Arthur Smith [13]
Byrd Smith
Charles A. Smith [2]
Ezekiel Smith
Paris Smith
Andrew Jackson Sowell [14]
John N. Sowell [15]
William C. Stiffey [5]
Arthur Swift [2]
Calvin S. Turner [2]
Samuel Turner
John B. Veach [2]

[1] Promoted on June 7 muster roll.
[2] Joined July 7, 1841.
[3] Joined December 4, 1841.
[4] Joined August 8, 1841.
[5] Joined May 24, 1841.
[6] Joined August 22, 1841.
[7] Joined September 25, 1841.
[8] Joined May 28, 1841.
[9] Joined August 18, 1841.
[10] Joined July 7. Served as second
 sergeant from July 7–26, 1841.
[11] Joined October 24, 1841.
[12] Joined August 12, 1841.
[13] Joined July 28, 1841.
[14] Joined June 8, 1841.
[15] Joined July 7.

Source: Compilation of Captain Callahan's
Minutemen Muster and Pay Rolls, Texas
State Archives.

Asa Jarmon Lee Sowell (1822–1877) and his brothers John and Andrew Jackson Sowell all served with Captain Callahan's 1841 Gonzales County Minuteman. This photo was originally published in Sowell's *Early Settlers and Indian Fighers of Southwest Texas.*

James Wilson Nichols (1820–1887), left a journal of his ranger experiences while serving under such captains as Mathew Caldwell, Jack Hays, and James Callahan. Originally published in Katherine W. McDowell (ed.), *Now You Hear My Horn.*

We went on and on until we struck the Colorado River high up near the mouth of the Concho or South Fork, thence on up to where Colorado City now stands, and where the trail left the river and bore out towards the plains.

The Indians had camped about one day and night at Big Springs, where the station Big Spring is now located on the railroad. Our guide Cockrell said that was the last water on the course the Indians were traveling until we struck Lost Creek on the plains, unless we found water at a spring on the side of a mountain near the edge of the plains some 80 miles distant.[57]

After camping that night, Captain Callahan asked Simon Cockrell to resume following the trail. His rangers loaded up all the water that they could carry and followed. The minutemen rode for two long days and reached the mountain about noon on the third day. To their chagrin, the rangers found that the little creek had gone dry. According to their scout, Lost Creek was still more than two days' ride ahead and their last water was the same ride back.

The rangers had used the last of their water that morning. Callahan put the situation to a vote. "Twelve voted to go on and eight voted to turn back, the rest not voting at all," wrote Jim Nichols. The following morning, Captain Callahan let those who so desired return back for Seguin while he led some of his men on. "It was a hot day and some of the men [were] already spitting cotton, some cursing, and nearly all fretting," recalled Nichols.[58]

They rode through lunch that day—their thirty-third day out from Seguín—and did not stop until evening. By mid-morning the following day, the rangers found that they had circled around and were approaching the same mountain where the command had decided to split the day before. Upon reaching the same dry creek, Nichols found "there was such a torrent of curses, enough to raise the hair of any Christian man's head."

Cockrell chose a different course and the company started out again. They had now been two days and nights without water and one day and night without food. Their horses had been four days without food. John R. King found his tongue so dry and swollen that he could scarcely close his mouth. Fortunately, Jim Nichols managed to kill a small antelope that evening, which the men devoured at camp.

Captain Callahan's men were on their way again the following morning, traveling until after lunch. They reached the foot of a mountain, "high and covered with scrubby brush, and several ledges of large rough scraggy boulders." The rangers tied their horses to a grove of live oak trees, where the horses found some grass to eat. Cockrell and Nichols climbed the mountain to try and spy out some nearby water.[59]

Jim Nichols' journal is missing pages at this point, but the Gonzales County Minutemen had been out on their scout for more than thirty days. The rest of Nichols' subheads indicate that the complete trip was a "forty-six days' scout." This would certainly have been sometime after July 11, on which date Calvin Turner joined Callahan's company.

Muster rolls of Callahan's expeditions do not show one of such duration, although it is possible that only the legal maximum of fifteen days was actually later submitted. Muster rolls submitted for services rendered during July and August, for example, have only two-day lapses between service. Callahan's third expedition was stated as July 7 through July 9, followed by another expedition from July 11 to July 26. The fifth expedition of Seguín rangers was from July 28 to August 6. The final service of the Gonzales County Minutemen is shown to be December 20, 1841.

The Indian depredations against Seguín were held in check as the constantly patrolling rangers kept most raiders away. "The marauding bands of Indians had ceased their operations and the Mexicans had made no attempt to regain Texas," wrote Jim Nichols.

According to A. J. Sowell's history of the early rangers, Captain Callahan's men did capture two more Mexican "regular horse thieves." The captain "condemned them to death without much ceremony." As with the wounded man later finished off near Rogue's Hollow, the accepted understanding among the Seguín rangers seemed to be that the only good horse thief was a dead horse thief—regardless of whether the perpetrator was Anglo, Indian, or Mexican.[60]

"In our day and time, this would look cruel and brutal," wrote Sowell, "but those were desperate times, and it was death to all horse thieves when caught."

CHAPTER 14

Enchanted Rock and Bird's Fort

October–December 1841

The Legend of Enchanted Rock

After operating with as many as forty-five men in August 1841, Captain Jack Hays trimmed his Béxar County Minutemen unit to a more efficient size. Muster and pay rolls show that he returned to the field with only nineteen privates under his command on September 1. Public debt papers for his September company show Hays to be "Capt. of Minute Men in 1841."[1]

All of the nineteen rangers now operating with Captain Hays had been under his command for the Uvalde Canyon expedition in late June, where Joseph Miller had been wounded. Hays' own hand wound and John Trueheart's chest wound from their recent July 24 Llano River fight were not serious enough to keep them from their horses in September.

Hays' rangers were out for a full month from San Antonio, disbanding again on October 1, 1841. The interesting thing about his command this particular month is that little has been recorded about what specifically his men did on this expedition.

Captain Hays was in San Antonio on September 14, 1841, on which date he signed discharge papers for one of his men. His note specifically says that the paper was signed "under my hand at the city of San Antonio on the 14th Sept. 1841."[2]

In August 1841, the citizens of San Antonio elected Hays to be the Béxar County surveyor. He had located numerous land titles throughout 1840. He employed deputy surveyors, but would

---

Capt. Hays' Béxar County Minutemen: Sept. 1–October 1, 1841

Captain:	William Isbell
John Coffee Hays	Joseph Miller *
	William H. Moore
Privates:	Robert Patton
Samuel Adams	Robert Pollett
S. P. Ball	Benjamin Prior
Antonio Coy	Benjamin Prior Jr.
Addison Drinkwater	John Trapnell
Archibald Fitzgerald	John O. Truehart
Peter Fohr	John Young
Damacio Galvan	
Nathaniel Harbert	* Discharged September 20, 1841.
Jacob Jackson Humphreys	

---

personally only locate five land certificates during the remainder of the year due to his obligations with his ranger command.[3]

There are many legends and tall tales of Jack Hays and his heroics on the Texas frontier. Muster rolls, pay rolls, military reports, and other documents keep pretty good tabs on this ranger leader for the first eight months of 1841. His only other recorded command during the balance of 1841 occurred on this expedition of September 1 to October 1, 1841.

Among the legends attached to Hays is that of Enchanted Rock, an engagement where he fought off Comanche attackers by himself for some time. If an action report was written by Captain Hays concerning this battle, it has long since disappeared. Contemporary newspapers also made no mention of any Enchanted Rock battle during the early 1840s. Historian Walter Prescott Webb, in fact, chose to skip past this Hays fight in his groundbreaking 1935 book, _The Texas Rangers_. In spite of the lack of significant direct evidence, John Coffee Hays himself told the tale often enough to at least make one consider it plausible.

The first published account is found in Samuel Chester Reid Jr.'s _The Scouting Expeditions of McCulloch's Texas Rangers_, which was published in Philadelphia in 1847. Reid learned of the exploits of Jack Hays around campfires during the Mexican War.[4]

The Enchanted Rock story was also told early on by John Caperton, who wrote a manuscript on the life of John Hays sometime after Hays moved to California. Caperton had first joined the rangers in 1848, and he heard the stories from Hays during that time. They traveled together for California in 1849, where Hays became the sheriff of San Francisco County, with Caperton as his deputy. It is possible that Caperton included his version of Enchanted Rock after seeing it in print from Reid's 1847 account, which he mentions in his text.[5]

It is not inconceivable that a minor Indian battle on the far extremes of the Texas frontier could escape newspaper attention. In researching the Texas Rangers from 1835 to this point, I have described several small engagements between Indians and frontiersmen that were not formally published in any newspaper. Some survive only in audited republic claims or other military papers. Aside from the Béxar County company under Hays, several other 1841 county minutemen companies have very little documentation of their scouts and skirmishes.

Perhaps Captain Hays wrote a report of his September 1841 expedition which has been lost with other adjutant general's records. Perhaps a minor shootout in which he captured no prisoners or gathered no significant intelligence did not warrant a detailed report from him. Remember that during his July 1841 expedition, one of his rangers was killed. He did not even mention this death in his report. Only Hays' pay roll and Caperton's sketch of Hays remain as testament to the man who did not return.

Reid wrote that Hays was "out with a party of some fifteen or twenty men." In A. J. Sowell's *Early Settlers and Indian Fighters of Southwest Texas*, he wrote that "Hays was on a scout with about twenty of his men near the head of the Pedernales at a place called then the 'Enchanted Rock.'" Published in 1900, Sowell certainly had had access to Reid's 1847 account. The number of men present for this expedition exactly matches Hays' September expedition. Caperton says that Hays was out "with 25 or 30 men" on this particular scout.[6]

The fact that Samuel Reid was told of the Enchanted Rock story in 1846 lends some credence to its authenticity. Concerning Jack Hays, "many were the stories that went the rounds in camp of his perilous expeditions, his wild and daring adventures, and his cool and determined bravery."[7]

Reid's source for the Enchanted Rock fight told him that this had happened "in the year 1841, or '42." With only about twenty men with him, Hays' September 1841 muster roll fits this count well. His other expeditions of 1841 are well documented, and his adventures in 1842 are more well known. The best fit for Enchanted Rock would be between September 1841 and early 1842, when comparatively little is known of the movements of Jack Hays' rangers.

By March 1842, Captain Hays had been ordered out by General Edward Burleson to pursue a Mexican force under General Rafael Vásquez which had invaded San Antonio. A search of audited republic claims and pension papers shows that Hays had no fewer than thirty-nine men under his direct command in March. Therefore, his muster roll of twenty men in September 1841 looks to be a better numeric fit to the party he had with him at Enchanted Rock.

It is obvious from Samuel Reid's hand-me-down version of Enchanted Rock that he had never personally seen the granite formation. He describes a hollowed-out bowl in the center of the hill "sufficiently large to allow a small party of men to lie in, thus forming a small fort, the projecting and elevated sides serving as a protection."[8]

Reid called Enchanted Rock "a high, round hill, very rugged and difficult of ascent." This rock is actually a solid granite mass, the second largest formation in the United States, falling only behind Stone Mountain near Atlanta, Georgia. It is not difficult to climb, with its sloping sides. There are many covered places for a person to hide, but also enough cover that others should have been able to slip up on a person hiding in the rocks.[9]

Llano County's granite mass is the subject of a number of old Indian legends. Comanche and Tonkawa Indians both held the rock in high reverence because of the powers they felt it held. They supposedly offered sacrifices at its base. Some believed that it was haunted by an Indian princess who threw herself off the rock when she saw her tribe being slaughtered by another. Enchanted Rock can take on a sinister look with the way it glitters on clear nights after a rainstorm. On cool nights after a very warm day, some have reported that the cooling surface can make creaking noises. This no doubt led to some early Indians believing that they could hear screams at night from the rock.[10]

The Reid account and the Caperton/Hays account at least agree on the basic facts. While out scouting west of San Antonio near the Pedernales, Captain Hays became cut off from his men when a band of Comanches attacked them.

According to Hays' biographer, his men made camp on the bank of nearby Crabapple Creek while scouting on a tributary of the Pedernales. The guards watched the horses and kept a sharp lookout for Indians at the camp. James Kimmins Greer says that Jack Hays went out alone the next morning to make a scout in the vicinity of Enchanted Rock. He was armed with only a rifle, two Colts acquired originally by the Frontier Regiment, and a bowie knife.[11]

He encountered three Indians on horseback and quickly found himself in a race for his life, as he later related to his friend John Caperton. As we have no direct account of this skirmish, I will leave the reader to peruse what Caperton claims to be straight from his friend Hays.

> Being mounted on a fine horse, he ran, and they took after him, and were presently joined by five or six more. They pursued him from point to point, his horse easily keeping in advance of theirs, and when they came near enough he would halt, and they would stop, and pass a shot with him.
>
> This continued for several miles, Major Hays going in the direction he thought his men would come from, but he saw nothing of them. His horse began to show fatigue, and the Indians were crowding him pretty closely. He could hear the yelling in every direction, and knew that he was in the vicinity of their large encampment.
>
> He rode on, the number of his pursuers increasing, and presently he saw before him in the valley a large rock standing alone, somewhat like a sugar loaf in shape, a celebrated peak, known as the "enchanted rock," so called from the curious lights that were sometimes seen about it, probably some electrical phenomenon. He made a dash for this rock, the Indians close by, they having run him eight or ten miles.[12]

Hays leaped off his horse and left him at the base of the hill. Shoving one of his Colt pistols back into his belt, he furiously scrambled up the face of Enchanted Rock as the Comanches wheeled their horses to a halt. According to the Caperton account, Hays reached the top and "found some loose rocks, which he hastily piled up to form a kind of shelter." As opposed to Reid's description of a large bowl that could safely hide a number of men, Caperton's account is more plausible. There are a number of small caves and indentures along the back sides of Enchanted Rock that would have offered good protection to an individual. Loose rocks could have certainly been found to pile up.

The Indians paused a brief while at the base of the little mountain as they prepared to take on "Devil Jack." They fired some shots up at him, but his rock hiding place made them ineffective. The first Comanches who tried to climb up the hill were sent scrambling when Captain Hays fired shots down at them.[13]

Hays was conservative, only firing when the Comanches advanced too close to his little rock hideout. To his good fortune, Captain Hays had acquired two of the army's Colt five-shooter pistols. Between firing his rifle and going through the reloading process, he therefore had five shots per pistol to dispense as needed during the reload.

There is no record of how many Indians he may have killed or wounded. Reid simply says that Hays "defended himself for three long hours," during which time "he felled them on all sides." The Caperton account makes no claim to the number of Comanche casualties. He contends that the captain held off his attackers "for an hour or two."[14]

Finally, Captain Hays must have sensed that the end was near for him. Despite their losses on the slopes of Enchanted Rock, the Comanches had continued to gather reinforcements from their camp some two miles away. Near the base of the rock, an estimated one hundred Indians had gathered. They began raising a terrible yell as they prepared for their final assault on the hill.

Fortunately for Hays, the remainder of his company had heard the cracks of his rifle and the yelling during the past hours. They made their way near the base of the granite hill and came to his aid. The Caperton/Hays account depicts the closing scene of Hays' ordeal.

Perhaps the most famous story of Texas Ranger Captain Jack Hays is his solo stand against Comanches in late 1841 from atop Enchanted Rock in present Llano County. While details of this battle exist only from his recounting of the battle to others, the Enchanted Rock story was in print as early as 1847. The fact that Hays sat for this oil painting years later in California lends some credibility that the battle was based on an actual event. The state of Texas erected a centennial marker on State Highway 16 in Llano County in 1936 for Enchanted Rock. Its inscription describes how Hays fought "while surrounded by Comanche Indians who cut him off from his ranging company."
Gift of Mrs. Roblay McMullins, Texas Ranger Hall of Fame and Museum.

Hays, lying there thought he was gone, as he could not resist a combined effort of this kind on the part of the savages. Just then, however, to his great relief, his men appeared in sight, having heard the firing and the yelling of the Indians. They fought their way through them, and compelled them to fall back, and thus rescued their commander.[15]

After surviving his tightest escape, John Coffee Hays was believed by the Indians to be leading a charmed life. To the Tejanos who served under him, he was commonly referred to as "*Capitan* [Kap-ee-tan] Jack." To the Indians, he was less reverently regarded as "Devil Jack."[16]

Being heavily outnumbered, Captain Hays' company likely departed the Enchanted Rock area quickly and made their way back to San Antonio for reinforcements. There is no muster roll evidence that Captain Hays took another ranger force into the field during the last three months of 1841. As of October 16, he was still in San Antonio, working to collect pay for his recent minuteman company. He likely continued to operate in the field in his roll as deputy county surveyor, as evidenced by a promissory note he wrote to John Twohig that day. He advised merchant Twohig to provision Benjamin Prior and his son with "what ever provisions that they may want." Hays promised to collect compensation when he collected the second half of his rangers' pay.[17]

The authenticity of Enchanted Rock will probably always be doubted by some. None, however, can contest the bravery and fighting skills of this unique Texas Ranger captain. And those who fought with him in the 1840s and heard the campfire stories about his solo fight at Enchanted Rock never spoke out against the veracity of his story.

His reputation was equally strong among his Indian foes. On a later occasion, some Indians came into San Antonio to make a treaty. Several chiefs were overheard as they pointed to Jack Hays and spoke of him. One chief pointed to his companion and said, "Blue Wing and I, no afraid go to hell together."[18]

Then, pointing to Captain Hays, the chief said, "*Capitan* Jack, great brave. No afraid go to hell by himself."

Major Bird's Fort on the Trinity

General Edward Tarrant's men had returned to Fort Inglish during early August from an expedition to the present Dallas–Fort Worth area. While some of his men had been discharged on August 11, a large number of the battalion remained in service into October under Colonel Robert Hamilton's supervision.

In mid-September, Tarrant carried out a plan to keep rangers active along the Trinity River. He would construct a fort from which his men could operate against the Indians in the Cross Timbers. Supply wagons from Fort Inglish and the Red River settlements could keep his men provisioned.

Major Jonathan Bird was ordered to head up the expedition to construct this new fort. On September 19, 1841, Colonel Daniel Montague mustered in a twenty-nine-man company under command of Captain Alexander W. Webb. Webb was among General Tarrant's men who had participated in the Village Creek fight in May. His company was organized to fill out the vacancies left by men who were not going back out into the field again. The companies of Andrew Fowler and David Key were largely broken up by August 11, while those of Captains Williams, Stout, Blair, Orton, and Lane would continue to serve into at least the first week of October. Some of Captain Webb's men had served under these other captains during Tarrant's past expedition.[19]

There were three men named Cox in Webb's company, although only John H. Cox and George H. Cox were brothers. John G. Cox was no relation to them. Wade H. Rattan was appointed quartermaster and commissary for the unit and would be responsible for supplying food to the men during their stay at Bird's Fort.[20]

George W. Wright, a resident of Lamar County, later wrote, "At the time Capt. Webb's company was made up for the purpose of erecting Bird's Fort, said company started from my house."[21]

Major Bird and Captain Webb's company were likely accompanied by one of the other units that was still in operation. They moved to the Trinity River and began construction of Bird's Fort near present Fort Worth in early October 1841. The site was about twenty-two miles west of Dallas, on the north side of the West Fork of the Trinity—about three miles east of the town of

Birdville (present Haltom City). By the time the last of Tarrant's original battalion was discharged on October 15, Webb's company, commonly known as the "Bird's Fort Company," was left alone to man and complete construction on the new fort.

The Trinity fort was in full operation by mid-October, as evidenced by the military papers of some of Webb's men. George Wright was discharged October 14, 1841, at "Fort Bird, Trinity" by Captain Webb and Major Bird. Private Wesley Askins, formerly of Captain Fowler's mounted gunmen, was discharged from the company on October 15, having completed his term of service as a substitute.[22]

Captain Webb's company apparently stayed with the fort through March 1842. Several families moved into the area during the fall of 1841. The first to reach there during the fall were the families of Hamp Rattan and Captain Mabel Gilbert, with a few men. A short time later the family of John Beeman arrived.[23]

Provisions for the Bird's Fort Company were handled by Hamp Rattan and Samuel Moss, the assistant commissary for the Third Regiment, Fourth Brigade of the Texas Militia. He purchased much of the company's corn from settler Daniel Slack, who lived near the Red River. Private Henry Hahn later confirmed the fact that Slack made a number of trips with his teams and wagons to haul corn out to Bird's Fort.[24]

Late in November 1841, Captain Alex Webb sent a wagon from Bird's Fort back to the Red River settlements for provisions. It was gone so long that Webb eventually decided to find out what was wrong. Taking Solomon Silkwood and Hamp Rattan with him, Captain Webb rode back along the path of the wagon toward Red River.

On the east side of Elm Fork, about a mile and a half southwest of where the city of Carrollton now stands, they encountered Indians. On Christmas Day 1841, Rattan was cutting down a large ash tree to get the honey in it. A small party of concealed Indians killed Rattan. Webb and Silkwood killed one of the Indians and escaped to reach their fort.[25]

There was a heavy snow during this time, which had left a good accumulation on the ground. It remained intensely cold for several days. Silkwood became sick and died from the exposure he had suffered on this little scout. A single ranger was again sent out to look for the wagon. He succeeded, and on December

Capt. Webb's "Bird's Fort Company": Sept. 19, 1841–March 19, 1842

Captain:
Alexander W. Webb [1]
First Lieutenant:
William Chisum [1]
J. B. Moore [1]
Second Lieutenant:
J. F. Redden [1]
First Sergeant:
King S. Custer [1]

Privates:
Charles Adams
John Adcock [1]
Isaac H. Beeman
James J. Beeman
John Beeman [1]
John H. Beeman
John S. Beeman
Sam H. Beeman
William H. Beeman
Lewis Bogard
Russell Bogard [1]
Crawford Brown
William H. Chadwell [1]
William Chisum
J. Rily Cole [1]
George H. Cox
John G. Cox [1]
John H. Cox [1]
Berry Crownover
Bly Dandy
Job Dean
John Columbus Guest [1]
Henry Hahn
James Harland [1]

Joshua E. Heath
Isaac Houston [1]
George Lampson
Henry Long
J. D. Lowery [1]
J. H. Manes [1]
William Martin [1]
Charles McPherson [1]
Daniel Montague [1]
Samuel Moss [1]
James R. O'Neal [1]
Daniel Rattan [1]
Thomas Rattan
Wade Hampton Rattan [1,2]
Joseph Reelor
C. Rogers [1]
Thomas Rollen
George W. Russell [1]
Solomon Silkwood
J. H. Tam [1]
Henderson Walker
Henson Walker
Landon Walker
James Wells
John Wells
Dirk Wilson

[1] Present for original muster roll. See McLean, *Papers*, XVIII: 338–9.
[2] Killed by Indians December 25, 1841.

Source: George W. Cox PD, R 146, F158–225. This roll shows each man serving between one and six months, without specific dates.

30, five days after the killing of Rattan, the wagon reached the scene.

A party returned to recover the body of Rattan. They found his faithful dog still guarding his master's body. The remains were conveyed to Bird's Fort, and were committed to the earth in a crude coffin which had been built from wood from an old wagon body. Hamp Rattan was survived by brothers John and Littleton Rattan. Hamp and Littleton had both been in the nearby Village Creek fight earlier in the year.

Another death happened sometime after the building of Bird's Fort. Robert Sloan was leading a scouting detachment of a company of Red River militiamen. He did not command the company but was leader of one of its squads, which had been divided up for scouting purposes.[26]

While on this scout, Sloan lost David (or Samuel) Clubb, who was from Illinois and a soldier in the 1832 Black Hawk War. Clubb was killed by Indians at a small lake on the Elm Fork of the Trinity, a short distance above its mouth and below the Keenan crossing.

Final Days of the Frontier Minutemen

By late 1841, the Texas Indian Wars were winding down. This is not to say that there were no more battles during the Republic of Texas years or that Indian depredations ceased. It is to say that the frontier systems that had been created and maintained out of necessity since October 1835 were not nearly as necessary. Many of the hostile tribes had been driven much farther away from the settlements. The Cherokees were largely gone, as were the Shawnees. The Comanches had suffered tough losses in 1840 and were not disturbing the Austin and San Antonio settlements with their past frequency.

The days when more than five hundred Red River militiamen were required to carry out a campaign into Indian territory were becoming a thing of the past. The Cherokee War of 1839—which had assembled more than one thousand Texans in East Texas––was a military buildup that would not be matched again. One well-equipped Texas Ranger company or a battalion could now range vast areas of Texas to deal with hostile groups.

Captain Joseph Daniels' Travis Guards remained in operation from Austin, moving out against Indians as situations warranted. In the fall of 1841, John Wahrenberger was attacked by Indians near the edge of Austin. Employed as Louis T. Cook's gardener, Wahrenberger was chased and slightly wounded by an arrow. He raced from a mill at the edge of town and collapsed exhausted on his employer's doorway. Cook fired on the pursuing Indians, dropping one of them and sending the others fleeing. They collected their wounded Indian, but did not push the fight. Captain Daniels' men were sent out the next day, but did not overtake these hostile Indians.[27]

On October 3, 1841, the Travis Guards were ordered out to apprehend Castro and Flacco, chiefs of the Lipan tribe which had been friendly to the Texas Rangers for so many years. A man named James Boyce was murdered by Indians on October 2, and blame was placed on a Lipan Indian of Castro and Flacco's tribe.[28]

Travis County Sheriff Alex MacFarlane "summoned Captain Daniels to call out the Travis Guards to assist in arresting Castro and Flacco." Daniels was to bring the chiefs in to answer charges "before some justice of the peace."

MacFarlane had no sooner dispatched his orders to Daniels than he retracted them. More than likely, cooler heads assured him that Flacco and his men had long defended Texan settlers from hostile Indians. Certainly, they must be taking the blame for the actions of another tribe's depredation. McFarlane decided to visit Chiefs Castro and Flacco himself. "In case of any resistance," he wrote Captain Daniels, "I will send you a message, when you will proceed to the camp of the Indians."

The *Texas Sentinel* of Austin reported in its Thursday, November 5, 1841, issue that "We had quite an alarm in town on Saturday night." This would have been October 31, 1841. A report made it into town that a party of Comanches had been discovered on Brushy Creek and were approaching town.[29]

It was later determined that this party, consisting of some three to four hundred Indians, had instead gone on toward Nashville-on-the-Brazos. The *Sentinel* reported that a party of one hundred citizens of Milam and Robertson counties were heard to have gone out to attack them, in cooperation with friendly Lipan and Tonkawa Indians.

The night after this attack, the Sixth Congress convened at Austin on November 1. Final preparations were underway to pass the reins of Texas leadership from Lamar back to Houston. Election day for the Republic of Texas had been September 6. In the capital city of Austin, the *Austin City Gazette* had favored Houston and his vice presidential running mate, frontiersman

Edward Burleson. Austin's other newspaper, the *Texas Sentinel*, had given its support to former Republic president David Burnet and General Memucan Hunt. Sam Houston, the hero of San Jacinto, was returned to power in Texas by the voters, in a margin of more than two to one over Burnet.[30]

Sam Houston rode into Austin on December 8. He was met outside of town by Captain Daniels' Travis Guards, which would serve as honor guards for the president-elect. President Houston and Vice President Burleson were inaugurated on December 13, 1841.[31]

Almost immediately upon the start of Houston's second term as president of Texas, the Texas Rangers and the country's entire military came under scrutiny. Secretary of State Anson Jones on December 22 proposed shutting down the Republic of Texas' military almost entirely. Her military was recommended "to act strictly on the defensive" toward any Mexican aggression.[32]

Further, Dr. Jones felt recommended to have "no troops kept in commission, except a few Rangers on the frontiers." A small sum of money would be required to keep the Indians conciliated. "It is much cheaper and more humane to purchase their friendship than to fight them."

The county minuteman system came under criticism by the end of 1841. Some complained to the Sixth Congress in early 1842 that this system had unfairly paid men during 1841. The chief justices were in no position to determine abuses. They had to take the word of the captains that muster rolls were fairly drawn up. Critics complained that the captains decided whether an "emergency" existed or not. Others complained that some of the minutemen were being used to guard surveyors' land in Indian territory and that others were even going on illegal cattle-stealing expeditions.[33]

The Sixth Congress ultimately sealed the deal on the county minutemen system by not appropriating any funds for this program to continue. By late December, therefore, most of the county ranging companies had ceased to operate. The final recorded expedition of Captain Eli Chandler's Robertson County Minutemen was a six-day scout with forty-four of his rangers, from October 29 to November 5, 1841. His muster roll was certified on November 22 by Robertson County Chief Justice Francis Stanton.

Captain Joseph Lilly's Paschal County Minutemen continued making scouts in October and November in small groups. Third Sergeant W. S. Keith went out in late September. He reported to Lilly on October 4, "We have discovered no signs of Indians whatever." Sergeant John Crownover led three other minutemen out in late November—William Truett, James Stout, and Robert Hinson. Upon returning on November 31, Crownover reported to Captain Lilly his men had "covered several areas and found nothing of anything animating danger."[34]

Captain James Callahan's Gonzales County Minutemen served through December 20. Captain George Erath's Milam County Minutemen were discharged on Christmas Eve, and Travis County's rangers under Captain George Dolson ended their field service on December 28.

Three areas remained under the active watch of a county ranging company as 1841 passed into 1842, despite the fact that official funding was allowed to cease. In these areas, the need for rangers to contest frontier injustices certainly negated whether the government actually wanted to pay for them. The people of these areas truly *needed* their protection.

The first of these areas was the Red River border. Captain William Becknell's rangers continued to operate for a full year in Red River County, through June 25, 1842.

The second area of continuing ranger operations was the disputed Nueces Strip. Following the capture of Philip Dimmitt and other men in the summer of 1841, the excitement along the Nueces had tamed a little. The September Refugio attack brought the need for rangers to the forefront once again. The Texas minutemen raised from San Patricio, in fact, had been charged by some individuals with being just as lawless as those they were supposedly out to attack.

President Lamar had ordered Colonel Bell to discharge some of these frontier companies and replace them with men more capable. Captain William Cairnes' "Western Spy Company," authorized by Bell, would operate into 1842 along the Nueces. The only minuteman company to serve beyond December was Captain John McDaniel's Refugio County company, which operated until February 24, 1842.

The third area that maintained a continual Texas Ranger presence was that of San Antonio de Béxar. Trading from this area and Mexico remained brisk, while depredations against the traders decreased. The reputation of "*Capitan* Jack" had grown in the Tejano and Indian communities.

Although there are no muster rolls to indicate field service for Hays' company between November 1841 and February 1842, he was not unnoticed.

The December 8, 1841, issue of the *Telegraph and Texas Register* gave much credit to Captain Hays and his rangers for keeping the Indians in check. His company had "almost completely broken-up the old haunts of the Comanches in the vicinity of Béxar."[35] The newspaper editor bragged on Hays highly, stating that the "protection and security resulting from the active enterprise of this excellent officer" was helping to extend the settlements around the San Antonio area.

Afterword

Captain Jack Hays had certainly become a role model in frontier fighting during 1841. He was respected by his peers and feared by his enemies. His rangers and minutemen were effective in quelling any threat, and with the Colt repeating revolver slowly making its way into their hands, the Texas Rangers would only become more efficient in combat.

The Lamar administration ended in December 1841, and he was replaced by his predecessor, Sam Houston, as president. Houston would condemn Lamar's Indian policies and his wasting of money. Under Lamar, the Cherokees and Shawnees had largely been purged from Texas. The Comanches had been aggressively attacked and driven further from the major settlements.

For all of its merits, the new county minuteman system of 1841 had certainly shown some flaws. While those units in most Texas counties operated for brief periods of time, others gave the ranging service a bad name. One such example was Captain William Cairnes, who commanded minutemen and other volunteer companies from San Patricio County during 1841 and into 1842, but would not survive much longer.

Cairnes' men had routed a trader camp during the final days of December 1841, killing one trader and taking off much of their camp supplies and mules. Months later, in March 1842, Cairnes was down to eight men, after having discharged his formal company. According to the chief justice of San Patricio County and to a report from the *Telegraph and Texas Register*, Cairnes and his men were attacked on March 7 near San Patricio on the Nueces.[1]

The former rangers with Cairnes were: William Snodgrass, Seth P. Marvin, William Wells, John White, Alanson T. Miles, Ewen Cameron, and one other man. Mexican troops under Ramón Valera attacked and killed Captain Cairnes, Miles, Snodgrass, White, and a fifth Texan. Marvin and Wells were captured. Only Ewen Cameron managed to swim the river and escape.[2]

Cairnes, after sustaining a mortal wound, reportedly killed one of his Mexican attackers. Colonel Henry Kinney was able to negotiate the release of Marvin the day after his capture. Wells was carried as a prisoner to Matamoros, although Kinney would later obtain his release as well.

During the late years of the Republic of Texas, the number of ranger versus Indian clashes began to decrease. Since 1839, there had been a sharp increase in expeditions more offensive in nature which sought to destroy the Indians and their entire villages. Some tribes were driven out of Texas, while others continued moving further from the settlements.

Statistics show that Texian casualties of the Texas Indian began to decline in 1840–1. Between 1835 and 1839, the number of Texan casualties in Indian combat increased ever year, with 1839 being the climax of action on the Texas frontier. Thereafter, the numbers of casualties began to decline in 1840 and 1841.

Year	Killed	Wounded
1835	2	3
1836	5	5
1837	25	4
1838	32	24*
1839	33	50
1840	15	21
1841	5	7

* The number of men wounded in 1838 fighting includes fourteen men whom I neglected to specifically list in the casualty list in the appendix of *Savage Frontier* Volume II.

In seven years, 117 men had been killed and 114 wounded in Indian encounters on the Texas frontier. These numbers do not reflect casualties of encounters with Mexican troops or civilians who were killed during Indian depredations against civilian homes or travelers. In return for these losses, the Texans boasted of killing and wounding several times this number of their Indian foes.

Technology was beginning to swing into the favor of the Texans by 1840 and 1841. Samuel Colt's .36 caliber "Paterson five-shooter" pistol with its revolving cylinder debuted in Texas battles during 1840 in small numbers. The Colt revolver and the subsequent Walker Colt—a .44 caliber six-shot revolver Samuel H. Walker helped Colt to design—would allow the Texas Rangers new freedom in fighting. With this new weapon, the Texans could continue to fire and charge on horseback. The Comanches would find that their foes were no longer the riflemen who had been forced to dismount to fight.

Such advancements during the final years of the Republic of Texas would forever change the old backwoodsman style of frontier fighting and influence future generations of Texas Rangers.

APPENDIX A

Texan Casualties of the Frontier Indian Wars

1840–1841

This compilation includes Texas Rangers, militiamen, and Frontier Regiment (First Infantry) soldiers killed *in the line of duty* during hostile encounters with Indian forces. Ranger losses to Mexican forces are not included. Among these would be ten former San Patricio Rangers under John Yerby who had deserted Captain Ownby's company. They ran afoul of Mexican Army soldiers and were killed on June 13, 1841.

Other casualties not listed are: men who were accidentally wounded and who subsequently died from these wounds during the course of a campaign; individuals killed during Indian depredations; and deserters who were killed by Indians after they left their companies on campaign.

1840

KILLED IN ACTION

Name:	Date Killed:	Action:
Henry Douglass	Feb. 28, 1840	Indian ambush near San Antonio
Richard L'Estrange	Feb. 28, 1840	Indian ambush near San Antonio
George W. Cayce	March 19, 1840	Council House Fight
William M. Dunnington	March 19, 1840	Council House Fight
Joseph L. Hood	March 19, 1840	Council House Fight
Frederick Kaminsky	March 19, 1840	Council House Fight
Hugh Miller Thompson	March 19, 1840	Council House Fight
Unnamed Hispanic man	March 19, 1840	Council House Fight
Robert G. Whitney	March 19, 1840	Council House Fight
Dr. Bell	August 9, 1840	Arenosa Creek Skirmish
Gotlip Wolf	August 12, 1840	Plum Creek Battle
4 unnamed soldiers	September 1840	Ambush on First Regiment

WOUNDED IN ACTION

Name:	Date Wounded:	Action:
William Kelly	Feb. 28, 1840	Indian ambush near San Antonio
C. A. Root	Feb. 28, 1840	Indian ambush near San Antonio
Mathew Caldwell	March 19, 1840	Council House Fight
_____ Carson	March 19, 1840	Council House Fight
Thomas Higginbotham	March 19, 1840	Council House Fight
George Thomas Howard	March 19, 1840	Council House Fight
Martin Kelly	March 19, 1840	Council House Fight
John C. Morgan	March 19, 1840	Council House Fight
James W. Robinson	March 19, 1840	Council House Fight
Edward Adams Thompson	March 19, 1840	Council House Fight
John Sutherland Menefee	August 9, 1840	Arenosa Creek Skirmish
C. Columbus DeWitt	August 12, 1840	Plum Creek Battle
James Gibson	August 12, 1840	Plum Creek Battle
Robert Hall	August 12, 1840	Plum Creek Battle
Nelson Lee	August 12, 1840	Plum Creek Battle
Henry E. McCulloch	August 12, 1840	Plum Creek Battle
James Wilson Nichols	August 12, 1840	Plum Creek Battle
Samuel H. Reed	August 12, 1840	Plum Creek Battle
Dr. Alonzo B. Sweitzer	August 12, 1840	Plum Creek Battle
Henry C. Winchel	August 12, 1840	Plum Creek Battle
J. L. Hill	October 25, 1840	Skirmish near Franklin

1841

KILLED IN ACTION

Name:	Date Killed:	Action:
John Bunyan Denton	May 24, 1841	Village Creek Battle
John Slein	July 24, 1841	Hay's Llano River Fight
A. T. Smith	August 5, 1841	Chandler's Cross Timbers Fight
George W. Heard	August 22, 1841	Indian ambush against rangers
Wade Hampton Rattan	Dec. 25, 1841	Indian ambush

WOUNDED IN ACTION

Name:	Date Wounded:	Action:
George M. Dolson	March 31, 1841	Hill Country skirmish
Thomas J. Smith	May 21, 1841	Wise County Indian Fight
John Griffin	May 24, 1841	Village Creek Battle
Henry B. Stout	May 24, 1841	Village Creek Battle
Joseph Miller	June 29, 1841	Hays' Uvalde Canyon Fight
John Coffee Hays	July 24, 1841	Hays' Llano River Fight
John O. Trueheart	July 24, 1841	Hays' Llano River Fight

APPENDIX B

Roster of 1841 Rangers and County Minutemen by Units

In 1841, three ranging companies were approved for the early months. Thereafter, the Texas government authorized twenty counties to employ companies of "minutemen" to range their frontier to maintain safety for the citizens. Although considered incomplete, this compilation shows the majority of the men who served in 1841 in these ranger or minuteman companies. Those men who served in mounted gunman companies operating under the authority of the Texas Militia are not listed here.

Key to Captains listed in this roster

Baker, Capt. John R.	Refugio County Minutemen
Becknell, Capt. William	Red River County Minutemen
Brookfield, Capt. William C.	Houston County Minutemen
Cairnes, Capt. William J.	San Patricio County Minutemen
Callahan, Capt. James H.	Gonzales County Minutemen
Chandler, Capt. Eli	Robertson County Minutemen
Creaner, Capt. Charles N.	Victoria County Minutemen
Daniels, Capt. Joseph	Travis Guards
Dolson, Capt. George M.	Travis County Minutemen
Erath, Capt. George Bernhard	Milam County Minutemen
Gage, Capt. David	Nacodoches County Minutemen
Greer, Capt. Thomas N. B.	Montgomery County Minutemen
Hays, Capt. John Coffee	Rangers/Béxar County Minutemen
Killough, Capt. Samuel B.	Robertson County Rangers
Lilly, Capt. Joseph D.	Paschal County Minutemen
Matthews, Capt. Mansell W.	Lamar County Minutemen
McDaniel, Capt. John	Refugio County Minutemen
Miles, Capt. Alanson T.	San Patricio County Minutemen
Ownby, Capt. James P.	San Patricio County Rangers
Pérez, Capt. Antonio	San Antonio Rangers
Price, Capt. John T.	Victoria County Rangers
Sowell, Capt. Joseph	Fannin County Minutemen
Webb, Capt. Alexander R.	Bird's Fort Rangers
Zumwalt, Capt. Adam	Victoria County Minutemen

Name	Captain
Acres, Harvey	Lilly
Adams, Charles	Sowell, Webb
Adams, John	Chandler
Adams, John F.	Killough, Chandler
Adams, John S.	Hays
Adcock, John	Sowell, Webb
Addison, Joseph J.	Killough
Addison, Oscar	Erath
Albritz, David	Sowell
Allen, John	Gage
Anderson, George	Miles, Cairnes
Anderson, Joel	Erath
Anderson, John	Erath
Anderson, John (2)	Matthews
Anderson, William	Gage
Anglin, William	Killough
Annibal, Bartlett	McDaniel
Antonio (Lipan Apache)	Hays
Ariola, Edward	Greer
Asberry, Spencer	Sowell
Attwell, William H.	Hays
Badgett, William	Ownby
Bailey, Aaron	Becknell
Bailey, Amos C. C.	Becknell
Bailey, James M.	Matthews
Bailey, William	Sowell
Baker, John	Callahan
Baker, John Reagan	Baker
Baker, William	Callahan
Ball, Elisha	Becknell
Ball, S. P.	Hays
Ballard, Ezekiel	Price, Ownby
Barton, David A.	Killough
Basil, R. W.	Ownby
Bass, Sam	Erath
Beasley, Charles	Chandler
Becknell, John C.	Becknell
Becknell, William	Becknell
Beeman, Isaac H.	Webb
Beeman, James J.	Webb
Beeman, John	Webb
Beeman, John H.	Webb
Beeman, John S.	Webb
Beeman, Sam H.	Webb
Beeman, William H.	Webb
Bell, Johnson	Erath
Bell, Stephen	Erath
Bennett, James	Miles
Berry, Tillman	Callahan
Bevins, James L. S.	Becknell
Binnion, Martin	Lilly
Birdwell, George	Matthews
Birdwell, Matthew R.	Gage, Matthews
Birdwell, Zachariah	Matthews
Bisbee, Ira	Callahan
Bishop, David	Becknell
Bishop, Joseph	Becknell
Black, John M.	Miles, Cairnes
Blackburn, Eli	Greer
Blackwell, Eli	Greer
Blackwell, John	Price, Ownby
Blair, Robert	Lilly
Blanton, Jacob	Becknell
Bloodworth, James C.	Greer
Boales, A. H.	Erath
Bobo, Lyn	Cairnes
Bogard, Lewis	Webb
Bogard, Russell	Webb
Bohannon, John M.	Lilly
Bolten, William	Greer
Boone, Daniel Jr.	Chandler
Boone, Mordecai	Chandler
Botham, John	Miles, Cairnes
Bowen, G. B.	Killough
Box, Thomas Wade	Matthews
Box, William Young	Matthews
Boyd, S. A. M.	Callahan
Brackeen, William T.	Matthews
Braden, A. G.	Chandler
Brannon, Merritt	Matthews
Bredkin, Ezeriah	Matthews
Brigham, Wiley B.	Matthews
Brinton, William	Becknell
Brookfield, William C.	Brookfield
Brown, Crawford	Webb
Brown, John W.	Miles, Cairnes
Brown, William	Becknell
Bruton, David	Lilly
Bruton, Isaac	Lilly
Bruton, John D.	Lilly
Bryant, Benjamin F.	Erath
Bryant, Jesse	Erath
Bryant, William	Erath
Buchannon, John E.	Greer
Buquor, Pasqual Leo	Hays
Burgess, Ewen	Ownby
Burke, Samuel	Matthews
Burkham, James	Becknell
Burns, Sam	Erath
Burrell, E. A.	Brookfield
Burriss, James M.	Lilly

Burriss, John R.	Killough	Coffman, Lovel	Becknell
Buttrell, William	Chandler	Cole, J. Riley	Webb
Byers, William W.	Greer	Colley, Canah C.	Callahan
Cahill, Michael	Baker, McDaniel	Collinsworth, James B.	Baker
		Colquie (Lipan Apache)	Hays
Cairnes, William J.	Price, Miles, Cairnes	Coltrin, William	Dolson
		Coots, Andew	Lilly
Callahan, James H.	Callahan	Coots, David	Lilly
Cameron, Ewen	Price, Miles, Cairnes	Copeland, Martin	Greer
		Copeland, Richard	Greer
Cameron, John	Ownby	Corkey, Henry P.	Gage
Campbell, Nathan	Erath	Costley, William	Sowell
Canfield, Israel	McDaniel	Cox, George H.	Webb
Capps, Harvey	Chandler	Cox, Hugh	Sowell
Cardinas, Jose Maria	Callahan	Cox, Jesse	Sowell
Carner, John	Killough	Cox, John G.	Webb
Carrington, Duncan C.	Greer	Cox, John H.	Webb
Carrington, W. D.	Greer	Cox, Joseph	Matthews
Carroll, John M.	Hays	Cox, William	Chandler
Carter, William	Erath	Coy, Antonio	Pérez, Hays
Casanavo, Cristano	Pérez	Crain, Allen A.	Callahan
Casey, John	Chandler, Gage	Crawford, George W.	Killough
		Creaner, Charles N.	Creaner
Cason, William	Gage	Crownover, Berry	Webb
Cass, James	Becknell	Crownover, John P.	Lilly
Castano, Luis	Pérez	Crunk, John W.	Gage
Cavitt, Volney	Killough	Custard, William	Erath
Chadwell, William H.	Webb	Custer, King S.	Webb
Chair, William	Gage	Dandy, Bly	Webb
Chandler, Eli	Chandler	Daniels, Joseph	Daniels
Chandler, John	Chandler	Davis, Daniel	Ownby
Chandler, Thomas	Gage	Davis, E. H.	Hays
Chapman, H. P.	Gage	Davis, John	Gage
Charty, Hezekiah	Gage	Davis, Samuel E.	Erath
Chatock, Henry	Erath	Dawson, William	Becknell
Chevallie, Michael H.	Hays	Day, James Milford	Callahan
Chisum, John E.	Lilly	Dean, Job	Webb
Chisum, William	Webb	Delgado, Martin	Hays
Chisum, William (2)	Webb	Denman, Colden	Newcomb
Clark, Benjamin S.	Becknell	Denyer, Samuel J.	Callahan
Clark, David	Becknell	Derrick, Simon	Matthews
Clark, Henry W.	Dolson	Dikes, Mark M.	Callahan
Clark, Thomas C.	Becknell	Dikes, Miles G.	Callahan
Clayton, Joseph	Killough	Dikes, W. M.	Callahan
Clements, Joseph D.	Callahan	Dincans, Stephen	Price, Ownby
Clifton, Henry H.	Lilly	Dixon, C. M.	Erath
Clinton, William	Callahan	Dolan, Joseph	Miles
Cobb, Clay	Greer	Dolson, George M.	Dolson
Cobb, David	Greer	Dove, James T.	Lilly
Cochran, Wilson W.	Gage	Downs, John S.	Greer
Cockrell, Simon M.	Callahan	Drew, Edward	Baker
Cody, Matthew W.	Baker, McDaniel	Drinkwater, Addison	Hays

Drumgold, Thomas	Chandler	García, Raphael	Pérez
Duggan, Michael	Miles, Cairnes	Garner, James M.	Sowell
Duncan, Green B.	Chandler	Garza, Leandro	Pérez
Duncan, Thomas	Chandler	Gaze, James	Ownby
Dunlap, George W.	Gage	Geary, George M.	Miles
Dunn, James	Killough	George, J. H.	Sowell
Eaton, Ransom	Erath	George, Stephen C.	Gage
Elliott, Jacob	Price	Gerard, F.	Miles, Cairnes
Ellison, Jesse	Chandler	Gibbons, W.	Dolson
Erath, George Bernhard	Erath	Gibson, William	Dolson
Eskridge, H. F.	Becknell	Gilbreath, John A.	Chandler
Espiniso, Pedro	Hays	Gonzales, Christopher	Miles
Estrevon, N.	Price	Gonzales, Raphael	Baker
Evans, Jesse	Becknell	Gooch, Benjamin F.	Matthews
Evans, William	Becknell	Gordon, Joseph H.	Sowell
Farías, Ensano	Pérez	Graham, John	Chandler
Faris, Isaac A.	Callahan	Granado, Francisco	Pérez, Hays
Faris, J. N.	Callahan	Graves, Robert C.	Lilly
Farmer, Kalib	Gage	Gray, J. N.	Lilly
Farris, Isham	Becknell	Gray, John	Erath
Farris, Warren A.	Gage	Grayson, Jackson	Gage
Ferguson, Alanson	Miles	Green, Berry	Gage
Ferguson, Alston	Gage	Green, George	Erath
Ferguson, Warrick	Gage	Greer, Andrew	Greer
Ferrill, Robert	Gage	Greer, Thomas N. B.	Greer
Findley, Jeremiah	Baker, McDaniel	Gregg, William	Becknell
Finley, William	Matthews	Griffin, Moses	Chandler
Fitch, Sterling	Erath	Griffin, Tim	Becknell
Fitzgerald, Archibald	Hays	Grigsby, John P.	Greer
Fitzgerald, Edward	Baker, McDaniel	Grim, Michael	Lilly
		Grimes, George W.	Greer
Flacco (Lipan Apache)	Hays	Groce, Jacob	Erath
Flint, David P.	Erath	Grubbs, G. H.	Hays
Flint, William F.	Killough	Guest, John Columbus	Webb
Flippert, Reuben	Killough	Guthrie, George W.	Price, Sowell
Flores, J. A.	Hays	Hackett, James	Miles
Fohr, Peter	Hays	Hagler, Lindsay S.	Miles
Foster, James	Callahan	Hahn, Henry	Webb
Fowler, David B.	Ownby	Hall, Benjamin	Becknell
Fowler, James G.	Ownby	Hall, Robert	Callahan
Fox, James	McDaniel	Hall, William A.	Callahan
Fox, John	McDaniel	Ham, Berry Lewis	Erath
Fox, Michael	Baker, McDaniel	Hamilton, William J.	Lilly
		Hammock, A. O.	Lilly
Fruster, G. L.	Ownby	Hancock, Thomas	Hays
Gage, David	Gage	Happell, Frederick W.	Callahan
Gahagen, John C.	Matthews	Harbert, Nathaniel	Hays
Galvan, Damacio	Hays	Hardisty, John	Chandler
García, A.	Price	Harland, James B.	Webb
García, Francisco	Pérez	Harris, Daniel	Becknell
García, Matias	Pérez	Harris, H. B.	Becknell
		Harris, John	Becknell

Harris, John W.	Greer	Jones, Henry W.	Lilly
Harrison, John W.	Dolson	Jones, Hiram	Lilly
Harrison, T. H.	Sowell	Jones, James M.	Becknell
Hastings, Marvin	Ownby	Jones, Jefferson Y.	Erath
Hawkins, Thomas M.	Gage	Jones, L. C.	Becknell
Hays, John Coffee	Hays	Jones, Martin	Lilly
Head, James A.	Chandler	Jones, Marvel C.	Lilly
Heard, George W.	Chandler	Jones, Thomas	Lilly
Heath, Joshua E.	Webb	Jones, Wiley	Erath
Heath, Thomas J.	Gage	Jordan, Levi	Lilly
Hefferon, John	Miles, Cairnes	Jordan, Samuel W.	Becknell
Hefflinger, James	Becknell	Jordan, Thomas	Matthews
Henderson, Hugh	Greer	Juan (Lipan Apache)	Hays
Henderson, Hugh G.	Callahan	Kattenhorn, Henry	Erath
Henry, H. R.	Killough	Keith, Gabriel	Lilly
Henry, J. D.	Killough	Keith, W. S.	Lilly
Henson, Absolom	Killough	Kennedy, Dennis	Ownby
Henson, David	Callahan	Kerner, John	Chandler
Hesskew, William A.	Hays	Kilgore, Samuel G.	Killough
Hill, Charles	Greer	Killough, Samuel B.	Killough
Hill, George W.	Chandler	Kimball, John N.	Becknell
Hill, James W.	Chandler	King, Baxter A.	Greer
Hill, L. B.	Sowell	King, Henry B.	Callahan
Hill, Samuel	Greer	King, Henry B. Jr.	Callahan
Hinson, Robert	Lilly	King, John N.	Lilly
Hogan, Robert	Erath	King, John R.	Callahan
Holden, Joshua	Dolson	King, Miles	Chandler
Houston, Isaac	Webb	King, Nathaniel	Lilly
Howith, Fletcher	Gage	King, Samuel C.	Greer
Howith, Tandy	Gage	King, William G.	Callahan
Hughes, Robert	Lilly	King, William H.	Erath
Hughes, Robert (2)	Lilly	Kinkannon, William P.	Callahan
Hughes, Russ	Lilly	Kirkland, Jonathan H.	Lilly
Hughes, W. V.	Lilly	Kitchell, Aaron	Chandler
Hughs, James M.	Gage	Ladd, John W.	Dolson,
Hulme, Robert S.	Gage		Newcomb
Humphreys, Jacob J.	Hays	Lakey, Henry	Erath
Hunt, Robert	Chandler	Lambert, Walter	Baker
Hunter, Samuel	Greer	Lampson, George	Webb
Hutchinson, John	Killough	Landford, W. G.	Greer
Isaacs, William	Erath	Lane, James	Chandler
Isbell, William	Hays	Lane, James F.	Gage
Jackson, Riley	Becknell	Lane, Robert L.	Gage
James, John	Miles	Lane, Thomas	Price, Ownby
Jamison, John	Ownby	Langston, Isaac	Becknell
Jasper, Selden L. B.	Brookfield	Lankford, P. S.	Sowell
Jeffries, James	Sowell	Lankford, William T.	Sowell
Jenkins, Silas W.	Price	Larimore, T. S.	Sowell
Jett, James Matthew	Hays	Larso, Carlos	Hays
Jett, Stephen	Hays	Leal, Joseph	Chandler
Johnson, James M.	Gage	Lee, Roswell W.	Sowell
Jones, Eli M.	Erath	Lees, George	Price

Legman, John	Ownby	McEvoy, Patrick	Miles, Cairnes
Lenard, James W.	Miles	McFarland, John W. B.	Baker,
Lennon, Thomas	Cairnes		McDaniel
Lilly, Harris B.	Lilly	McGrew, Hardin R.	Chandler
Lilly, Joseph D.	Lilly	McKay, Daniel	Erath
Linam, James W.	Cairnes	McKeen, John B.	Erath
Lockemy, Hugh	Chandler	McKeen, William H.	Erath
Lockwood, C.	Sowell	McKeen, Z.	Erath
Long, Henry	Webb	McKenzie, John	Cairnes
Long, Joseph	Erath	McLaughlin, Joseph	Greer
Longbotham, John	Greer	McLennan, Neil	Erath
Love, Andrew C.	Chandler	McLennon, John	Erath
Love, William M.	Chandler	McMahon, Andrew	Killough
Lovejoy, C. A.	Gage	McMaury, James L.	Chandler
Lowery, J. D.	Webb	McMullin, Edward	Chandler
Luckie, Samuel H.	Hays	McMurry, M. C.	Chandler
Lusk, Robert O.	Matthews	McPherson, C. T.	Sowell
Lynn, John	Killough	McPherson, Charles	Webb
Mahan, Patrick	Miles, Cairnes	McPherson, James	Miles, Cairnes
Makinster, F. H.	Ownby	Merritt, James	Erath
Manes, J. H.	Webb	Middleton, Thomas J.	Greer
Manning, Charles	Erath	Miles, Alanson T.	Miles, Cairnes
Marlin, John	Chandler	Milford, Joseph	Cairnes
Marlin, Samuel Wilson	Chandler	Miller, A. J.	Gage
Maroney, Peter	Sowell	Miller, John C.	Gage
Marsh, Joseph S.	Ownby	Miller, Joseph	Hays
Martain, Joseph S.	Callahan	Milligan, John H.	Lilly
Martin, Bailey	Killough	Milligan, Reece P.	Lilly
Martin, Silas	Sowell	Milligan, Thomas S.	Lilly
Martin, William	Sowell, Webb	Milligan, William G.	Lilly
Marvin, Seth P.	Miles, Cairnes	Mills, John	Cairnes
Masten, J. W.	Killough	Mills, Lawson F.	Miles, Cairnes
Mather, Joseph	Chandler	Milner, John L.	Hays
Matthews, Barton W.	Matthews	Mitchell, Edward	Greer
Matthews, James D.	Chandler	Mitchell, James	Greer
Matthews, Joseph J.	Matthews	Mitchell, John	Gage
Matthews, Mansil Walter	Matthews	Mitchell, Memnon A.	Chandler
Matthews, Robert E.	Matthews,	Monroe, Daniel	Erath
	Chandler	Montague, Daniel	Webb
Matthews, William O.	Matthews	Moody, James	Gage
Maximillian, A.	Greer	Moody, Joseph	Sowell
Maxwell, Thomas	Gage	Moore, Calvin	Sowell
McAdams, J. J.	Lilly	Moore, J. B.	Callahan
McCafferty, Francis	Ownby	Moore, James	Gage
McCanless, J. P.	Killough	Moore, Peter	Gage
McCarty, William M.	Matthews	Moore, William H.	Hays
McColler, Sam	Becknell	Moore, William W.	Erath
McCrary, Wilson	Becknell	Morgan, John C.	Hays
McCulloch, Benjamin	Callahan	Morris, Ross	Erath
McCustion, John C.	Killough	Moss, James H.	Sowell
McDaniel, John	Baker	Moss, Samuel	Webb
McDonnell, E. M.	Ownby	Mouser, Henry	Sowell

Mozier, Adam	Price
Murray, Thomas W.	Miles
Murry, Alfred	Erath
Myers, Gibson	Sowell
Nanny, Charles W.	Chandler
Neal, Benjamin F.	Baker, McDaniel
Neill, Andrew	Callahan
Neill, John C.	Miles, Cairnes
Netherly, Abner	Matthews
Newcomb, James W.	Dolson, Newcomb
Nichols, George W.	Callahan
Nichols, James W.	Callahan
Nichols, John W.	Callahan
Nichols, Thomas R.	Callahan
Nidiver, John	Matthews
Northington, Mentor W.	Lilly
Nugent, John	Becknell
Nutt, Samuel A.	Killough
Odom, William H.	Killough
O'Neal, James R.	Webb
Osborne, B. W.	Becknell
Oustal, John	Matthews
Owens, L. S.	Matthews
Ownby, James P.	Ownby
Page, Andrew J.	Gage
Page, E. G.	Gage
Page, John M.	Gage
Parish, Jefferson C.	Sowell
Parker, Isaac G.	Gage
Parks, Joseph B.	Miles, Cairnes
Parmer, William	Gage
Pate, William H.	Ownby
Patrick, William W.	Chandler
Patterson, David	Dolson, Newcomb
Patton, James M.	Sowell
Patton, Robert	Hays
Peck, L. L.	Callahan
Pendegrast, L. Baker	Killough, Chandler
Pendergrast, T. J.	Sowell
Pepes, Samuel	Hays
Pérez, Antonio	Pérez
Perez, Canato	Pérez
Perez, Pablo	Pérez
Perez, Pedro	Hays
Perry, James	Hays
Pertle, William J.	Becknell
Philey, Bartes	Becknell
Philpot, Joseph P.	Greer

Pickett, W. M.	Lilly
Pieratt, Ary	Price
Plasedonce (Lipan Apache)	Hays
Plummer, Francis	Baker
Plummer, Joseph E.	Baker
Pollett, Robert	Hays
Porter, James	Erath
Porter, Robert H.	Chandler, Erath
Powers, Elijah	Chandler, Sowell
Pratt, H. M.	Ownby
Price, George W.	Callahan
Price, John	Becknell
Price, John T.	Price
Prior, Benjamin	Hays
Prior, Benjamin Jr.	Hays
Quinn, Patrick	Miles, Cairnes
Ragan, William	Gage
Ramsay, Thomas W.	Gage
Randall, O. W.	Gage
Rattan, Daniel	Webb
Rattan, Thomas	Webb
Rattan, Wade Hampton	Webb
Rayburn, R. J.	Greer
Rayford, Robert	Erath
Raymond, Charles H.	Killough, Chandler
Raymond, Nathaniel C.	Erath
Redden, J. F.	Webb
Reed, A. H.	Gage
Reed, Elijah	Killough
Reed, William W.	Chandler
Reeder, William	Sowell
Reelor, Joseph	Webb
Reid, James B.	Gage
Reily, James	Greer
Rice, James Ogden	Dolson, Newcomb
Rice, William P.	Killough
Richardson, Willard	Baker, McDaniel
Ricks, George W.	Dolson
Rinehart, Henry	Dolson, Newcomb
Ringo, James J.	Becknell
Ringo, Peter	Becknell
Ritchey	Matthews
Robbins, John	Greer
Robbins, William	Greer
Roberts, James B.	Callahan
Roberts, Jeremiah	Callahan

Roberts, William W.	Chandler	Smith, Ezekiel	Callahan
Robertson, Haziel	Killough	Smith, French	Miles, Cairnes
Robertson, Richard	Gage	Smith, George W.	Killough, Lilly
Robertson, Sterling Clack	Killough	Smith, Henry M.	Gage
Robinson, Daniel	Erath	Smith, J. P.	Gage
Robinson, John L.	Greer	Smith, James	Gage, Erath
Rodgers, John K.	Becknell	Smith, M. B.	Greer
Rogers, A. G.	Greer	Smith, Paris	Callahan
Rogers, C.	Webb	Smith, Thomas F.	Sowell
Rogers, E. C.	Lilly	Smith, Tom T.	Erath
Rogers, Joseph	Killough	Smith, William	Ownby
Rogers, Joseph	Price	Snalum, Thomas C.	Greer
Rogers, Robert	Greer	Snodgrass, William	Price, Miles,
Rogers, Stephen N.	Greer		Cairnes
Rollen, Thomas	Webb	Sowell, Andrew Jackson	Callahan
Ross, Shapley P.	Erath	Sowell, Asa J. Lee	Callahan
Rouche, Peter	Price, Miles	Sowell, John N.	Callahan
Rozier, William M.	Ownby	Sowell, Joseph	Sowell
Rupley, William	Price	Standifer, Price	Erath
Russell, George W.	Webb	Starnes, Aaron	Lilly
Rutherford, John H.	Matthews	Starnes, Titus	Lilly
Rutherford, Thomas M.	Matthews	Steele, Robert	Chandler
Salinas, Martin	Pérez, Hays	Stem, Isaac Phillip	Price
Sánchez, Antonio	Pérez, Hays	Stevens, Isham	Becknell
Sapp, A. P. D.	Miles	Stewart, Samuel	Lilly
Sassaman, C. R.	Dolson	Stiff, Jesse	Sowell
Scott, John T.	Sowell	Stiffey, William C.	Callahan
Seale, Eli	Chandler	St. John, Edmund Jr.	McDaniel
Seale, Joshua	Chandler	St. John, Edmund Sr.	McDaniel
Sealy, David	Chandler	St. John, Edward	Baker
Senan, James W.	Miles	St. John, James	McDaniel
Sevier, Charles	Chandler	St. John, William	McDaniel
Seymore, James	Sowell	Stokes, Guy S.	Erath
Shaw, James	Erath	Stone, Berry A.	Gage
Shelly, Abram	Sowell	Stout, Berryman Oliver	Ownby
Sherman, Charles	Miles	Stout, James S.	Lilly
Sherrill, Arthur	Zumwalt	Stout, William B.	Becknell
Shockley, J. M.	Dolson	Strickland, Joseph	Sowell
Silkwood, Solomon	Webb	Strother, John L.	Chandler
Simmons, Edward C.	Gage	Stroud, Ethan A.	Killough
Skinner, John K.	Becknell	Stroud, Mandrid	Killough
Slein, John	Hays	Sullivan, Daniel	Erath
Sloan, J. S.	Lilly	Sullivan, Giles O.	Erath
Small, William B.	Hays	Sullivan, John	Erath
Smith, A. T.	Erath	Swift, Arthur	Callahan
Smith, Andrew	Killough	Sypert, Thomas	Chandler
Smith, Arthur	Callahan	Tally, John R.	Baker
Smith, Byrd	Callahan	Tam, J. H.	Webb
Smith, C. C.	Greer	Tankersly, James	Lilly
Smith, Charles	Baker,	Tankersly, Richard	Lilly
	McDaniel	Tankersly, William	Lilly
Smith, Charles A.	Callahan	Taylor, Franklin R.	Miles, Cairnes

Taylor, Jacob	Gage	Webb, David R.	Dolson
Teal, Richard S.	Erath	Webb, Jesse J.	Killough
Thomas, Josiah	Gage	Weeks, Henry D.	Miles, Cairnes
Thomas, W. G.	Erath	Welch, Charles	Killough,
Thompson, Francis	Erath		Chandler
Thompson, John S.	Erath	Welch, John	Killough
Thompson, Josiah	Erath	Wells, James	Webb
Thompson, M. D.	Erath	Wells, John	Webb
Thompson, Thomas	Erath	Wells, William	Gage, Miles,
Thruston, J. P.	Sowell		Cairnes
Tibble, John	Dolson	Whalen, Henry	Miles, Cairnes
Timmons, Thomas	Gage	Wheeler, Thomas J.	Miles, Cairnes
Tivey, Joseph A.	Erath	Wheeler, William	Erath
Tivus, M.	Killough	Wheelock, E. Louis Ripley	Chandler
Todd, Charles	Ownby	Whelan, Michael	Baker,
Tom (Lipan Apache)	Hays		McDaniel
Trapnell, John	Hays	White, John B.	Miles, Cairnes
Travieso, Melchor	Pérez, Hays	Wilkins, William	Erath
Tresten, J. Louis	Price	Wilkinson, James	Erath
Trueheart, James L.	Hays	Wilkinson, John	Erath
Trueheart, John O.	Pérez, Hays	Williams, W.	Gage
Truett, William	Lilly	Wilson, Dirk	Webb
Turner, Calvin S.	Callahan	Wilson, Isaac	Becknell
Turner, Elisha W.	Lilly	Wilson, J. N.	Becknell
Turner, Samuel	Callahan	Wilson, James	Miles, Baker,
Turnham, Joseph P.	Erath		McDaniel
Twitty, William C.	Sowell	Wilson, John	Miles, Cairnes
Tyus, Roll	Killough	Wilson, John (2)	Baker
Underwood, Elias	Sowell	Winkler, Clinton M.	Killough
Vandyke, John	Gage	Wood, C. L.	Gage
Van Horn, William H.	Miles	Woodson, John M.	Matthews
Vanzant, James	Killough	Woolfolk, R. S.	Erath
Vanzant, Neri	Chandler	Wyatt, Robert	Gage
Vardeman, S. W.	Gage	Wychard, Samuel	Sowell
Vardeman, William	Gage	Yerby, John H.	Ownby
Vasquez, Florencio	Hays	York, Harrison	Chandler
Veach, John B.	Callahan	Young, Andrew S.	Matthews
Walker, Henderson	Webb	Young, Jesse	Greer
Walker, Hiram	Gage	Young, John	Hays
Walker, Landon	Webb	Zumwalt, Adam	Zumwalt
Walker, Skeaugh	Killough		
Walker, Thomas	Miles		
Wardlow, James	Lilly	*Note: No muster rolls available for the*	
Warmel, Benjamin	Brookfield	*1841 companies of Charles Creaner,*	
Wash (Lipan Apache)	Hays	*Joseph Daniels, or Adam Zumwalt.*	
Watrous, Nathaniel H.	Dolson		
Watson, John M.	Matthews		
Weaver, Abner	Becknell		
Weaver, Green	Becknell		
Weaver, Larkin	Becknell		
Weaver, Tinsley	Becknell		
Webb, Alexander W.	Webb		

Chapter Notes
Volume III

Abbreviations to the Republic Claims Papers, 1835–1846.
Texas State Library and Archives Commission, Austin.

AC   Audited Claims are those military-related claims submitted to the Comptroller or Treasurer of the Republic of Texas that were audited, approved and paid by the republic government.

PD   Public Debt Claims are claims for services provided between 1835 and 1846 that could not be paid until after Texas' annexation in 1846. These were largely paid between 1848 and the early 1860s, mainly from the 1850 Boundary Compromise money Texas was paid for its lost territory.

PP   Republic Pension Papers were generally filed from the 1870s to the early 1900s by veterans who served in the Texas Revolution and other republic-era military units.

UC   Unpaid Claims are those documents which do not fit in one of the above categories or those whose final payment disposition is unknown.

PROLOGUE

1. Walter Prescott Webb, *The Texas Rangers: A Century of Frontier Defense* (Austin: University of Texas Press, 1991), 84–85. Utley, Robert M. *Lone Star Justice: The First Century of The Texas Rangers* (New York: Oxford University Press, 2002), 4.

CHAPTER 1
THE COMANCHES

1. Newcomb, W. W. Jr. *The Indians of Texas: From Prehistoric to Modern Times* (Austin: University of Texas Press, 1961), 155–60. Gary Clayton Anderson, *The Conquest of Texas: Ethnic Cleansing in the Promised Land, 1820–1875* (Norman: University of Oklahoma Press, 2005), 20–24. Handbook of Texas Online, s.v. "Comanche Indians," http://www.tsha.utexas.edu/handbook/online/articles/CC/bmc72.html (accessed July 26, 2006).

2. *Journals of the House of Representatives of the Republic of Texas: Fifth Congress*, Appendix (Austin: Gazette Office, 1841), 133.

3. Anderson, *The Conquest of Texas*, 128, 181.

4. *Journals, Fifth Congress*, Appendix, 133.

5. Gerald Swetnam Pierce, *Texas Under Arms: The Camps, Posts, Forts, and Military Towns of the Republic of Texas* (Austin, Tex: Encino Press, 1969), 37.

6. Nelson Lee, *Three Years Among the Comanches: The Narrative of Nelson Lee, The Texas Ranger* (1859; repr., Norman: University of Oklahoma Press, 1957), 13–14.

7. John H. Jenkins and Kenneth Kesselus, *Edward Burleson: Texas Frontier Leader* (Austin, Tex: Jenkins Publishing Co., 1990), 219–21.

8. Ibid., 220.

9. Ibid., 221–22.

10. Gerald Swetnam Pierce, *The Army of the Republic of Texas, 1836–1845* (Dissertation from the University of Mississippi, copyright 1964, on file in the Texas Room of the Houston Public Library), 182–3. See also (Karl) Hans Peter Marius Nielsen Gammell, *The Laws of Texas, 1822–1897* (Ten volumes; Austin, Tex: The Gammel Book Company, 1898), II:381–6.

11. Pierce, *The Army of the Republic of Texas*, 181–83.

12. Johnston to Fisher in *Journals, Fifth Congress*, Appendix, 134–35.

13. James T. DeShields, *Border Wars of Texas* (1912; repr., Austin, Tex: State House Press, 1993), 288–89.

14. Nance, Joseph M. *After San Jacinto: The Texas-Mexican Frontier, 1836–1841*. Austin: University of Texas Press, 1963, 93.

15. Karen R. Thompson (Editor), *Defenders of the Republic of Texas* (Austin, Tex: Daughters of the Republic of Texas via Laurel House Press, 1989), 27–32.

16. Pierce, *Texas Under Arms*, 155.

17. Benjamin A. Vansickle UN, R 257, F 445; Durst & Company PD, R 150, F 445; John Durst PD, R 150, F 556-88.

18. Malcolm D. McLean, *Papers Concerning Robertson's Colony in Texas* (Published by the University of Texas at Arlington, Arlington, Tex: The UTA Press, 1991). XVII:523–27.

19. Thompson (ed.), *Defenders*, 188–93.

20. Ibid., 163-69. Those joining Captain Lewis from Company G were: Third Sergeant Edward Smith, Fourth Corporal Henry Sandculer, and Privates T. W. Brown, John Brown, Michael Campbell, Daniel Carlin, John Dalton, Lewis Duval, Peter Davison, Thomas Dening, Albert Germar, Thomas Haskins, Wilson C. Hamilton, Conrad Lundell, Thomas O'Brien, John Quinn, Michael Riley, James Simms, Hiram Summers, Joseph Sleeter, and Henry Ward.

21. McLean, *Papers Concerning Robertson's Colony*, XVII:523–27.

22. Ibid.

23. Amelia W. Williams and Eugene C. Barker, *Writings of Sam Houston* (Austin: The University of Texas Press, 1938-43), 425–27.

24. Pierce, *Texas Under Arms*, 20–21.

25. Jefferson Y. Jones PD, R 165, F 245.

26. Jenkins, *Edward Burleson*, 226.

27. Ibid., 227–8.

28. For reference, see Handbook of Texas Online, s.v. "Plácido," http://

www.tsha.utexas.edu/handbook/online/articles/PP/fpl1.html (accessed July 26, 2006).

29. *Constitution and By-Laws of the Travis Guards: Adopted March First, 1840*. Austin: Cruger and Bonnell's Print, 1840. From the collections in the Center for American History, The University of Texas at Austin.

CHAPTER 2
THE COUNCIL HOUSE FIGHT

1. Rena Maverick Green (editor), *Memoirs of Mary A. Maverick. Arranged by Mary A. Maverick and her son George Madison Maverick* (1921; repr., Lincoln: University of Nebraska Press, 1989), 38.

2. Charles M. Robinson III, *The Men Who Wear the Star. The Story of the Texas Rangers* (New York: Random House, 2000), 61–62.

3. Ibid., 62. Webb, *The Texas Rangers: A Century of Frontier Defense*, 84–85.

4. Frederick Wilkins, *The Legend Begins: The Texas Rangers, 1823–1845* (Austin, Tex: State House Press, 1996), 65–66.

5. Ibid., 67. Thomas W. Knowles, *They Rode for the Lone Star. The Saga of the Texas Rangers. The Birth of Texas–The Civil War* (Dallas, Tex: Taylor Publishing Company, 1999), 97.

6. Donaly E. Brice, *The Great Comanche Raid: Boldest Indian Attack of the Texas Republic* (Austin, Tex: Eakin Press, 1987), 22–23.

7. Green (editor), *Memoirs of Mary A. Maverick*, 25.

8. McLeod to Lamar, in *Appendix to the Journals of the House of Representatives: Fifth Congress*, 136–9. McLeod's report is the principal official source of the Council House Fight. DeShields in his *Border Wars of Texas* (288–94) gives more accounts. See also Brown, *Indian Wars*, 77–8. Another good source for the Council House Fight is Paul N. Spellman, *Forgotten Texas Leader: Hugh McLeod and the Texan Santa Fe Expedition* (College Station: Texas A&M University Press, 1999), 46–50. Unless otherwise noted, the direct quotes are taken from McLeod's letter from *Appendix*.

9. DeShields, *Border Wars of Texas*, 290.

10. Green, *Memoirs of Mary Maverick*, 29.

11. Spellman, *Forgotten Texas Leader*, 49.

12. Wilkins, *The Legend Begins*, 79; Green, *Memoirs of Mary Maverick*, 28; Brown, *Indian Wars*, 77.

13. Green, *Memoirs of Mary A. Maverick*, 28.

14. Ibid., 27.

15. McLeod to Lamar, in *Appendix to the Journals of the House of Representatives: Fifth Congress*, 136-39; Green, *Memoirs of Mary Maverick*, 29.

16. Green, *Memoirs of Mary A. Maverick*, 29–30.

17. Ibid., 32–33. See also DeShields, *Border Wars of Texas*, 293.

18. Green, Memoirs of Mary Maverick, 30; Brown, *Indian Wars*, 78; McLeod to Lamar, in *Appendix to the Journals of the House of Representatives:*

Fifth Congress, 136-39.

19. Utley, *The First Century of The Texas Rangers*, 27.

CHAPTER 3
SPRING EXPEDITIONS

1. Green, *Memoirs of Mary A. Maverick*, 36; Wilkins, *The Legend Begins*, 79–80; Brown, *History of Texas*, II: 177; DeShields, *Border Wars of Texas*, 293–4.

2. Green, *Memoirs of Mary A. Maverick*, 36.

3. *Telegraph and Texas Register*, April 22, 1840.

4. Brice, *The Great Comanche Raid*, 25–26; Green, *Memoirs of Mary A. Maverick*, 40–41.

5. *Telegraph and Texas Register*, April 22, 1840.

6. Howard to Fisher, April 6, 1840, from John S. Ford's "Memoirs," II: 227. This letter continues as the primary source unless otherwise noted.

7. Ibid., 228.

8. See Handbook of Texas Online, s.v. "Cornelius Van Ness" http://www.tsha.utexas.edu/handbook/online/articles/VV/fva9.html (accessed August 3, 2006).

9. Green, *Memoirs of Mary A. Maverick*, 38–40.

10. Howard to Fisher, April 6, 1840, from John S. Ford's "Memoirs," II: 229. This same source is used until next footnote is shown.

11. Brice, *The Great Comanche Raid*, 25–26; Green, *Memoirs of Mary Maverick*, 30–31.

12. Green, *Memoirs of Mary Maverick*, 31.

13. George Bernard Erath as dictated to Lucy A. Erath, *The Memoirs of Major George B. Erath, 1813–1891* (1923; repr., The Heritage Society of Waco, 1956), 57.

14. Pierce, *Army*, 188.

15. Brice, *The Great Comanche Raid*, 59.

16. Nance, *After San Jacinto*, 271.

17. Ibid., 271–72.

18. Ibid., 304–5.

19. *Journals of the Sixth Congress, Republic of Texas*, III: 408.

20. Army Correspondence, April 2, 1840.

21. Daniel Jackson AC, R 164, F 259. Carter Boland PD, R 138, F 280–325.

22. Jenkins, *Edward Burleson*, 234–35.

23. Ibid., 235.

24. Nance, *After San Jacinto*, 329.

25. Buckman Canfield PD, R 142, F 374.

26. Pierce, *Texas Under Arms*, 115.

27. Jenkins, *Edward Burleson*, 236–7.

28. E. B. Nichols UN, R 255, F 36.

29. Brice, *The Great Comanche Raid*, 27.

30. Pierce, *Army*, 188–89.

31. William Physick Zuber, *My Eighty Years in Texas* (Austin: University of Texas Press, 1971), 107–8; McLean, *Papers*, XVII, 565–66.

32. Jenkins, *Edward Burleson*, 240.

33. Alpheus A. Bogart PD, R 138, F 186; Richard Williams PD, R 197, F 36–39.

34. Uriah Case AC, R 143, F 61–62.

35. Zuber, *My Eighty Years in Texas*, 107–8.

36. McLean, *Papers*, XVII: 569–70.

37. Zuber, *My Eighty Years in Texas*, 107–8.

38. McLean, *Papers*, XVIII:123.

39. Zuber, *My Eighty Years in Texas*, 108–9.

40. William R. Sanders PD, R 184, F 9–26.

41. John C. Pool PD, R 180, F 27.

42. Zuber, *My Eighty Years in Texas*, 108–9.

43. Ibid., 108-9.

44. Abram Helm AU, R 160, F 637.

45. Zuber, *My Eighty Years in Texas*, 109.

46. Ibid., 109–10.

47. Craner Foard PD, R 153, F 278; William H. Fowler PD, R 153, F 639.

48. McLean, *Papers*, XVIII: 56–57.

49. Pierce, *Texas Under Arms*, 179.

50. William Gordon Cooke AU, R 120, F 479.

51. John Daniels PD, R 147, F 602–10.

52. William Gordon Cooke AU, R 120, F 477–79.

53. Pierce, *Texas Under Arms*, 158.

54. Levi Jordan UN, R 252, F 676–77.

55. John Baldin PD, R 135, F 230; Pierce, *Texas Under Arms*, 43.

56. Green, *Memoirs of Mary A. Maverick*, 37.

57. Ibid., 37.

58. Jenkins, *Edward Burleson*, 238; Thompson (ed.), *Defenders*, 114.

59. Pierce, *Texas Under Arms*, 140–41.

60. Edward S. Ratcliffe AU, R 129, F 669.

61. Nance, *After San Jacinto*, 315.

62. Ibid., 316.

63. Pierce, *Texas Under Arms*, 66; DRT, *Defenders*, 109–15.

64. Nance, *After San Jacinto*, 316.

65. Nance, *After San Jacinto*, 319–20; *Telegraph and Texas Register*, July 1, 1840.

66. Nance, *After San Jacinto*, 320–21.

67. George B. Erath PD, R 157, F639–41.

68. Jenkins, *Edward Burleson*, 240.

69. Ibid., 239.

70. Handbook of Texas Online, s.v. "James Decatur Cocke," http://www.tsha.utexas.edu/handbook/online/articles/CC/fco8.html (accessed January 21, 2005); James D. Cocke AU, R 19, F 7–17.

71. John A. Settle PD, R 184, F 498; A. F. James PD, R 164, F 328–9.

72. Samuel Purcell PD, R 180, F 656–62; Larkin B. Smith PD, R 186, F 656; Larkin B. Smith UN, R 256, F 563; William H. Henderson PD, R 43, F 595.

73. "Reminiscences of Western Texas," by Miles Squier Bennett. Contained in the Valentine Bennett scrapbook, The Center for American History, The University of Texas at Austin.

74. DeShields, *Border Wars of Texas*, 317.

75. Wilbarger, *Indian Depredations*, 397–401; DeShields, *Border Wars of Texas*, 316.

76. Wilbarger, *Indian Depredations*, 400.

77. Ibid., 402–4.

78. DeShields, *Indian Depredations*, 269–70.

79. Jenkins, *Edward Burleson*, 241.

80. *Telegraph and Texas Register*, July 8, 1840.

81. DRT, *Defenders*, 174; McLean, *Papers*, XVII: 573; *Telegraph and Texas Register*, July 8, 1840.

82. Lester to Lamar, July 16, 1840, in *Lamar Papers*, 3: 419.

83. DRT, *Defenders*, 38–43.

84. John James PD, R 164, F 370.

85. Cunningham to Clendenin, July 9, 1840, in *Appendix to the Journals of the House of Representatives: Fifth Congress*, 151. Cunningham's report is the primary source in this section unless otherwise noted.

86. John James PD, R 164, F 370.

87. Cunningham to Clendenin, July 9, 1840, in *Appendix to the Journals of the House of Representatives: Fifth Congress*, 151.

88. Robert Barkley PD, R 135, F 451–53. Handbook of Texas Online, s.v. "Nicholas Adolphus Sterne," http://www.tsha.utexas.edu/handbook/online/articles/SS/fst45.html (accessed August 3, 2006).

89. John F. Graham PD, R 157, F 9–10; Adolphus Sterne PD, R 188, F 12.

90. Reuben Webb PD, R 157, F 12; J. L. Shields UN, R 256, F 329.

91. Nance, *After San Jacinto*, 322–23.

92. Ibid., 322–24.

93. Green, *Memoirs of Mary A. Maverick*, 35.

CHAPTER 4
THE GREAT COMANCHE RAID

1. Brown, *Indian Wars*, 79.

2. Anderson, *The Conquest of Texas*, 185–87.

3. Ibid., 187.

4. Brice, *The Great Comanche Raid*, 28. Handbook of Texas Online, s.v. "Linnville Raid of 1840," http://www.tsha.utexas.edu/handbook/online/articles/GG/fgr3.html (accessed August 3, 2006).

5. Pierce, *Texas Under Arms*, 82–83.

6. DeShields, *Border Wars*, 305.

7. Brown, *Indian Wars*, 79.

8. Ibid., 79.

9. Jenkins, *Recollections*, 62; Morrell, *Flowers and Fruits in the Wilderness*, 63.

10. Boethel, Paul C. *A History of Lavaca County* (Austin: Von Boeckmann–Jones, 1959), 9.

11. Boethel, *A History of Lavaca County*, 33; Henry Bridger PE, R 248, F 678; Isaac K. Zumwalt UN R 258, F 482.

12. Brice, *The Great Comanche Raid*, 29; Boethel, *A History of Lavaca County*, 33; Brown, *Indian Wars*, 79.

13. Morrell, *Flowers and Fruits in the Wilderness*, 63.

14. Ibid., 64–65.

15. Brown, *Indian Wars*, 79.

16. W. D. Miller account from September 9, 1840 *Telegraph and Texas Register*. As authenticated by Benjamin McCulloch, "Capt. of Gonzales Comp." and David Murphree of Victoria. Reprint from the August 17, 1840 *Austin City Gazette*. Hereafter referenced as Miller account from September 9, 1840, *Telegraph and Texas Register*. Handbook of Texas Online, s.v. "Washington D. Miller," http://www.tsha.utexas.edu/handbook/online/articles/MM/fmi29.html (accessed July 25, 2006).

17. Rose, *The Life and Services of Gen. Ben McCulloch*, 54–55. See "Reuben Ross" article, The Handbook of Texas Online.

18. Brown, *Indian Wars*, 79; Brice, *The Great Comanche Raid*, 29.

19. Miller account from September 9, 1840, *Telegraph and Texas Register*.

20. Brown, *Indian Wars*, 79.

21. Brice, *The Great Comanche Raid*, 30.

22. Linn, *Reminiscences of Fifty Years in Texas*, 338–89.

23. Brown, *Indian Wars*, 79–80; Brice, *The Great Comanche Raid*, 30.

24. Brice, *The Great Comanche Raid*, 30.

25. McDowell, *Now You Hear My Horn: The Journal of James Wilson Nichols,* 56–57; Brice, *The Great Comanche Raid*, 31.

26. Brown, *Indian Wars*, 80; Brice, *The Great Comanche Raid*, 31.

27. Brice, *The Great Comanche Raid*, 31.

28. *Telegraph and Texas Register*, September 2, 1840.

29. Brown, *Indian Wars*, 80; Brice, *The Great Comanche Raid*, 32; "Linnville Raid of 1840," The Handbook of Texas Online.

30. Brice, *The Great Comanche Raid*, 99.

31. *Telegraph and Texas Register*, September 2, 1840.

32. Linn, *Reminiscences of Fifty Years in Texas*, 342.

33. Brice, *The Great Comanche Raid*, 32; Linn, *Reminiscences*, 341.

34. *Telegraph and Texas Register*, September 2, 1840.

35. W. D. Miller to the *Austin City Gazette*, August 17, 1840. See also September 9, 1840 *Telegraph and Texas Register*.

36. Brown, *Indian Wars*, 80.

37. Kerr to Moore from Gulick, *Lamar Papers*, 3: 428–29.

38. Brown, *Indian Wars*, 80; Taylor, *The Cavalcade of Jackson County*,

415.

39. Brice, *The Great Comanche Raid*, 34.

40. W. D. Miller to the *Austin City Gazette*, August 17, 1840. See also September 9, 1840 *Telegraph and Texas Register*.

41. Ibid.

42. William Riley Wood PE, R 246, F 712.

43. W. D. Miller to the *Austin City Gazette*, August 17, 1840. See also September 9, 1840, *Telegraph and Texas Register*.

44. Anonymous eyewitness account published in the *Austin Sentinel*, from Ford's "Memoirs," 233–34.

45. Rose, *The Life and Services of Gen. Ben McCulloch*, 56.

46. W. D. Miller to the *Austin City Gazette*, August 17, 1840. See also September 9, 1840 *Telegraph and Texas Register*.

CHAPTER 5
"IF WE CAN'T WHIP 'EM, WE CAN TRY!"

1. Rose, *The Life and Services of Gen. Ben McCulloch*, 56.

2. Jenkins, *Edward Burleson*, 248.

3. Ibid., 248-49. This is the source of the next paragraph, as well.

4. Ibid., 250.

5. W. D. Miller to the *Austin City Gazette*, August 17, 1840. See also September 9, 1840, *Telegraph and Texas Register*.

6. Brown, *Indian Wars*, 80; Lee, *Three Years Among the Comanches*, 17.

7. Brown, *Indian Wars*, 80.

8. Ibid., 80–81.

9. Ibid., 81.

10. General Huston to Archer, August 12, 1840, in *Appendix to the Journals of the House of Representatives: Fifth Congress*, 141–43.

11. Brazos (pseud.), *The Life of Robert Hall* (Austin: Ben C. Jones and Company, Printers, 1898), 54.

12. Brown, *Indian Wars*, 81.

13. McDowell, *Now You Hear My Horn: The Journal of James Wilson Nichols,* 59.

14. Ibid., 59.

15. Brown, *Indian Wars*, 81.

16. General Huston to Archer, August 12, 1840, in *Appendix to the Journals of the House of Representatives: Fifth Congress*, 141–43.

17. Ibid., 141–43.

18. Jenkins, *Recollections*, 63.

19. McDowell, *Now You Hear My Horn: The Journal of James Wilson Nichols,* 72–74.

20. Brown, *Indian Wars*, 81.

21. McDowell, *Now You Hear My Horn: The Journal of James Wilson Nichols,* 61.

22. Brazos (pseud.), *The Life of Robert Hall*, 53.

23. Jenkins, *Recollections*, 64-65.

24. Brown, *Indian Wars*, 81.

25. General Huston to Archer, August 12, 1840, in *Appendix to the Journals of the House of Representatives: Fifth Congress*, 141-43.

26. Brown, *Indian Wars*, 81.

27. Brice, *The Great Comanche Raid*, 97.

28. Ibid., 40.

29. Gotlip Wolf was the only tax-paying citizen of Harris County by the name of Wolf, Wolfe, or deWolfe showing in early Republic records during 1839. He does not appear in any further Republic claims records after 1839, indicating that he may have been deceased.

30. This text of this article is listed in Ford, "Memoirs," 230.

31. Brown, *Indian Wars*, 81.

32. General Huston to Archer, August 12, 1840, in *Appendix to the Journals of the House of Representatives: Fifth Congress*, 141-3.

33. Rose, *The Life and Services of Gen. Ben McCulloch*, 56-7.

34. McDowell, *Now You Hear My Horn: The Journal of James Wilson Nichols*, 61.

35. Ibid., 62.

36. Morrell, *Flowers and Fruits in the Wilderness*, 65.

37. Sowell, *Texas Indian Fighters*, 418.

38. Rose, *The Life and Services of Gen. Ben McCulloch*, 56.

39. Brown, *Indian Wars*, 81.

40. McDowell, *Now You Hear My Horn: The Journal of James Wilson Nichols*, 63.

41. Ibid., 61.

42. Morrell, *Flowers and Fruits in the Wilderness*, 65-66.

43. Boethel, Paul C. *A History of Lavaca County*. Austin: Von Boeckmann-Jones, 1959.

44. Brown, *Indian Wars*, 82.

45. Ibid., 82.

46. Rose, *The Life and Services of Gen. Ben McCulloch*, 56.

47. McDowell, *Now You Hear My Horn: The Journal of James Wilson Nichols*, 63.

48. Brazos (pseud.), *The Life of Robert Hall*, 54-5.

49. Lee, *Three Years Among the Comanches*, 17.

50. Brown, *Indian Wars*, 82.

51. General Huston to Archer, August 12, 1840, in *Appendix to the Journals of the House of Representatives: Fifth Congress*, 141-3.

52. McDowell, *Now You Hear My Horn: The Journal of James Wilson Nichols*, 61.

53. Jenkins, *Recollections*, 65.

54. McDowell, *Now You Hear My Horn: The Journal of James Wilson Nichols*, 64.

55. Brown, *Indian Wars*, 82.

56. McDowell, *Now You Hear My Horn: The Journal of James Wilson*

Nichols, 63.

57. Brown, *Indian Wars*, 82; Brazos (pseud.), *The Life of Robert Hall*, 55.

58. Brown, *Indian Wars*, 82.

59. Rose, *The Life and Services of Gen. Ben McCulloch*, 58.

60. McDowell, *Now You Hear My Horn: The Journal of James Wilson Nichols,* 64-65.

61. Rose, *The Life and Services of Gen. Ben McCulloch*, 58.

62. Brice, *The Great Comanche Raid*, 42.

63. Jenkins, *Recollections*, 66.

64. Ibid., 66.

65. Ibid., 66-67.

66. Ibid., 67.

67. Rose, *The Life and Services of Gen. Ben McCulloch*, 58–9.

68. McDowell, *Now You Hear My Horn: The Journal of James Wilson Nichols,* 65–6.

69. Jenkins, *Recollections*, 66.

70. Brown, *Indian Wars*, 82.

71. McDowell, *Now You Hear My Horn: The Journal of James Wilson Nichols,* 67.

72. Ibid., 70.

73. Linn, *Reminiscences of Fifty Years in Texas*, 342–44.

74. Brice, *The Great Comanche Raid*, 99.

75. McDowell, *Now You Hear My Horn: The Journal of James Wilson Nichols,* 69-70.

76. Brazos (pseud.), *The Life of Robert Hall,* 55.

77. Brice, *The Great Comanche Raid*, 47.

78. McDowell, *Now You Hear My Horn: The Journal of James Wilson Nichols,* 70–71.

79. Brice, *The Great Comanche Raid*, 46.

80. Ibid., 60–61.

81. Ibid., 62.

82. General Huston to Archer, August 12, 1840, in *Appendix to the Journals of the House of Representatives: Fifth Congress*, 141–43.

83. Brice, *The Great Comanche Raid*, 48.

84. General Huston to Archer, August 12, 1840, in *Appendix to the Journals of the House of Representatives: Fifth Congress*, 141–43.

85. Jenkins, *Edward Burleson*, 258.

86. John Harvey biographical sketch, Louis Wiltz Kemp Papers, San Jacinto Museum of History.

87. Morrell, *Flowers and Fruits in the Wilderness*, 63.

88. Brazos (pseud.), *The Life of Robert Hall,* 56–57.

89. Ibid., 57.

90. Nichols called the friendly Indians "Lipans" versus Tonkawas. McDowell, *Now You Hear My Horn: The Journal of James Wilson Nichols,* 73.

91. Ford, "Memoirs," 230–31.

92. Brown, *Indian Wars*, 82.

93. McDowell, *Now You Hear My Horn: The Journal of James Wilson Nichols,* 71–72. Jenkins, *Recollections,* 67–68.

94. Linn, *Reminiscences of Fifty Years in Texas*, 343–44.

95. McDowell, *Now You Hear My Horn: The Journal of James Wilson Nichols,* 72.

96. Brazos [pseud.], *The Life of Robert Hall,* 57–58.

97. Pierce, *Army*, 195.

98. Huston to Archer, September 28, 1840, in *Appendix to the Journals of the House of Representatives: Fifth Congress*, 143–44.

99. Brown, *Indian Wars*, 82.

CHAPTER 6
MOORE'S COMANCHE VILLAGE RAID

1. Jenkins, *Edward Burleson*, 258.

2. Rose, *The Life and Services of Gen. Ben McCulloch*, 59.

3. Pierce, *Army*, 196, citing Oliver to Ira R. Lewis letter from the Ira R. Lewis Papers, University of Texas Library.

4. Jenkins, *Edward Burleson*, 258–59.

5. Ibid., 259–60.

6. Nance, *After San Jacinto*, 329.

7. DRT, *Defenders of the Republic of Texas*, 259.

8. DRT, *Defenders*, 259. Nance, *After San Jacinto*, 329.

9. McLeod to Lamar from Gulick, *Lamar Papers*, 3: 437.

10. Lewis Beardsley PD, R 136, F362; Samuel Purcell PD, R 180, F 24; John Daly PD, R 147, F 485; William H. Henderson PD, R 43, F 595; John R. Slocomb PD, R 186, F 245–49.

11. Kerr to Moore from Gulick, *Lamar Papers*, 3: 439.

12. McLean, *Papers*, XVIII: 53.

13. George B. Erath PD, R 151, F 639.

14. McLean, *Papers*, XVIII: 115.

15. George B. Erath PD, R 151, F 639–41.

16. McLean, *Papers*, XVIII: 57.

17. DeShields, *Border Wars of Texas*, 306.

18. Pierce, *Army*, 197.

19. Ibid., 197–98.

20. *Telegraph and Texas Register*, September 3, 1840.

21. Mathew Caldwell's public debt papers (R 142, F 111–12, shows "B. C. Ackland" to have served as the company's first lieutenant. These 1853 papers, however, do not state that they were transcribed directly from a muster roll, and most likely were done solely from memory. The actual spelling was certainly meant to be early ranger C. B. Acklin, who had fought at Plum Creek just weeks prior under Caldwell. James Callahan's public debt papers (R 142, F 254–55) include sworn testimony from Jeremiah Roberts and Tillman Berry that Callahan was elected and served as "first lieutenant" of Caldwell's 1841 company.

22. Mathew Caldwell PD, R 142, F 126; Daniel Grady PD, R 156, F 660–64; Rufus Taylor PD, R 190, F 493.

23. In his report, Major Howard only lists Caldwell and Cunningham as commander of the volunteers, but in his unpaid claims, Howard would later relate that Cunningham commanded the "whites" and Flores the "Mexicans" from San Antonio. See George T. Howard UN, R 252, F 312–13.

24. Ford, *Memoirs*, II: 235–36.

25. Jenkins, *Recollections*, 187–88.

26. Ford, *Memoirs*, II: 236.

27. Ibid., 188.

28. Jenkins, *Recollections*, 187–88.

29. Ibid., 189–90.

30. Ford, *Memoirs*, II: 236–37.

31. Jenkins, *Recollections*, 191.

32. Ford, *Memoirs*, II: 237.

33. John Hemphill AU, R 160, F 659–62; Mathew Caldwell PD, R 142, F 126.

34. Howard to Lamar from Gulick, *Lamar Papers*, IV: Part I, 231. This is the source for the quotes that follow until the next citation.

35. Pierce, *Army*, 199.

36. *Telegraph and Texas Register*, September 3, 1840.

37. Pierce, *Army*, 199.

38. Brice, *The Great Comanche Raid*, 49–50.

39. McLean, *Papers*, XVIII: 118. This quotation in the next paragraph is also from this source.

40. Pierce, *Army*, 199–200.

41. Brown, *Indian Wars*, 83; Henry W. Baylor PD, R 136, F 262–72.

42. Brown, *Indian Wars*, 83.

43. Webb, *The Texas Rangers*, 45; Robinson, *The Men Who Wear the Star*, 59; Wilkins, *The Legend Begins*, 87.

44. Brown, *Indian Wars*, 83; John H. Moore report, published in the *Austin City Gazette* on November 11, 1840.

45. Brice, *The Great Comanche Raid*, 50; Pierce, *Army*, 200.

46. Pierce, *Texas Under Arms*, 119.

47. *Telegraph and Texas Register*, November 18, 1840; Jenkins, *Recollections*, 174.

48. Jenkins, *Recollections*, 171. Wilkins, *The Legend Begins*, 86–87.

49. Brice, *The Great Comanche Raid*, 50.

50. Ibid., 50–51.

51. Pierce, *Army*, 200. Brown, *Indian Wars*, 83.

52. Brice, *The Great Comanche Raid*, 51.

53. Brown, *Indian Wars*, 83.

54. John H. Moore report, published in the *Austin City Gazette* on November 11, 1840.

55. Ibid.

56. Brown, *Indian Wars*, 84.

57. John H. Moore report, published in the *Austin City Gazette* on November 11, 1840.

58. Brown, *Indian Wars*, 83.

59. John H. Moore report, published in the *Austin City Gazette* on November 11, 1840.

60. Jenkins, *Recollections*, 172–73.

61. Brown, *Indian Wars*, 84.

62. *Telegraph and Texas Register*, September 3, 1840. Brice, *The Great Comanche Raid*, 62–63.

63. John H. Moore report, published in the *Austin City Gazette* on November 11, 1840; Brown, *Indian Wars*, 84; Anderson, *The Conquest of Texas*, 190–1.

64. John H. Moore report, published in the *Austin City Gazette* on November 11, 1840.

65. Brice, *The Great Comanche Raid*, 53.

66. Jenkins, *Recollections*, 173.

67. John H. Moore report, published in the *Austin City Gazette* on November 11, 1840.

68. Ibid.

69. Pierce, *Army*, 201.

70. Dewitt C. Lyons PD, R 169, F 645; Thomas Lubbock PD, R 169, F 479.

71. Jenkins, *Recollections*, 174–76.

72. Anderson, *The Conquest of Texas*, 191.

73. Brice, *The Great Comanche Raid*, 56–57.

CHAPTER 7
THE GREAT MILITARY ROAD

1. McLean, *Papers*, XVIII: 57, 123.

2. Sherrod Roland UN, R 256, F 53.

3. John R. Craddock UN, R 249, F 628–35.

4. Stout gives the date as December 1841, but 1840 is most likely the correct date. See Gulick, *Lamar Papers* 4: William B. Stout to Lamar, # 2465, # 274–75. Jason Wilson AU, R 116, F 591-92; John Nidiver PD, R 137, F530-64.

5. Pierce, *Army*, 202.

6. Ibid., 203.

7. Nance, *After San Jacinto*, 93.

8. McLeod to Archer, October 1, 1840, in *Appendix to the Journals of the House of Representatives: Fifth Congress*, 155–57.

9. Pierce, *Army*, 204–5.

10. Ibid., 205.

11. McLean, *Papers*, XVIII: 146.

12. McLeod to Archer, October 1, 1840, in *Appendix to the Journals of the House of Representatives: Fifth Congress*, 155–57.

13. Pierce, *Texas Under Arms*, 150-51.

14. Ibid., 29–30.

15. Cooke to Archer, November 14, 1840, in *Appendix to the Journals of*

the House of Representatives: Fifth Congress, 325.

16. McLean, *Papers*, XVIII: 146.

17. Ibid., 147.

18. Pierce, *Army*, 206–7.

19. Pierce, *Texas Under Arms*, 32.

20. Nance, *After San Jacinto*, 97.

21. Pierce, *Texas Under Arms*, 80–81.

22. McLean, *Papers*, XVIII: 177–78.

23. Pierce, *Army*, 208.

24. Ibid., 208–9.

25. McLeod to Archer, December 17, 1840, in *Appendix to the Journals of the House of Representatives: Fifth Congress*, 376.

26. Ibid., 378–79.

27. McLean, *Papers*, XVIII: 52–53.

28. Ibid., 52–53.

29. Allen to Archer, December 14, 1840, in *Appendix to the Journals of the House of Representatives: Fifth Congress*, 380–81. This letter is also the source for quotes in the following two paragraphs.

30. McLean, *Papers*, XVIII: 169.

31. Howard to Branch T. Archer, Army Papers.

32. Nance, *After San Jacinto*, 383.

33. de la Teja, Jesús F., ed., *A Revolution Remembered: The Memoirs and Selected Correspondence of Juan N. Seguín* (Austin: State House Press, 1991), 87–91.

34. Ibid., 39–40.

35. Ibid., 176–78.

36. Nance, *After San Jacinto*, 383–84.

37. Ibid., 384.

38. Ibid., 398.

39. Dimmitt to Executive Department, January 13, 1841, Army Papers.

40. Gammell, *Laws of Texas*, II:475–76.

41. Nance, *After San Jacinto*, 399.

CHAPTER 8
THE NEW FRONTIER "MINUTE MEN"
1. Greer, *Texas Ranger*, 37–40.

2. Caperton, "Sketch of Colonel John C. Hays," 8–9.

3. Hays to Lamar from Gulick, *Lamar Papers*, IV: Part I, 232–3; Caperton, "Sketch of Colonel John C. Hays," 8.

4. Caperton, "Sketch of Colonel John C. Hays," 9. Caperton says that original pay was $30 per month, but republic records show the actual payment to be $3 per day.

5. Webb, *The Texas Rangers*, 85.

6. Caperton, "Sketch of Colonel John C. Hays," 10.

7. Hays to Lamar from Gulick, *Lamar Papers*, IV: Part I, 232.

8. Wilkins, *The Legend Begins*, 91-92.

9. Stephen Dincans UN, R 250, F 376–79.

10. Isaac P. Stem PD, R 25–26. Price to Archer, January 23, 1841, Army Papers.

11. Gillen to McLeod, January 10, 1841, Army Papers.

12. Hays to Lamar from Gulick, *Lamar Papers*, 4: Part I, 232.

13. Price to Archer, Army Papers, January 23, 1841.

14. Ibid.

15. Frederic Giroud AU, R 36, F 116.

16. Nance, *After San Jacinto*, 252–59.

17. Pierce, *Army*, 215.

18. McLean, *Papers*, XVIII: 63–64, 179; citing January 20, 1841, *Telegraph and Texas Register* article.

19. Morehouse to Archer, Army Papers, December 31, 1840.

20. McLean, *Papers*, XVIII: 180, citing January 26, 1841, *The Morning Star* of Houston article.

21. J. Sauls PD, R 184, F 90.

22. George B. Erath AU, R 29, F 585.

23. Erath, *The Memoirs of Major George B. Erath,* 57.

24. John C. Pool PD, R 180, F 24; Neill McLennan PD, R 172, F 569–75; Lewis H. M. Washington AU, R 110, F 587.

25. William Morgan PD, R 175, F 424; Albert Gallatin PD, R 154, F 599.

26. McLean, *Papers*, XVIII: 64.

27. Pierce, *Texas Under Arms*, 158–59.

28. Ibid., 47.

29. William Morgan PD, R 175, F 424.

30. Erath, *The Memoirs of Major George B. Erath,* 57–58.

31. DeShields, *Border Wars of Texas*, 322.

32. Nance, *After San Jacinto*, 400.

33. Nance, *After San Jacinto*, 400–1. Nance does not list General Tarrant's Fourth Brigade.

34. DeShields, *Border Wars of Texas*, 320.

35. Pierce, *Army*, 210.

36. Gammell, *Laws of Texas*, II:574–75.

37. Ibid., II:646–48.

38. Pierce, *Texas Under Arms*, 17.

39. Boethel, *A History of Lavaca County*, 31.

40. Erath, *The Memoirs of Major George B. Erath,* 58.

41. Army Correspondence, Box 401–1308. William Charles Brookfield PD, R 140, F 190–95.

42. Http://genforum.genealogy.com/yeary/messages/46.html, referenced July 14, 2006. In a September 21, 1999, posting, descendant Teresa Yeary gives a complete military listing of John Yeary's army service dates which she received from the National Archives. Other John and Mary Yeary genealogy information is largely from son Walter Yeary's privately published "The Family Called Yeary."

43. Strickland, Rex Wallace. "History of Fannin County, Texas, 1836–

1843." *Southwestern Historical Quarterly,* Vol. XXXIV: July 1930, 39–40. See also Brown, *Indian Wars,* 85. The fact that such source refer to John Yeary as "Captain Yeary" might also indicate that he held command of a small militia company for some time in Texas.

44. *Lamar Papers,* 4, Part 1: 235.

45. McLean, *Papers,* XVIII: 241–43. The paragraph which follows is also from this source.

46. *Journals of the Sixth Congress, Republic of Texas,* III: 409.

47. Ibid., 409–10.

48. McLean, *Papers,* XVIII: 183.

49. DRT, *Defenders,* 179.

50. Ibid., 179.

51. Cazneau to Lamar, from Gulick, *Lamar Papers,* 3: 495–96.

52. McLean, *Papers,* XVIII: 184; quoting from the Thursday, March 4, 1841, edition of the *Texas Sentinel* in Austin.

53. Pierce, *Texas Under Arms,* 28.

54. Ibid., 81.

55. Ibid., 28.

56. Ibid., 80–81.

57. McLean, *Papers,* XVIII: 185; quoting from the Thursday, March 4, 1841, edition of the *Texas Sentinel* in Austin.

58. Nance, *After San Jacinto,* 402–3.

59. Ibid., 420.

60. Nance, *After San Jacinto,* 421.

61. Forster to Cooke, Army Correspondence, Texas Archives.

62. Nance, *After San Jacinto,* 410.

63. *Journals of the Sixth Congress, Republic of Texas,* III: 411.

64. Nance, *After San Jacinto,* 408–10.

65. Ibid., 411–2.

66. Hays to Lamar from Gulick, *Lamar Papers,* 4: Part I, 232.

67. Nance, *After San Jacinto,* 412.

68. P. L. Buquor, "An Episode of 1841," from the *Floresville Chronicle.* Contained in Ford, "Memoirs," 243–47.

69. Ibid., 246.

70. Caperton, "Sketch of Colonel John C. Hays, Texas Ranger," 14–5.

71. *Journals of the Sixth Congress, Republic of Texas,* 3: 411.

72. Ford, "Memoirs," 246.

73. *Journals of the Sixth Congress, Republic of Texas,* 3: 411.

74. Nance, *After San Jacinto,* 414.

75. Hays to Lamar from Gulick, *Lamar Papers,* 4: Part I, 233.

76. Ibid., 233.

77. Nance, *After San Jacinto,* 415.

CHAPTER 9
THE LEWIS EXPEDITION

1. Pierce, *Texas Under Arms,* 47.

2. *Journals of the Sixth Congress, Republic of Texas*, 3: 412.

3. Brown, *Indian Wars*, 84.

4. Ibid., 84.

5. Ibid., 84.

6. *Journals of the Sixth Congress, Republic of Texas*, 3: 413. It should be noted that Thomas I. Smith is referred to as "colonel" in some accounts. This honorary title was often used by a person's contemporaries to recognize the fact that they had commanded any group of men as a captain. There is no evidence that Smith served any command role in 1841 other than leading groups of surveyors.

7. Account of Newton C. Duncan, published in McLean, *Papers*, XVIII: 198–200. Two of Duncan's older brothers served under Captain Chandler.

8. *Journals of the Sixth Congress, Republic of Texas*, 3: 413–14.

9. Pierce, *Texas Under Arms*, 10. William Bugg PD, R 141, F 219–21. Anson G. Neal AU, R 129, F 441–42.

10. Dewitt C. Lyons PD, R 169, F 639. James P. Longly AC, R 169, F 167.

11. Colden Denman PD, R 149, F 85.

12. Pierce, *Texas Under Arms*, 9.

13. *Journals of the Sixth Congress, Republic of Texas*, 3: 414.

14. "Biography of Cicero Rufus Perry, 1822–1898. Captain, Texas Rangers." Special collections of Daughters of the Republic of Texas Library, San Antonio, Tex.

15. Ibid.

16. *Journals of the Sixth Congress, Republic of Texas*, 3: 414-15.

17. "Biography of Cicero Rufus Perry."

18. Anderson, *Conquest of Texas*, 136–38.

19. *Journals of the Sixth Congress, Republic of Texas*, 3: 414-15.

20. John Twohig PD, R 192, F 114.

21. "Biography of Cicero Rufus Perry."

22. Ibid.

CHAPTER **10**

THE VILLAGE CREEK EXPEDITION

1. H. H. Clifton PD, R 144, F 292–96.

2. Brown, *Indian Wars*, 85. See also www.kentuckystewarts.com/-Alexander/BioCharlesSStewart.htm. Referenced August 28, 2003.

3. Stout to Lamar, *Lamar Papers*, 4, Part 1: 276.

4. See www.kentuckystewarts.com/Alexander/BioCharlesSStewart.htm. Referenced August 28, 2003.

5. *Journals of the Sixth Congress*, 416.

6. Brown, *Indian Wars*, 85.

7. James Bourland PD, R 138, F 562.

8. Stout, Henry. "Account of the Death of John B. Denton." *The Weekly Gazette*, Fort Worth, Friday, July 1, 1887.

9. James Bourland PD, R 138, F 563; Samuel Burk PD, R 141, F 334–62.

10. Pierce, *Texas Under Arms*, 80–81; Brown, *Indian Wars*, 86.

11. Brown, *Indian Wars*, 86.

12. *Journals of the Sixth Congress*, 416.

13. Ibid., 416. Stout, "Account of the Death of John B. Denton."

14. *Journals of the Sixth Congress*, 416.

15. Ibid., 416.

16. Stout, "Account of the Death of John B. Denton."

17. *Journals of the Sixth Congress*, 416–17.

18. This and the following quotations are from Stout, "Account of the Death of John B. Denton."

19. Brown, *Indian Wars*, 86; Ed. F. Bates, *History and Reminiscences of Denton County* (1918; repr., Denton: Terrill Wheeler Printing, Inc., 1976), 18–19.

20. Bates, *History and Reminiscences of Denton County,* 20.

21. Brown, *Indian Wars*, 86.

22. Bates, *History and Reminiscences of Denton County,* 20.

23. Stout, "Account of the Death of John B. Denton."

24. Brown, *Indian Wars*, 86.

25. *Journals of the Sixth Congress*, 417.

26. Bates, *History and Reminiscences of Denton County,* 20–21.

27. *Journals of the Sixth Congress*, 417.

28. Brown, *Indian Wars*, 86.

29. Ibid., 86.

30. Stout, "Account of the Death of John B. Denton."

31. Bates, *History and Reminiscences of Denton County,* 22.

32. Stout, "Account of the Death of John B. Denton." See also Sowell, *Rangers and Pioneers of Texas*, 10.

33. Brown, *Indian Wars*, 87.

34. Bates, *History and Reminiscences of Denton County,* 22.

35. *Journals of the Sixth Congress*, 418-19.

36. Ibid., 418.

37. Stout, "Account of the Death of John B. Denton."

38. *Journals of the Sixth Congress*, 418.

39. Brown, *Indian Wars*, 87.

40. *Journals of the Sixth Congress*, 418. Brown, *Indian Wars*, 87; Stout, "Account of the Death of John B. Denton."

41. Bates, *History and Reminiscences of Denton County,* 23.

42. Stout, Henry. "Account of the Death of John B. Denton." *The Weekly Gazette*, Fort Worth, Friday, July 1, 1887.

43. Bates, *History and Reminiscences of Denton County,* 23–25.

44. Brown, *Indian Wars*, 87.

45. *Journals of the Sixth Congress*, 419. Stout, "Account of the Death of John B. Denton."

CHAPTER 11

"ACTIVE AND ENERGETIC MEASURES"

1. *Journals of the Sixth Congress, Republic of Texas*, 3: 419.

2. David Gage PD, R 154, F 537.

3. This and the following quotation are from *Journals of the Sixth Congress, Republic of Texas*, 3: 419.

4. Ibid., 3: 419–20.

5. Ibid., 3: 420.

6. McLean, *Papers*, XVIII: 198; *Journals of the Sixth Congress, Republic of Texas*, 3: 420.

7. *Journals of the Sixth Congress, Republic of Texas*, 3: 420.

8. McLean, *Papers*, XVIII: 198. *Journals of the Sixth Congress, Republic of Texas*, 3: 420.

9. This and the following quotations are from *Journals of the Sixth Congress, Republic of Texas*, 3: 421.

10. Brown, *Indian Wars*, 87. For the earliest count, there is an anonymous eyewitness account, apparently by Captain Daniel M. Crist, written from Fort Houston on August 3, 1841. It was published in the *Red Lander* and again on September 2, 1841, in the Austin's *Texas Centinel*. See McLean, *Papers*, XVIII: 329–30.

11. Stout to Lamar, *Lamar Papers*, 4, Part 1: 276.

12. Author's research of audited military claims and public debt papers of militiamen who served under Key and Lane. For Fort DeKalb, see Pierce, *Texas Under Arms*, 97–99.

13. Brown, *Indian Wars*, 87.

14. Most of the company letters from this Tarrant expedition can be verified through the Republic of Texas public debt papers in the Texas State Archives. For example, James M. Merrill PD, R 173, F 366, shows that Merrill was furloughed on August 10 at DeKalb by Capt. D. P. Key, Capt. Comp. A Volunteers. Hiram Baker PD, R 135, F 76, shows that he was discharged from James Blair's Company F on October 15. See Joseph W. Ellett PD, R 151, F 416 for his discharge, in which Captain Lane states that his company was "known by Co. C." Captain Fowler's unit being Company D and Captain Williams' being Company F are assumptions. Oftentimes, the companies were numbered in order of their tenure in service, which would fit the pattern established here.

15. Anonymous account, apparently written by Captain Daniel Crist on August 3, 1841, from Fort Houston. This letter was subsequently published in the *Red Lander* and again in Austin's *Texas Centinel* on September 2, 1841. See McLean, *Papers*, XVIII: 329-30.

16. Brown, *Indian Wars*, 87.

17. Brown, *Indian Wars*, 87. Wilbarger, *Indian Depredations*, 434. William Cox AU, R 21, F 223–24.

18. Wilbarger, *Indian Depredations*, 434–35.

19. Ibid., 435.

20. Henry Stallings UN, R 256, F 692.

21. John Emberson PD, R 151, F 592.

22. John Emberson PD, R 151, F 588–602.

23. William Cox AU, R 21, F 223–24.

24. Joseph W. Ellett PD, R 151, F 416; David Lane PD, R 167, F 251.

25. William M. Williams, PD R 197, F195–329.

26. Wiatt W. Kennedy PD, R 166, F 23, shows Lindley still in command as of December 21, 1841.

27. H. B. Elliott PD, R 151, F 488–491.

28. Ramsay served from July 11–August 8, 1841. Wyatt served from July 10–August 8, 1841. Thomas W. Ramsay PD, R 181, F 151; Robert Wyatt PD, R 198, F 647.

29. Robert J. Gwin PD, R 158, F 194.

30. Daniel M. Crist PD, R 146, F 674. Isaac Powers PD, R 158, F 481. The Burnet County where Captain Crist's men mustered into service is not the present Burnet County in Central Texas, but was rather a temporary, judicial county of eastern Texas.

31. Pierce, *Texas Under Arms*, 84.

32. Anonymous eyewitness account, apparently by Captain Daniel M. Crist, written from Fort Houston on August 3, 1841. It was published in the *Red Lander* and again on September 2, 1841, in the Austin's *Texas Centinel*. See McLean, *Papers*, XVIII: 329–30.

33. John Henry Brown in *Indian Wars*, 87, later wrote that this was the East Fork.

34. McLean, *Papers*, XVIII: 329–30.

35. Brown, *Indian Wars*, 87.

36. McLean, *Papers*, XVIII: 329–30.

37. Brown, *Indian Wars*, 87–8.

38. McLean, *Papers*, XVIII: 329-30.

39. James S. Ghormsley PD, R 155, F 275–77. Isaac Powers PD, R 158, F 479. Brown, *Indian Wars*, 88.

40. Pierce, *Army*, 219.

41. Green, *Memoirs of Mary A. Maverick*, 49.

42. Ibid., 49–50.

43. Pierce, *Army*, 219–20.

44. Ibid., 221–22.

45. Spellman, *Forgotten Texas Leader*, 58–60.

46. Wilkins, *The Legend Begins*, 103.

47. Green, *Memoirs of Mary A. Maverick*, 22. See John C. Hays' PD, R 160, F 379–482.

48. *Journals of the Sixth Congress, Republic of Texas*, 3: 422. Wilkins, *The Legend Begins*, 104.

49. Hays to Lamar in *Lamar Papers*, 4, Part I, 234.

50. *Journals of the Sixth Congress, Republic of Texas*, III: 422.

51. Caperton, "Sketch of Col. John C. Hays," 16. Slein is not named in the sketch, but he is the one new man to the company. Hays' account of the Uvalde Canyon fight and his July 24 Llano fight are mixed together, a product of his friend John Caperton trying to recall the stories many years later in 1879. The Caperton account would have the reader believe that Hays was shot in the finger

and that "the other man" fighting with him was killed in the Uvalde Canyon battle. Hays' own battle report of August 13, 1841, shows that he was wounded in the hand and that another ranger was shot in the breast. Hays' July 1 report for the Uvalde Canyon battle shows that no one other than Joseph Miller was wounded in that battle.

52. Hays to Lamar in *Lamar Papers*, 4, Part I, 234. The words I chose to leave out in the passage below would have read: "Hays and his two companions were soon wounded, but not totally disabled." In both this 1844 account to Lamar and in the stories he related to John Caperton, Jack Hays indicated that he and two companions were wounded in this Uvalde Canyon Fight. Caperton, "Sketch of Col. John C. Hays," 16–8. It is important, however, to note that neither of these two sources give any specific dates. Further, a study of Hays' own after-action reports to the government indicates which battle he was actually wounded in. His July 1, 1841, report states very clearly that "But one of my command was wounded—Mr. Miller, and he not severely." *Journals of the Sixth Congress, Republic of Texas*, 3: 422. To Caperton, he related that he was wounded by a shot in the finger during what Caperton understood to be the Uvalde fight. The wound actually occurred on July 24, 1841, during a second Indian battle. Hays wrote in his after-action report from this battle that one man of his command was "wounded in the hand" and another was shot in the chest. *Journals of the Sixth Congress, Republic of Texas*, 3: 423–24.

CHAPTER 12
THE GULF COAST MINUTEMEN

1. Stem testimoney from Stephen Dincans UC, R 250, F 376–79.

2. Nance, *After San Jacinto*, 423–24.

3. See Handbook of Texas Online, s.v. "John Reagan Baker," http://www.tsha.utexas.edu/handbook/online/articles/BB/fba32.html (accessed August 8, 2006).

4. Chabot, *Texas Expeditions of 1842, Vol. I: Corpus Christi and Lipantitlan*, 31–2. Nance, *After San Jacinto*, 424.

5. See Handbook of Texas Online, s.v. "Ewen Cameron," http://www.tsha.utexas.edu/handbook/online/articles/BB/fba32.html (accessed August 8, 2006).

6. William M. Rozier PE, R 236, F 564-65.

7. Nance, *After San Jacinto*, 424.

8. Kinney to Lamar, *Lamar Papers*, 4, Part I: 212.

9. William M. Rozier PE, R 236, F 565.

10. Nance, *After San Jacinto*, 425–26.

11. Ezekiel Ballard UN, R 248, F 288-294; Stephen Dincans PD, R 250, F 362.

12. McKinney to Lamar, *Lamar Papers*, Item No. 2420, 4, Part I: 211. Ezekiel Ballard UN, R 248, F 289.

13. William M. Rozier PE, R 236, F 565–66.

14. Nance, *After San Jacinto*, 424–25, 466. William M. Rozier PE, R 236, F 566.

15. Stephen Dincans PD, R 250, F 362–63. William M. Rozier PE, R 236,

F 567–68.

16. *Journals of the Sixth Congress, Republic of Texas*, III: 424–25.

17. Nance, *After San Jacinto*, 427–28.

18. Ibid., 445–46.

19. See Handbook of Texas Online, s.v. "Philip Dimmitt," http://www.tsha.utexas.edu/handbook/online/articles/BB/fba32.html (accessed August 8, 2006).

20. *Journals of the Sixth Congress, Republic of Texas*, 3: 425–27. Nance, *After San Jacinto*, 446.

21. Nance, *After San Jacinto*, 447–49.

22. *Journals of the Sixth Congress, Republic of Texas*, 3: 425–27.

23. Nance, *After San Jacinto*, 449.

24. *Journals of the Sixth Congress, Republic of Texas*, 3: 425–27.

25. Ibid., 3: 430–31.

26. Nance, *After San Jacinto*, 449.

27. Ibid., 457–58.

28. Ibid., 458–59.

29. Ibid., 459–60.

30. Ibid., 460–62. Handbook of Texas Online, s.v. "Anderson Hutchinson," http://www.tsha.utexas.edu/handbook/online/articles/HH/fhu52.html (accessed August 8, 2006).

31. Nance, *After San Jacinto*, 462–65.

32. Jones to Lamar, August 18, 1841, in L*amar Papers*, 3: 563–65.

33. Nance, *After San Jacinto*, 470–71.

34. *Journals of the Sixth Congress, Republic of Texas*, 3: 431; Nance, *After San Jacinto*, 475.

35. Nance, *After San Jacinto*, 475.

36. McKinney to Lamar, *Lamar Papers*, Item No. 2420, 4, Part I: 211.

37. Nance, *After San Jacinto*, 466–68.

38. Ibid., 468–69.

39. Ibid., 482–83.

40. Ibid., 483–84.

41. *Journals of the Sixth Congress, Republic of Texas*, 3: 435–37.

42. Nance, *After San Jacinto*, 484.

43. *Journals of the Sixth Congress, Republic of Texas*, 3: 431.

44. Ibid., 3: 432.

45. Ibid., 3: 432.

46. Ibid., 3: 433–34.

47. Nance, *After San Jacinto*, 486.

48. Baker Muster and Pay Rolls, Texas State Archives.

49. Nance, *After San Jacinto*, 491–92.

50. Harvey Rucker PD, R 183, F 375, 383.

51. Nance, *After San Jacinto*, 497.

52. Ibid., 497–98.

CHAPTER 13
"BRAVO TOO MUCH"

1. Gulick, *Papers*, 4: No. 2164, 34.

2. Pierce, *Texas Under Arms*, 24.

3. McLean, *Papers*, XVIII: 259.

4. From *Texas Sentinel*, Austin, Thursday, July 8, 1841.

5. *Journals of the Sixth Congress, Republic of Texas*, 3: 422; McLean, *Papers*, XVIII: 331–32, reprints the August 19, 1841, *Texas Centinel* of Austin.

6. John J. Tumlinson PD, R 191, F 688–89.

7. Gulick, *Papers*, IV: No. 2164, 34.

8. *Journals of the Sixth Congress, Republic of Texas*, 3: 422–23.

9. Erath, *The Memoirs of Major George B. Erath*, 58. McLean, *Papers*, XVIII: 331–32, reprints the August 19, 1841, *Texas Centinel* of Austin.

10. *Journals of the Sixth Congress, Republic of Texas*, 3: 423.

11. Erath, *The Memoirs of Major George B. Erath*, 57–58.

12. It should be noted that there were two competing newspapers, the *Austin* (Texas) *Sentinel* and the *Texas Centinel*, in Austin during 1841. McLean, *Papers*, XVIII: 331–32, reprints the August 19, 1841, *Texas Centinel* of Austin.

13. DeShields, *Border Wars of Texas*, 344.

14. Ibid., 344–45.

15. 1841 Army Correspondence, Texas Archives.

16. Stout to Lamar, *Lamar Papers*, 4, Part 1: 277.

17. Maverick, *Memoirs*, 22–23.

18. *Journals of the Sixth Congress, Republic of Texas*, 3: 423.

19. Caperton, "Sketch of Col. John C. Hays," 18. Caperton wrote that Hays had 120 men on this expedition and "15 or 20 of the Lipan tribe of the Indians." Although his numbers are exaggerated, he does at least correctly follow up the June 29 Uvalde Canyon fight with two basic truths: 1) Hays very quickly returned to the field with a larger force than what he had fought with two weeks prior; and 2) this force was accompanied by some of Flaco's Lipans to the Llano River. After this point, Caperton apparently again mixes two fights, as he claimed that Hays "lost 20 or 30 of his men." Frequent mixings of expeditions and such exaggerated losses have caused some historians to look past the Caperton–Hays recollections altogether.

20. *Journals of the Sixth Congress, Republic of Texas*, 3: 423.

21. Ibid., 3: 423-24.

22. Hays to Lamar in *Lamar Papers*, 4, Part I, 234.

23. Webb, *The Texas Rangers*, 71.

24. *Lamar Papers*, 4, Part I, 235. In Caperton, "Sketch of Col. John C. Hays," 20–21, this episode is also detailed.

25. Caperton, "Sketch of Col. John C. Hays," 20.

26. *Journals of the Sixth Congress, Republic of Texas*, 3: 424.

27. Caperton, "Sketch of Col. John C. Hays," 16. The nature of these wounds fit perfectly with Hays' August 13 action report for the July 24 Llano battle. Hays' own muster roll does show that John Slein was killed on July 24. To further complicate this battle to researchers, see Hays to Lamar in *Lamar*

Papers, Vol. 4, Part I, 234–5. In 1844, he related to Lamar that "several men were wounded, but none killed." Caperton, as previously related in the Uvalde Canyon June 29 fight, mixes the details of Hays' June 29 and July 24 Comanche fights. With such conflicting accounts of the same battles, it is no wonder that the battles of Jack Hays are sometimes considered more legend than fact.

28. *Journals of the Sixth Congress, Republic of Texas*, 3: 424.

29. Caperton, "Sketch of Col. John C. Hays," 18.

30. *Journals of the Sixth Congress, Republic of Texas*, 3: 424.

31. Hays to Lamar in *Lamar Papers*, 4, Part I, 235.

32. McLean, *Papers*, XVIII: 331–32, reprints the August 19, 1841, *Texas Centinel* of Austin.

33. McLean, *Papers*, XVIII: 332–33, reprints the August 24, 1841, *Morning Star* of Houston.

34. Ibid., XVIII: 333.

35. Ibid., XVIII: 336.

36. Pierce, *Texas Under Arms*, 176–77.

37. Wilbarger, *Indian Depredations*, 407.

38. Ibid., 409–11.

39. Hugh Cox PD, R 146, F 269; Jesse Cox PD, R 146, F 289.

40. Wilbarger, *Indian Depredations*, 410–12.

41. DeShields, *Border Wars of Texas*, 314–15.

42. Wilbarger, *Indian Depredations*, 414.

43. DeShields, *Border Wars of Texas*, 315.

44. Wilbarger, *Indian Depredations*, 432.

45. Ibid., 432–33.

46. Ibid., 433.

47. Sowell, *Rangers and Pioneers of Texas*, 21–22.

48. The Handbook of Texas Online, s.v. "Callahan, James Hughes," http://www.tsha.utexas.edu/handbook/online/articles/CC/fca16.html, (referenced September 9, 2003). James H. Callahan, R 142, F 254–25.

49. McDowell, (ed.). *Now You Hear My Horn: The Journal of James Wilson Nichols*, 83.

50. Sowell, *Rangers and Pioneers of Texas*, 193.

51. McDowell, (ed.). *Now You Hear My Horn*, 83. The Nichols and Sowell accounts agree to the basics of Milford Day being the head scout in tracking the Mexican horse thieves.

52. Ibid., 84.

53. Ibid., 84–85. Sowell, *Rangers and Pioneers of Texas*, 193.

54. McDowell, (ed.). *Now You Hear My Horn*, 85.

55. Ibid., 85–86. Sowell, *Rangers and Pioneers of Texas*, 193–94.

56. McDowell, *Now You Hear My Horn*, 25–26.

57. Ibid., 26–7.

58. Ibid., 28.

59. Ibid., 28–31.

60. This and the following quote are from Sowell, *Rangers and Pioneers of Texas*, 194.

CHAPTER 14
ENCHANTED ROCK AND BIRD'S FORT

1. John C. Hays AC, R 160, F 378-493.

2. Ibid., R 160, F 446.

3. Greer, *Texas Ranger*, 51–2.

4. Robinson, *The Men Who Wear the Star*, 66–67.

5. Wilkins, *The Legend Begins*, 203–4; See Caperton, "Sketch of Col. John C. Hays."

6. Reid, *McCulloch's Texas Rangers*, 111; Sowell, *Texas Indian Fighters*, 334-35.

7. Reid, *McCulloch's Texas Rangers*, 112.

8. Ibid., 111.

9. Reid, *McCulloch's Texas Rangers*, 111. Wilkins, *The Legend Begins*, 204. A. J. Sowell's account of Enchanted Rock is obviously lifted from Reid, as Sowell very closely describes the hill as having a bowl at the top in which "a dozen or more men can lie." Sowell, *Early Settlers and Indian Fighters of Southwest Texas*, 334–35.

10. Handbook of Texas Online, s.v. "Enchanted Rock Legends," http://www.tsha.utexas.edu/handbook/online/articles/EE/lxe1.html (accessed November 10, 2003).

11. Greer, *Texas Ranger*, 52.

12. Caperton, "Sketch of Col. John C. Hays," 30.

13. Ibid., 31.

14. Reid, *McCulloch's Texas Rangers*, 111; Caperton, "Sketch of Col. John C. Hays," 31.

15. Caperton, "Sketch of Col. John C. Hays," 31. Caperton lists that Ad Gillespie was second in command of Hays' company at the time of Enchanted Rock, but here he is mistaken on dates. Gillespie did not serve with Hays at all in 1841. He joined the company on September 13, 1842, just in time for the Somervell Campaign.

16. Reid, *McCulloch's Texas Rangers*, 111–12.

17. John C. Hays AC, R 160, F 439.

18. Reid, *McCulloch's Texas Rangers*, 112.

19. McLean, *Papers*, XVIII: 338–9.

20. John H. Cox PD, R 146, F 293–94.

21. Eli J. Shelton UN, R 256, F 314.

22. George Wright PD, R 258, F 429; Wesley Askins PD, R 151, F 122.

23. Jackson, *Sixty Years in Texas*, 378–79.

24. Daniel Slack PD, R 186, F 191.

25. Jackson, *Sixty Years in Texas*, 379.

26. Ibid., 378–79.

27. DeShields, *Border Wars of Texas*, 345.

28. Looscan, "Capt. Joseph Daniels," 26."

29. McLean, *Papers*, XVIII: 352.

30. Nance, *After San Jacinto*, 480.

31. Pierce, *Texas Under Arms*, 11.
32. Robinson, *The Men Who Wear the Star*, 66.
33. Pierce, *Army*, 214.
34. 1841 Army Correspondence, Box 1215–13.
35. Nance, *After San Jacinto*, 473-74.

AFTERWORD

1. Nance, *After San Jacinto*, 498.
2. Kinney to Lamar, *Lamar Papers*, 4: Part I: 211.

BIBLIOGRAPHY

DOCUMENTS, MANUSCRIPTS AND COLLECTIONS

Aldrich, Armistead Albert. Papers. Center for American History, University of Texas, Austin.

Appendix to the Journals of the House of Representatives: Fifth Congress. Printed at the Gazette Office for the Republic of Texas, Austin, 1841.

Army Papers, Republic of Texas. Archives and Library Division, Texas State Library in Austin, Texas.

"Biography of Cicero Rufus Perry, 1822–1898. Captain, Texas Rangers." Special collections of Daughters of the Republic of Texas Library, San Antonio, Tex.

Caperton, John C. "Sketch of Colonel John C. Hays, The Texas Rangers, Incidents in Texas and Mexico, Etc. from materials furnished by Col. Hays and Major John Caperton." Typescript version. Original prepared in 1879. The original copy is housed in the Bancroft Library at the University of California at Berkley. A typescript copy of this 77-page manuscript was obtained from the University of California in 1922 and is part of the James T. DeShields Papers, Center for American History, University of Texas at Austin. DeShields used Caperton's sketch as a source for articles on Hays which he ran in the 1880s. Caperton's manuscript includes some obvious exaggerations and it suffers from a lack of accurate dates. It is obvious, however, that Hays himself was consulted for this document, as descriptions of the various battles match closely the testimony offered up by Hays to President M. B. Lamar in 1844. It is doubtful that Caperton could have had a copy of this document, unless he had obtained it or the same stories firsthand from Hays.

Constitution and By-Laws of the Travis Guards: Adopted March First, 1840. Austin: Cruger and Bonnell's Print, 1840. From the collections in the Center for American History, The University of Texas at Austin.

Ford, John S. "Memoirs." Typescript of Ford's manuscript. 7 volumes. Center for American History, The University of Texas at Austin.

General Land Office of Texas: records and papers collection.

Journals of the Fourth Congress of the Republic of Texas. Austin, Tex: Von Boeckmann-Jones Co. Printers, 1930.

Journals of the House of Representatives of the Republic of Texas: Fifth Congress, Appendix. Austin: Gazette Office, 1841.

Journals of the Sixth Congress, Republic of Texas. Austin: np, 1842.

Muster Rolls of the Texas Army and the Texas Militia, courtesy of the Texas State Archives. See individual chapter footnotes and appendices for those referenced.

Nicholson, James. Papers. Center for American History, University of Texas, Austin.

Republic Claims Papers, 1835–1846 (microfilmed). Texas State Library and Archives Commission, Austin.

Yeary, Walter. "The Family Called Yeary." Privately published genealogical history of John and Mary Yeary's descendants. See http://genforum.genealogy.com/yeary/messages/46.html, referenced July 14, 2006.

BOOKS

Aldrich, Armistead Albert. *History of Houston County, Together with Biograhical Sketches of Many Pioneers*. San Antonio, Tex: The Naylor Co., 1943.

Anderson, Gary Clayton. *The Conquest of Texas: Ethnic Cleansing in the Promised Land, 1820–1875*. Norman: University of Oklahoma Press, 2005, 128, 181.

Aubrey, Betty Dooley and Claude Dooley. *Why Stop? A Guide to Texas Historical Roadside Markers*. Houston, Tex: Lone Star Books, Fourth Edition, 1999. Reprint, 1978.

Bates, Ed. F. *History and Reminiscences of Denton County*. Denton, Tex: McNitzky Printing Company, 1918. Reprint. Denton: Terrill Wheeler Printing, Inc., 1976.

Bennett, Miles Squier diary from Valentine Bennett Scrapbook, The Center for American History, University of Texas at Austin. Also includes "Experiences on the Western Frontier, Republic of Texas, 1838–1842," sketch by Miles S. Bennett.

Biographical Directory of the Texan Conventions and Congresses, 1832–1845. Austin, Tex: Book Exchange, 1941.

Biographical Gazetteer of Texas. Austin, Tex: W. M. Morrison Books, 1987.

Boethel, Paul C. *A History of Lavaca County*. Austin: Von Boeckmann-Jones, 1959.

Brazos [pseud.]. *The Life of Robert Hall*. Austin: Ben C. Jones and Company, Printers, 1898.

Brice, Donaly E. *The Great Comanche Raid: Boldest Indian Attack of the Texas Republic*. Austin, Tex: Eakin Press, 1987.

Brown, John Henry. *History of Texas*. St. Louis, Missouri: L. E. Daniell, 1892.

Brown, John Henry. *Indian Wars and Pioneers of Texas*. 1880. Reprint. Austin, Tex: State House Press, 1988.

Carter, W. A. *History of Fannin County, Texas*. Bonham, Tex: Bonham News, 1885. Reprint. Honey Grove, Tex: Fannin County Historical Society, 1975.

Chabot, Frederick C. *Texas Expeditions of 1842. Volume I: Corpus Christi and Lipantitlan*. San Antonio: Artes Graficas, 1942.

de la Teja, Jesús F., ed., *A Revolution Remembered: The Memoirs and Selected Correspondence of Juan N. Seguín*. Austin: State House Press, 1991.

DeShields, James T. *Border Wars of Texas*. 1912. Reprint. Austin, Tex: State House Press, 1993.

Erath, George Bernard as dictated to Lucy A. Erath. *The Memoirs of Major George B. Erath, 1813-1891*. Austin, Tex: Texas State Historical Society, 1923. Reprinted by The Heritage Society of Waco in 1956.

Ericson, Carolyn Reeves. *Nacogdoches—Gateway to Texas: A Biographical Directory, Vol. I*. Nacogdoches, Tex: Ericson Books, 1977.

Fehrenbach, T. R. *Lone Star: A History of Texas and the Texans*. Reprint. New York: American Legacy Press, 1983.

Ford, John Salmon, edited by Stephen B. Oates. *Rip Ford's Texas*. Austin: University of Texas Press, 1994.

Gammell, (Karl) Hans Peter Marius Nielsen. *The Laws of Texas, 1822–1897*. Ten volumes. Austin, Tex: The Gammel Book Company, 1898.

Gonzales County History. Published by Gonzales County Historical Commission and Curtis Media Corp., 1986.

Greer, James Kimmins. *Texas Ranger: Jack Hays in the Frontier Southwest*. College Station, TX: Texas A&M University Press, 1993. This book was originally published by E.P. Dutton and Company, Inc. as *Colonel Jack Hays: Texas Frontier Leader and California Builder* in 1952.

Groneman, Bill. *Battlefields of Texas*. Plano: Republic of Texas Press, 1998.

Gulick, Charles A. Jr., Winnie Allen, Katherine Elliott, and Harriet Smither. *The Papers of Mirabeau Buonaparte Lamar*, 6 Volumes, 1922. Reprint. Austin, Tex: Pemberton Press, 1968. (Referenced in chapter notes as *Lamar Papers*.)

History of Houston County: 1687-1979. Compiled and edited by the History Book Committee of Houston County Historical Commission of Crockett, Texas. Tulsa, Okla.: Heritage Publishing Company, 1979.

Jenkins, John H. and Kenneth Kesselus. *Edward Burleson: Texas Frontier Leader*. Austin, Tex: Jenkins Publishing Co., 1990.

Jenkins, John Holland. *Recollections of Early Texas: The Memoirs of John Holland Jenkins*. Edited by John Holmes Jenkins III. Austin: University of Texas Press, 1958. Reprint. 1995.

Knowles, Thomas W. *They Rode for the Lone Star: The Saga of the Texas Rangers. The Birth of Texas–The Civil War*. Dallas, Tex: Taylor Publishing Company, 1999.

Koury, Michael J. *Arms For Texas: A Study of the Weapons of the Republic of Texas*. Fort Collins, Colo.: The Old Army Press, 1973.

Ladd, Kevin. *Gone to Texas: Genealogical Abstracts from The Telegraph and Texas Register 1835–1841*. Bowie, MD: Heritage Books, 1994.

Lee, Nelson. *Three Years Among the Comanches: The Narrative of Nelson Lee, The Texas Ranger*. 1859. Reprint. Norman: University of Oklahoma Press, 1957.

Linn, John J. *Reminiscences of Fifty Years in Texas*. New York: Sadler, 1883.

Green, Rena Maverick. (editor) *Memoirs of Mary A. Maverick. Arranged by Mary A. Maverick and her son George Madison Maverick*. San Antonio: Alamo Printing Co., 1921. Reprint. Lincoln: University of Nebraska Press, 1989.

McDowell, Catherine W. (ed.). *Now You Hear My Horn: The Journal of James Wilson Nichols, 1820-1887*. Austin: University of Texas Press, 1961.

McLean, Malcolm D. *Papers Concerning Robertson's Colony in Texas*. Published by the University of Texas at Arlington. Arlington, Tex: The UTA Press. Volume XVII (1991, covering December 1838–August 10, 1840).

Moore, Stephen L. *Taming Texas: Captain William T. Sadler's Lone Star Service*. Austin, Tex: State House Press, 2000.

Muster Rolls of the Texas Revolution. Austin: Daughters of the Republic of Texas, 1986.

Nance, Joseph M. *After San Jacinto: The Texas-Mexican Frontier, 1836–1841*. Austin: University of Texas Press, 1963.

The New Handbook of Texas. Austin: The Texas State Historical Association, 1996, Six Volumes.

Newcomb, W. W. Jr. *The Indians of Texas: From Prehistoric to Modern Times*. Austin, Tex: University of Texas Press, 1961.

Pierce, Gerald Swetnam. *The Army of the Republic of Texas, 1836-1845*. Dissertation from the University of Mississippi, copyright 1964, on file in the Texas Room of the Houston Public Library.

———. *Texas Under Arms: The Camps, Posts, Forts, and Military Towns of the Republic of Texas*. Austin, Tex: Encino Press, 1969.

Purcell, Robert Allen. *The History of the Texas Militia*. Austin: University of Texas Press, 1981.

Robinson, Charles M. III. *The Men Who Wear the Star: The Story of the Texas Rangers*. New York: Random House, 2000.

Rose, Victor M. *The Life and Services of Gen. Ben McCullough*. Philadelphia: Pictorial Bureau of the Press, 1888. Facsimile Reproduction. Austin, Tex: The Steck Company.

Smithwick, Noah. *The Evolution of a State/Recollections of Old Texas Days*. Austin: University of Texas Press, 1983.

Sowell, A. J. *Texas Indian Fighters. Early Settlers and Indian Fighters of Southwest Texas*. 1900. Reprint. Austin, Tex: State House Press, 1986.

———. *Rangers and Pioneers of Texas*. 1884. Reprint. Austin, Tex: State House Press, 1991.

Spellman, Paul N. *Forgotten Texas Leader: Hugh McLeod and the Texan Santa Fe Expedition*. College Station: Texas A&M University Press, 1999.

Taylor, Ira T. *The Cavalcade of Jackson County* (Texas). San Antonio: The Naylor Company, 1938.

Thompson, Karen R. (Editor). *Defenders of the Republic of Texas*. Austin, Tex: Daughters of the Republic of Texas via Laurel House Press, 1989.

Utley, Robert M. *Lone Star Justice: The First Century of The Texas Rangers*. New York: Oxford University Press, 2002.

Webb, Walter Prescott (Editor-in-Chief). *The Handbook of Texas*: *A Dictionary of Essential Information* (Three Volumes). Austin: The Texas State Historical Association, 1952.

———. *The Texas Rangers: A Century of Frontier Defense*. Austin: University of Texas Press, 1991.

Wilbarger, John Wesley. *Indian Depredations in Texas.* 1889. Reprint. Austin, Tex: State House Press, 1985.

Wilkins, Frederick. *The Legend Begins: The Texas Rangers, 1823–1845.* Austin, Tex: State House Press, 1996.

Williams, Amelia W. and Eugene C. Barker. *Writings of Sam Houston.* Austin: The University of Texas Press, 1938-43.

Winfrey, Dorman, and James M. Day. *The Texas Indian Papers, 1825-1843.* Four volumes. Austin, Tex: Austin Printing Co., 1911.

Yoakum, Henderson. *History of Texas From its First Settlement in 1685 to its Annexation to the United States in 1846.* Two volumes. New York: Redfield Publishers, 1855. Reprint. Austin, Tex: Steck Company, 1935.

Zuber, William Physick. *My Eighty Years in Texas.* Austin: University of Texas Press, 1971.

ARTICLES AND NEWSPAPERS

Austin City Gazette. See source notes from individual chapters for dates.

Austin Sentinel. See source notes from individual chapters for dates.

Davis, Andrew. "The Story of the Fight and Captain Denton's Death." Special to *The Dallas News*, October 6, 1900.

Looscan, Adele B. "Capt. Joseph Daniels." *Texas Historical Association Quarterly* 5, no. 1 (1901-1092): 19–21.

The Morning Star (of Houston). See source notes from individual chapters for dates.

Pierce, Gerald S. "Burleson's Northwestern Campaign." *Texas Military Monthly* 6, no. 3 (Fall 1967): 191–201.

Stout, Henry. "Account of the Death of John B. Denton." *The Weekly Gazette*, Fort Worth, Friday, July 1, 1887.

Strickland, Rex Wallace. "History of Fannin County, Texas, 1836–1843." *Southwestern Historical Quarterly,* 34 (July 1930).

Telegraph and Texas Register. See source notes from individual chapters for dates.

Texas Centinel (Austin). See source notes from individual chapters for dates.

Index